Erie Water West

ERIE WATER WEST

*A History
of the Erie Canal
1792-1854*

RONALD E. SHAW

UNIVERSITY OF KENTUCKY PRESS

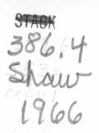

TO Glyndon G. Van Deusen
Teacher, Author, Friend

Preface

THE ERIE CANAL has long been celebrated in song, folklore, and fiction. Shortly after the turn of the twentieth century its history was told in a comprehensive engineering study. More recently it has attracted attention for its contribution to American economic growth.

I have attempted to give a balanced account of the history of the Erie Canal during the period 1792-1854 that brings together such varied aspects as its political sponsorship and opposition, construction and operation, travel and commerce, and its social and cultural significance. I have tried here to show the place of the Erie Canal in the lives of the generations that planned, constructed, and first traveled upon it, and have sought to explain why many saw it as the wonder of their age.

Any discussion of the Erie Canal requires designation in time. Today the canal passing boats and barges through gigantic locks between the Hudson River and Lake Erie is the Erie Barge Canal, construction of which began in 1905. Though its route is much the same as that of the Erie Canal of the nineteenth century, it represents the last of three major phases of Erie Canal history. Here I am concerned with the first two phases: the construction and use of the original canal, completed in 1825 and often called the "old Erie Canal" or "Clinton's Ditch"; and the enlarged or "improved Erie" on which construction began in 1836 and was completed in 1862.

This study, however, closes with the year 1854 as that year saw the climax of the major political contest between the Democrats and Whigs over the enlargement of the canal, and as the consolidation of the New York Central Railroad only a year earlier marked the transition from the Canal Era to the Railroad Age in New York. Moreover, in the 1850s New Yorkers turned their attention increasingly away from state conflicts over internal improvements toward the national problem of slavery and the threat of civil war.

Research for this study has been supported by grants from the Penrose Fund and the Johnson Fund of the American Philosophical Society and by research grants from Miami University. The latter institution also provided a Summer University Research Fellowship in 1958.

I am indebted to Glyndon G. Van Deusen for encouragement and criticism in my initial work on this subject. I also wish to acknowledge the unstinting assistance of Richard N. Wright, secretary of the Canal Society of New York State, who loaned research materials, provided illustrations, and sought to save me from published error. To Albert E. Gayer of Schenectady I am grateful for permission to use his extensive personal canal collection and for the energetic tours on which he guided me over parts of the remains of the Erie Canal.

I wish to acknowledge the generous assistance of members of the staffs of the Library of Congress, the Columbia University Library, the New York Public Library, the New-York Historical Society, the New York State Library, the Utica Public Library, the Jervis Public Library in Rome, the Onondaga Historical Society, the

Cornell University Library, the Rochester Public Library, the University of Rochester Library, the Buffalo Public Library, the Buffalo and Erie County Historical Society, and the Miami University Library. Particular thanks are due Margaret B. Andrews, Assistant Librarian in Charge of Special Collections at the University of Rochester, for assistance spanning many years.

I owe a special debt to my wife, Judith M. Shaw, for her help in research and typing and for her critical judgment which have made the preparation of this book a shared endeavor. For errors of fact or interpretation, however, I alone am responsible.

Miami University   Ronald E. Shaw
November, 1965

Contents

Illustrations

ABBREVIATIONS USED IN THE NOTES

BECHS—Buffalo and Erie County Historical Society
CUL—Columbia University Library
LC—Library of Congress
NYHS—New-York Historical Society
NYPL—New York Public Library
NYSL—New York State Library
RPL—Rochester Public Library
URL—University of Rochester Library

I. *The Prophecy*

1

Up the Mohawk to the West

THE ERIE CANAL was the work of that remarkable generation in America who made the period between 1815 and 1860 an age of great national expansion. New York expansionists saw in the Mohawk gap in the Appalachian chain an opportunity to bring the Great Lakes heartland close to the growing metropolis at the mouth of the Hudson. The scheme was bold. They proposed a canal which would strike out ahead of the older society of eastern New York, penetrate the frontier, and create a new mold for the future of the Old Northwest. They sought to close the great compass formed by the Mississippi and the St. Lawrence by some twenty degrees, thereby bringing its northern arm through American soil for the fulfillment of their dreams of national growth. In this the builders of the Erie Canal belonged with their age. They shared the optimism of the founding fathers who saw in their naked land the raw materials of future strength and expansion. Their prophecy was part of the basic American pattern which was, as it always has been, one of optimistic vision.

Canal-minded men in New York traded largely in futures before the culmination of their efforts in 1825. The history of the colonial province and of three decades of statehood ended for the most part at the wilderness backdrop which crowded the Mohawk and hugged the Hudson at the Catskills. Revolutionary War clashes in New York had revolved chiefly around the struggle for the Hudson-Mohawk valley and Lakes George and Champlain, while the dismal conflicts of the War of 1812 were contested over a largely unsettled frontier in western New York.

Neil Adams McNall's history of the Genesee Valley finds only 23,148 people settled in the six counties nearest to the Genesee River between the Pennsylvania boundary and Lake Ontario in 1810.[1] As late as 1820 population began to dribble off into isolated settlements westward of Lake Oneida. These hamlets were served by roads which were often only lines of penetration through the frontier. Westward from Albany, the Mohawk and Schenectady Turnpike served the thriving commerce of Yankee, Dutch, and German settlers in the lower Mohawk Valley. Over the next sixty-eight miles to Utica, travelers followed the Schenectady and Utica Turnpike. At Utica the best road turned south, passed through Manlius below Syracuse, and joined the Great Western Turnpike, the route of which is followed by U.S. 20 today. This major artery across the state carried the traveler through the beautiful Finger Lake villages from Skaneateles to Geneva and Canandaigua and continued west through Bloomfield, Avon, LeRoy, and Batavia to Buffalo.

There were other choices west of Utica, however, for the turnpike era had brought 4,000 miles of roads into operation in New York by 1822.[2] South of the Mohawk route, the Cherry Valley Turnpike followed a westward path from Albany through Cooperstown and Sherburne.

[1] Neil Adams McNall, *An Agricultural History of the Genesee Valley 1790-1860* (Philadelphia, 1952), p. 66n.
[2] Joseph Austin Durrenberger, *Turnpikes: a Study of the Toll Road Movement in the Middle Atlantic States and Maryland* (Valdosta, 1931), p. 158.

Two major roads reached western New York by routes to the north. From Manlius a turnpike followed the Oswego River to Oswego on Lake Ontario. There fleet schooners plied to Lewiston in the Niagara gorge, where a short land journey saw the traveler to Black Rock and Buffalo. The second alternative to the north lay in departing from the Great Western Turnpike at Auburn to take the road to the falls of the Genesee at Rochesterville, and from there to traverse the famous Ridge Road to Lewiston. The Genesee country could also be approached from the south by the Susquehanna-Bath turnpike which came from eastern New York by way of Ithaca or by a second turnpike which followed the Susquehanna and the Cohocton valleys and passed through the present site of Elmira.[3] From Bath other roads led north to Batavia and westward through the southern tier of counties to Lake Erie. Many travelers en route to northern Ohio turned southwest from Genesee through Cattaraugus County in preference to the longer route through Batavia and Buffalo.

The existence of scattered settlements and the poor connections by roads made for an uneven advance against the wilderness. At the end of the first two decades of the nineteenth century no town in western New York exceeded a population of 6,000 and most were smaller by half.[4] Nearly eight million acres of land in ten upper western New York counties lying along the future route of the Erie Canal were occupied in 1816 by only 194,951 inhabitants and only a tenth of this land was under cultivation.[5] The neat white villages suckling at the Finger Lakes were older communities, but they averaged

[3] McNall, *History of the Genesee Valley*, pp. 70-74.

[4] *Census for 1820* (Washington, 1821), pp. 10-12.

[5] *A Serious Appeal to the Wisdom and Patriotism of the Legislature of the State of New York; on the Subject of a Canal Communication between the Great Western Lakes and the Waters of the Hudson, by a friend of his country* (printed privately, 1816), p. 5.

only 2,000 souls each in 1820. The Holland Land Company's great tract in western New York was well settled along the Great Western Turnpike and most of James Wadsworth's lands along the lower Genesee had been sold by 1820.[6] But Batavia, the seat of the Holland Company's land office, contained only 200 inhabitants in 1818 and the courthouse served also as the church.[7] In 1820 a population of only 1,502 were settled at the falls of the Genesee where eight years earlier a solitary house marked the fording place. Only two partially constructed cabins existed in 1820 at the future Lockport. Except for the tri-weekly stages, contact between northwestern New York and the outside world came from Lake Ontario ports of Ogdensburg, Oswego, Sodus Bay, Charlotte, and Lewiston. It was uncertain which of the tiny villages of Buffalo or Black Rock would become the major port of transfer from western New York to Lake Erie.

Where the land was settled in the "Western District," clearing proceeded slowly and could require the labor of a generation.[8] The first log cabins were more often simple, crude, and primitive. Benjamin Coates, a traveler passing west in 1819, recorded the "gradual deterioration of the stile of useful and elegant improvement of the country, from about Onondaga to Lake Erie," where he saw farm houses neglected in cleanliness and repair and seldom white.[9] Around the houses often were found the blackened trunks of trees scorched by fire in the process of clearing the land for cultivation. Whole forests flaming against the black of night made an awesome impression upon the traveler from the east.

[6] McNall, *History of the Genesee Valley*, pp. 74-75.

[7] John M. Duncan, *Travels through Part of the United States and Canada in 1818-1819* (Glasgow, 1823), II, 23.

[8] McNall, *History of the Genesee Valley*, p. 85.

[9] Benjamin Coates, "Journal of a Trip to Niagara, 1817," MS, URL.

At the same time, the presence of the red man testified to the gradual retreat of the wilderness. In colonial days the Six Nations held sway to the headwaters of the Mohawk, and through the formative years of the canal project their remnant remained on reservations in western New York. Red Jacket and his Seneca brethren, dressed in long blue frock coats with bright red sashes about their waists, lounged on the streets of Buffalo. The Tuscaroras camped on "Lewiston Mountain." Near Utica were the Onondagas, and the primitive, bark-covered houses of the Cattaraugus tribe lined the creek that bore their name in southwestern New York.

Travel by road through this frontier was at best tedious, more often grueling. The open "stage wagon" was little more than a roofed box crossed by four seats. Baggage went on behind or was stuffed under seats and knees. Trusting to the leather springs of the wagon, the traveler crossed corduroy roads which jolted him mercilessly or floated beneath him in the rainy seasons. Where the corduroy was absent, quagmire mud or enveloping clouds of dust were certain alternatives. "Probably the Roads from Utica to Canandaigua were never worse," wrote Joseph Ellicott, Holland land agent in Batavia in 1808. "The Stage was the best part of four days wading along this Mud Turnpike from the former to the latter place."[10] Over such roads, oxen or horses pulled the heavy freight wagons carrying from two to six tons beneath their canvas tops. In 1814, Robert Fulton wrote that it cost $2.00 to send a barrel of flour 130 miles overland; the same barrel could go by water from Albany to New York City for 25¢, a distance of 160 miles.[11] Smith H. Salisbury, editor of

[10] Ellicott to Paul Busti, December 17, 1808, Joseph Ellicott Letterbooks, BECHS.

[11] Cited in David Maldwyn Ellis, *Landlords and Farmers in the Hudson-Mohawk Region 1790-1850* (Ithaca, 1946), p. 134.

the year-old Buffalo *Gazette* in 1812 called for improvement of the road west of the Genesee. "The government of this state must bend its attention westward," he wrote from the little village at the mouth of Buffalo Creek, ". . . while the clouds of legislative favor drop marrow and fatness on the eastern, southern and middle districts of the state, not a solitary cent has rolled to the westward of Oneida castle."[12]

Men of the time saw the key to the development of western New York in the improvement of the roads or other means of transportation to eastern markets. Improvements in transportation, writes Professor McNall of the Genesee Valley, opened new markets and in turn changed the agricultural pattern. "Few significant improvements," he noted, ". . . were made before the opening of the Erie Canal."[13]

With these conditions in the west, the first efforts to improve transportation to the interior understandably centered on the Mohawk-Oswego water route to Lake Ontario, a well-known route recognized as improvable since colonial times. The distance from the head of the Mohawk at Fort Stanwix (Rome) to Lake Ontario was less than fifty miles. River travelers left the Mohawk and portaged their bateaux over two miles of flats to Wood Creek which flowed into Oneida Lake. Out of Oneida Lake ran the Oneida River, joining the Seneca River after about twenty miles. Up the Seneca River to the west, navigation was possible to the falls between Seneca and Cayuga lakes; downstream to the north, the waters of the Seneca and the Oneida formed the Oswego River which dropped over a hundred feet in the twenty-four miles to Lake Ontario. Where these watercourses were navigable,

[12] Buffalo *Gazette*, January 29, 1812.
[13] McNall, *History of the Genesee Valley*, p. 89.

long, shallow "Durhams" carried cargo inland, powered by rivermen who put their shoulders to the flattened heads of long, iron-shod poles and facing rear, walked the craft treadmill fashion slowly upstream. For boats moving downstream, wing dams helped to deepen the river channels and allow easier passage.

But at innumerable points the Mohawk-Oswego route was checked and endangered with falls, undergrowth, and clogged channels. The Cohoes Falls near the mouth of the Mohawk were impassable for any craft, and their interference compelled river traffic to make its lower terminus at Schenectady. The rapids at Little Falls fifty-six miles west of Schenectady, required a mile portage of boats and supplies "over a road as rough, rocky and bad as the imagination can conceive. . . ."[14] There were other rapids, such as those at German Flats, shifting sandbars, and recurrent times of low water, all of which severely limited the navigation of the Mohawk. The two-mile portage at Rome between the Mohawk and Wood Creek, and the brook-level waters which that creek offered at its origin made for an arduous transfer to Oneida Lake. The rapids of the Oswego were perhaps the most difficult of all. Yet over much of the route weight could be floated when the water was high, and the way was short in comparison to the long overland journey to Lake Erie.

The sea-going Dutch of New Netherland stumbled into this land of rivers and lakes and carried with them the Dutch pattern of society which had brought garden and canal to a peak of development in seventeenth-century Holland.[15] They were thus particularly qualified to take a major hand in improvements so patently desirable. The

[14] *Report of the Directors of the Western and Northern Inland Lock Navigation Companies* (Albany, 1796), p. 5.

[15] Lewis Mumford, *Technics and Civilization* (New York, 1934), pp. 120-23.

author of an essay on the origin of the Erie Canal, published in 1825, wrote that "there are many now living who can recollect that their fathers spoke with fond anticipations of the intercourse which would take place at a future day, with the western country by means of an inland navigation, after the manner of the Netherlands. . . ."[16] In this pattern of living, water and wood, horse and harness, boat and canal would combine to spread the pleasing picture of the Dutch garden over the landscape of New York. Working with English and native Americans, the New York Dutchmen would make water communications the heart of their society.

The English colonials early recognized the strategic importance of developing such a society. While the Dutch were contemplating the remaking of America on the Dutch model, Cadwallader Colden, surveyor general of New York, sent a memorial to Governor William Burnet in 1724 with perhaps the first recognition of a possible water connection between the Hudson and the Great Lakes. He did not mention a canal, but he introduced considerations which became the nodes of almost all future discussions involving the beginning of the New York canal system.

The burden of Colden's memorial was the superiority of the province of New York over New France in capturing the inland fur trade. The lakes with their natural outlet through the St. Lawrence, together with the Mississippi and its branches, presented to him *"such a Scene of inland Navigation as cannot be parallel'd in any other Part of the World."*[17] His means of reaching the interior

---

[16] *Facts and Observations in Relation to the Origin and Completion of the Erie Canal* (New York, 1825), p. 3.

[17] Quoted in Henry W. Hill, *An Historical Review of Waterways and Canal Construction in New York State, Buffalo Historical Society Publications,* XII (Buffalo, 1908), 10.

was the conventional one long traveled by Indian canoe from the Mohawk to Oneida Lake and Lake Ontario; but his faulty geography led him to speculation depending "upon further Discovery" which implied the future route of the Erie Canal. He wrote of "a river which comes from the Country of the *Sennekas*," the head of which "goes very near to Lake Erie and probably may give a very near passage into that Lake, much more advantageous than the way the French are obliged to take by the great fall of the Jagara [Niagara]. . . ." At the outset, then, the prize was the trade of the lakes, the competitor was the possessor of the St. Lawrence, and the English ace in the hole was in the potential advantage of an inland water route to Lake Erie.

New York provincials were given further cause to look to the development of their back country as they were caught up in the American Revolution. The Revolution, like the later War of 1812, brought military demands for achieving a better system of transportation than the roads could provide. Roads in which wagons buried themselves hub-deep in mud slowed the campaigns of Colonials and British alike. The direction of the campaigns themselves emphasized the strategic importance of control of the Susquehanna, Hudson, and Mohawk rivers and Lakes Champlain and Ontario.

As the Revolution drew to a close, Washington saw in the development of these natural waterways bonds of union which would keep the western settlers safe from a commercial dependence upon the British and Spanish at "the flanks and rear of the United States." Washington toured the waterways of eastern New York in 1783, traveled up the Mohawk to Fort Stanwix and crossed over Wood Creek to Oneida Lake. Writing to the Marquis de Chastellux of his journey, he described the "vast inland navigation of these United States," and added, "Would to God we may have wisdom enough" to improve it. The following year, Washington wrote to a member of Congress and sketched broadly the policy of internal improvement which he believed the nation must pursue. In very general terms, he included the improvement of the waterways of New York: "Extend the inland navigation of the eastern waters; communicate them as near as possible with those which run westward; open these to the Ohio; open also such as extend from the Ohio towards Lake Erie; and we shall not only draw the produce of the western settlers, but the peltry and fur trade of the lakes also, to our ports; thus adding immense increase to our exports, and binding these people to us by a chain which can never be broken."[18] For the sake of the nation, Washington urged improvement of the natural advantages enjoyed by New York and Pennsylvania, but his more immediate interest was in drawing the trade of the interior to the Potomac and Virginia rather than to the Mohawk and the Hudson.

Two years after Washington's New York tour the attention of the New York legislature was drawn to the navigation of the Mohawk by one Christopher Colles, the first of many native Irishmen to be associated with the New York canals. Colles had been the principal engineer on the improvement of the River Shannon and came to America seeking similar employment.[19] Although unsuccessful, his memorial to the legislature urged the removal of the obstructions in the Mohawk, and a pamphlet by

[18] Above quotations from Washington are cited in David Hosack, *Memoir of De Witt Clinton: with an Appendix, Containing Numerous Documents, Illustrative of the Principal Events of His Life* (New York, 1829), pp. 275, 277, 278-79.

[19] Colles to Charles J. Ingersoll and Richard Stockton, January 17, 1814, Christopher Colles Papers, NYHS.

his hand in 1785 was directed to "the speedy settlement of the waste and unappropriated lands on the western frontier of the State of New York." For the improvement of the Mohawk he proposed a private company capitalized at £13,000 to be granted 250,000 acres of western lands when the necessary works were completed. His company never materialized, but the prophecy he made should his plan be adopted added to a growing vision which would lead to the Erie Canal:

By this, the internal trade will be increased—by this also, the foreign trade will be promoted—by this, the country will be settled—by this, the frontiers will be secured—by this, a variety of articles, as masts, yards, and ship timber may be brought to New York, which will not bear the expense of land carriage. . . . By this, in time of war, provisions and military stores may be moved with facility in sufficient quantity to answer any emergency; and by this in time of peace, all the necessaries, conveniences, and if we please, luxuries of life, may be distributed to the remotest parts of the great lakes . . . and to the smallest branches of the numerous rivers which shoot from these lakes upon every part of the compass.[20]

In 1787 a bill was introduced in the New York legislature for making improvements in the navigation of the Mohawk which contained the interesting phrase "and for extending the same, if practicable, to Lake Erie," but like the proposal of Christopher Colles, it went no further.

It was not until the 1790s that the improvement of the Mohawk-Oswego water route was finally begun. A joint committee in the state legislature was appointed to report on opening navigation between the Mohawk and Wood Creek and between the Hudson and Lake Champlain by

[20] Quoted in Tacitus [De Witt Clinton], *The Canal Policy of the State of New York; Delineated in a Letter to Robert Troup, Esquire* (Albany, 1821), p. 12.

contract with a private company. The favorable report of this committee led in 1791 to the first canal law in New York state, authorizing the necessary exploration, survey, and estimates for these improvements. The result was the incorporation in 1792 of two private companies that would not only seek to accomplish these limited goals but attempt a project of still broader scope.

The companies were formed chiefly through the exertions of Elkanah Watson and Philip Schuyler. Watson became famous for his contributions to agricultural reform and his early advocacy of the county fair, but in the years after the Revolution he was best known in New York as an eager propagandist for canals. He later wrote a history of the New York canals in which he emerged as the exclusive projector of the canal policy of the state.[21] In 1784, Watson had made a visit to the Netherlands where he was fascinated by the Dutch countryside and "enchanted" by canal travel. A two-day visit to Mount Vernon in 1785 during which Washington described his plans for a canal connecting the Potomac with the Ohio made Watson Washington's "canal disciple." During the next three years he traveled through the Southern states, visiting as he went the sites of proposed canals. With this background he journeyed in 1788 up the Mohawk Valley to Fort Stanwix. There he became convinced that by improving and joining the Mohawk with Wood Creek, the state of New York would "divert the future trade of Lake Ontario and the Great Lakes above, from Alexandria [Virginia] and Quebec to Albany and New York."[22] The

[21] Elkanah Watson, *History of the Rise, Progress and Existing Conditions of the Western Canals in the State of New York* (Albany, 1820), pp. 5-19; Robert Troup, *A Vindication of the Claim of Elkanah Watson, Esq. to the Merit of Projecting the Lake Canal Policy* (Geneva, 1821), Appendix, p. 2.

[22] Watson, *History of the Western Canals*, pp. 15-16.

memoirs of a second and more prolonged journey to Oswego and to Seneca Lake in 1791 produced a glowing confidence in the growth of the West through inland navigation and an enthusiasm which he conveyed to the public in his canal articles in the New York *Journal and Patriotic Register* and the Albany *Gazette*.[23] Watson's plans for the improvement of the Mohawk, Seneca, and Oswego rivers by building short canals, and by deepening and clearing their channels went far beyond those of the joint committee appointed in the legislature of 1791.

General Philip Schuyler of Albany, meanwhile, had likewise caught a vision of water improvements in New York. He had heard Gouverneur Morris speculate at Saratoga during the Revolution of a water connection between the Hudson and the "great western seas." He had seen the new canals of England on a visit there in 1761. Wealthy and public-spirited, with title to thousands of acres of land in New York, he became, as Dixon Ryan Fox has described him, "the chief patron of internal improvements" in the state.[24] Schuyler's political prestige as Federalist leader in the state senate carried Watson's plans into the act of 1792 that incorporated the two private canal companies to begin the first canal construction in New York.

The act of 1792 incorporated the Western Inland Lock Navigation Company and the Northern Inland Lock Navigation Company. The first was to open a navigable waterway from Albany to Lakes Seneca and Ontario, while the second was to improve the waters between the Hudson and Lake Champlain. Both companies were

[23] "For the New York Journal and Patriotic Register May 12, 1792," Journal of 1791, Elkanah Watson Papers, NYSL.

[24] Dixon Ryan Fox, *The Decline of Aristocracy in the Politics of New York* (New York, 1919), p. 151.

authorized to take subscriptions for a thousand shares at $25 a share, and each was to be given a grant of $12,500 by the state. Schuyler became president of both companies and Watson was a director. The Northern company began work on a canal near Stillwater in 1793 and made limited improvements between Fort Edward and Lake Champlain, but failing, it was soon dissolved. The Western company had more success as it struggled for more than a decade to improve the Mohawk route to the west.[25]

Wealthy landholders, merchants, and bankers were most prominent among the backers of the Western company. Among them were the Holland Land Company, Robert Troup as agent for the Pulteney estate, LeRoy, Bayard & Company, and land speculators such as Samuel Ward, Melancton Smith, and Daniel McCormick. Nearly half of the directors of the company were landholders hoping for a rise of land values as a result of their canal investments.[26] New York City businessmen such as John Murray, Nicholas Low, and Daniel Ludlow were stockholders and the Quaker merchant, Thomas Eddy, served for a time as treasurer. Between 1792 and 1795, 743 shares were sold, of which 240 were later forfeited.[27] By 1801 nine calls upon the shareholders had been made for further assessments. The state gave liberally to these fledging efforts at privately sponsored improvements. The legislature followed its initial gift with the purchase in 1795 of 200 shares at $50 a share and in 1796 granted the company a loan of $37,500.

[25] Nathan Miller, "Private Enterprise in Inland Navigation; the Mohawk Route Prior to the Erie Canal," *New York History*, XXXI (1950), pp. 398-413.

[26] *Ibid.*, p. 403.

[27] *Ibid.*, p. 402.

The Western company excavated canals, constructed locks, and cleared obstacles from the Mohawk River and Wood Creek, hampered always by a shortage of money and the novelty of the project. "In a country where improvements in water navigation have never been prosecuted to any extent," Barent Bleecker complained to the stockholders in 1794, "it is not in the least possible to procure mechanics and laborers the least conversant with the business."[28] Frederick de Zeng, a superintendent at Little Falls, explained the delay of his contractors, "making the reasonable allowance, it being the first work of the kind in the Country."[29]

First the Western company built a small canal and five locks measuring 74 by 12 feet at Little Falls where the river fell thirty-nine feet in three-quarters of a mile. By 1797, two miles of canal 37 feet wide and 4 feet deep and two locks were completed at Rome to open navigation between the Mohawk and Wood Creek.[30] On the second of October of that year, an empty bateau carrying the American flag led a tiny procession through the works traversing in an hour what formerly had required a day to perform. Wood Creek itself was cleared and shortened, navigation of the Mohawk was improved, and another mile and a quarter of canal and two locks were finished in 1798 at Wolf Rift in German Flats. These improvements made it possible in times of sufficient water for new Durham boats as long as sixty feet and carrying sixteen tons to supplant those carrying only a ton and a half used heretofore on the river. The cost of transportation from

[28] Bleecker to the Stockholders of the Western Canal Company, January 4, 1794, Philip Schuyler Papers, NYPL.

[29] De Zeng to Schuyler, August 17, 1793, Philip Schuyler Papers, NYPL.

[30] *Report of the Directors of the Western Inland Lock Navigation Company* (Albany, 1798), pp. 9 ff.

Albany to Seneca Lake was reduced from $100 to $32 a ton and that from Albany to the Niagara by half.[31] Down the canals came furs, lumber, pot and pearl ashes, wheat, and salt, and up them moved boats "principally laded with European or Indian productions or manufactures."[32]

Against these achievements was the fact that the Western company found the portage around Cohoes Falls between Schenectady and Albany completely beyond its resources. Nothing was done on the Oswego River and little was attempted between Lakes Oneida and Seneca. Low water in the Mohawk frequently made that capricious stream impassable between Utica and Rome, and even with the company's works in operation the river boats could never supplant wagon carriage on the land. The farmers of the Mohawk Valley and the settlers around the Finger Lakes and in the Genesee Valley more often sent their goods to Albany by road than by water.[33]

The canal builders of this period must be judged to have left a record more of failure than of success. When no competent American engineer could be found, the companies sent vainly to England for aid and finally secured the part-time services of William Weston, an Englishman who was then employed in Pennsylvania on the Schuylkill and Susquehanna Canal. But Weston could not visit the works until 1795. Schuyler himself felt compelled to superintend the canal operations in spite of his increasing enfeeblement by gout, his duties in the state senate, and without, as he wrote to Weston in 1793, "the

[31] *Ibid.*, pp. 24-32; J. Murdock to Arthur Noble, July 5, 1798, Philip Schuyler Papers, NYPL; Watson to the Albany *Argus*, June 14, 1818, Elkanah Watson Papers, NYSL.

[32] Resolutions of a Meeting of the Directors of the Western Canal Company, February 14, 1803, Philip Schuyler Papers, NYPL.

[33] Ellis, *Landlords and Farmers*, p. 84; McNall, *History of the Genesee Valley*, p. 98.

least practical experience in the business."[34] Schuyler and Watson quarreled over Schuyler's salary and his "tyrannical manner," ultimately causing Watson to withdraw from company affairs.[35] De Witt Clinton, who held only one share of stock but spoke for the Republican supporters of his uncle, Governor George Clinton, accused Schuyler of using the canal to benefit his Federalist friends, "to enlist the passions of a party on the side of hydraulic experiments."[36]

Labor proved always in short supply, and some of the Irishmen employed became embroiled in riots with each other and with neighboring townsmen. More than 400 men were employed at a time and workers were brought from Pennsylvania, Vermont, Connecticut, and Canada. An attempt was even made to hire Indians in 1796, but they quit after two days and on one occasion they threatened the men on Wood Creek by their "hostile disposition." The annual "sickly time" so decimated the ranks of the laborers that the blockhouse of Fort Schuyler was turned into a hospital.

Constant problems of supply and supervision plagued the work, and De Zeng was accused of embezzling the Western company's money through fraudulent accounts. First wood, then brick, and then stone were used for the locks, some of which were rebuilt four times. A satisfactory mortar could not be devised. Not until 1803 did Benjamin Wright discover limestone near Oneida Lake

[34] Schuyler to Weston, April 16, 1793. Schuyler paid $100 to David Rittenhouse for a leveling instrument. Receipt, May 31, 1793, Philip Schuyler Papers, NYPL.

[35] Schuyler to Watson, November 16, 1792; Watson to Thomas Eddy, November 27, 1800, Elkanah Watson Papers, NYSL.

[36] Marcellus [De Witt Clinton] to Schuyler in New York *Journal*, July 24, 1793; "On the Canal Company," Draft, De Witt Clinton Papers, CUL.

suitable for the locks. Both merchants and boatmen protested the high tolls, which were raised steadily as the financial condition of the company worsened.

Whatever benefits the company's backers may have looked for in their land speculations or commercial interests from the improvement of the Mohawk route to the interior of the state, the balance sheet of the company remained profitless. The first dividend of 3 percent was paid in 1798 and the next did not come until 1813. By 1803, eleven years after incorporation, the Western company's revenues amounted to less than $10,000 after expenditure of more than $400,000.[37] In that year plans were underway to eliminate the last of the portages between Schenectady and Seneca Lake, but five years later the company relinquished its rights to make further improvements west of Oneida Lake.[38] Little more was done than to keep the works in repair. Although ill health increasingly limited Schuyler's direction of company affairs, the aging general served as president until 1803, promising to "exert what remains of my ability to promoting the Interest of the W. Canal company and that of the Community, for they are mutual."[39] The accounts of the company were finally closed when the state purchased its property for the Erie Canal in 1820.

Both the difficulties and the dreams of the inland lock navigation companies were in microcosm those of the Erie Canal. Their directors saw themselves in the vanguard

[37] Julius Rubin, "An Innovating Public Improvement: The Erie Canal," in Carter Goodrich, ed., *Canals and American Economic Development* (New York, 1961), pp. 22-23.

[38] Miller, *New York History*, XXXI, 408; Minutes of the Meeting of the Directors of the Western Inland Lock Navigation Company, July 6, 1803, Philip Schuyler Papers, NYPL. A dividend of 4½ percent was paid in 1815. Albany *Gazette*, February 16, 1815.

[39] Schuyler to John Murray, January 22, 1803, Philip Schuyler Papers, NYPL.

of the canal movement in Europe and America. Their letters, reports, and petitions told of the need to settle western New York, the rivalry of the St. Lawrence and other routes to the interior, and the public blessings which would result from their private labors. Their failures gave a foretaste of the engineering problems which must be solved in building a canal through the Mohawk Valley and gave clear indication that such a work in that day was beyond the resources of private enterprise alone.

Clinton, Watson, Troup, Eddy, Jeremiah and Stephen Van Rensselaer, Gouverneur Morris, Benjamin Wright, Gideon Granger, Jonas Platt, Simeon De Witt, and many others bent on improving the navigation of the Mohawk at the turn of the century, would be intimately involved with the New York canals for the remainder of their lives. Their experiences in canal making were being stored for future use. Limited as was their success, the efforts of these men to develop an inland water empire served as the first major step to the development of a greater project that would go far beyond Seneca Lake and Oswego, reaching its destination on the shores of Lake Erie.

2

Jesse Hawley's "Genesee Canal"

PERHAPS the first conception of an interior route for a canal to Lake Erie, following the vague reference by Cadwallader Colden, was expressed in 1800 by the statesman-traveler, Gouverneur Morris. Recently returned from his post as minister to France and a speculator in "Genesee Lands," the exotic Morris traveled to the wild backcountry of New York. He visited General Schuyler in Rome and saw the improvements already made along the Mohawk. Then, standing on the shore of Lake Erie, he counted nine vessels riding at anchor. "Does it not seem like magic?" Morris wrote subsequently to a correspondent abroad.

Hundreds of large ships will in no distant period bound on the billows of those inland seas. At this point commences a navigation of more than a thousand miles. Shall I lead your astonishment to the verge of incredulity? I will: know then, that one-tenth of the expense borne by Britain in the last campaign, would enable ships to sail from London through Hudson's River into Lake Erie. As yet, my friend, we only crawl along the outer shell of our country. The interior excels the part we inhabit in soil, in climate, in every thing. The proudest empire in Europe is but a bauble compared to what America *will* be, *must* be, in the course of two centuries, perhaps of one.[1]

Just what passage for a canal across New York Morris envisioned would be strongly contested by all who contributed to the early steps toward the adoption of an interior route direct from the Mohawk to Lake Erie. Simeon De Witt, the surveyor general of New York, wrote later of his chance meeting with Morris in the fall of 1803 at an inn in Schenectady when the latter discoursed upon the "project of tapping Lake Erie . . . and leading its waters in an artificial river, directly across the country to the Hudson River." Although De Witt thought it a "romantic thing, and characteristic of the man," he told others of the scheme, among them James Geddes who was a judge and surveyor of Onondaga County. Geddes found Morris optimistic at the prospect of a canal direct to Lake Erie which would avoid the greater lockage required to descend to Lake Ontario and rise again to the Lake Erie level, but so ignorant was Morris of the country to be crossed "and his pertinacity was such, that it was almost impossible to call his attention to the impracticability of such a thing."[2]

But Geddes did, by his later account, discuss the "probable track of such a canal" west of the Genesee River with Jesse Hawley in February of 1805 when Hawley boarded at the home of Geddes' relatives in Geneva.[3] And it was Jesse Hawley who first published a plan for "A canal from the foot of Lake Erie into the Mohawk."

Jesse Hawley was a merchant in Geneva in partnership with one Henry Corl and engaged in forwarding flour to the New York market. Sending cargoes by wagon and

[1] Hosack, *Memoir of De Witt Clinton*, p. 257. Julius Rubin, a recent authority on the origins of the Erie Canal, presents the view that Morris meant an overland or interior route for the canal. Rubin, "An Innovating Public Improvement," pp. 26-28.

[2] Hosack, *Memoir of De Witt Clinton*, p. 266; *Laws of the State of New York, in Relation to the Erie and Champlain Canals* (Albany, 1825), I, 42, cited hereafter as *Laws*.

[3] Monroe *Democrat*, December 29, 1835.

in the long Durham boats that passed through the locks of the Western Inland Lock Navigation Company, he was forced to pay higher transportation charges when the Mohawk fell in the summer months. Early in April of 1805, Hawley worried over this state of affairs with Colonel Mynderse in Seneca Falls, whose mills ground the flour that Hawley purchased. Lamenting the inability to draw water from Lake Ontario into Wood Creek and the Mohawk, as Hawley himself later described the birth of his great idea, he "sat in a fit of abstraction for some minutes—then took down De Witt's map of the State, spread it on the table and sat over it with my head reclined in my hands and my elbows on the table, ruminating over it, for—I cannot tell how long—muttering *a head of water;* at length my eye lit on the falls of Niagara which instantly presented the idea that Lake Erie was *that head of water.*"[4] His friends thought his notion of using water from Lake Erie a "whimsical vagary," and in December of 1806 the failure of his business partner led him to flee to Pittsburgh to escape their debts. There Hawley wrote an essay in the Pittsburgh *Commonwealth* proposing the project of connecting Lake Erie, the Mohawk, and the Hudson by canal.

Returning to New York to relieve a friend who had provided bail in suit over Hawley's obligations, Hawley surrendered himself in Canandaigua and taking advantage of a twenty-month confinement "within the gaol limits" of the county for debt, he began a series of fourteen essays describing not only a canal from Lake Erie to the Mohawk but improvements over the entire continent as well. His own account continued: "There I was!—in a Debtor's Prison for the relief of my bail; betrayed and defrauded by my partner; broken down and almost destitute in

4 Ontario *Messenger,* January 27, 1841.

despondency at the thought that hitherto I had lived to no useful purpose of my own;—accompanied with many pensive reflections that I never want to recall. Recovering myself, I resolved to publish to the world my favorite, fanciful project of an overland canal, for the benefit of my country, and endure the temporary odium that it would incur."[5]

This prescient debtor, without formal education beyond that of a country school, gathered a few books and maps and by "laborious study" sought "to review the inland waters of this continent and suggest modes of their improvement. . . ." Hawley's essays were published in the Genesee *Messenger* in 1807 and 1808, signed "Hercules," and they made him the first publicist for the Erie Canal. He insisted that his project was no one's but his own, and until he died in 1841 he sought to establish himself as the originator of the project for an overland canal.[6] De Witt Clinton gave it as his opinion that Hawley's essays were the first suggestion "in a tangible shape" of the Erie Canal though Gouverneur Morris had earlier thrown out "hints" of the project.[7]

Hawley's remarkable proposals emerged from an age of water transportation in which navigation offered the

[5] *Ibid.* In 1825, Hawley explained the writing of his essays in a letter published in that paper, July 19, 1825: "They were written when all my private prospects in life were blighted; and I was indeed 'induced to write them' from a wish to render some use to society for my existence. . . . It was a new, unexplored, and hard subject to write on, for I could not find a treatise on canals."

[6] For Hawley's defense of his claim see letters by Hawley, Geddes and others in Rochester *Telegraph*, July 19, 1825; Monroe *Democrat*, October 13, December 29, 1835; Ontario *Messenger*, January 27, 1841; Rochester *Daily Democrat*, July 30, 1841; Rochester *Daily Advertiser*, December 6, 1842. Rubin cites conflicting sources on "Morris's originating role" in "An Innovating Public Improvement," p. 259, n. 24.

[7] Benjamin Wright to Hawley, July 22, 1835, Jesse Hawley Papers, NYHS; Clinton to Jesse Hawley, February 22, March 22, 1822, Henry O'Reilly Papers, RPL.

"most cheap, familiar, and extensive intercourse with distant places." Moreover, the route he proposed for his "Genesee Canal," though never examined by himself, was very nearly that which was adopted after years of survey. His estimated cost of six millions was within a million dollars of the final expenditure. The projected canal began in the West near the mouth of the Niagara River, ran parallel with that river for a few miles, was carried over the Tonawanda Creek and the Genesee River by aqueducts, flowed into Mud Creek and the Seneca River, and finally entered the Mohawk at Utica. Hawley advertised a canal built on an inclined plane which would fall from the elevation of Lake Erie to the Mohawk, "pitched and gauged to any dimension required," in a fashion that would characterize the canal proposals for the next five years.

The advantages foretold in these essays anticipated with accuracy the development of the state once the canal was a reality. The trade of Upper Canada would pay for canal repairs; mail and passage boats would make the muddy perils of spring and autumn travel ordeals of the past for thousands of travelers; emigration would be made easier, and mill seats along the course of the canal would pay the wages of the lock-tender. Most phenomenal of all would be the new face brought to the land. The Finger Lake region would be laced with canals and connected to the Oswego River, "enhancing the value of many millions of acres of land adjacent to their navigation." New York City would cover "its island" with buildings and population. Albany would "cut down her hills and fill her valleys," and the harbor at Buffalo would "exchange her forest trees for a thicket of marine spars." In short, wrote this eager propagandist, "no situation on the globe offers such extensive and numerous advantages to inland navigation by a canal as this."[8] So favored a condition Hawley attributed to the hand of God: "Nor do I conceive the idea to be vain, or even incorrect in saying that it appears as if the Author of nature . . . had in prospect a large and valuable canal . . . to be completed at some period in the history of man, by his ingenuity and industry."

But who should build such a canal? Heretofore the efforts to improve the Mohawk route had been made chiefly by private investors aided by the state, but Hawley now proposed that the national government should construct the work. He judged the undertaking to be beyond the reach of individual capital and to remain so for a century to come. Foreign aid he would not tolerate, for he feared that foreign capitalists would levy a perpetual and parasitic toll. Corporate bodies were to him inimical "to the common interest" and tended toward monopoly. Living in Jeffersonian America, he sketched in Jacksonian fashion the problems of an America in which Hamiltonian economics would come of age:

The government which grants charter-parties, cedes so much of its jurisdiction—creates and erects so many little demisovereigns within itself. This it does at its own expense. . . . The joint interests of incorporate bodies, like partnership, produces a concert of measures. Being derived from government by an emanation of political power, they are very subject to react on the parent of its existence. Fifty men associated for a common purpose, can out machinate five hundred unassociated; and one bank association, *may* bribe two-thirds of the representation of the whole state. They must, indeed pay for it, but others must pay them in turn; and like the special immunities, the whole must come out of the people.[9]

8 Hosack, *Memoir of De Witt Clinton*, p. 323.
9 *Ibid.*, pp. 324-25.

The prophecy of Hawley's essays, like that to be characteristic of the entire canal movement, was by and large a prophecy of nationalism and democracy. He believed that only a "patriotic government, with a productive revenue" could be relied upon to build the canal. Significantly too, he applied the litmus of national interest to justify his proposals. He looked to "political considerations, the consequences of which cannot be estimated by the rule of pence." Our growing nation, destined to spawn "ten times" as many new states, must be bound together by water communications which would secure the states from dismemberment.

Lastly, these far-ranging essays charted the coming of the canal era to America. Hawley traced improvable water-courses through every state of the union and gave emphasis to those which would link to his Genesee Canal. His eye glimpsed even a canal across the Isthmus of Darien. He little realized the rapidity with which his proposed canals would be attempted, and like men in any period of change, he tempered incredulity in the future with faith in the past:

Although, I have an ardent wish to live and see many of them effected, yet, by accident, I may be writing for a subsequent age: And I have that reliance on the American character, already established for its inventive genius and enterprise, which gives me even grateful expectations that . . . my countrymen are capable of encountering many difficulties and apparent impossibilities, by which many improvements . . . will be undertaken and completed in a future day. . . . it would be a burlesque on civilization and the useful arts, for the inventive and enterprising genius of European Americans, with their large bodies and streams of fresh water for inland navigation to be contented with navigating farm brooks in bark canoes.[10]

[10] *Ibid.*, pp. 328, 337.

Only five years later Jesse Hawley was making application to De Witt Clinton for a position as an engineer on the Erie Canal.[11] Within as many decades two canals from Lake Erie to the Ohio River, a canal from the Maumee River to the Wabash in Indiana, a ship canal at the falls of St. Mary, two canals improving navigation between Lake Michigan and the Mississippi, and the Raritan Canal between the Raritan and the Delaware rivers were completed along routes foreseen in the essays by "Hercules."

Hawley's public proposal for a waterway which would follow the long interior route from the Mohawk to Lake Erie met with understandable skepticism and his essays received only limited circulation. But as interest grew, a deep difference of opinion was manifested as to the best path by which the trade of the lakes could be drawn to the Hudson. Questions of practicability, expense, safety, ease of travel, and direction of trade awaited answer. At the same time, such a prospective bonanza affected basic interests of land values and political power, and inevitably brought a varied local response.

The controversy on the question of the route of the Erie Canal began the moment the first action was taken in February of 1808 by the New York legislature. Joshua Forman, member of the assembly from Onondaga County, and Benjamin Wright, a representative from Oneida County, "hatched up" a canal resolution which was presented by the former and seconded by the latter. They called for a survey and exploration of the most eligible and direct route for a canal between the Hudson and Lake Erie to be financed by Congress. These two Federalists from central New York were each known by the title of "Judge," and they shared a room in Albany. Forman had been elected to the assembly on a "canal tick-

[11] Elijah Hawley to Clinton, April 26, 1813, De Witt Clinton Papers, CUL.

et," with a Democratic Republican, George McWhorter. Wright had surveyed more than a hundred miles on the Ontario route for the Western Inland Lock Navigation Company. They had with them a copy of Ree's *Cyclopedia* which told of the success of English canals, and they were eager to take advantage of the opportunities seemingly offered by Jefferson's message of 1807 to Congress which recommended the application of surplus revenues to canals and turnpikes. Although Hawley could later show that Forman was in possession of the first numbers of his essays, both Forman and Wright professed to have been ignorant of them and to have persuaded themselves of the superiority of the interior over the Ontario route to Lake Erie.

Forman made an able speech advocating a canal direct to Lake Erie and sketched the path which it might follow. Its cost he estimated at ten millions, a "bagatelle to the value of such a navigation" in the settlement of western New York, the enrichment of New York City, and as a "bond of union between the Western and Atlantic states."[12] He had little confidence that Congress would ever undertake such a waterway, but he hoped that his resolution would induce the state to explore the route, "which, if proposed as a work of the state, would not have been listened to at all." So skeptical was the legislature of the resolution, that the $600 provided for the survey was to be divided by the surveyor general between the interior route and the better known Ontario route at his own discretion.

Simeon De Witt, the surveyor general in 1808 and long a shareholder in the Western Inland Lock Navigation Company, so favored the traditional route to Lake Ontario that he looked upon an interior canal to Lake Erie as "a separate

[12] Hosack, *Memoir of De Witt Clinton*, p. 345.

work," perhaps to be undertaken after a canal to Lake Ontario had been completed. Nevertheless, to carry out the directive of the legislature he dispatched a letter to Joseph Ellicott who was agent of the Holland Land Company at Batavia and the man west of the Genesee whose opinion as to the feasibility of a canal direct to Lake Erie would carry the most weight. "Should such a thing be brought about," added De Witt unnecessarily, "the Holland Company will doubtless be much benefitted by it."[13]

Word of the proposed interior route had already reached Ellicott in his frontier outpost. Ellicott had seen the possibility of a canal through western New York as early as 1805. He was a shrewd manager of the Holland Company's affairs and was far ahead of his superiors in recognizing the value of the canal to the development of western New York.

Title holder to the greater part of New York west of the Genesee, the Holland Company had taken an active, though cautious, part in the earliest attempts to open the region to settlement. Theophile Cazenove and Paul Busti, the successive agents for the company residing in Philadelphia, had initially sought to combine the interests of the Western Inland Lock Navigation Company with those of the land company in the passage of an act to secure an extension of the right of alien land holding in the state. But the Dutch had refused to make the loan of $250,000 demanded by the canal company and only the efforts of Aaron Burr and some well-placed bribery finally secured the passage of the Alien Act of 1798, opening the way for continued land sales in western New

13 De Witt to Ellicott, June 13, 1808, Frank H. Severance, ed., *The Holland Land Co. and Canal Construction in Western New York, Buffalo–Black Rock Harbor Papers, Journals and Documents, Buffalo Historical Society Publications,* XIV (Buffalo, 1910), 3; cited hereafter as *HLC-WNY Canal Documents.*

York.[14] Company aid was also promised to the Erie
Turnpike Company in 1807, but Busti believed such projects were premature and gave his promise of assistance
only to avoid "exciting public clamour" against the Dutch
speculators. But now that Forman's canal resolution of
1808 offered the prospect of a waterway built and maintained by Congress or the state, Ellicott and Busti found
the canal project a nice combination of public good and
private gain.[15]

To no one's surprise, Ellicott's long and detailed reply
to the surveyor general favored an interior route for the
canal which crossed the Holland Purchase. He advised
against the Ontario route with its plan for a canal around
Niagara Falls, believing the solid rock along the Niagara
River would make such a canal impossible. To Busti in
Philadelphia, Ellicott pointed out that an interior canal
would pass through swamp land "totally unfit for cultivation" unless it be drained, while with a canal the 40,000-
acre tract might net a tidy profit of a million dollars. Thus
the company readily offered a cession to the state of
alternating lots of 160 acres adjoining the canal, totaling
over 18,000 acres.[16]

Together with the proferred land cession, the sage land
agent of Batavia gave hard-headed arguments for the
superiority of the interior route. He calculated that 244
feet less lockage would be required than that by the
Ontario route. He feared that the Ontario route would

[14] Paul D. Evans, *Holland Land Purchase, Buffalo Historical Society
Publications,* XXVIII (Buffalo, 1924), 207-14.

[15] Busti to Ellicott, June 6, 1807, April 12, 1810, Robert Troup to
Ellicott, January 15, 1807, Henry O'Reilly Papers, NYHS.

[16] Ellicott to Busti, July 16, 30, 1808, Ellicott to De Witt, November
9, 1808, Joseph Ellicott Letterbooks, BECHS; Ellicott to David Evans,
October 20, 1808, *HLC-WNY Canal Documents,* p. 17. If the canal
were to be constructed by a company, Ellicott pledged the Holland
Company to a land grant and himself to a subscription of $2,500.

actually turn to the advantage of Canada, "whereby the Trade of all the Western World would be lost" to New York. A canal by the Ontario route, he warned, would lead to "other Evils of a political Nature . . . highly injurious to the Harmony and Prosperity of the United States."[17] Ellicott's report to De Witt gave a solid boost to the prospects for an interior canal, provided a favorable survey could be run from the Seneca River to the Genesee.

By agreement with the sponsors of the Forman resolution, De Witt appointed James Geddes to run the surveys authorized by the legislature. Geddes, it will be recalled, had discussed the canal project with Gouverneur Morris and claimed to have communicated Morris' plan to Jesse Hawley. At De Witt's direction he spent the summer of 1808 and all the $600 surveying the lands between the Mohawk and Lake Ontario and along the Niagara River. He turned finally in December to the critical part of the interior route, "the spot of great difficulty and uncertainty" between the Genesee River and Mud Creek (Palmyra), where it was presumed that high ground intervened. With an explorer's excitement he pronounced the interior route practicable. To his "great joy and surprise" Geddes found the only problem that of carrying the water of the Genesee across the Irondequoit Valley. And here the canal could be carried "on a surface not surpassed, perhaps in the world, for singularity," over a series of ridges, "in many places of just sufficient height and width for its support." An artificial embankment 68 feet in height and more than 500 yards in length would be needed, but given money, labor, and time, the work could be accomplished. "While traversing these snowy hills in December, 1808," Geddes later wrote to his friend, William Darby, "I little

17 Ellicott to Busti, December 17, 1808, Joseph Ellicott Letterbooks, BECHS.

thought of ever *seeing* the Genesee waters crossing this valley on the embankment now constructing over it. I had, to be sure, lively presentiments, that *time* would bring about all I was planning, that boats would one day pass along on the tops of these fantastic ridges, that posterity would see and enjoy the sublime spectacle, but that for myself, I had been born many, very many years too soon. There are those, sir, who can realize my feelings on such an occasion, and can forgive, if I felt disposed to exclaim *Eureka,* on making this discovery."[18]

Since by December the young surveyor had already expended the original appropriation for the survey, he was reimbursed the additional seventy-three dollars which had enabled him to make the discovery most critical to the success of the interior route.

Geddes made his report to the surveyor general in 1809, detailing first the path of a canal from Oneida Lake to Lake Ontario and along the Niagara River to Lake Erie, and second, in more general terms, the path of an interior canal from Oneida Lake to Lake Erie. His survey convinced him that both routes were possible, but his report went further than a technical description of each. He reported the "obstinate" insistence by the advocates of the interior route that with the use of Lake Ontario "there would be danger of the whole lake trade being diverted" to Canada.[19] On the other hand, he noted the cheaper conveyance claimed for shipments by lake than by canal, "the grand desideratum in all such works." This he countered with the estimate of Robert Fulton that a ton could be carried 150 miles by canal for $1.50 as compared to the $5.25 charge per ton on salt carried between the lake ports of Oswego and Lewiston. Disinterested as

[18] *Laws,* I 44.
[19] *Ibid.,* p. 31.

Geddes sought to be, the tone of his report favored the interior route, even though he admitted that he had driven no leveling pegs in any part of his work, "or attended to that nicety requisite for the actual staking out of a canal. . . ."[20] What had been the visionary scheme of Gouverneur Morris, the publicized plan of Jesse Hawley, and the legislative proposal of Joshua Forman now became the basis for determined action by the state or national governments.

Assistance from the national government seemed almost assured when Secretary of the Treasury Albert Gallatin made his famous report on internal improvements to the Senate in April of 1808, even before Geddes made his report to the surveyor general of New York. With payment of the national debt in sight, Jefferson and Gallatin proposed a national system of roads and canals which Jefferson believed could be authorized through an amendment to the Constitution. Gallatin asked for an annual appropriation of two millions a year for ten years toward projected improvements throughout the nation. Prominent among them was a canal to connect the Hudson River with Lake Champlain, a canal to connect the Hudson with Lake Ontario at Oswego, and a canal around the Niagara Falls.[21] Gallatin was promisingly specific in his proposal to apply more than three millions in national funds to canals between the Hudson and Lake Erie. Although he did not mention the interior route set forth by Jesse Hawley, the Canandaigua debtor and the secretary of the treasury offered a remarkable parallel in their plans to make canals between the Hudson and Lake Erie part of a national system.

Joshua Forman was quick to capitalize on such favor-

20 *Ibid.*, p. 32.
21 Henry Adams, *The Life of Albert Gallatin* (New York, 1879), p. 351.

able prospects for national aid. Being in New York on business, he journeyed on to Washington "almost entirely to converse with Mr. Jefferson on the subject."[22] He was introduced to Jefferson by a New York congressman, and "in as laconic a manner" as possible he promptly reported New York ready to receive a share of the surplus revenues in view of the "important advantages" offered to the nation by a canal direct from Lake Erie to the Hudson. But the New Yorker found Jefferson "not a little surprised" at so early a call on his proposed fund for internal improvement. For all the recommendations of Gallatin's report, Jefferson thought their project a century ahead of its time. "Why sir," said Jefferson, "here is a canal for a few miles, projected by George Washington, which if completed, would render this a fine commercial city, which has languished for many years because the small sum of 200,000 dollars necessary to complete it, cannot be obtained from the general government, the state government, or from individuals—and you talk of making a canal 350 miles through the wilderness—it is little short of madness to think of it at this day."[23]

In part because worsening relations with England and

22 Hosack, *Memoir of De Witt Clinton*, p. 346.
23 *Ibid.*, p. 347. Jefferson later wrote to Clinton in 1822 affirming the conversation of 1808 and added: "and many, I dare say, still think with me that New-York has anticipated, by a full century, the ordinary progress of improvement. This great work suggests a question, both curious and difficult, as to the comparative capability of nations to execute great enterprises. It is not from greater surplus of produce, . . . for in this New-York is not beyond some other states; is it from other sources of industry additional to her produce? This may be;—or is it a moral superiority? a sounder calculating mind, as to the most profitable employment of surplus, by improvement of capital, instead of useless consumption? I should lean to the latter hypothesis, were I disposed to puzzle myself with such investigations; but at the age of 80, it would be an idle labour, which I leave to the generation which is to see and feel its effects. . . ." Jefferson to Clinton, December 12, 1822, *Ibid.*, pp. 347-48.

France were soon to carry the nation into the War of 1812 Congress never provided the requested funds. But the prospect of national aid from the administration of Thomas Jefferson had enabled the New Yorkers to launch the Erie Canal.

3

Survey and Report

WHILE IT appeared unlikely that the Forman resolution and the surveys of 1808 would yield tangible federal aid, a fresh boost to the prospects for a canal to Lake Erie came in March of 1810 as the promoters of the failing Western Inland Lock Navigation Company revived their efforts for support. Thomas Eddy, the company treasurer, called upon Jonas Platt, who was a Federalist senator from the Western District and also candidate for governor running on a platform of "Platt and Commerce" in those days of the Embargo and restrictions in European trade.[1] Eddy's object was to interest the legislature in new explorations for a company-constructed canal from Oneida Lake to the Seneca River. But Platt, who had himself been long associated with the canal company's projects, astonished the lobbyist with a more sweeping proposal: "why not make application at once for a canal to connect the waters of Lake Erie with the waters of the Hudson River?" Eddy feared that the legislature would be so frightened by the proposal that he "would lose even what I am sent here to obtain," but together they devised a plan for the state to set up a board of commissioners to explore the two routes to Lake Erie preparatory to constructing a canal.

What was needed for the success of their plan was the

support of a prominent Democratic Republican to counter the predominantly Federalist complexion of the canal company. De Witt Clinton was the available man. He was nephew of Governor George Clinton, former mayor of New York, a land speculator, naturalist, and educator and the ascendant leader of the Republicans in the state senate. Moreover, it was Clinton who, as a shareholder of the Western canal company, had publicly attacked Schuyler for using the company to the advantage of the New York Federalists in 1793. At Platt's behest, Clinton consented to back a canal resolution provided the names of the commissioners be left blank. Platt then introduced a resolution to appoint a board of commissioners to examine and survey the entire interior route from the Hudson to Lake Erie as well as that to Lake Ontario and around the Niagara Falls, and to report on the most eligible path. Clinton seconded it and it passed both senate and assembly by unanimous vote.[2] Three thousand dollars were appropriated to defray the cost of the survey. How far the canal idea had spread since the timid response given to Joshua Forman's resolution of 1808!

The seven-man board of commissioners was given a nice political balance; the entire canal project might stand or fall on their reputations. Gouverneur Morris, Stephen Van Rensselaer, William North, and Thomas Eddy were Federalists; Simeon De Witt and Clinton were Republicans, and Peter B. Porter led the Tammany faction known as "Martling Men," Republicans, but politically opposed to Clinton.[3] At the same time these men knew each other

[1] New York *Evening Post*, April 10, 1810.

[2] Rubin, "An Innovating Public Improvement," p. 40.

[3] Only North and Porter among the commissioners had not been stockholders in the Inland Lock Navigation companies. North was an heir to the Von Steuben estate and Porter was a landholder on the Niagara River. Miller, *Enterprise of a Free People*, p. 218, n. 32.

well; they had dealt with each other in business, politics, and land speculation, and as men of substance they presented a strong claim to public confidence.

Divisions among the commissioners over the rival routes to Lake Erie did not become manifest until the success of the canal itself was more assured. Peter B. Porter, one of the most prominent of the commissioners, worked zealously for the canal although his personal interests centered upon the use of the Ontario route. Such a route would mean a canal through his own lands at Black Rock, three miles down the Niagara River, following the portage path over which his brother Augustus had long held a monopoly.[4] As a member of Congress in 1810, Porter had made a widely publicized speech in the House where he sought unsuccessfully to secure national aid for a canal constructed on the Ontario route as part of the Gallatin plan.[5] But Porter's name was affixed to all the reports of the commissioners even as they increasingly recommended the interior route.

The commissioners put themselves vigorously to their task of exploration. Morris and Van Rensselaer, carrying with them Hawley's essays, Ellicott's letter and map, and the report of Geddes, covered the ground from Albany to Buffalo. The other commissioners examined once more

[4] Tacitus, *Canal Policy*, p. 24.

[5] Porter's bill in the House was accompanied by a bill in the Senate sponsored by John Pope of Kentucky. Neither was passed. Porter anticipated the day when the United States would turn from foreign concerns to national development. Since the commercial restrictions of the Napoleonic wars had led the American people to develop their own internal resources, a "great inland commerce" would become more profitable than any foreign commerce America could enjoy. He feared the division of America "into great distinct sections" separating Americans into agriculturalists on the one side and merchants and manufacturers on the other. Such a danger might be averted, said Porter, by "opening a great navigable canal from the Atlantic to the western states." Hosack, *Memoir of De Witt Clinton*, pp. 359-74.

the advantages of the Ontario route.[6] Geddes and Benjamin Wright served as surveyors and mapped out the line of the canals. In March of 1811, when public expectation was reported to be "on tip toe," the commissioners made their report.[7] They declared for the interior route.

This first serious examination of the entire ground proved such a canal entirely feasible. Looking westward, the canal could follow the "vale of rich soil" along the Mohawk and be fed with waters from the river or the Canada, Schoharie, and Oriskany creeks. From the summit level at Rome to the outlet of Canandaigua Lake, four lakes lay higher than any canal which might be constructed to Lake Erie, furnishing a "copious supply of water." From the Canandaigua outlet to Lake Erie, which the commissioners called the "dry division," the land was essentially a plain. There a canal could be supplied by the Genesee River, cut through the steep ridge marking the rise in elevation from Lake Ontario to Lake Erie, and then use the bed of the Tonawanda Creek itself to reach the Niagara River which in turn would be followed to Lake Erie.

Although the Tonawanda Creek was so favorably situated as to be converted into a canal, the commissioners' conviction that the beds of rivers could not serve as a canal militated against the use of the Oswego River and the Ontario route. If that route were followed they foresaw the necessity of constructing a horse "rail-way" for the twelve miles between the falls of the Oswego and Lake Ontario. Furthermore, they feared that the use of

[6] See John Hartshorne Eddy, "Diary describing a tour of inspection of the Commissioners appointed in 1810, to examine into the navigation of the western parts of the State of New York between the Hudson River, and Lakes Ontario and Erie, June 30 to July 16, 1810," MS, NYPL.

[7] New York *Evening Post*, February 7, 1811; Tacitus, *Canal Policy*, p. 24; *Laws*, I, 48-69.

Lake Ontario would destroy the very purpose of the entire
canal project. Articles once afloat on Lake Ontario, they
believed, "will, generally speaking, go on to Montreal."

Professor McNall's study of the Genesee Valley has
shown that the factors influencing the selection of a
market for the products of western New York were more
complex than the commissioners knew. Montreal was a
"more satisfactory" market by reason of cheaper transportation on Lake Ontario and the St. Lawrence than that
offered by the water route to Albany. At the same time,
the Montreal market was subject to embarrassments from
Canadian trade restrictions and flour shipped to it arrived
in Europe later than that from competing regions. Road
transportation to Albany, more expensive though it was,
made that Hudson River city still the "favorite market"
for the farmers of the Genesee Valley.[8]

When the canal commissioners made their report in
1811, the difference in transportation costs between Montreal and Albany seemed reason enough for their opposition to the Ontario route. Lumber, furs, flour, pot and
pearl ashes did find a market in Canada. James Wadsworth, landholder in the Genesee Valley, looked upon the
St. Lawrence as the "natural out-let" for the produce of
his region, and he remained cool to the canal project until
1818 when he finally despaired of British trade policies.
In February of 1811, a New York merchant reminded a
friend at the Genesee that the projected canal would be
"the means of retaining the affections of our western
brethren, who are now trading principally with their
Canadian neighbors, and from continued intercourse they
may soon fancy their interest inseparable."[9]

Joseph Ellicott's partiality for his "inland route" rested

[8] McNall, *History of the Genesee Valley*, pp. 98-102.
[9] Quoted in New York *Evening Post*, February 1, 1811.

on concern for his company's lands to be sure, but as the canal project matured, the question of a Canadian or American market became decisive in his thinking. In June of 1810, Ellicott reported that the "great men of the nation" favored the Ontario route and a canal around the Niagara Falls.[10] In view of this, Ellicott, on whose financial support Clinton relied for success in "all future operations," cooled perceptibly. "I have therefore much less opinion of this great object than I formerly had," he wrote to Busti in Philadelphia, "because I am of the opinion that if the products of the country contiguous to Lake Erie are once carried to Lake Ontario that is [sic] natural channel is Montreal and Quebec. . . ." Ellicott stated candidly the course he would follow: "Should this Canal ever be undertaken, and the Oneida and Ontario route be preferred I shall not subscribe anything towards carrying on the work; because, I am pursuaded [sic] that it will be more advantage at once to make Montreal our market; and it makes no difference to us what Market we go to; the great object is to go to such a Place where we can make the most profits, being the governing Principles with those who have anything to dispose of."[11]

Already a marked increase of "foreign gold" made its appearance in the coffers of the Holland Company. The Canadian firm of Borrekins and Company had established a post at Great Sodus for the purchase of produce and another had been set up at the mouth of the Genesee River. Ellicott was confident that new posts would be set up between the Genesee and the Niagara "as soon as the Settlers on the Holland Purchase may have produce to spare." By August of 1810, Ellicott had made up his mind.

10 Ellicott to Paul Busti, June 9, 1810, Joseph Ellicott Letterbooks, BECHS.
11 *Ibid.*

News came that a barrel of potash could be carried from any port on Lake Ontario to Montreal for three dollars. If the canal were made by either route, it would be useless in the face of such competition. "I am therefore of the opinion that Montreal will be our Market," wrote Ellicott to Busti as he surveyed the commercial future of western New York.[12] The goal of the commissioners was to counter this alarming possibility as they planned for the Erie Canal.

Ironically, the phase of the New York canal movement which had begun with Thomas Eddy's efforts to revive the fortunes of the Western canal company produced the firm decision by the commissioners in 1811 that construction must be by public authority alone. On this question, "more important, perhaps, than any other," the commissioners entered "their feeble protest against a grant to private persons or companies," fearing individual or corporate speculation.[13] Since a national interest was at stake and other states would share in the benefits of a canal through New York, the commissioners anticipated the "prudent munificence" of Congress in sharing the costs to be incurred. Their language here reflected the youthfulness of the Republic with all its uncertainties over the relationship between state and nation. To determine the proper contribution of state and national governments,

[12] Ellicott to Paul Busti, August 11, 1810, Joseph Ellicott Letterbooks, BECHS. Busti continued in this thinking well into 1811. Busti to Ellicott, May 17, 1811, *HLC-WNY Canal Documents*, p. 19. Lyman Spalding, growing up in western New York, later to live at Lockport on the Erie Canal, related an experience of the winter of 1809-1810. His father sent him with a party of men to the mouth of the Genesee River from his residence at Scipio on the east shore of Cayuga Lake to "get out pipe staves for the Quebec Market" by sleigh. Shortly thereafter his father moved to the mouth of the Genesee itself to trade in the Montreal market. Lyman A. Spalding, *Recollections of the War of 1812 and Early Life in Western New York* (Lockport, 1949), p. 5.

[13] *Laws*, I, 68.

thought the commissioners, "the proportion, the conditions, the compact in short, must be the result of treaty," arrived at by "negociation."

If much of the report of 1811 was cautious, tentative, and calculating, there was also much to alarm rather than to convince the skeptical. It was penned by the ebullient Gouverneur Morris as president of the board of commissioners and still proposed an "inclined plane" canal from Lake Erie. Morris saw a "glowing hue" in the prospect of such a canal "fed by pure water from lakes, provided mounds and aqueducts be made over intervening vallies, or the canal be carried around them." The elevation of Lake Erie 565 feet above the Hudson allowed a drop of six inches to the mile and the canal was to consist of a yard of excavation to bring its depth to four and a half or five feet of water. Such a canal was estimated to cost only five million dollars.[14] Projected on this plan, the canal seemed fantastic to anyone familiar with the undulating landscape of western New York.

The work of the commissioners bore fruit in the passage of the first canal law by the legislature in April of 1811. By its provisions, the commissioners were reappointed, Robert Livingston and Robert Fulton were added to their number, and now $15,000 was appropriated for their use. They were authorized to seek the aid of other states and of Congress, receive land grants and seek out loans, and to negotiate for the purchase of the interests of the Western Inland Lock Navigation Company. Early in May, five of the commissioners met in New York. Clinton and Fulton were named to communicate with the Lock Navigation Company. Simeon De Witt and Van Rensselaer were to seek land cessions for the path of the canal. Clinton and Livingston were given the task devis-

14 *Ibid.*, pp. 60, 65, 67.

ing a plan to secure national assistance. Morris and William North were to report on the best terms on which money could be borrowed, while Eddy and Fulton began the search for an engineer.[15] The canal project was visibly in motion.

By the end of the year Clinton and Morris were in Washington to appeal to Congress for aid. President Madison was willing enough to lend his support, though the New Yorkers found him "embarrassed by scruples derived from his interpretation of the Constitution." Madison sent to Congress a copy of the act of the New York legislature, noting that the canal enterprise included "objects of national, as well as more limited, importance," and he reminded the legislative branch of the "signal advantages" to be derived from a "general system of internal communication and conveyance." At the Treasury Department, Gallatin was eager to prosecute the New York canal as part of his earlier plan, but he believed that the national treasury would allow assistance only in the form of land grants which might "be afterwards redeemed by cash, when the treasury should be in a more prosperous condition." For its part, Congress proved slow to respond to the appeal from New York.

A committee was appointed in the House to deal with the petition of the New Yorkers and Madison's message regarding it. Its members offered some hope if the New York canal were made part of a general system benefiting many states. Quickly the New Yorkers drafted a bill providing tempting land grants to states from Massachusetts to Georgia and inland to Ohio, Kentucky, and Tennessee, to be ceded as soon as designated canals within their borders should be completed. By this grand log-roll,

[15] Extract from the Minutes of the meeting of the Canal Commissioners, May 4, 1811, Peter A. Porter Papers, BECHS.

Clinton and Morris hoped for a grant to New York of four million acres "so soon as a canal shall be opened from Lake Erie to Hudson's river," which could be pledged as security for loans at the rate of two dollars an acre. But the committee delayed and the bill never reached the House. Some favored a constitutional amendment, which the New Yorkers feared was more for the purpose of aiding the National Bank than canals, and the commissioners noted the "baleful effect" of state jealousy in raising an opposition to the measure. Moreover, Morris wrote that Congressman Peter B. Porter "hangs back" as it appeared that the canal would follow the interior route rather than that by his own lands.[16] The New Yorkers were finally put off by the claim, which they believed "more plausible than solid," that every national resource might be required to support a war.[17]

With much bitterness, the commissioners were forced to conclude that national aid was not forthcoming. They reported that hostile or jealous congressmen hoped "that the envied state of New York will continue a supplicant for the favor and a dependent on the generosity of the Union, instead of making a manly and dignified appeal to her own power," and they added with a show of independence, "It remains to be proved, whether they judge justly who judge so meanly of our councils."

In spite of an imminent war with Britain involving an area where New York was particularly vulnerable, the commissioners plunged ahead with their work and made a second report to the New York legislature in 1812. The Buffalo *Gazette*, though representing a certain location of conflict, found this report "the most important and in-

[16] Morris to Clinton, January 18, 1812, De Witt Clinton Papers, CUL; *Laws*, I, 92.
[17] *Laws*, I, 94.

teresting Paper our country's recent history can boast of."[18] Indeed, Clinton argued, the prospect of war made the canal project all the more imperative.[19]

The matter of Canadian rivalry for Western trade still remained a paramount consideration in the need for a canal. Miffed at the unwillingness of the officials of the Michigan Territory to come to the aid of New York in the building of an interior canal out of preference to the Ontario route, and finding "men of influential character" preaching the same doctrine in New York, the commissioners again spelled out the dangers of trusting the trade of the West to the temptations of Montreal. The obdurate fact was there. It was cheaper to ship by lake from Ogdensburg to Montreal than to go by canal from the "difficult and dangerous port of Oswego" to Rome on the Mohawk route to the Hudson. Moreover, the commissioners reiterated their concern for the people of western New York who enjoyed few harbors on Lake Ontario. These isolated souls would be benefited most by a canal "dug at a distance from lake Ontario," and in a comparison of transportation costs by land or by canal the effect of an inland canal would be the same "as if Lake Erie were brought within forty miles of Hudson's river."

The report of 1812 chipped away at the plan for an inclined plane first advocated by Morris and Hawley. The 83-foot embankment required to cross the Seneca River by such a plan had already proved impossible. Now the project would combine both inclined plane and level canal. After the commissioners had "taken pains to extend investigation, increased the number of surveys, and accumulated the knowledge of facts," they raised their estimate of the cost of the canal to six million dollars, a

18 Buffalo *Gazette*, May 5, 1812.
19 Tacitus, *Canal Policy*, pp. 26-27.

"trifling weight" to the million souls of New York. Here the commissioners were blunt. New York had been rebuffed in its appeal to Congress and had been offered scant prospect for assistance from other states. She was now "at liberty to pursue the maxims of policy." These, said the commissioners, seemed "imperatively to demand that the canal be made by her, and for her own account, as soon as circumstances will permit."[20]

Perhaps just because it seemed so certain that New York must build alone, the commissioners showed little patience for those whose caution or realism led them to the side of conservatism. After calculating the cost, they sought to estimate the toll which might be collected and they levied this effusion of sarcasm against the timid:

Things which twenty years ago a man would have been laughed at for believing, we now see. . . . Under circumstances of this sort, there can be no doubt that those microcosmic minds which, habitually occupied in the consideration of what is little, are incapable of discerning what is great, and who already stigmatize the proposed canal as a romantic scheme, will, not unsparingly, distribute the epithets, absurd, ridiculous, chimerical, on the estimate of what it may produce. The commissioners must, nevertheless, have the hardihood to brave the sneers and sarcasms of men, who, with too much pride to study, and too much wit to think, undervalue what they do not understand, and condemn what they cannot comprehend.[21]

By their own calculations of the increased cultivation of the regions opened up by an Erie Canal, the commissioners foresaw 250,000 tons of goods annually brought down from the West within twenty years. A toll of $2.50

[20] *Laws,* I, 72; see also Morris to Harmanus Bleecker, February 28, 1812 (copy), Gouverneur Morris Papers, CUL.
[21] *Laws,* I, 79.

a ton on boats "going and returning" would make an annual revenue of $1,250,000. Scale down the estimate to half that amount, said the commissioners, and there would still be $600,000 to pay the interest at 6 percent on a canal costing even ten millions.

How long might such a canal serve the state and hold "a key to the commerce of our western world?" Here the report of the commissioners could set no end: "And even when . . . our constitution shall be dissolved and our laws be lost, . . . after a lapse of two thousand years, and the ravage of repeated revolutions, when the records of history shall have been obliterated, and the tongue of tradition shall have converted (as in China) the shadowy remembrance of ancient events into childish tales of miracle, this national work shall remain. It will bear testimony to the genius, the learning, the industry and intelligence of the present age."[22] Against the background of its times, the report of 1812 is an amazing document. Though our national institutions were scarcely established, though we were in the severest diplomatic embarrassments abroad and still contending with a wilderness land at home, these men were sanguine of the future. "Whether this subject be considered with a view to commerce and finance, or on the more extensive scale of policy," they concluded, "there would be a want of wisdom, and almost of piety, not to employ for public advantage those means which Divine Providence has placed so completely in our power."[23]

But wishing did not make it so. The War of 1812, with its feeble operations centering on the New York frontier, brought canal plans nearly to a stop. Stephen Van Rensselaer, one of the commissioners, was placed at the

[22] *Ibid.,* p. 81.   [23] *Ibid.,* p. 72.

head of the New York militia and the war brought a decline to Clinton's political career. Clinton became the unsuccessful peace candidate for the presidency in 1812, supported by Republicans opposed to Madison and by the Federalists, and three years later he was removed from the office of mayor of New York City which he had held throughout the war. Although an act was passed in June of 1812 which allowed the commissioners to borrow five million dollars and to continue their surveys, its enabling provisions were repealed in 1814. Still, the commissioners were ready to attempt a loan in Europe on the very eve of the war; and the day after war was declared, Platt introduced a bill to purchase the rights of the Western Inland Lock Navigation Company. The commissioners appointed an English (!) engineer "preferably to any other" because "an Englishman speaking the same language, and habituated to the same usages and manners, will more easily acquire information among us, and be less liable to imposition."[24] And in their report of 1814 they proposed extending their project to the valley of the Susquehanna.

Although Commodore Macdonough had not yet exhibited his tactical brilliance on Lake Champlain, the commissioners announced in 1814 that grants had been made by the great land holders of the state whose property would appreciate through the influence of the canal. The Holland Company donated 100,632 acres; 2,500 acres came from the company of LeRoy, Bayard and McEvers, and 3,500 were given by John Grieg in behalf of the Hornby estate. Robert Troup promised a large grant from the Pulteney estate as soon as it was in his power to make it. Public notice of these donations was the culmination of a

[24] *Ibid.,* p. 103.

long negotiation between the land companies and the commissioners.

The agents of the Holland Land Company were completely opportunistic during the vicissitudes of the early stages of canal planning. When it appeared that the canal was not going to follow the path through company lands marked out by Ellicott, Busti found his "zeal for the success of the undertaking . . . much abated."[25] But if anything developed, he wished to be in on the ground floor. He cautiously authorized in 1812 the grant of half a township, upon the condition that the canal be put into operation within twenty years, and operate for ten years more.

The commissioners could not accept this form of grant, and Thomas Eddy wrote to his friend in Batavia requesting a larger quantity of land, specifically located on the Holland Purchase. Perhaps unfairly, the Holland Company was made the bellwether for the future of the canal project. If the company grant "should amount to something considerable," Eddy promised, the legislature would commence the work. But "if unfortunately *you should fall short of what might be reasonably expected from you, the whole plan would be frustrated.*"[26] The commissioners could twist an arm.

Ellicott responded with a neat scheme whereby the company could gain a reputation for generosity at no loss, and even at a profit to themselves. He refrained from forwarding Busti's offer to the commissioners and proposed a substitute donation; he would give the state a large body fo land between the Allegheny River and the

[25] Paul Busti to Joseph Ellicott, March 4, 1812, *HLC-WNY Canal Documents*, pp. 21-22; Ellicott to Busti, May 20, 1820, Joseph Ellicott Letterbooks, BECHS.

[26] Eddy to Joseph Ellicott, July 10, 1812, *HLC-WNY Canal Documents*, pp. 25-26.

northern boundary of Pennsylvania. At this location, 115,000 acres at 25¢ an acre would be the equivalent of 11,500 acres worth $2.50 an acre in Busti's original proposal near the canal line. In the transaction, the company would be relieved of ten times as much taxable land in mountains that could never be sold. "It would also appear to be vastly more liberal," Ellicott added, "because the quantity of land is so much greater, and neither the commissioners nor the public have any knowledge of the difference in quality."[27] Busti concurred. To make assurance doubly sure, he urged Ellicott to take care that since he had been requested to make surveys for the canal, he "would contrive to make the canal follow the track" through Batavia, the seat of the Holland Company land office.[28] The 100,632-acre grant so eagerly announced by the commissioners in 1814 was virtually unsalable land located in the mountains of southwestern New York.

This promising arrangement for the company finally soured. The commissioners appeared at first pleased, but they wanted something more. They requested the ground fifty feet in width through which the canal would actually be cut, and in addition, free quarrying and wood cutting rights along the canal. In prolonged negotiations, Busti balked at the generosity of the company being made "a model of imitation for everything" and refused to grant the canal path unless all owners of such lands made equal concessions. By 1815, because of the difficulties of war, the entire canal project appeared to have collapsed. "The Canal bubble it appears, has at length exploded," wrote

[27] Ellicott to Busti, July 21, Ellicott to Eddy, August 19, 1812, *HLC-WNY Canal Documents*, pp. 28, 32-33. Ellicott was actually willing to make both donations, believing that if the canal were a success, the company would be repaid fourfold for its grant.

[28] Busti to Ellicott, August 1, 1812, *HLC-WNY Canal Documents*, p. 30.

Ellicott to Busti, and the deed granting the lands south
of the Allegheny River was cancelled.[29]

The temporary collapse of the canal project was undoubtedly due largely to the travails of war, but Clinton
saw the suspending act of 1814 as the fruit of growing
political opposition to himself and to the canal as well.
The canal issue could not fail to become enmeshed in the
three-way political division of New York among Clintonians, Madisonians, and Federalists. The powerful Tammany Society branded Clinton's alliance with the Federalists in 1812 as disloyal to the Republican cause.[30]
Porter, the Martling leader, found it possible to serve his
own political interests, while opposing those of Clinton,
all without publicly opposing the canal. Martin Van
Buren backed Governor Daniel Tompkins against Clinton,
but voted against the suspending act of 1814 on the canal.
Governor Tompkins endorsed the canal reports but so
favored the Ontario route that Clinton found him "the
insidious enemy of the Erie Canal."[31]

At the same time, sectional opposition to a canal
through western New York began to appear in both the
eastern and southern parts of the state where it was foreseen that the canal could not be an unmixed blessing. A
pamphlet by Samuel Beach of Jefferson County, entitled
*Considerations against Continuing the Great Canal West
of the Seneca,* though it appeared somewhat later, reflects
the dissent of southern New York. Writing under the
pseudonym of Peter Ploughshare, Beach complained that
while the canal would carry the western New Yorker's

[29] Ellicott to Busti, August 12, 1815, *HLC-WNY Canal Documents,*
p. 38.

[30] Robert Reineke, "Political Aspects of the Origin and Building of
the Erie Canal" (unpublished master's thesis, Colgate University, 1951),
p. 41.

[31] Tacitus, *Canal Policy,* p. 26.

produce to market, it would ruin those markets by inviting the competition of farms in Michigan and Ohio. "I should like to know," he asked, "whether my little farm in the county of Jefferson has got to be taxed from year to year, for the purpose of enabling the farmers on the shores of Lakes Erie, Huron and Michigan to bring their produce to market for nothing. . . ."[32] Beach deprecated the commissioners' fears that articles once afloat on Lake Ontario would go on to Montreal and reminded them of the obstacles in the navigation of the St. Lawrence. He found it foolish to build a canal parallel to Lake Ontario, passing through a lake port such as Rochester which was equally susceptible to the alleged dangers of Canadian rivalry for American trade. Contrary to the conclusion of the commissioners, Beach argued persuasively that the Oswego River could be improved at a fraction of the expense of an interior canal to Lake Erie. Meanwhile, other critics of the proposed canal thought it simply beyond the resources of the state.[33] Voices like these would reach a crescendo when the war was over and the debate was focused on the floor of the legislature.

Officially, canal prospects appeared to have reached bottom in 1814. But the future would show that the commissioners had launched a program which would be carried by its own momentum and the force of circumstance. In only two years following the end of the war the canal project would snowball into the long-awaited law by which construction could begin.

[32] Peter Ploughshare [Samuel Beach], *Considerations against Continuing the Great Canal West of the Seneca* (Utica, 1819), pp. 4-5, 13; see also George Tibbits to Benjamin Tibbits, June 13, 1828, in Hosack, *Memoir of De Witt Clinton*, p. 488.

[33] Cadwallader D. Colden, *Memoir, . . . at the Celebration of the Completion of the New York Canals* (New York, 1825), p. 41.

4

From Prophecy into Law

THE SURGE of national expansion which followed the successful termination of the war added to older pressures in New York for the inauguration of the canal. The war itself had turned on the control of the very waterways which the New York canal system would unite. Military embarrassments on the Niagara frontier were attributed in part to the bad roads between Washington and Buffalo, as cannon worth $400 at Washington had cost $2,000 to transport to Lake Erie.[1] Furthermore, the failure to annex Canada to the United States meant that the geopolitical realities which gave the outlet of the Great Lakes to a foreign power would remain for the foreseeable future.

Once more the stockholders of the Western Inland Lock Navigation Company helped to reinvigorate the canal project. They were more than ever convinced of its necessity, and they were also eager to sell their unproductive holdings to the state. In New York City, where most of them lived, Clinton, Eddy, Platt, William Bayard, Cadwallader Colden, and John Swartwout sent invitations to about a hundred "respectable citizens" to meet at the City Hotel on the next to the last day of 1815, hoping there to win public support for the canal. Bayard took the chair, John Pintard (Clinton's life-long friend) served as secretary, and Platt addressed the meeting. Platt sought to remove the lingering suspicion of a canal by an inclined-plane, and Clinton was put at the head of a committee to petition the legislature for the immediate commencement of the great waterway.[2]

Clinton's memorial, bearing thousands of signatures from New York City and throughout the state, became the most publicized of some thirty appeals sent to the legislature in 1816. A thousand copies were printed "for the information of the public," and Clinton later claimed it to be "the basis for the whole canal system."[3] Clinton's petition was grounded upon the axioms of the canal era, by which canals "united cheapness, celerity, certainty and safety" in transportation. The ideal of a harmonious, water-connected society seemed particularly applicable to New York. An interior canal to Lake Erie would extend 300 miles "through the most fertile country in the universe," and when joined with the Great Lakes, it "would perhaps convey more riches on its waters than any other canal in the world." The canal plan was shown to be entirely practicable; no longer was there talk of an inclined plane, but instead the New York memorial proposed sixty-two locks to allow a rise and fall of 625 feet in the canal. The cost was put at $20,000 a mile, or six million dollars for a canal to be completed in "ten or fifteen years."[4]

The New York memorial deplored the continuing "contrariety of opinion" over the now tiresome question of the route. In pages of close argument, Clinton opposed a

[1] Caroline E. MacGill and others, *History of Transportation in the United States before 1860* (Cambridge, 1948), p. 59; Colden, *Memoir of the New York Canals*, p. 42.

[2] Minutes, December 30, 1815, De Witt Clinton Papers, NYHS.

[3] Clinton to John Sergeant, August 17, 1825, De Witt Clinton Papers, CUL.

[4] *Laws*, I, 131.

canal around the Niagara Falls and another from Oswego to Albany if such should be built to the exclusion of an interior route to Lake Erie. He would risk the competition of an Ontario route with all its loadings and unloadings of cargo if canals by both routes could be constructed, but "if a canal is cut around the falls of Niagara, and no countervailing nor counteracting system is adopted in relation to Lake Erie, the commerce of the west is lost to us for ever." Even more important, an "Erie Canal" would "diffuse the blessings of internal navigation over the most fertile and populous parts of the state," while the Ontario route "would be a circuitous by-road, inconvenient in all essential respects." Clinton rhapsodized over the transformation awaiting the line of the canal as agriculture blossomed, factories sprang up, and cities were created. "It remains," he concluded, "for a free state to create a new era in history, and to erect a work more stupendous, more magnificent, and more beneficial than has hitherto been achieved by the human race."[5]

Canal meetings were called up and down the state in 1816. Editor Salisbury in Buffalo, who spoke for a village then numbering more than a thousand souls, called for action in January and in February announced a Niagara County meeting at the inn of Gaius Kibbe.[6] Seven days later a petition was on its way to Albany, prophetic of future wealth to be derived from the canal, emphasizing the need for strengthening the frontier after "the melancholy experience of the late war," and (in spite of Porter's local prestige) warning against any choice of the Ontario route.

A canal gathering at Canandaigua was attended by a particularly notable group. Robert Troup, Gideon Granger,

[5] *Ibid.*, pp. 140-41.
[6] Buffalo *Gazette*, January 30, 1816.

John Grieg, John Nicholas, Nathaniel Howell, Nathaniel Rochester, and Myron Holley were among the most prominent men in the western part of the state. The resolutions of their memorial to the legislature clustered around the now familiar pattern: impending prosperity, the dangers of the Ontario route, the increased value of western lands, and the great bond of union that could be so easily fashioned.[7]

In Batavia, James W. Stevens called upon the state to squeeze land donations out of every landholder whose lands would appreciate in value because of the canal. With arguments which made him an early Henry George, he wished the legislature to buy for speculation the sites of future cities at the crossing of the Genesee and the Seneca Rivers and land in Ohio and Michigan as well.[8] What the public created, so should it reap.

But Joseph Ellicott was preeminently cautious in his reaction to the new impetus behind the canal movement. Prompted by Clinton, he joined in the meeting at Buffalo and directed William Peacock, his agent at Mayville, to convene a similar one at that seat on Chautauqua Lake. At the same time, he wrote Chauncey Loomis in the senate chamber at Albany to learn just what kind of a law might be produced by this influx of petitions. Still unsettled were questions of route and apparently plan as well, for reports had it that the idea of an inclined plane was not yet dead. He warned Clinton that if the Ontario route was still in the winds, the West would be ready with a remonstrance against it. Unwilling to see precipitate action, Ellicott advised Clinton that what was wanted was not a law to begin construction as Clinton's New York memorial had proposed, but a law which would appoint commis-

[7] Hosack, *Memoir of De Witt Clinton*, pp. 426-27.
[8] Stevens to Clinton, February 26, 1816, De Witt Clinton Papers, CUL.

sioners with power to explore and survey so that accurate calculations of expense could be made.[9]

Practicality went with simplicity in Ellicott's character and expressed itself in nativist antipathy to foreign engineers. "Have no foreigners in the business," he wrote to Loomis, "they make everything cost double what it might, and really have not as much knowledge of constructing objects of this nature as many Americans that may be obtained." The sober Quaker, Thomas Eddy, was writing at the same time to Clinton that a first-class engineer should be employed, "but he ought not to be a Frenchman."[10]

∠ The legislature could not remain deaf to such vigorous clamor for action on the canal when it convened in February of 1816; but it could delay⁷. Governor Tompkins, from whom leadership might have been expected, was unable to move, even though it was an election year and he was considered vice presidential timber. Described by Clinton as "profoundly ignorant on the subject," and influenced by Porter in favor of the Ontario route, Tompkins gave only lukewarm support to the canal in his opening address: "It will rest with the Legislature, whether the prospect of connecting the waters of the Hudson with those of the western lakes and of Champlain, is not sufficiently important to demand the appropriation of some part of the revenues of the State to its accomplish-

[9] Ellicott to Clinton, February 21, 1816, *HLC-WNY Canal Documents,* p. 49. It is interesting to note that after what was regarded by the friends of the canal as an initial defeat, this plan was finally followed.

[10] Ellicott to Chauncey Loomis, February 14, 1816, *HLC-WNY Canal Documents,* pp. 46-47; Ellicott wrote the same to Clinton and urged "employing Americans solely . . . ; the truth is [he added] the laying out of a path for the canal, requires neither conjurors nor wizards; practical nature is everything that is necessary." Ellicott to Clinton, February 21, 1816, *HLC-WNY Canal Documents,* p. 49. Eddy to Clinton, February 28, 1816, De Witt Clinton Papers, CUL.

ment, without imposing too great a burden upon our constitution."[11]

At this, Clinton was furious. He regarded the charge as an evasion by which the advocates of neither route would be offended and the onus of financial extravagance would be placed upon the legislature.[12] Clinton, in contrast to Tompkins, had made the canal his own. He had been a commissioner since 1810; he had toured the entire line of the canal, publicized his authorship of the New York memorial, and after his removal as mayor of New York City, he had staked all upon the canal issue. "We are all united on this subject, except the Martling Men," he wrote to Ellicott. "We have a good cause and let it not be our fault if it is not crowned with success."[13]

Governor Tompkins found himself in difficult straits indeed. To keep the support of Porter and the Martling Men, he must equivocate; if he came out for the interior route, he would alienate Porter; if for the Ontario route he would lose support in the West. He was extricated from this predicament, at least in part, by the opposition still shadowing the growing outburst of canal enthusiasm and, so Michael Burnham of the New York *Evening Post* believed, by the skillful political handiwork of Martin Van Buren. Clinton supported Tompkins for the governorship over the Federalist Rufus King as a "less evil," and Tompkins was reelected in the spring.

∠ In the legislature there was still sufficient opposition to postpone for over a year the authorization of a state constructed canal. The counties along the Hudson and on Long Island which feared the competition of new regions to the West were opposed, and the counties of the southern

11 *Laws*, I, 116.
12 James Renwick, *Life of De Witt Clinton* (New York, 1840), p. 249.
13 Clinton to Joseph Ellicott, February 3, 1816, *HLC-WNY Canal Documents*, pp. 41-42.

tier could be counted in the negative. The beginnings of the business recession which would become a panic in 1819 were threatening, and it seemed risky to launch so broad a project in a period of economic instability.[14] Many, such as Martin Van Buren, were pro-canal but anti-Clinton and were reluctant to assist a measure which must almost certainly raise his political stock. It was clear that when the legislature took up the canal question, it would be divided.

The commissioners appointed under the act of 1810 brought in their final report on March 8 and recommended legislative approval for an immediate beginning of the canal.[15] Thirteen days later, Jacob Rutsen Van Rensselaer introduced a bill in the assembly to authorize construction of a canal by the interior route.

The tactics of the opposition were rather to postpone than to reject the measure outright. On the motion of William A. Duer of Dutchess County, the assembly decided to permit only surveys and estimates by the close vote of 55 to 52. Then with the adoption of a tax upon lands bordering the canal, advocates of immediate construction were successful in pushing through amendments going far beyond mere survey. The section between Rome and the Seneca River was actually to be commenced and the commissioners were to be given authority to borrow two million dollars on the credit of the State. In such form the bill passed the assembly by the impressive majority of 91 to 18. But in the senate, Martin Van Buren, who was the anti-Clintonian ally of Tompkins and who claimed to be convinced that more information was

---

[14] Nathan Miller, *Enterprise of a Free People: Aspects of Economic Development in New York State During the Canal Period, 1792-1838* (Ithaca, 1962), pp. 66-70.

[15] *Laws*, I, 117. The signature of Gouverneur Morris was withheld from this report.

needed, moved to expunge all that part of the bill after the fifth section. This authorized only additional surveys and a further report to the legislature. The amendment carried, and now recast into a form which would postpone the actual beginning of the canal, the bill passed the senate, 19 to 6.

The assembly at first refused to concur. The senate would not recede. It was the last day of the session and the alternatives were half a loaf or none. The assembly yielded and on April 17, 1816, the canal bill became law. "After all the expectations raised respecting the Great Canal, it is still 'hope deferred,' " wrote James Geddes to Clinton.[16] But again commissioners were appointed, including Clinton, Ellicott, Stephen Van Rensselaer, Samuel Young, and Myron Holley. Gouverneur Morris was not reappointed, and a few months later death ended his distinguished public career. The commissioners were to survey the canal route, estimate its cost, and apply to Congress and others for aid with the $20,000 appropriated for their use. And the division in the assembly had been close—close enough to foreshadow the day when construction would begin.

The commissioners began their new duties in May. They elected Clinton their president, divided the canal into three great divisions, and assigned an engineer to each. To assist Geddes on the western section, they appointed William Peacock, who, working under Ellicott's direction, was to survey a route which would pass for forty miles through the lands of the Holland Company.

Relieved that Gouverneur Morris had been dropped from the board of commissioners, Geddes now explored a new and more northerly route which forever gave up

[16] Geddes to Clinton, April 24, 1816, De Witt Clinton Papers, CUL.

Morris' *"grand* idea of drawing water from Lake Erie."[17] Throughout the summer and fall of 1816 the survey parties moved out across the state, taking levels, placing locks, and recording every detail for the report to the legislature. When they finally put down their instruments, they and the commissioners were confident that apprehension over the obstacles to be encountered was unwarranted. But since the engineer on the eastern section, Charles Broadhead, was unable to complete his survey of the Mohawk Valley in time, the commissioners were forced to rely on William Weston's reports of twenty years earlier. Clinton was exuberant over the "general sentiment in favor of the Erie Canal" found along the route, and he wrote optimistically to John Pintard that the surveys would now place it "beyond the reach of cavil."[18]

The Holland Company continued its interest, but wavered between lack of confidence, optimism, and conditional support. On the whole Ellicott and Busti were confident that the company could not lose. Even if the canal were never completed, the construction gangs would need provisions from company lands, and the "mere idea of a canal" would bring new settlers. "Roads and Canals whenever opened will be beneficial to the lands, and provided the Company has not to pay the piper, never oppose the pleasure of the settlers in running a race over a new Road or having a rowing match on a Canal or pond," wrote Busti in a jocular vein to Ellicott.

Memorials continued to pour in upon the legislature,

[17] *Ibid.* Peacock and Ellicott recommended a route through the Holland Company lands passing near Batavia, which required an elevation of the canal 74 feet above Lake Erie and 148 feet of additional lockage.
[18] Clinton to Ellicott, August 18, 1816, *HLC-WNY Canal Documents,* pp. 64-65; Clinton to Pintard, August 18, 1816, De Witt Clinton Papers, NYPL.

and the canal took an increasingly more prominent place in public prints. The Buffalo *Gazette* demanded in January of 1817, that the State "go forward perseveringly to commence, *and prosecute with vigor, the Canal from Erie to the Hudson*," in order that "the great, all important object" be accomplished.[19] Clinton himself took up his pen again to continue his "ATTICUS" letters, which had first appeared in the New York *Evening Post* in 1811, to popularize the project. In 1816 he wrote three more letters now presenting the canal as the "child of the people" and the special interest of no person or party or section.[20] Addressing those in the western part of the state, Clinton wrote that the canal was "an object of such magnitude, that the blind may see it," and to the people of New York City he predicted that their metropolis "will stand when the canal shall be finished, unrivalled by any city on the face of the earth." What was more, he appealed to his city friends to care for the civilization of the frontiersmen of the interior. "Is it with you a subject of no consideration," he asked, "whether the millions of people, who are settled or may settle upon the waters of the great lakes, shall be a virtuous or vicious generation, whether they be civilized or savage?"

It was an anonymous author who published in 1816 the most elaborate of all the demands for a beginning of the canal.[21] In his pamphlet, whose long title began with the words *A Serious Appeal,* he recapitulated the steps already taken in the canal project. He sought to quiet fears raised by earlier plans and assured his readers that "the commencement of the canal will neither disturb the existing

[19] Buffalo *Gazette,* January 28, 1817.
[20] Atticus [De Witt Clinton], *Remarks on the Proposed Canal from Lake Erie to the Hudson River* (New York, 1816), p. 11.
[21] *A Serious Appeal to . . . the Legislature of the State of New York. . . .*

condition of things, nor bow down the people with taxes."

But it was readily apparent in the pages of this persuasive pamphlet that to change the existing order of things was the very purpose of the Erie Canal. Its author put his pencil to paper and found that a barrel of flour costing $1.50 to ship from Lake Erie to Montreal could go to New York by canal for 55¢. A ton of sugar delivered at Buffalo from Montreal could be transported thence for $25; from New York by canal, it would come for $5.50. He calculated the annual surplus production of wheat from the borders of the Great Lakes at 128 million bushels and found himself staggered by his own figures. When calculation "swells into millions, the mind becomes bewildered," he confessed, ". . . and we dread most to promulge our opinions at the very moment we are most firmly persuaded of their certainty." Still, he allowed himself to repeat the fanciful notion fast becoming popular that in winter the frozen canal would "furnish a commodious, level, direct and certain road." Without a canal, he feared for the future of western New York; neglect might "attach it to Canada." With a canal it would be saved for the Union; the canal would spread "happiness and virtue" and "raise up adorers to God, where the panther and the wolf now prowl." Spurred by the challenge of building a canal, New York would form a school of engineers; she "would become the focus of the sciences, and the polar star of every valuable improvement throughout the Union." If challenge would evoke so happy a response, the opportunity, at least, was fast approaching, for it was becoming increasingly clear that New York must build her canal alone.

No other state found itself able to contribute to a canal in New York and a renewed appeal by the commissioners to Congress was unsuccessful. But the New Yorkers watched with care the progress of Calhoun's "Bonus Bill" in the national legislature in the session of 1816-1817. The bill would set aside for internal improvements the dividends of the stock held by the United States in the National Bank, and Calhoun specifically included aid to a canal between the Great Lakes and the Hudson.[22] The share of New York would be $90,000 a year for twenty years, which amounted to a fourth of the total expense of the canal, or enough to pay all the interest on a loan for the purpose.[23]

Ellicott wrote to Micah Brooks in the House, suggesting what bordered on blackmail. If Congress did not aid the New York canal, "the State will unquestionably retain the jurisdiction, police, and supreme control over it, and may exercise that control in such a manner as to be extremely injurious to the U.S. territories, and exclusively beneficial to the State."[24] Meanwhile, Clinton journeyed again to Washington to lobby for this new prospect of national assistance. He repeated familiar arguments for the national advantages of the Erie Canal and carefully subordinated the benefits to New York.[25]

The Bonus Bill squeaked through the House by a majority of two. When the clerk announced the vote, a member was heard to exclaim, "New York has carried it!" The measure succeeded in the Senate as well, only to fall before President Madison's constitutional scruples. The New Yorkers were crestfallen. "After swallowing the National Bank and the Cumberland Road," Clinton wrote

[22] Miller, *Enterprise of a Free People*, p. 51.
[23] Clinton to King, December 13, 1817, Rufus King Papers, NYHS.
[24] Ellicott to Brooks, December 30, 1816, *HLC-WNY Canal Documents*, pp. 84-85. The state administration, he wrote, would be "ever so viciously inclined by having the sole control of such a navigable communication."
[25] Miller, *Enterprise of a Free People*, p. 53.

bitterly to Rufus King, "it was not to be supposed that
Mr. Madison would strain at Canals but so it is. . . ."[26]
The New York *Evening Post* put the veto down to Madi-
son's fear of the rivalry of New York over Virginia.[27]
Ellicott had thought the Bonus Bill would provide an
excellent "entering wedge" for larger grants.

Disappointed in the quest for national support, the
commissioners continued their efforts at home to secure
further donations for the canal. They appointed agents
all across the state to receive subscriptions in land or
money and secured agreements from nine-tenths of the
land owners along the canal to donate land. The Holland
Company again offered lands in the southwestern part
of the state, and, in addition, the actual site of the
canal to a width of four rods.[28] Ellicott imbibed some
of the enthusiasm of the other commissioners, but Busti
in Philadelphia could not bring himself to be confident
in the success of the canal. He wrote to Ellicott in
February of 1817, "The more I consider the nature of
the undertaking and compare it with the temper of our
state and general government, the more I grow incredu-
lous of its ever be[ing] perfected if begun."[29] As it was,
although the company reserved the site of the canal from
sale to the public, two years elapsed before the state
finally accepted the company's land grant; and for all the
company's pains, the canal did not follow Ellicott's route
through the Tonawanda swamp but Geddes' route to the
north instead. Altogether only 106,136 acres of land were

[26] Clinton to King, December 13, 1817, Rufus King Papers, NYHS.

[27] New York *Evening Post*, March 29, 1817.

[28] Paul Busti to Joseph Ellicott, February 22, 1817, *HLC-WNY Canal
Documents*, p. 121; *Laws*, 1, 311.

[29] Busti to Ellicott, February 22, 1817, *HLC-WNY Canal Documents*,
p. 120. See also Busti to Ellicott, October 31, 1816, January 23, 1817,
ibid., pp. 78, 98.

finally contributed in support of the canal, 100,000 of which were ceded by the Holland Company, and the latter tract was finally sold for $28,000.[30]

Their labors under the canal law of 1816 finished, the commissioners brought in their report to the New York legislature, complete with maps and profiles, in February of 1817. Though the Bonus Bill was still being debated in Congress, the time for argument in New York appeared to be past. The commissioners confined their remarks chiefly to explicit information regarding the route, the character of the soil and landscape, and estimates for every mile to be done. As the only real precedent in the United States was the Middlesex Canal, twenty-seven miles long, between Boston and the Merrimac River, the commissioners had examined it and made it their model; but in actuality they had very few standards by which to judge their plans. The dimensions they set forth seem lilliputian to the modern eye. They recommended a canal 353 miles long, from Albany to Lake Erie, 40 feet wide at the surface, 28 feet wide at the bottom, and 4 feet deep. The seventy-seven locks were each to be 90 feet long, 12 feet wide, and sufficient to accommodate boats of 100 tons. The cost was estimated at $13,800 per mile making a total of less than $5,000,000. For another short canal from the Hudson to Lake Champlain, the additional expense would be $871,000. The day after the report was submitted, Myron Holley sat down and wrote to Ellicott: "My mind is so completely settled and satisfied that I cannot but believe that . . . the Legislature will be disposed to take efficient measures for the accomplishment of this great work."[31]

[30] Miller, *Enterprise of a Free People,* p. 58.
[31] Holley to Ellicott, February 18, 1817, *HLC-WNY Canal Documents,* p. 118.

Events did move rapidly in Albany. A joint committee on canals reported on the work of the commissioners and introduced a bill in the assembly on March 18, only three days short of a year from the act of 1816. The joint committee made explicit what had been implicit since the passage of the assembly version of the act of 1816. Construction would begin on the middle section of the Erie Canal, only seventy-seven miles long and so level that but six locks would be required. Here the work would be relatively easy and the expense incurred would be only $853,186.[32] In addition, the committee recommended for immediate construction the short Champlain Canal, which would cost an almost equal amount and would help to win the support of the northern counties to the bill. Initially then, the appropriation to be authorized would not exceed one and a half millions, and the work could be regarded as experimental. Although the joint committee recorded its "perfect conviction" that both the Erie and the Champlain canals could be made without "any serious inconvenience to the financial operations of the state," it admitted "that it is due to the counsels of prudence, to bring the solidity of their conviction to the touchstone of experiment, before the whole system is undertaken."[33] The middle section of the Erie Canal would extend water navigation from the Mohawk to the Seneca River, and if "after a fair trial of the experiment" it should be decided to stop there, "yet these partial operations" would be sufficiently worthwhile to justify passage of the bill.

⌐ After a month of contentious debate, an act was passed and at last construction could begin,⌐ The famous Canal Law of 1817 created a Canal Fund consisting of appro-

[32] *Laws*, I, 245-46.
[33] *Ibid.*, p. 281.

priations and grants from all sources and managed by a board composed of the lieutenant governor, the comptroller, the attorney and surveyor generals, the treasurer, and the secretary of state.[34] These commissioners of the Canal Fund, as they were called, were given charge of all the financial operations of the canal, and the canal was thus placed under the direct supervision of the highest officers of the state. As these offices were elective, the canal became subject ultimately to the authority of the polls. Moreover, the duties and powers of the board were carefully circumscribed. They might borrow on the credit of the state, which gave a firm base to the entire project, but not more than $400,000 in any one year. A tax was placed on salt, steam boat travel, and lands lying within twenty-five miles of the canal. For the executive functions of actual construction, the act continued the former canal commissioners in their offices while relieving them of responsibility for the financial management of the canal. The canal commissioners were empowered to begin construction of the Champlain Canal and on the line of the Erie Canal between the Mohawk and Seneca rivers.

< Rapidly as events moved to produce this epochal act, passage of the canal bill was not easily achieved. In that day of limited journalism, Myron Holley charged many of its difficulties in the legislature to its not being sufficiently understood, and the New York *Evening Post* reported that the majority of the people of the state did not know enough of the merits of the question even to form an opinion.[35] Sectional differences within the state became increasingly acute as enactment of the bill appeared imminent. Once the bill was introduced in the assembly innumerable attempts were made to reject it outright,

[34] *Ibid.*, pp. 358, 364.
[35] New York *Evening Post*, April 17, 1817.

amend it into harmlessness, or postpone the beginning of construction. They centered, understandably, upon the question of how the canal should be financed, which in turn led to a stormy dispute over the inequalities in the expected benefits from the canal.

The bill as it was introduced provided for payment of the $300,000 interest on the initial construction loan by "partial taxation" or local assessment of cities and counties supposedly to be most benefited by their location near the canal. Since these lands might increase in value as much as four hundred times, and most of the money would be expended there, the special tax of a mill on a dollar seemed justified. So it was argued by Assemblymen Ford of Herkimer County, Rochester of Monroe, Ostrander of Albany, Eldrich of Madison, Duer and Pendleton of Dutchess, and Williams of Columbia. Moreover, the recent study of the New York canals by Nathan Miller finds political finesse in this portion of the bill as it was first proposed by the canal commissioners.[36] Taxing of Western lands held by Federalist speculators in the East enabled Federalists such as Duer and Pendleton to support the canal bill in spite of the hostility of voters along the Hudson and in New York City. Bearing much of the costs of construction themselves, they were rescued from the charge of legislative favor certain to be leveled against them. Nathaniel Pendleton, who carried the burden of the debate in favor on the bill, could move to the broader benefits of the canal as he calculated that the cost of carrying a ton from Buffalo to Albany would be reduced from $100 to $10.50, wiping out the advantage of Montreal and saving the citizens of the state a million dollars a year.[37]

[36] Miller, *Enterprise of a Free People*, pp. 68-70.
[37] Hosack, *Memoir of De Witt Clinton*, p. 54.

Local opposition to the bill in eastern New York rested in the legislative representatives from New York City, Emmott, Sharpe, Sargeant, and Romaine. Myron Holley wrote to his father on April 3 that they opposed the canal with "malignant hostility" out of fear of taxation to pay for it.[38] They stood steadfastly opposed to the principle of special assessments to such cities as their own, and to the bill as a whole. New York was already "drained to the last pore," complained Sharpe. "Depend upon it," said Emmott, "if we vote for the canal this day, we mortgage the State forever." The New York delegation reflected the views of tradesmen, mechanics, and laborers of the city rather than its mercantile interests which had been represented in the New York memorial of 1816. The former were fearful of taxation, suspicious of the interests of a landed or moneyed aristocracy, and contemptuous of the canal as a "visionary project."[39] Their representatives remained obstructionist to the end, refusing the optimism of those who assured them that New York would be raised by the canal to a position as the leading city of the Union. At a critical point in the assembly debate, Elisha Williams of Columbia County on the lower Hudson admonished the leader of the New York delegation: "If the canal is to be a shower of gold, it will fall upon New-York; if a river of gold, it will flow into her lap." The accuracy of this prediction was questioned then, as it has been by historians to this day.[40]

By the close vote of 52 to 51 in the assembly, support of the canal through local assessments was defeated. But William Duer substituted the clause of the act of 1816

[38] Holley to Luther Holley, April 3, 1817, Myron Holley Papers, NYSL.

[39] Rubin, "An Innovating Public Improvement," pp. 62-63.

[40] See below, Chapter 15.

taxing lands along the canal twenty-five miles from either side, all but $10,000 of the State auction duties was taken from the support of the foreign poor in New York City, and the bill passed by the comfortable margin of 64 to 36.

In the senate the opposition again sought to alter, weaken, or defeat the bill. A motion to include a canal around the falls of the Oswego raised once more the prickly question of the Ontario route and was defeated by a single vote. Again it was the representatives from New York City who formed the core of the opposition. Peter Elmendorf contended that the national government should construct the canal if it were to be done at all. Peter R. Livingston raised the spectre of General Schuyler's "splendid schemes" for canals, feared to hurt American industry by allowing cheap English manufactures to reach the West, and thought conditions too depressed to begin such a work. "You will find it a ditch that will bury you all," he warned.[41]

Supporters of the canal bill in the senate said less than their allies in the assembly. George Tibbitts of Rensselaer County, who was accounted the "master spirit" behind the passage of the bill, answered the fears and alarms of those who spoke against it. But paradoxically, the margin of victory in the upper house was provided by Martin Van Buren, the anti-Clintonian who had moved to reduce the act of 1816 to one of survey and estimate only and who had it still within his power to defeat the bill. "Now the scene is entirely changed," Van Buren assured the senate.[42] The requisite information was at hand, and unless the report of the commissioners was a "tissue of fraud or misrepresentation," the plan for the canal was practicable

[41] Albany *Gazette and General Advertiser*, April 17, 1817.
[42] *Ibid.*

in every respect. Skillfully he traversed the record since the commissioners had first been appointed in 1810. He reminded his listeners of the popular support given the reports of the commissioners in 1811, 1812, and 1814, and of the petitions which had flooded the legislature after the war. The same bill had passed the popular branch of the legislature two years in succession; no one could longer doubt but that the people had expressed themselves in its favor. To fail now was to recede from measures already taken. For himself, the Fox of Kinderhook considered this the most important vote he had ever given. Summing up the six years of careful investigation to which the project had been subjected, Van Buren made it a point of honor for the state to bring the plan to fruition. When he had finished speaking, Clinton himself crowded in to press his hand. Moreover, it was Van Buren who made a vital change in the bill as it came from the assembly. He moved to build the canal on the "credit of the people of this state" rather than merely on the credit of the Canal Fund. Thus, the shrewd political leader of the anti-Clintonians was equally successful in opposing Clinton and supporting the canal, but in aiding the latter he moved in such a way that his Democratic followers could claim to have put the canal on a sounder basis than its Clintonian advocates.[43] On April 15, the day of adjournment, the canal bill passed the senate by a vote of 18 to 9. Five of the ayes were the votes of anti-Clintonians.

[43] Miller, *Enterprise of a Free People*, p. 45; Rubin, "An Innovating Public Improvement," p. 62. A recent study by Alvin Kass interprets this episode of 1816-1817 as an example of Van Buren's "realistic" rather than "theoretical" approach to politics and concludes, "It would be unfair to discount completely the sincerity of the reasons Van Buren proffered for his initial antagonism toward the canal. On the other hand, it would also be the height of naivete to disregard the circumstances surrounding his change of mind." Alvin Kass, *Politics in New York State 1800-1830* (Syracuse, 1965), pp. 129-30.

One more hurdle remained—the approval of the Council of Revision, which held the veto power under the state constitution. The five-man council was split with Justices Platt and Yates for the bill and Acting Governor Taylor and Chief Justice Thompson opposed. The deciding vote was held by Chancellor James Kent who was unconvinced of the wisdom of the project under the conditions of the time. In the middle of the heated argument over the bill, Tompkins, who had been elected to the vice presidency in March, entered the council chamber. Speaking informally he advised against the bill. "The late peace with Great Britain," he said, "was a mere truce, and the credit and resources of the State should be employed, not in great civil works like this, but in preparing for war." Chancellor Kent took immediate interest. Pressing Tompkins further, he brought from him the prediction that war would be resumed within two years. Instantly the Chancellor was on his feet. "Then if we must have a war, or have a canal," exclaimed Kent, "I am in favor of the canal! I vote for the bill!"[44]

The geographical distribution of the votes on the canal bill reflected the sectional opposition to the project. In the senate the bill met almost solid opposition from New York City and its environs, and in the assembly the representatives from the counties of New York, Delaware, Putnam, Washington, and Warren gave all but one of their recorded votes against it.[45] Two assemblymen from Ulster and Sullivan split their votes to give one for and one against. Although most of the other counties were registered for the bill, enough votes from them were cast in the negative to show that geography alone did not deter-

[44] William Kent, *Memoirs and Letters of James Kent, LL.D.* (Boston, 1898), pp. 168-70.
[45] *Laws,* I, 349-57.

mine the vote on the canal. One vote each in the assembly from the counties of Genesee, Onondaga, Cayuga, Saratoga, Jefferson, and Lewis was cast against the bill.

Paradoxically, construction of the canal passed into law on the solid support of the Federalists who were out of power in New York and through the sponsorship of Clinton as a Republican maverick. Although the Federalists found themselves "mere spectators" while rival Republican factions battled for power, it was the Federalist assemblymen, William Duer, Abraham Van Vechten, T. J. Oakley, and Elisha Williams, who carried the canal bill through the lower house. George Tibbitts, Federalist nominee for lieutenant governor in 1816, was one of its ablest proponents in the senate. It had the support of Federalist Judge Jonas Platt in the crucial Council of Revision. J. Rutsen Van Rensselaer, Federalist landholder from Columbia County, had even offered to form a company to construct the canal in return for a liberal allowance in payment or in tolls.[46] To these men and a majority of their party, Clinton had made himself acceptable, for all his Republican inheritance and his support of Governor Tompkins in 1816.

Within his own party, Clinton's position was anything but secure. His collaboration with Federalists, his opposition to Madison, his "lukewarm" support for the War of 1812 as mayor of New York, and withal his cold and formal manner turned Republican regulars against him. His political sins, wrote Samuel R. Betts to Van Buren, were "red like crimson."[47]

Governor Tompkins was elected to the vice presidency

[46] *Ibid.*, 285-86; Van Rensselaer to Clinton, March 11, 1817, De Witt Clinton Papers, CUL.

[47] Betts to Van Buren, February 24, 1817, Martin Van Buren Papers, LC.

in 1816, and his Republican followers backed Peter B. Porter for the gubernatorial vacancy which was created. Porter possessed a passable military record and enjoyed the support of Van Buren, Robert Swartwout, and other Republican leaders. But as the Republican state convention of March 25 approached, popular support swung to Clinton, a shift shaped in good measure by the influence of the canal. "This result has been brought about by Mr. Clinton's being continually kept before the public eye, without an opponent, and the desire of having the canal made," Enos Throop complained to Van Buren.[48] The day before the nomination, a gathering of the Sons of St. Patrick in Albany celebrating their patron's day toasted the canal as Clinton's work, and the Albany *Register* reported the current of opinion in favor of Clinton to be as irresistible as "the cataract of Niagara."[49]

When the Republican convention met in Albany, Van Buren, Sharpe, Sargeant, Elmendorf, and other anti-Clintonians pushed hard for Porter's nomination, but after an eight-hour caucus and a midnight vote, Clinton won nomination as governor easily, 85 to 41.[50] Thus when the canal bill was debated in April, Clinton's ascendancy in the state was already clear. He had made the canal his hobby and its progress had been tied closely to his political fortunes. The sixty-four members of the assembly voting for the canal bill were chiefly Clintonians and Federalists.[51] The thirty-six voting against were chiefly his opponents. In the senate, Elmendorf and Peter R. Livingston opposed the canal as they opposed all things

[48] Throop to Van Buren, March 15, 1817, Martin Van Buren Papers, LC.

[49] Quoted in New York *Evening Post*, March 31, 1817.

[50] Jabez D. Hammond, *The History of Political Parties in the State of New York* (4th ed.; Syracuse, 1852), I, 439.

[51] *Ibid.*, p. 441.

Clintonian. The representation from New York, voting almost to a man against the bill, had been selected by Tammany Hall as anti-Clintonians. Van Buren's departure from the anti-Clintonian ranks on the canal issue and his success in carrying five others with him can be explained by his honest appreciation of the canal project and the fact that when the canal bill reached the senate, the political die had been cast.

In the election of the following May, Porter withdrew from the contest and the Federalists put up no opposing candidate against Clinton. From a position in 1815 as "a sort of political *Bohan Upas,* with whom the slightest intercourse would contaminate," as the eye-witness historian Jabez D. Hammond later observed, Clinton had risen in only two years to unanimous election as governor of New York. A majority of Clintonians, backed by the Federalists, were elected to the assembly as well. As the canal was so largely a work of Clinton's hands, so also it served in his political redemption.

But the political struggle was only the surface manifestation of deeper social currents. The public support for Clinton's political aspirations found its origin in the desire to link the Great Lakes and the Atlantic by water, and in the vision of what New York might become once the canal was completed. The Albany *Gazette* exulted in May of 1817: "We believe the commencement of this splendid project will be hailed by the great body of the people of this state, as the dawning of an era which will be productive of more durable renown and glory to New York, than has been imparted to her by anything she has accomplished since the first settlement of the country."[52]

At long last the Erie Canal was a project whose time

[52] Albany *Gazette and General Advertiser,* May 15, 1817.

had come. For more than a decade the canal themes had been repeated over and over again. The potential productivity of the uninhabited Western lands, the pressing need for communication, the visions of private and public gain, the fear of Canadian rivalry—all formed a nexus of ideas which carried the canal project through personal politics to public program.

II. *The Grand Canal*

5

Forty Feet Wide and
Four Feet Deep

THE ERIE CANAL was dug with an eye to drama. As
soon as construction of the middle section was
authorized, preparations were begun all along the line
from Utica on the Mohawk to the Seneca River. On July
4, three days after Clinton had taken the oath of office as
governor, the canal commissioners broke soil in an auspi-
cious ceremony at Rome.

The time was set at sunrise. Visiting dignitaries and
local residents gathered at the village in the hazy dawn
and moved in procession to the canal line. Samuel Young
alone represented the commissioners. The three chief
engineers, Benjamin Wright, James Geddes, and Charles
G. Broadhead, stood by while Judge Joshua Hathaway of
Rome presided. Judge John Richardson, first to take up
a contract on the canal, waited with his hand upon a
plow behind a heavy team of oxen while most of the
company leaned expectantly on the shovels which they
had brought for the celebration.

As the sun rose, cannon from the United States Arsenal
boomed and Richardson opened a furrow on the canal
line. Judge Hathaway began the ceremony with a brief
salutation and Commissioner Young addressed the gathering:

We have assembled to commence the excavation of the Erie Canal. This work when accomplished will connect our western inland seas with the Atlantic ocean. It will diffuse the benefits of internal navigation over a surface of vast extent, blessed with a salubrious climate and luxurious soil, embracing a tract of country capable of sustaining more human beings than were ever accommodated by any work of the kind.

By this great highway, unborn millions will easily transport their surplus productions to the shores of the Atlantic, procure their supplies, and hold a useful and profitable intercourse with all the maritime nations of the earth.

The expense and labor of this great undertaking bear no proportion to its utility. Nature has kindly afforded every facility; we have all the moral and physical means within our reach and control. Let us then proceed to the work, animated by the prospect of its speedy accomplishment, and cheered with the anticipated benedictions of a grateful posterity.[1]

Hathaway handed a spade to Young, who passed it to Judge Richardson, who plunged it into the soft earth. The cannon boomed again and the whole throng fell to the digging, "each vying with the other," reported the Utica *Gazette*, "in this demonstration of the joy, of which all partook on that interesting occasion."[2] The earth had been turned.

But to build the canal a host of new decisions had yet to be faced. The five-man board of commissioners were to expend the canal funds "in the most prudent and economical manner" and recommend the measures which would best fulfill the intentions of the act of 1817. They

---

[1] Oswald T. Backus, "Rome, Romans and the Canals," *Memorial of the Centennial Celebration of the Turning of the First Shovelful of Earth in the Construction of the Erie Canal* (Rome, 1917), pp. 55-56; Hosack, *Memoir of De Witt Clinton*, p. 455.

[2] Utica *Gazette*, July 15, 1817. Judge Hathaway later took a contract for excavating a mile and a quarter of the canal. *Laws*, II, 513.

must devise a blueprint for construction, gain the approval of the legislature, and see to its execution. Like the assembly of a machine, the entire canal must be completed before it could be fully tested and the total benefits be realized. Popular support must be sustained over years of effort.

When operations were begun in 1817 the canal board was composed of De Witt Clinton, Stephen Van Rensselaer, Joseph Ellicott, Myron Holley, and Samuel Young. Two of them, Holley and Young, were designated acting commissioners and devoted all their time to canal affairs. Ellicott's responsibilities with the Holland Land Company compelled him to resign within a year, and Ephraim Hart of Oneida County was appointed by Clinton temporarily in his place. Henry Seymour was elected over Hart to fill this vacancy in March of 1818 and was made acting commissioner on the middle section of the canal. William C. Bouck was added to the board as an acting commissioner in 1821.

The efficiency with which the commissioners acted is remarkable. Although they were dominated by Clinton, who was notorious for his lack of political tact and who was believed by many to be using the canal project to serve his political advancement, they were men of strong character, and more than one possessed political ambitions. They were divided by party affiliation; Holley and Van Rensselaer supported Clinton, and Young, Seymour, and Bouck were among Clinton's political opponents. A majority vote was necessary for them to act as a board. In spite of some notable conflicts, however, their divisions of opinion did not inhibit the steady progress of construction. Holley and Young served as salaried acting commissioners and as members of the legislature at the same time, the former in the assembly and the latter in the senate, without issue being made of their dual functions. Their annual reports reveal able and impartial service to the state in positions of political pressures and personal friction.

In their first progress report the commissioners took pride that New York possessed "the genius, the skill, the enterprise, and all other means" required for the completion of the canal.[3] Indeed, the eight years of construction between 1817 and 1825 saw the achievement of an outstanding engineering feat. A narrow ribbon of water 363 miles long, 40 feet wide at the top, and 4 feet deep was created between Albany and Lake Erie, with an additional twenty-two miles of canal connecting the Hudson River and Lake Champlain. In overcoming the 565 feet of elevation of Lake Erie over the Hudson at Albany, the Erie Canal followed a combined ascent and descent of 675 feet. The canal had eighty-three locks with lifts ranging from six to twelve feet, and a succession of eighteen aqueducts which became the marvels of the day.[4]

At the outset the canal line had been divided into three sections with engineers and surveyors assigned to each. Since operations were first begun on the middle section, the ninety-four miles of construction between the Mohawk and Seneca rivers became the proving ground for the work in the west and east which followed. Benjamin Wright, chief engineer for the section, advertised for sealed bids and a thousand men were on the line by October. First the surveyors drove rows of red stakes sixty feet apart marking out the land to be cleared. Between them, two more rows were driven forty feet apart to show the exact line of excavation. Borers followed to sink holes twelve

[3] *Laws*, I, 380.
[4] *Ibid.*, pp. 198, 268, 377-80; Noble E. Whitford, *History of the Canal System of the State of New York* (Albany, 1906), I, 798, II, 1030.

feet into the earth to discover the nature of the soil to be removed. Last came the diggers and levelers. The commissioners were elated to discover that a summit level of sixty miles could be made from a point west of Rome to a short distance below Utica and on this level fifty-eight miles were under construction by January of 1818.[5] But to establish so long a level with the primitive instruments of the day was thought by many to be beyond the skill of American engineers. In the season of 1818, Wright and Geddes set out to run a series of test levels between Rome and Syracuse. While Wright laid off the canal line west of Rome, Geddes ran a test level on a circuit near Oneida and Onondaga lakes extending nearly a hundred miles. When Geddes' survey returned to the canal line laid off by Wright, the difference at the junction was less than one and a half inches.[6]

Although no adequate engineering training was available in the United States, the canal became a school of engineering in itself. A small group of engineers bore the responsibility for the technical decisions on the canal. Benjamin Wright, the oldest and most experienced, was valued for his critical judgment though he irritated the commissioners by his refusal to subordinate his private business affairs to his canal duties.[7] James Geddes, who had run the original surveys of 1810 and worked with the commissioners ever since, was assigned to Wright and became one of the leading engineers with particular responsibility for designing the mechanical structures on the canal. David Thomas, a taciturn Quaker, shared Clinton's botanical interests and was particularly skillful

[5] *Laws,* I, 373.

[6] Whitford, *History of the Canal System,* I, 788-89.

[7] Clinton later wrote that "to him we are indebted more than to any other Engineer." Clinton to Caleb Newbold, Jr., November 23, 1825, De Witt Clinton Papers, CUL.

as a mapmaker. Nathan S. Roberts, like most of the engineers, began as a surveyor, laid out much of the canal line and found his highest achievement when he designed the series of five "double combined locks" placed side by side to carry the canal up an elevation of seventy-six feet over the rock ridge at Lockport. Roberts also trained John B. Jervis, whose autobiography gives perhaps the most personal glimpse into the making of an engineer of the Erie Canal.[8]

A young man of twenty-two in 1817, Jervis began as an axeman and target carrier in Roberts' survey party walking seven miles a day through the "Rome swamp." Roberts taught him the rudiments of leveling, he read two books on surveying, served a winter weighing stone, and was assigned as an assistant to David S. Bates on a section of the canal near Canastota. Bates had been a land surveyor of note, but knew less about leveling for a canal than did Jervis. When Bates moved to another part of the canal in 1818, Jervis was made resident engineer of the section. Jervis' own account of his rise as an engineer is oppressive in its earnestness, but after eight years on the Erie Canal he became chief engineer for the Delaware and Hudson Canal, designed the Croton Aqueduct in New York City, and went on to a career in railroading.

By 1821 Charles G. Haines could boast in his introduction to a volume of canal documents: "For accuracy, despatch and science, we can now present a corps of engineers equal to any in the world. . . . The canal line is now one of the most excellent schools that could be divised [sic], to accomplish men for this pursuit."[9] Nor did these engineers have the assistance of a modern state

[8] John B. Jervis, "Autobiography," MS, Jervis Public Library, Rome.

[9] New-York Corresponding Association, for the Promotion of Internal Improvements, *Public Documents, Relating to the New-York Canals* (New York, 1821), p. xlii.

construction service which could provide heavy equipment and a state-employed labor force already skilled and experienced.

The commissioners let the canal contracts on the best terms they could secure to private contractors who furnished their own tools and hired their own labor. They gave contracts for sections as short as one-fourth of a mile so that men of moderate means could engage in the work. Funds were advanced to them under bond in order that they might procure teams, equipment, and supplies. More than fifty contractors were at work on the first fifty-eight miles let out and new ones continually applied. Some failed, but the great majority profited from the enterprise and having successfully completed one contract applied for another. Clinton believed the system was practiced with "extraordinary success," decidedly preferable to the hiring of laborers directly by the state.[10]

Nativist in outlook, the commissioners noted with pride that very few of the contractors were foreigners who had recently arrived in America and that the majority were "native farmers, mechanics, merchants and professional men" who resided near the canal.[11] Tradition has it that Irish immigrants built the Erie Canal and many sons of Erin may have been added to the labor force. But the commissioners reported in 1819 that three-fourths of the workers were "born among us," and the half a million

[10] Clinton to A. D. Murphy, September 24, 1821, De Witt Clinton Papers, NYSL. An excellent primary account of the work of these contractors can be found in Canvass White's notebook, "Examination of that part of the Erie Canal extending from the Nine mile Creek to the Seneca River," dated December 10, 1818. MS, Canvass White Papers, Cornell University Library.

[11] *Laws,* I, 403. See also Myron Holley to Clinton, August 9, 31, 1817, May 19, 1818, Samuel Young to Clinton, August 11, 1817, De Witt Clinton Papers, CUL. One Timothy Hunt of Boston had worked on the Middlesex Canal and contracted in 1817 for part of the Erie Canal. Schenectady *Cabinet,* September 10, 1817.

work reports now preserved in the New York State Library
in Albany show, for the period after 1828, most canal
workers to have been recruited locally.[12] It seems probable that the labor force on the Erie Canal reflected the
national backgrounds, Irish and others, of the inhabitants
who resided along the canal line.

Laborers on the canal received from $8 to $12 a month
or 50¢ a day.[13] Contractors were paid at the rate of
10¢ to 14¢ per cubic yard for the excavation of earth, with
higher allowances for shale or rock. For the excavation
of marl the commissioners paid as high as 75¢; and for
breccia, a particularly hard rock, as high as $2.00. For
embankments, 16¢ to 25¢ a cubic yard was given and
locks and culverts were contracted from 75¢ to $1.50
per perch.[14] In many instances these allowances were so
liberal that some contractors sublet their work to others
and pocketed the profit. The principal engineers received
a salary from $1,500 to $2,000 a year and assistant engineers $4.00 a day. The salary of the acting commissioners
was set in 1819 at $2,500, which was reduced to $2,000
in 1820.[15] More than this, Joseph Ellicott advised Clinton,
would create in uneducated minds the idea that the commissioners were "aggrandizing themselves on the canal
funds."[16]

Relationships among the builders of the Erie Canal
were personal and direct. A set of overall specifications
applicable to every contract was drawn up for grubbing,

[12] Walter B. Smith, "Wage Rates on the Erie Canal, 1828-1881,"
Journal of Economic History, XXXIII (September 1963), p. 305.

[13] Albany *Gazette*, August 25, 1817; Buffalo *Republican Press*, August
21, 1822; Rochester *Telegraph*, October 16, 1821, July 9, 1822.

[14] Albany *Gazette*, August 25, 1817; Buffalo *Gazette*, September 23,
1817; *Laws*, I, 376, 446, II, 160. Myron Holley to Clinton, August 31,
1817, May 19, 1818, De Witt Clinton Papers, CUL.

[15] *Laws*, I, 428-29, 516, II, 200-10.

[16] Ellicott to Clinton, April 2, 1818, *HLC-WNY Canal Documents*,
p. 135.

clearing, and excavating, and for the construction of embankments, towpaths, fences, waste weirs, locks, and culverts.[17] Beyond this, each contract was suited to the requirements of the individual situation. The engineers boarded in homes near the canal and Myron Holley, who was appointed treasurer of the canal board and who, of all the commissioners, devoted himself most fully to the construction of the canal, drove his carriage slowly up and down the line paying the contractors out of his strong box in small bills drawn on local banks.[18]

Although the contracts were drawn in such a way as to require inspection and approval by the superintending engineer before any contractor received his pay, monthly payments were advanced pro rata unless some deception was discovered in the works. If deception was discovered, payments were suspended and the letter of the contract was enforced. Each contract really embraced a tiny canal, divided where possible so that it could be filled with water and drained independently of any other. Before settlement, each contractor's portion was filled with water, and if leaks developed, they were repaired at the expense of the contractor. Contractors for locks were required to warrant their work for five years, though enforcement of this provision must have been well-nigh impossible.[19]

Spurred by the need for resourcefulness to profit on contracts which went to the lowest bidder, contractors produced ingenious answers to the challenge of building

[17] New-York Corresponding Association, *Public Documents,* pp. 294-310.

[18] Albany *Gazette,* November 1, 1819. The commissioners of the Canal Fund issued canal stock which was taken by banks at a premium and the money was then deposited in banks near the sites of operations.

[19] Myron Holley to Clinton, May 19, 1818, De Witt Clinton Papers, CUL. Extra claims for expenses were usually made in settlement of contracts and, wrote Jervis, "it was by no means rare for ingenious contractors to swell these claims to large amounts." Jervis, "Autobiography," Jervis Public Library.

a canal which often traversed a wilderness. Within the first six months they learned that the use of the plow and scraper was superior to the European method with spade and wheelbarrow. Three men with horses or oxen could excavate a mile of canal in a season, and the constant passage of men and animals over the banks made them more compact and less subject to later settling. Wet ground, however, could be dug only by spade and wheel-barrow, but even here there was improvement. Jeremiah Brainard of Rome invented a new wheelbarrow in which bottom and sides were made of a single board bent to a semicircular shape, and which was lighter, more durable, and easier to unload than any used before.[20]

Between two and three thousand men and seven hundred horses were at work on the middle section from Utica to the Seneca River in the summers of 1818 and 1819. By the latter year a new method had been found for clearing trees from the land. A comparatively small contrivance was perfected by which a man could bring down a tree of any height without touch from axe or saw. The machine consisted of an endless screw connected with a roller, cable and crank, and applied the principles of both screw and lever. It was placed about a hundred feet from the base of the tree to be felled and the cable was secured far up the trunk. By turning the crank the tree was easily top-pled and made ready to be dragged away by oxen.[21]

Tree stumps were cleared by application of a larger machine, but with little more effort. A pair of wheels sixteen-feet high were connected by an axle thirty-feet long to make a giant stump puller. A third wheel fourteen-feet high was spoked into the axle in the middle, around which a rope was wound several times to produce an

---

[20] Clinton to J. Bigelow, April [?], 1819, De Witt Clinton Papers, CUL.

[21] *Laws,* I, 404.

eight-fold gain in power. The stump was hooked to the wheel by a heavy chain, oxen or horses pulled at the rope, and the stump was out. Seven men and a team of oxen using the stump puller could grub thirty to forty stumps in a day.[22]

Clinton was besieged by inventors and well-wishers giving advice and offering machines for canal construction. One inventor designed a "mud machine" for excavation, another proposed a method of avoiding all locks, and Henry Persse, an Irish correspondent, advised Clinton on operating the canal. Amos Eaton, who was a geologist and a professor at the Rensselaer School at Troy, proposed that the banks of the canal be sowed with crabgrass to prevent them from washing.

Fortunately, most of the materials needed for construction were found near the canal. The engineers discovered a muck called "the blue mud of the meadows" which served as a canal lining to prevent water seepage.[23] A high grade of limestone which was discovered near Medina provided excellent facing for the locks and other structures where stone was required. Furthermore, a particular variety known as "meagre limestone" became the welcome answer to the pressing need for a suitable water cement. Until this resource was discovered, construction was hampered by the poor quality of ordinary lime mortar on which the engineers were forced to rely. Clinton had read about Roman cement in the *Repository of the Arts,* had procured some samples, and wrote to Samuel Latham Mitchill, as "the Delphic Oracle of New York" to know if New York limestone and basalt could be used.[24]

[22] *Ibid.,* pp. 404-405.

[23] Madeline Sadler Waggoner, *The Long Haul West* (New York, 1958), p. 79.

[24] Clinton to Mitchill, July 14, 1817, De Witt Clinton Papers, CUL.

But the utilization of this meagre limestone was chiefly the work of Canvass White of Whitesboro, a young engineer whose reputation was made on the New York waterways. White grew up on a farm in Oneida County while that area was still a frontier, and he had served as a lieutenant in the New York Volunteers in the War of 1812. He possessed a real flair for things mechanical, and as the canal began to involve the interests of his kinsmen in central New York, he became an assistant to Benjamin Wright on the surveys of 1816 and 1817. Soon his abilities caught the interest of Clinton. At the governor's request, but on his own funds, White went to England to examine the hydraulic works there. He traveled some four hundred miles in the British Isles observing canals, aqueducts, tunnels, and especially underwater cements.[25] Returning to the canal in New York the young surveyor became an assistant engineer on the middle section. In 1818, after repeated experiments with varieties of limestone, he found a type in Madison County that when made into a quick-lime cement, had the particular virtue of hardening under water. The cement was prepared by calcining the stone, then reducing it to a powder and mixing it with water and sand to form a mortar. Once under water, the cement became increasingly hard with age. Abundantly available and easily prepared, this limestone produced a cement superior to any found in America. It was applied in 1819 to all construction where mortar was needed, and over 400,000 bushels were used on the canal.[26]

White took out a patent on his discovery in 1820 and followed this with a second patent the next year for a

---

[25] William P. White, "Canvass White's Services," in *Canal Enlargement in New York State, Buffalo Historical Society Publications,* XIII (Buffalo, 1909), 353-66; Canvass White to Captain Hugh White, January 21, 1818, Canvass White Papers, Cornell University Library.

[26] *Laws,* II, 216-17.

further improvement.[27] At first the commissioners officially regarded the discovery as their common property and avoided recognition of White's claims. Under their encouragement, contractors supplied large quantities of cement to the state without payment of royalty. When White brought successful suit, the contractors applied to the state for relief. An attempt was made in the legislature to purchase the patent rights for the state for $10,000 and thus end the controversy. Although the measure passed the assembly and had the backing of Clinton, it ultimately failed and White turned to private development of the cement business based on his canal discoveries.[28] The discovery and application of this cement in New York is one of the epochal achievements of the building of the Erie Canal.

In keeping with the assertion running through canal literature that the builders were "planning for posterity," the canal was built to last. Specifications for all major structures called for the use of stone and iron, although wood was used for the trunks of aqueducts on a plan developed by one Cady, a carpenter of Chittenango. The locks, which measured 90 by 15 feet and cost $1,000 per

[27] Letters Patent, February 1, 1820, Specifications for Letters Patent, February 1, 1820, Petition to the Hon. John Q. Adams, February 16, 1821, Canvass White Papers, Cornell University Library.

[28] *Laws*, I, 448-49, II, 216-17; Whitford, *History of the Canal System*, I, 98. Canvass White enlisted the aid of his brother, Hugh White, and at Chittenango on the canal line, he developed a prosperous cement business. There he prepared the stone and shipped the finished cement by canal at considerable profit. To meet rising competition, he emphasized the production of "a good and cheap article." "As no reliance can be placed on the patent," he wrote to his brother, "our only protection will be in honesty and punctuality." (May 16, 1825, Canvass White Papers, Cornell University Library.) The business prospered at least until 1840 and many thousands of bushels were produced annually. Canvass White to Hugh White, September 25, 1825, August 8, 1826, September 12, November 22, 1829, April 18, October 14, 1830, Canvass White Papers, Cornell University Library. Erie Canal Waybill for the boat *Bridgewater*, June 29, 1826, Hugh White Papers, Cornell University Library.

foot of rise, had particular solidity. The following excerpt from the report of the commissioners in 1819 suggests the quality of the work called for throughout the canal:

> The foundations of these eight locks, are to consist of a solid flooring of hewed timber, one foot thick, and covered with well jointed three inch plank, over which, within the chamber, will be laid another flooring, of two inch plank, accurately fitted together with water joints, and spiked down, so as to prevent leakage: and this foundation is to be strongly supported and guarded by piling. The lock walls are to be sustained by several massy butresses [*sic*], to be laid in water-cement, and thoroughly grouted—to have all the faces, ends, and beds, of each stone, laid in front of the wall, together with the hollow quoins, the lock culverts and the ventilators, well cut—and the whole to be sufficiently cramped together with iron, and the best construction, and properly fitted, secured, and hung.[29]

In December of 1818 water was let into the first job taken by Judge Richardson extending for three-fourths of a mile west of Rome. Myron Holley and the engineers passed through the canal in a horse-drawn boat. However, during the first season of construction the rains and frosts so retarded the work that only $200,000 could be applied to the canal. In 1818 more than $466,000 was expended and in 1819 nearly $600,000 was devoted to the work.[30]

The requisite funds were raised through a series of canal loans offered by the state between 1817 and 1820. The loans were taken chiefly by investors who sub-scribed in small amounts. Those floated before 1822 bore 6 percent interest and were redeemable in 1837. Some of these investors of more limited means contributed their money unknowingly. It was their deposits in the

[29] *Laws*, I, 413-14.
[30] *Ibid.*, II, 285-87.

Bank for Savings in New York City that made it possible
for that institution to hold almost 30 percent of the
outstanding canal stock by 1821. Later loans attracted
the funds of wealthier American investors such as John
Jacob Astor and the firms of LeRoy, Bayard & Company,
and Prime, Ward and King. Foreign investors, notably
English capitalists, took increasing amounts of canal stock
after 1822, though foreigners did not exceed Americans
in their holdings until 1829. Nothing succeeded like
success. As construction progressed, confidence in the
canal was strengthened, and the money became more
readily available. The final loans in 1825 brought pre-
miums of from 8 to 19 percent.[31]

By 1820 the middle section was completed and the
canal was navigable for a full ninety-four miles from
Utica to Montezuma on the Seneca River. The experimental phase of canal building in New York was over.
Great excitement came to the tiny canal-side villages as
water filled ever longer stretches of the canal for the first
time. On October 23, 1819, the commissioners, together
with a band and some fifty notables and friends, boarded
the *Chief Engineer* and 'sailed' behind a single horse from
Utica to Rome. While church bells pealed, they glided
serenely between neatly fenced banks crowded with
cheering spectators. On the following Fourth of July,
just three years after the canal was begun, the ceremony
was repeated in a procession of seventy-three boats at
Syracuse to celebrate the completion of the entire section.[32] The correspondents who sent news of these cele-

[31] An analysis of the canal loans offered by the state from 1817 to
1825, from which the above paragraph is taken, is found in Miller,
Enterprise of a Free People, Chapters V-VI.

[32] *Laws*, I, 437. On November 24, 1819, the Champlain Canal was
also navigable although not entirely completed. Hosack, *Memoir of De
Witt Clinton*, pp. 456-57.

brations throughout the state recorded the drama of these events in emotional accounts. "To see the first boat launched, to be among the first that were borne on the waters of a canal which is to connect the great chain of western lakes with the Hudson, and which will be one of the most stupendous works the world has ever known . . . ," wrote one, "produced emotions which those only who felt them can conceive."[33]

The opening of navigation ushered in the canal era. New Yorkers were introduced to the fascination of canal travel and the seemingly limitless advantages of water transportation. The completion of the middle section was more than an engineering triumph. In their annual report of 1820 the commissioners suggested the future meaning of the canal as the heart of the new style of society which they were helping to create: "The novelty of seeing large boats drawn by horses, upon waters artificially conducted —through cultivated fields, forests and swamps, over ravines, creeks and morasses, and from one elevation to another, by means of ample, beautiful and substantial locks, has been eminently exhilerating [sic]. The precision of the levels, the solidity of the banks, the regularity of the curves, the symmetry of the numerous and massive stone works, the depth of the excavation in some places, the extent of the embankments in others, and the impression produced everywhere along the line, by the visible effects of immense labor, have uniformly afforded gratification mingled with surprise."[34]

A sense of satisfaction was well justified by the experience of the first three years of canal construction in New York. In a pioneering effort, the commissioners, engineers,

[33] Rochester *Telegraph*, November 2, 1819.
[34] *Laws*, I, 455-56.

and contractors had devised the means of building a canal through a wilderness. Procedures had been established, inventions had been perfected, and the results augured well for the success of the whole of the Erie Canal. But the western section, most important of all, had been scarcely begun.

6

The Politics of Construction

IN THE popular mind, the Erie Canal was known more commonly as the "Grand Canal," the "Great Western Canal," or the "Big Ditch." And, as a matter of fact, legislative authorization for construction west of the Seneca was not yet given. The middle section had put the plans of the commissioners to the "touchstone of experiment," said Clinton in 1819, and there could not "exist a doubt of the feasibility of the work, or of the ability of the state" to complete them. When the middle section was nearly navigable, Clinton recommended to the legislature that a law should be passed "authorizing the completion of the whole work as soon as possible."[1]

Clinton repeated his admonition that while it cost $100 a ton to carry goods from Buffalo to Albany, only one-fourth of the expense would carry the same goods from Buffalo to Montreal. Again his goal was to bring the trade of the west to New York and to offer new markets to manufacturer and farmer alike. He reemphasized the function of the canal as a bond of union and the key to the preservation of American liberty. A majority of the members of the legislature supported him and the completion of the canal was authorized in April of 1819.[2]

But which section would next be completed? Canal goods piled up at Utica and suffered spoilage for want of

transportation to Albany. On the other hand Robert Troup
spoke for the people along the western section of the
canal when he wrote to Clinton in 1818 urging the
advantages of turning next to the west.[3] In February of
1819 the Joint Committee on Canals in the legislature,
acting on the advice of the commissioners, recommended
the beginning of the western section. Since the eastern
section was in many respects the most difficult it would
be well to have additional experience in the west. Furthermore, the commissioners advised that the sooner the
western section was completed the sooner commercial
connections to Montreal would be severed and the tide of
Western commerce would set towards New York.[4] But a
still more fundamental reason dictated the immediate
beginning of construction west of the Seneca.

Clinton was most concerned with the political opposition of those in New York who had long been unsym-
pathetic to the interior route and who wished to see him
down. And for Clinton, 1820 was an election year. In the
face of this threat, the commissioners immediately let
contracts for the sixty-three miles between the Seneca
River and Rochester, and for the twenty-six miles between
Utica and Little Falls.[5]

The governor made public his fears in his annual address to the legislature in January of 1820. He told of the
"exertions of insidious enmity" which sought to combine

[1] *Laws,* I, 394. Clinton wrote confidently to Rufus King in January,
"Our Canal improvements will be prosecuted with vigor and the Legislature will pass favorable laws on the subject this session. . . . The opposition to internal navigation is entirely paralized [*sic*]." January 24,
1819, Rufus King Papers, NYHS.

[2] *Laws,* I, 433-35.

[3] Troup to Clinton, December 18, 1818, De Witt Clinton Papers, CUL.

[4] *Laws,* I, 425.

[5] Clinton to Joseph Ellicott, March 11, September 25, 1818, February
19, 23, 1819, *HLC-WNY Canal Documents,* pp. 130, 144, 157; *Laws,*
I, 438.

an ever greater proportion of the population against the
further extension of the canal as each locality strove to
gain the advantage over western rivals. He told of the
attempts being made to halt the canal at the Seneca River
and he warned that similar attempts would be renewed
when it reached the Genesee. In furthering their "selfish
designs" the perpetrators of these acts of political sabotage
would "destroy the great fabric of internal improvement."
It was partly to forestall such attacks that the middle
section of the canal had been constructed first. Now,
promised Clinton, "By operating in both directions, a
solemn pledge is given of our determination to finish the
whole canal. . . ."[6]

The political struggle of the years 1819 and 1820 over
the completion of the western section of the canal was
essentially a new phase of the struggle which had marked
the inauguration of the canal in 1817. Opposition from
the southern counties continued to deplore the improvement of a route regarded as unnecessary and from which
it was believed the southern counties could not benefit.[7]
A protest was heard in Albany that the canal would see
the decline of that port as canal trade went directly to
New York City.[8] Peter B. Porter and his political friends
on the Niagara frontier still nourished the hope that by the
use of the Ontario route instead of the western section, the
partially completed canal could be made an adjunct of
the Niagara River rather than of Buffalo Creek.[9]

[6] *Laws*, I, 438-39.
[7] Ploughshare, *Considerations against Continuing the Great Western
Canal*.
[8] Albany *Gazette*, October 26, 1818.
[9] Clinton to Joseph Ellicott, February 19, 1819, *HLC-WNY Canal
Documents*, p. 157; The Black Rock Harbor Company, *Documents Relating to the Western Termination of the Erie Canal; with Explanations
and Remarks* (Black Rock, 1822), p. 53; Buffalo Harbor Committee,
*Documents and Brief Remarks, in Reply to the Pamphlet Written by
General Porter* (Buffalo, 1823), p. 7. Porter's plans for improvements

Shrillest of the voices still raised against the canal was that of Mordecai Manassas Noah, editor of the New York *National Advocate* and long a spokesman for Clinton's Tammany opponents in New York City. Noah denounced the report of the canal commissioners in 1817 as a "Budget of Blunders"; he found a single mile of the canal that would cost nearly two millions, and warned his readers of a bridge just completed in London that had cost "*near a million pounds sterling.*"[10] The canal would become a "monument of weakness and folly." The men of Tammany Hall fought the canal in 1817 and 1818 as Clinton's canal, designed to pass the door of every man who possessed a vote and to be abandoned when it could no longer serve Clinton's political purposes. "It is now said that the Canal project is the people's," wrote Noah in 1817, "it was not so formerly—THE PROJECT IS CERTAINLY INDIVIDUAL—If it succeeds, the ground will be again shifted, and it will be the grand project of an individual."[11] In spite of the obvious advantages certain to come to New York City from the completion of the canal, only Cadwallader Colden of all the New York delegation in the legislature spoke in its favor.[12]

In his fulminations, Noah spoke for the most extreme elements in a faction of the Republican party which went well beyond Tammany Hall in membership and which was known by 1819 as the Bucktails, from the furry decoration of Tammany hats. This faction was grappling with Clinton for control of the party and of the state.

---

in the Niagara River were called "Peter Ploughshare" projects. Buffalo *Journal*, January 1, 1822.

[10] Quoted in the Albany *Gazette*, August 4, 1817.

[11] Quoted in [Gideon Granger], *The Address of Epaminondas to the Citizens of the State of New York* (Albany, 1819), p. 9.

[12] Holley to Clinton, March 25, 1818, Myron Holley Papers, NYSL; Albany *Gazette*, February 12, 1818.

At its head stood Martin Van Buren. Opposing Clinton put the Bucktails too often in the unenviable position of opposing the canal. But for his part, Clinton lacked the political skill to win their support for his administration.

Clinton's political forces had fallen rapidly into disarray after his nearly unanimous election as governor in 1817. He was politically vindictive by nature and refused to conciliate those who had backed Porter. He was unwilling and unable to place himself at the head of the Republican party in whose name he acted. Dependent as he was upon Republicans who still regarded his sins against the party as unforgivable, he stood, as Van Buren saw him, "on a giddy eminence on which the difficulties of preservation are so great & distressing that many men would prefer political prostration as a choice of evils."[13] Never willing to follow a caucus decision out of party loyalty, Clinton's followers deserted the Republican caucus candidate in a critical choice of speaker of the assembly in 1819. A series of unwise removals and appointments brought accusation from the Bucktails that he had proscribed Republicans and allied himself again with Federalists. It was widely believed that he sought to create a personal party, loyal to himself alone. One Nathan Williams, who had formerly supported both Clinton and the canal, summed up a general Republican disillusionment when he wrote to Van Buren: "I confess myself among those who were deceived by Mr. Clinton—not as to his talents . . . nor as to . . . measures . . . but in his whole course as a politician. It is all too evident that he has acted a direct hostility to the republican party."[14] After the spring of 1819 the two factions of the Republican party dropped the fiction of

[13] Van Buren to G. A. Worth, March 19, 1818, Martin Van Buren Papers, LC.

[14] Williams to Van Buren, December 9, 1819, Martin Van Buren Papers, LC.

cooperation. Two distinct parties, Bucktail and Clintonian, emerged in New York with the Federalists holding
the balance of power between them.

Clinton had also incurred the hostility of a large
number of Federalists. Having acquiesced in his election
in 1817, they expected more in patronage than they had
received. Some had hoped that Clinton would, in the
spirit of the "Era of Good Feelings," appoint worthy men
to office regardless of party. But Clinton refused to support the able Federalist, Rufus King, for the United States
Senate. As a result, the Federalists divided; King and a
party known as "high minded Federalists" opposed Clinton, while others continued their support. Writing in the
New York *Evening Post,* a critic who signed himself an
"Old Federalist" judged that Clinton had been "weighed
in the balance and found wanting." "He is the political
Ishmael of our times," wrote this disillusioned Federalist;
"he is a sort of *political pirate* sailing under his own black
flag and not entitled to use that of either party."[15] By July
of 1819 Van Buren was writing that "the whole state is in
motion from Buffalo to Mantauk point & from the St.
Lawrence to the Atlantic," and the Little Magician concluded that Clinton's "influence is utterly destroyed & his
reelection put out of the question."[16] A portion of the
Federalists and a personal following of favored Republicans constituted the shaky political groundwork upon
which Clinton sought support for the progress of the Erie
Canal.

Two New York Bucktails, Ulshoeffer and Meigs, protested when the assembly proposed to respond to Clinton's
speech to the legislature in 1818 with praise for the canal,

15 New York *Evening Post,* April 1, 1819.
16 Van Buren to G. A. Worth, April 22, 1819, Martin Van Buren
Papers, LC.

but the first telling effect of Bucktail opposition came when Clinton sought to secure the election of Ephraim Hart to fill the vacancy on the canal board left by the resignation of Joseph Ellicott. But Henry Seymour, the Bucktail candidate, defeated Hart by a single vote. In this case, the Federalists sought out Van Buren, agreed to back Seymour, and revealed their willingness to act in coalition with the Bucktails rather than the Clintonians.[17] Not only was Clinton deprived of the services of an able man, but Seymour's election meant that two of the three acting commissioners on the canal were now Bucktails.

As the legislative session of 1819 progressed, moreover, the Bucktails speedily found it more expedient to drop their opposition to the canal. So popular had the canal become that no party could openly oppose it and still gain office. Especially was this true in the western district where Clintonians were dominant and where the Bucktails hoped to penetrate. The act of 1819 authorizing completion of the canal thus emerged out of the combined support of bitterly opposed factions, which were divided, however, on little more than the contest for place and office.

The address of the Clintonians in the legislature to their constituents, bearing sixty-two signatures, publicized this paradoxical state of affairs. They reminded the voters that although there was no longer hostility to "the great and magnificent enterprise of connecting . . . the waters of the Hudson and the Western and Northern Lakes," a relentless war was being waged against Clinton's administration. They branded Bucktail support of the canal as an attempt to steal the fruits of Clintonian labors. "A new contest has arisen on this subject," announced Gideon

---

[17] Hammond, *Political Parties*, I, 497; Kass, *Politics in New York State*, pp. 77, 104.

Granger, in a pamphlet deriding the Bucktails; "the opposition wish to create the belief that these splendid and all important improvements, are not in any considerable degree to be ascribed to the talents, exertions, and influence of Mr. Clinton."[18] In a "twinkling of time," Granger observed with accuracy, the Bucktails had been transformed into friends of the canal.

Conflict between Bucktails and Clintonians erupted in the canal board itself when Clinton and Samuel Young became involved in mutual recriminations in the fall of 1819. The rupture grew out of suspicions imputed to Clinton that Young was privately interested in contracts let on the Champlain Canal. But the angry exchange of letters which ensued produced a clash of personalities, allegations against Young for failure to perform his duties as secretary of the board and acting commissioner, and charges that Young's official duties were compromised by his political opposition to Clinton.[19] Clinton addressed Young as a "blackguard," "dastardly accuser," and author of "audacious calumnies" and asserted that Young's conversion from an enemy to a friend of the canal had dated from his appointment as commissioner. Young, on the other hand, accused Clinton of "contumely" and "slander" and of excluding the other commissioners from credit for their joint achievements in building the canal. A complete break in personal relations between the two men resulted, though they continued to serve together on the board for two more years.

Most of Clinton's political enemies, even Mordecai Noah, now supported the canal, and some of his friends

[18] Granger, *Epaminondas,* p. 36.

[19] Young to Clinton, October 12, December 20, 1819, Clinton to Young, October 18, 1819, February 25, 1820, James Geddes to Stephen Van Rensselaer, November 8, 1819, De Witt Clinton Papers, CUL.

with whom the canal had made him popular now deserted him. One of the latter was Joseph Ellicott. Ellicott's interest in the canal remained undiminished in 1818 and 1819. He assured Clinton that there would be no difficulty in the gift of the canal site through the company's lands, no matter which route was chosen for the western section. The Holland Company again offered its donation of 100,000 acres in the mountains of southwestern New York, and it was finally accepted by the state in 1819.[20] With Clinton's encouragement, Ellicott strengthened the wavering desire of his nephew, David Evans, to run for the senate as a Clintonian in the western district. But Ellicott, who believed Clinton partly responsible for the failure of a Buffalo bank, moved out of the Clintonian camp in 1819, and his nephew, after election, moved into the Bucktail opposition.[21]

When the question of renewed expenditure on the canal arose in 1820, opposition was directed not against the canal but against its Clintonian sponsorship. Two resolutions, which the Clintonian Myron Holley noted "of evil omen," were pushed through the assembly early in March. The first was introduced by Erastus Root, Bucktail from Delaware County, and provided for the collection of the local tax on lands lying within twenty-five miles of the canal as had been authorized by the act of 1817.[22] The second and more important, offered by George Tibbitts who had left the Federalists to join the Bucktails, directed

20 Clinton to Joseph Ellicott, March 11, 1818, *HLC-WNY Canal Documents*, p. 131; Ellicott to Clinton, March 18, 1818, Joseph Ellicott Letterbooks, BECHS; J. Vanderkamp to Ellicott, October 26, 1819, Letters to Joseph Ellicott, BECHS; New York *Evening Post*, April 16, 1819; *Laws*, I, 435-37.
21 Ellicott to Paul Busti, May 10, 1819, Joseph Ellicott Letterbooks, BECHS; Niagara *Patriot*, November 30, December 26, 1819.
22 This tax had been suspended in 1818.

that disbursements be made exclusively on the eastern section and on the Champlain Canal until they were completed. The resolutions went to the Joint Committee on Canals, and the committee in turn asked the commissioners for an opinion. The commissioners divided along party lines. The Clintonians, Clinton, Van Rensselaer, and Holley, formed a majority and submitted a lengthy report recapitulating the dangers inherent in the resolutions.[23] Seymour and Young, Bucktails, dissented and did not sign the report. With the commissioners divided on the question, the joint committee was unwilling to interfere, and the resolutions were defeated.

Now the Bucktails jockeyed to gain credit for backing the canal. Young introduced a bill in the senate which directed that after a specified appropriation was made for the Champlain Canal, the remainder of the available funds would be divided between the eastern and western sections. Van Buren proposed a minor alteration, and on the twelfth of April, 1820, the measure passed into law.[24]

The Clintonians nonetheless claimed the law as their own. At the opening of the legislative session in November of 1820, Clinton noted that "the public sentiment is now united in favor of the measure," and, citing the

[23] *Laws*, I, 459-81. The commissioners argued that the local tax would be inconvenient to collect and impossible to assess at that time. Against the second resolution they argued that contracts had already been let on the western section, that the western section would provide valuable experience, that such a course would threaten the western section with abandonment, that grants of land in the West had already been accepted and that the resources of the state would be increased most rapidly by the completion of the western section first.

[24] By the terms of the law one-fourth of the appropriations for future operations was to be expended upon the Champlain Canal, and the remaining three-fourths was to be divided equally between the eastern and western sections of the Erie Canal. *Laws*, I, 517. As a token of the unabated interest of those whose future was linked with Lake Ontario, the first $25,000 derived from land sales marked for the Canal Fund was set aside for the improvement of the Oswego River. *Laws*, I, 509.

propitious circumstances for construction, anticipated that the canal would be finished in three more years.[25] The friends of the canal in both parties might well exult that the canal would go on.

A political syllogism was at work. The prime objective of the Bucktails was the defeat of Clinton and Clinton's popularity was bound up with the progress of the canal. It was therefore inevitable that the canal should figure conspicuously in the political campaigns of 1819 and 1820, even though Bucktail legislative opposition had ceased. Popular concern over the welfare of the Erie Canal was coming to exercise a telling influence in the annual race for office.

The progress of the middle section of the canal had evoked well-nigh universal acclaim in western New York. Hezekiah A. Salisbury, for example, edited the Niagara *Patriot* in unrestrained opposition to Clinton; but he stood solidly behind the canal. On the eve of the spring campaign in 1819 for the election of the legislature, he gave fair warning to any who would make the canal a political issue. "As the canal is obviously a work of the first importance to the state, and will need, in its progress, our united energies to prosecute it effectually," he wrote, "it should be kept perfectly distinct from any political question that may arise, in the present unsettled state of parties in this state."[26] The Clintonians, as was to be expected, held to their pose as the exclusive friends of the Erie Canal. Within little more than a month after Salisbury's appeal to keep the canal nonpartisan, the *Patriot* reported that the "man worshippers in this quarter" were "spurring their hobby horses at full speed" to turn the

[25] Charles Z. Lincoln, ed., *Messages from the Governors*, II (Albany, 1909), 1045.
[26] Niagara *Patriot*, February 16, 1819.

canal to political profit.[27] In the local campaign that followed, the canal was very much involved.

To fill one of the assembly seats from Niagara County, the Clintonians nominated Oliver Forward while the Bucktails nominated Archibald S. Clarke. David M. Day, editor of the Clintonian Niagara *Journal,* did not hesitate to inject the canal issue into the race. He published correspondence to show that Clarke and Porter had "hitched their political teams" and appealed to the voters to withhold their ballot from any man who opposed the canal.[28] From his columns, "ATTICUS" urged the electorate to remember the canal as they voted: "Judge Forward is not only a firm friend of the present administration of the national and state governments, but an advocate of the overland route of the Great Western Canal. But can we say this of Judge Clarke? We have no evidence that would justify us in saying so. His declarations are equivocal. Why do certain persons in the northern towns, in the views of a certain interest proclaim that they will support him? Because say they, he will use his influence to divide the country, and divert the Western section of the canal into Lake Ontario, through the Oswego River. Let the people pause and reflect."[29] Clarke quickly affirmed his continued loyalty to the Grand Canal, and Salisbury decried the campaign which was spreading such accusations. But undoubtedly the canal was part of the reason why Forward went to the assembly and Clarke stayed home.

Clintonians and Federalists favorable to Clinton again won a majority in the assembly in 1819. At the same time, the Bucktails gained so many seats that the Federalist New York *Evening Post* could look to Clinton's political future and predict flatly "He is lost."[30] The Clintonian

[27] *Ibid.,* March 23, 1819.
[28] Niagara *Journal,* April 27, 1819.
[29] *Ibid.*   [30] New York *Evening Post,* May 19, 1819.

success again had come from the western district and again the southern part of the state had gone solidly against him. "The canal is a sore subject to the Bucktails," wrote Charles G. Haines to Clinton after the election. With the governorship at stake the following year, the canal was certain to come up again.

The Bucktails nominated the popular Tompkins for governor in 1820, whose place Clinton had taken when Tompkins resigned to become vice president. Tompkins was vulnerable because of his inability to account for money expended under his governorship during the War of 1812, but the Bucktails quickly made clear their record on the canal. In February, the address of the Bucktail members of the legislature to their constituents reminded the public that the canal acts for which the Clintonians claimed exclusive credit had been passed by an anti-Clintonian senate.[31] In western New York, the Niagara County convention, which met to select a Bucktail nominee for the senate, pledged its canal support without equivocation: "*Resolved,* that we observe with the highest satisfaction the successful progress of internal improvements, and the evident intention of all parties to accelerate their completion—that we consider the practice, pursued by the admirers of Governor Clinton, of depriving the authors of the project of Canal intercommunication, of the laurels so justly due them, to adorn the brow of 'unchastened ambition,' as sycophantic, disgusting and dishonest—and that we look upon the insinuations of his Excellency, that the opposers of his administration are inimical to the Grand Canal, as illiberal, undignified and unfounded."[32]

Nevertheless, "The Canal in Danger!" became the

[31] Address of the Bucktail Members of the Legislature, February, 1820, MS, Martin Van Buren Papers, LC.
[32] Niagara *Patriot,* February 15, 1820.

Clintonian watchword throughout the western district. Clinton was made the father of the canal and his friends the only guardians of its future.[33] Handbills signed by "Eighteen respectable citizens of Rochester" carried the alarm. Their special evidence that Bucktail hostility remained unchanged was the unwillingness of Young and Seymour to sign the report of the commissioners in 1819 recommending immediate completion of the western section.

The Rochester *Telegraph* sounded the same tocsin. Editor Everard Peck warned that the "ultimate object" of the Bucktails was "the destruction of the Grand Canal!"[34] Peck traced the Bucktail record. Root, head of Tammany Hall, was "deadly hostile" to the great work. Noah had turned his wit and ridicule against it. George Tibbitts, Bucktail assemblyman, had sponsored the resolution to suspend further operations on the western section. The report of the commissioners, devoid of Bucktail signatures, was in the *Telegraph* office for all to see. The backers of Tompkins were "secretly plodding [*sic*] the destruction of one of the greatest projects which has ever been devised."

The Bucktails answered with evidence to erase the impression that the canal was a Clintonian achievement alone. Had not Van Buren spoken eloquently in behalf of the act of 1817 and received the congratulatory hand-clasp of Clinton himself? Had not anti-Clintonians held the majority in the upper house of the legislature that had brought the canal to its present success? Had not Young introduced the bill which divided appropriations equally between the western and eastern sections until they were completed? Handbill answered handbill to demonstrate that "the great body of the Republican party have uni-

[33] Rochester *Telegraph*, April 25, 1820; Rochester *Gazette*, February 13, 1821.
[34] Rochester *Telegraph*, April 4, 1820.

formly, and from its commencement, been the warm advocates of the Grand Canal."[35]

When the votes were taken on the last Tuesday in April, a majority of the electorate remained loyal to Clinton, if not to his Clintonian followers. Clinton carried the western and eastern districts and with them was reelected governor.[36] His victory was a personal victory and only a few members of the legislature rode in on his coattails. Instead, the Bucktails added a comfortable majority in the assembly to the one they already enjoyed in the senate. "We have scotched the snake not killed it," wrote Van Buren. "One more campaign & all will be well."[37] But Clinton's friend, Haines, reported from New York that the Bucktails felt Tompkins' defeat "to the pith of their bones." Now, he added, "the bucktails will make great exertions to prosecute the canals—and will make great exertions to induce the people to believe that they are friendly to their completion. All this is infamous nonsense."[38] But mend their record on the canal the Bucktails did, and speedily.

In November the senate passed, without opposition, a bill appropriating $1,000,000 annually for two years to be added to the $600,000 regularly appropriated each year for canal construction.[39] The second section of the bill, however, carried a sleeper. It authorized the appointment

[35] *Ibid.*, April 18, 1820; Niagara *Patriot*, April 18, 1820.

[36] Hammond, *Political Parties*, I, 532-33; Rochester *Telegraph*, June 6, 1820; Niagara *Patriot*, May 16, 1820. Clinton carried the counties of Ontario, Genesee, Niagara, and Chautauqua by large majorities and every other county on the canal line. Allegheny and Catteraugus voted for Tompkins along with the other counties of the southern tier. Oswego County also gave a majority to Tompkins. Clinton won by the narrow majority of 1707 in the state.

[37] Van Buren to G. A. Worth, June 1, 1820, Martin Van Buren Papers, LC.

[38] Charles G. Haines to Clinton, May 24, 1820, De Witt Clinton Papers, CUL.

[39] *Laws*, II, 50-52.

of an additional canal commissioner and added significantly that the commissioners should hold their offices
"during the pleasure of the two houses of the legislature,
subject to be removed by concurrent resolution of the
two houses."[40] The law was thus double-barreled. It
would make good the Bucktail pledge of friendship for the
canal, and it would effectively remove the canal from its
Clintonian sponsorship. It would give the Bucktails, who
controlled both houses of the legislature, absolute sway
over the composition of the canal board, and it placed
canal expenditures in their hands. Moreover, they could
not lose because the swarms of boats already crowding
the more than ninety miles of navigable canal offered
proof that the canal would soon pay for itself many times
over.

Jesse Hawley, then a Clintonian member of the assembly from Rochester, is authority that a more Machiavellian
scheme was afoot.[41] The real motive of the Bucktails,
charged Hawley, was to trap the fifty-five Clintonians of
the assembly into amending the second section of the bill
in an attempt to preserve the Clintonian control of the
canal board. The Bucktails would allow the amendments
to pass the assembly, after which the senate would "non
concur" and the bill would die. Thus the Bucktails would
stand before the electorate as sponsors of generous support
to the canals without cost to themselves, and the Clintonians would bear the odium of causing the defeat of the
bill.

If this were the strategy, the plan yielded bitter fruit to
its makers. The Clintonians swallowed the bill whole and
wrested from the Bucktails much of the credit for its
passage. Gideon Granger, Clintonian senator, convinced

[40] *Ibid.*
[41] Hawley to Hamilton White, March 10, 1839 (copy), Henry O'Reilly
Papers, RPL.

Clinton that there would be greater glory in celebrating a completed Erie Canal as governor than in attempting to keep control over one which never reached Lake Erie at all. When the bill came upon the assembly floor in February of 1821, the astounded Bucktails witnessed Granger, Clinton, and the Council of Revision force the measure into law in two hectic days.[42] The Bucktails, "their countenances turned as blue as a December cloud," could do nothing but acquiesce. After four caucuses and five ballotings, the Bucktail William C. Bouck was elected as the new commissioner, and the canal board was directed to contract for the whole two millions immediately so that the next session of the legislature could not in good faith repeal the law. In no legislative session did Dame Fortune ever turn her smile more favorably upon the Erie Canal.

The Clintonians were jubilant and Clinton wrote to his correspondents that the whole canal would be completed by 1823 "at the farthest."[43] Myron Holley expressed to his father his satisfaction at the passage of the bill. "Ever since the canal was begun, the dearest hopes of its friends have been precarious till this Spring," he wrote. "Since the passage of the great appropriation law . . . those hopes may be regarded as sure and steadfast, relating to its entire completion."[44] To make prospects even better, in the spring elections of 1821 the Clintonians gained a majority in the senate and the Bucktail majority in the assembly was reduced.

Newspapers from one end of the state to the other took note that the canal was emerging from the political woods. "Well may opposition cease, to a work . . . upon which, in

[42] *Laws*, II, 27-28, 50-52.
[43] Clinton to R. H. Rose, April 10, 1821, Clinton to E. A. Brown, March 6, 1821, De Witt Clinton Papers, CUL.
[44] Myron Holley to Luther Holley, June 20, 1821, Myron Holley Papers, NYSL.

great degree depends the future prosperity, grandeur and glory of New York, and the nation," concluded the Clintonian *Commercial Advertiser* in New York.[45] To pro-canal Bucktail editors in western New York, the passage of the bill was like a soaking rain after a long drought. "But the People are now undeceived," declared Dauby of the Rochester *Gazette*: "They see that the Canals can go on without the aid of Mr. Clinton and his friends—that Republicans know what is for their interest as well as Mr. Clinton . . . and that they are determined to spare no pains in promoting that interest. What a pity it is that the prophecies of the Clintonians respecting the Canals should so soon have fallen into disrepute. . . . These great works are not yet stopped, and they must hunt up for some other device to amuse or alarm the people before the next election."[46]

If any doubts remained over Bucktail support for the canal, they were mitigated as the continued progress of the canal was made secure in the constitutional convention which met in the summer and fall of 1821. The movement for the convention came from the people and its goal was the elimination of the more glaring impediments to democratic government in New York. Van Buren and the Bucktails backed it to the hilt, but it was opposed by embarrassed Clintonians who would be forced out of office by the proposed reforms. As the convention approached, pressure also grew to put the canals under the specific protection of the constitution. In June, the New York *Evening Post* recommended that the new constitution insure against the canals "ever being sold, or passing out of the hands of the state."[47] In August, the New York *Commercial Advertiser* printed a panegyric to the canals

[45] New York *Commercial Advertiser*, November 14, 1821.
[46] Rochester *Gazette*, February 13, 1821.
[47] New York *Evening Post*, June 20, 1821.

as "an immense PUBLIC PROPERTY," which the convention must place "beyond the reach of party views, and party animosities."[48]

The convention was a Bucktail gathering, but in addition to abolishing the undemocratic Council of Appointment and the Council of Revision and broadening the suffrage, the new constitution guaranteed the Canal Fund.[49] For the latter achievement, Clinton and his followers could claim little, if any, credit at all. Indeed, Clinton's opposition to the convention would lead him to retire when his term expired. His followers would be driven from both houses of the legislature, their seats to be taken by Bucktails who would back the canal as well as constitutional reform.[50]

The Two Million Bill, as the appropriations law of 1821 came to be called, made note in its preamble of the "great advantages" for construction from the lowered wages and prices arising out of the hard times following the panic of 1819. Overexpansion in credit land purchases, the failure of unsound western banks, and the collapse of markets at home and abroad had their effect in New York as in the rest of the nation. The greater portion of the farmers west of the Seneca River were in debt for their lands, and it was a common report that reduced prices hardly paid them for carrying their produce to market. The only resource for money was "by getting a job on the canal," ran the complaint of "PHOCION" in the Rochester *Gazette* in 1820.[51] Intense competition forced down the bids as

[48] Quoted in Schenectady *Cabinet*, August 29, 1821.
[49] Charles Z. Lincoln, *The Constitutional History of New York* (Rochester, 1906), I, 691, 713-15.
[50] Robert V. Remini, *Martin Van Buren and the Making of the Democratic Party* (New York, 1959), p. 7.
[51] Rochester *Gazette*, October 10, 1820. Holley reported that this was Ambrose Hall, "a shaving lawyer" who had come from Massachusetts. Myron Holley to Orville Holley, October 30, 1821, Myron Holley Papers, NYSL.

men in need of money applied for contracts on the newly
begun western section, and the commissioners reported
"a reduction in prices of nearly every kind of labor required on the canals." Construction costs were 30 to 40
percent cheaper in 1820 and in July of 1821 excavation
contracts were taken as low as four cents per cubic yard.[52]

Although the commissioners had let contracts in small
sections so that employment would be open to men of
limited means, the concept of public works as a palliative
in time of depression had not yet emerged. Instead the
prevailing belief held that prosperity would come to all
when the great work was done.

Phocion's complaint about the stringencies of the times,
however, contains at least a glimpse of the more modern
point of view. With a demand for aid he mixed resentment at the manner in which the canal had become an
instrument of Clintonian patronage, a charge undoubtedly
carrying some truth, although John B. Jervis observed in
his unpublished Autobiography that "in selecting the contractors no notice was taken of their politics," and Holley
asserted that nearly half of the contractors on the western
section were Bucktails.[53] Nonetheless, all of the engineers
were Clintonians and whole stretches of the canal line
were reported to be in the hands of an uninterrupted
succession of Clintonians, many of whom "underlet" the
work at profit to themselves.[54] "How comes it about,"

[52] *Laws*, I, 7; Albany *Gazette*, May 25, 1820; Buffalo *Republican
Press*, July 24, 1821; Myron Holley to Luther Holley, June 20, 1821,
Myron Holley Papers, NYSL.

[53] Myron Holley to Orville Holley, October 30, 1820, Myron Holley
Papers, NYSL.

[54] The Albany *Argus* announced in 1819 after the Bucktails gained a
majority among the acting commissioners: "A majority of the canal commissioners are now politically opposed to the governor, and *it will not
be necessary for a person who wishes to obtain employment on the canal
as agent, contractor, or otherwise, to avow himself a Clintonian.*" Quoted
in Hammond, *Political Parties*, I, 497.

demanded Phocion, "that a noisy Clintonian by the name of Scovel, of Palmyra, should have jobs on the Canal to the enormous amount of nearly seventy thousand dollars, when there were more than five hundred mechanics, unable to obtain a job to the amount of a single dollar?" The answer, he alleged, lay in Mr. Scovel's willingness to send his helpers out into the county carrying pamphlets promoting the election of Holley to the assembly and Clinton to the governorship. Phocion advocated essentially a program of public works relief: "The Canal should be let out in small jobs, to relieve the necessities of as many as possible. In this way the honest labouring man would be fairly rewarded for his services and would be placed beyond the reach of the merciless grasp of the mammoth speculators and it would be the means of saving hundreds of Farmers, who are more or less indebted, from bankruptcy and ruin."[55]

While there was no idea of economic pump-priming, canal expenditures must have had that effect when the eastern and western sections of the Erie Canal and the Champlain Canal were all under construction, and as the operation of the middle section created new employment. Nine thousand men were at work on the canals in 1821.[56] Many along the line of the western section turned to building boats in anticipation of the day when they would be sold for use on the canal.[57] Land speculation accompanied the canal everywhere. Clinton retained land holdings in central and western New York, Holley bought land in Lyons and sought to make it the seat of a new county, and Elkanah Watson turned to the development of Port

[55] Rochester *Gazette*, October 10, 1820.

[56] Buffalo *Patriot*, October 16, 1821. They were distributed as follows: 5,000 between Utica and Schenectady, 2,500 west of the Seneca River, and 1,500 on the Champlain Canal.

[57] Niagara *Journal*, June 12, 1821; Rochester *Telegraph*, July 10, 1821.

Kent on Lake Champlain and to speculation in lands in Michigan.[58]

So strong was confidence in the ability of the state to meet its engagements that the depressed times following the Panic of 1819 had little effect upon the efforts of Commissioners of the Canal Fund to raise money by the sale of canal stock.[59] Expenditures on the Erie and Champlain canals steadily increased, and between 1821 and 1824 the commissioners paid out more than a million dollars yearly.[60] The average expenditure on the Erie Canal of $26,241 per mile must have had dramatic impact in the sparsely settled counties west of the Seneca River, the largest of which contained a population of only 61,185 in 1822.[61] With the fresh infusion of canal appropriations after 1821, the Erie Canal came to its most cherished destination, western New York.

[58] Clinton to Elijah Miles, September 27, 1823, Clinton to William Smith, December 12, 1823, Clinton to John W. Harpur, April 22, 1824, De Witt Clinton Papers, CUL; Myron Holley to Luther Holley, November 11, 1821, Myron Holley to Orville Holley, January 23, 1822, Myron Holley Papers, NYSL; Petition to the Legislature for a canal from Port Kent to the Hudson River, "Peru Lands," MS, Elkanah Watson Papers, NYSL.

[59] New York *Evening Post*, May 28, 1819, January 16, March 9, 1821; Albany *Gazette*, August 25, October 17, 1820; Miller, *Enterprise of a Free People*, p. 108.

[60] *Laws*, II, 285-87.

[61] [Sterling Goodenow], *A Brief Topographical and Statistical Manual of the State of New York* (New York, 1822) pp. 32, 63-65. Ontario County contained 61,185 inhabitants; Genesee, 40,200; Monroe, 28,855; Niagara, 7,322; and the new county of Erie, 15,668. Expenditures on the middle section of the canal averaged $12,000 per mile, on the eastern section, $18,000, and from Schenectady to Albany, $30,000. Clinton to John Sergeant, November 27, 1825, De Witt Clinton Papers, CUL.

7

The Canal Comes West

WESTWARD from the long Rome summit level, the completed line of the middle section was lowered near Syracuse to the lake country. There it passed over a lower summit from Nine-Mile Creek to the Skaneateles Outlet on its way to the Seneca River. The numerous streams abounding in central New York were laced to the canal by feeders and kept it plentifully supplied with water. At the beginning of the western section, the canal crossed over the Seneca River by a towpath bridge and passed through the Cayuga marshes to the village of Lyons where it took the waters of the Canandaigua Outlet and Mud Creek. After following the valley of Mud Creek to its headwaters at Palmyra, the canal was dependent for its water supply upon the Genesee River which was 130 feet above the Seneca River and 36 feet above Mud Creek.[1] A series of natural ridges solved the problem of carrying water from the Genesee River down the valley of Mud Creek to the Cayuga marshes, requiring only an embankment to be built across the valley of Irondequoit Creek at Mann's Mills. The discovery of these natural ridges was the cause for James Geddes' elation on his survey of 1808. They were the key to the western section of the Erie Canal.

Plans in 1817 called for the canal to cross the Genesee

River behind a dam ten feet high with a bridge for a towing path, but an aqueduct was later found preferable. From the Genesee River to Lake Erie the canal followed Geddes' route along the famous Ridge Road rather than the more southerly route passing near Batavia, which had been traced out by William Peacock at the behest of Joseph Ellicott. The choice was a difficult one and the public presses of Rochester and Batavia maintained a lively difference of opinion as to the respective merits of the routes involved.[2] In Buffalo the southern route was favored because it would guarantee that the termination of the Erie Canal would be at the mouth of Buffalo Creek rather than at the rival port of Black Rock on the Niagara River. By either route a ridge had to be crossed, for between the northern ridge which paralleled the shore of Lake Ontario and a southern ridge running from near Avon to the eastern tip of Lake Erie, a middle ridge lay like the bisector of a huge parallelogram.[3] The southern route was shorter and less expensive and passed nearer the larger settlements on the state road to Buffalo. But by this path the canal was required to rise seventy-five feet above Lake Erie and the consequent shortage of water induced the commissioners to direct the line northward. By cutting through the middle ridge near Eighteen Mile Creek, the canal would remain always lower than the lake, though it relied for its water supply primarily on the waters of Tonawanda Creek, Skejaquada Creek, and Buf-

[1] *Laws,* I, 28, 452.

[2] Rochester *Telegraph,* August 3, September 28, November 19, 1819. Still a third and more southerly route was advocated by Thomas Tufts and a group from Batavia. Tufts and others to Clinton, December 30, 1818, De Witt Clinton Papers, CUL. Elijah Hawley wrote to Clinton that although he would be benefited by it, this route could not be supplied by water. Hawley to Clinton, January 30, 1819, De Witt Clinton Papers, CUL.

[3] John H. Eddy, *Map of the Western Part of the State of New York* (Newark, 1811).

falo Creek "rather than the fluctuating waters of Lake Erie."[4] The canal therefore crossed the Genesee at Rochester and followed the northern ridge for sixty-three miles to the point where it crossed the middle ridge, then turned south through the Tonawanda swamp, and joined the Tonawanda Creek for twelve miles in its passage to the Niagara River. To use the water of Lake Erie whenever the level of the lake should make it available, the canal between the Niagara River and Lockport was carefully constructed with a drop of one inch to the mile.

The long levels across the Cayuga marshes and from the Genesee River to the "mountain ridge" needed only mile on mile of digging, the construction of towpath on one side and bank on the other, and the building of locks, culverts, waste weirs, bridges, and fences. For these tasks the procedures were by now well established, although still subject to difficulty and delay. The line through the Cayuga marshes was dug in water from six inches to a foot in depth, and sickness struck nearly every contractor as the work progressed in 1820 and 1821. The canal was navigable through the marshes by the spring of 1822. As new stretches of the canal were finished they brought the same excitement that had characterized the completion of the middle section. When the canal reached Lyons in June, editor H. T. Day of the Lyons *Advertiser* recorded the "liveliest sensations of joy and hope" felt by those who witnessed "the successful execution of an undertaking, so arduous, so extensive, and in our country, so novel; . . . and more than any thing else occupying the thoughts of a great community."[5]

---

[4] David Thomas to Clinton, June 8, 1821, November 1, 1822, De Witt Clinton Papers, CUL. The commissioners asked Benjamin Wright to choose between the two routes and he answered in favor of the northern. Albany *Gazette*, November 15, 1819.

[5] Quoted in the Rochester *Telegraph*, June 11, 1822.

While the scattered settlements of western New York read of the novelty of navigation on the portion of the canal already completed, they were equally fascinated by the great edifices taking shape among them. Three great engineering problems faced the builders of the western section of the canal, exclusive of the harbor which must be constructed at its termination. The canal must pass high in the air over the valley of Irondequoit Creek; the Genesee River must be spanned; and the "mountain ridge" must be scaled and cut to make water available for the long level from Lockport to the Genesee.

The valley of Irondequoit Creek presented the most spectacular challenge and the commissioners were no less daring in their proposal. Examination of the soil led them to conclude first of all that an embankment would not be feasible. They therefore announced contracts in 1821 for the construction of a wooden aqueduct, sixty feet in height, which would carry the canal for a quarter of a mile across the valley.[6] When this was erected, earth of a suitable variety would be brought in boats to provide a permanent base. The following season, however, they reconsidered, and fearful lest such a structure be unable to withstand the winds they accepted an offer to build the whole embankment of stone and earth.[7] Nine hundred piles were sunk deep in the quicksand of the valley bottom to sustain a semicircular culvert which carried Irondequoit Creek 245 feet under the embankment. Workers brought earth of sufficiently cohesive texture from miles around to build the mound a full seventy feet high.[8]

In the season of 1822, while sweating teamsters found the going ever more arduous at the pyramiding top of the

[6] *Laws*, II, 10.
[7] *Ibid.*, 60, 106.
[8] *Ibid.*, 60-61.

embankment, the level line from Rochester to Pittsford was easily completed. Genesee water flowed into the canal from Rochester to the embankment on the second of July. Two days later the village of Rochester celebrated the forty-sixth anniversary of the nation's independence. Ardent republicanism and sentimental fraternalism were typical of any frontier celebration of a national birthday, but now there was something more. *"The Erie Canal— Great! Stupendous! Magnificent!"* toasted an enthusiastic patriot while "parties of pleasure" sailed gaily on the new waterway.[9] Almost immediately, loaded canal boats ran back and forth to Pittsford meeting the wagons that had hauled their freights the two miles around the embankment to Hartwell's Basin until the summer drought prevented navigation further east.

The embankment was done in October. With the waters of the Genesee River supplying the canal across its narrow summit as far as the Seneca River, 180 miles of navigation were open from Rochester all the way to Little Falls. Yet it was an uneasy victory. For many weeks the commissioners drained the structure nightly and posted a constant watch for fear that the entire pile would dissolve in one great torrent onto the forest and farmhouses below.[10]

At the Genesee River itself, the construction of one of the longest aqueducts on the canal was well underway. Nine hewn-stone arches of fifty-foot span were being raised in the swift current of the river and a smaller arch was in progress at each end. In all the aqueduct would carry the canal a distance of 802 feet.[11] The central piers were sunk six inches into the rock of the river bottom,

9 Rochester *Telegraph,* July 9, 1822.
10 *Ibid.,* November 26, 1822, December 30, 1822.
11 *Laws,* II, 67, 100-101.

and from this anchorage the parapets of the aqueduct were so fastened with bolts and bars of iron that it must stand or be swept away altogether.

The village clustered at the two ends of the aqueduct that busy year of 1822 was nearly as new as the edifice under construction. Twelve years earlier its site had been only a fording place. Now as it became a focal point of canal activity, it took the appearance of a summer hive. A visitor in 1821 counted from one vantage point eighteen houses being built at one time, and more than one hundred new houses were added before the year was out.[12] "We now hear the 'busy hum' of a village containing nearly four thousand inhabitants," boasted the editor of the Monroe *Republican* in September of 1823.[13] The numerous mills and shops, which took their power from the falls cascading in a ninety-six-foot drop a short distance below the aqueduct, could look forward to certain expansion. Situated on the east bank of the Genesee, the "Rochester Aqueduct Nail Factory" capitalized on its proximity to the great work.[14]

Best of all, the end of the lean years seemed at hand. Advertisements such as that for "FIFTY LABORERS" to work in the Genesee feeder at ten dollars a month offered ready employment, and the days when "Cash for wheat" meant twenty-five cents to the bushel were over.[15] The Monroe *Republican* heralded the new prosperity with a banner announcement: "*Good Times*—The period for which the farmers have been so long looking has at length arrived.

---

[12] P. Stansbury, *A Pedestrian Tour of Two Thousand Three Hundred Miles, in North America* . . . , (New York, 1822), p. 92; "Journal of a Trip to Niagara, 1822," MS, URL.

[13] Monroe *Republican*, September 9, 1823. The population of Rochester doubled between 1820 and 1822 and added a transient labor force of 400. Rochester *Telegraph*, September 24, 1822.

[14] Rochester *Telegraph*, April 6, 1824.

[15] *Ibid.*, October 16, 1821.

Wheat was selling in our village on Saturday last, at *one* dollar a bushel."[16]

The hothouse growth of the town was not without its pains. One of the first shocks came with the announcement in 1821 that convicts from the Auburn State Prison were to be employed in hewing stone for the aqueduct. "Who can contemplate without horror," cried the *Republican,* "one hundred and fifty convicts, in the constant view of the children and youth of this populous settlement, pouring the sound of curses and profanity into the ears of all who may be attracted by the novelty of the scene to visit their encampment?"[17] The *Telegraph,* on the other side of the political fence, suggested that less concern was felt for public morals than for making political capital by attacking the Clintonian building of the canal. Nevertheless, the *Telegraph* continued to give notice of the numerous escapes from the force.

The aqueduct was completed in September 1823 after an expenditure of $83,000. Now that the canal had reached the west bank of the Genesee where most of the merchants lived and worked it was time for Rochester's first real canal celebration.[18] A line of decorated boats passed across the aqueduct on October 6 in ceremonial procession while the band played the Masonic ode, "The Temple's Completed," and the local militia fired their salutes. The procession continued slowly to the western outskirts of the village and returned to the aqueduct. There the celebrants heard an oration, after which the leading citizens retired to Christopher's Mansion House for feasting and toasting. The venerable Colonel Rochester, who presided at the table, toasted the aqueduct as

16 Monroe *Republican,* March 25, 1823.

17 Quoted in Rochester *Telegraph,* July 31, August 7, 1821.

18 Blake McKelvey, "Rochester and the Erie Canal," *Rochester History,* XI (July, 1949), 5-6.

"the most stupendous and strongest work in America," and other worthies paid tribute to the greatness of the village, state, and nation rising from the waters of the Erie Canal.[19] Their celebration accorded well with the judgment of Francis Hall, an earlier visitor to Rochester, when he observed, "Here are no memorials of the past, for the whole country is of today."[20]

Hall's observation was even more fitting for the feverish activity then in progress at the crossing of the "mountain ridge," where the operations were not only the most extensive of anywhere on the line of the canal but where a brand new city was in the act of creation. To surmount the ridge the commissioners decided to carve out a channel through the solid rock of the ridge itself.

Work began in 1822, but it soon became evident that carving the channel was beyond the resources of individual contractors. Accordingly, the state itself took over their function in 1823. Contractors were given wages to act as overseers while the commissioners hired the laborers and directed operations. Here was the first assumption of public works by the state on the Erie Canal, and perhaps, the first such project in the history of the United States.

A thousand men were employed by the commissioners to cut a deep, straight, clean-cornered trough for seven miles through the ridge, two miles of it through solid rock.[21] The channel was 27 feet wide and varied from 13 to 30 feet in depth.[22] In addition, a towpath was chiseled from the side of the cutting. Over the heads of the workers, high wooden-armed derricks swung baskets loaded with the rock blasted from the bottom of the excavation.

[19] Rochester *Telegraph*, October 14, 1823; Monroe *Republican*, October 7, 1823.

[20] Francis Hall, *Travels in Canada, and the United States, in 1816 and 1817* (Boston, 1818), pp. 118-19.

[21] Rochester *Telegraph*, May 6, 1823.

[22] *Laws*, II, 64.

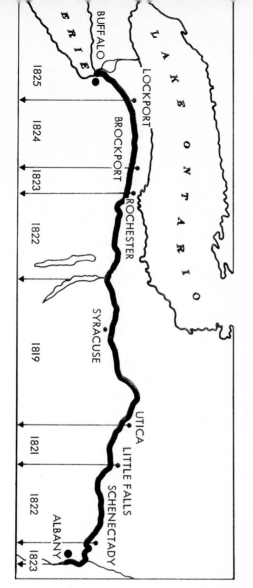

THE ERIE CANAL, SHOWING THE STAGES OF COMPLETION, 1819-1825

Based on a map prepared by the
Canal Society of New York State

EXCAVATING THE DEEP CUT WEST OF LOCKPORT, 1825

*Courtesy of the Canal
Society of New York State*

Flying pieces of stone from the drills and blasting frequently endangered the workers' lives, and accidents were numerous. The rocky bottom of the excavation had to be drained after every rain before blasting could go on, and near the top of the ridge the rock became so flinty that even large explosions produced little effect. Progress was often frustratingly slow.

At the eastern extremity of the deep cutting, a double flight of five locks was constructed to carry boats up and down the sixty-six foot rise in the canal. They were the work of Nathan B. Roberts, whose plan was chosen from several advanced by the other engineers. The acceptance of his plan by the commissioners, he later said, was the greatest event of his career.[23] With something of the appearance of a cataract, the locks stood at the head of a natural basin, flanked by steep banks a hundred feet high on either side. The long herringbone arms of the lock gates at each step emphasized the suggestion of a waterfall. Besides the immense quantities of timber, cement, and coping iron accumulated for the construction of the locks, fifty thousand feet of facing stone were imported to the site. They have almost invariably been chosen by authors from that day to this to illustrate any work on the Erie Canal.

Within little more than seven months a new village was born at the center of this intense activity. In July of 1821 (two months after the first contracts were let) only three families resided there. By January of 1822, 337 families (exclusive of the transient laborers on the canal) had established permanent residences at the village of Lockport.[24] In all there were fifty buildings. Those within

23 Whitford, *History of the Canal System*, I, 798.
24 Buffalo *Journal*, January 15, 1822. One of them was the brother-in-law of Myron Holley. Myron Holley to Luther Holley, June 20, 1821, Myron Holley Papers, NYSL.

range of flying stone from the excavating were protected by long tree trunks leaned against each side of the buildings so as to meet at the top.[25] Four stores, two apothecary shops, five taverns, and several "groceries" were serving the public, and the Lockport *Observatory* gave its weekly account of life and labor in the new settlement.[26]

All was bustle and vigor as Lockport sprouted to become a village of 1,500 by 1825. But here, too, rapid growth was accompanied by acute growing pains. Newcomers scrambled for lots, shortages drove prices high, and the Irish laborers engaged in lusty combat over Old Country loyalties. On the twelfth of July, 1824, the "Orangemen" from Protestant Ulster set out to celebrate a national holiday. Three-hundred "Catholics," whose affections were centered in the southern part of the Emerald Isle, turned out to disperse them, armed with guns, cudgels, and other instruments of persuasion. Sufficiently overawed, the Ulstermen attempted to return to work on the canal. But as they did so their fellow-Irish of different faith marched through the village behind drum and fife and a battle soon developed. Only when the militia had been called out and the citizens had begun to arm was peace restored.[27]

It was not until June of 1825 that the works which had given rise to these phenomena were completed. When they were finished, the inhabitants, who must have taken part in celebrations all along the line, concluded their work with appropriate flourish. Four hundred "brethren of the *mystic tie*" from the Lockport and surrounding Masonic lodges laid the capstone at the top of the combined locks on the morning of the twenty-fourth. An

25 Spalding, *Recollections*, p. 16.
26 Buffalo *Journal*, January 15, 1822.
27 Buffalo *Patriot*, July 20, 1824.

estimated four to five thousand spectators crowded about the locks as the procession was formed. The Masons, attired in full regalia, descended to the foot of the locks and from there they lined the staircased walls of the whole structure. An ode was sung and the Rev. Francis H. Cuming of Rochester delivered the address of the day. The capstone then slipped into place and the work was complete.[28]

While costly delays retarded the work at Lockport, the uncompleted portions of the canal west to the Niagara River and all the way east to the Hudson were opened. Boats began to traverse the nineteen miles from Rochester west to Brockport, the country seat of Hial Brockway, in October of 1823, and the remaining distance west to Lockport was open to traffic by September of the following year. For the entire distance from Rochester to Lockport the canal followed a single level. West of Lockport, the digging was delayed somewhat by poor roads where the canal turned south through the Tonawanda swamp. Near the mouth of Tonawanda Creek a dam was constructed and the slow moving stream was widened, deepened, and lined with towpath and bank to become part of the canal. By 1824 boats were passing for twelve miles along the length of the creek and entering the Niagara River through a lock.

While the western portions of the canal were being completed, work had proceeded apace on the line east of Utica. When the canal was finished east to Little Falls, the *Chief Engineer* again became the first boat down the canal, but this time it was guided into the lock at Little Falls by a steersman who had taken Washington from West Point to New York and Elizabethtown during

[28] Rochester *Telegraph*, June 7, 21, 28, 1825; Buffalo *Emporium and General Advertiser*, July 9, 1825.

the Revolution.[29] Along the eighty-six miles from Little Falls to Albany, which remained to be done in 1822, the canal followed the twisting valley of the Mohawk River on a line between the river and the crowding hills, which was more difficult to locate than any other on the canal. It ran close by the south bank all the way to Alexander's Mills (later Rexford), four miles below Schenectady. There the canal crossed the river by an aqueduct to the north side and, after twelve miles, recrossed the river again as it turned south to Albany. At Little Falls, a spectacular stone aqueduct 1,184 feet long, rose on a massive central arch of 70 feet and two smaller arches of 50 feet each to carry a navigable feeder from the Mohawk River into the canal. This aqueduct served to feed water to the canal, but more important to the local citizens, it carried the canal to the village of Little Falls which lay on the north side of the river.[30]

If the western section of the canal boasted the most imposing structures, that portion of the canal between Schenectady and Albany required an equal or greater application of engineering skill. There the gorge of the Mohawk narrowed and deepened briefly as the river rushed downward in descents as steep as eight and a half feet to the mile. "How we shall get a line from Schenectady to the Hudson I am most anxious to know," wrote Henry Seymour to Clinton.[31] Benjamin Wright proposed a plan for tunneling through the rocky gorge, but it was not adopted for fear of adding years to the work.[32] In some places the canal clung to a narrow ledge above the water,

[29] New York *Evening Post*, November 10, 1821.

[30] *Laws*, II, 110; Benjamin Wright to Clinton, May 1, 1821, De Witt Clinton Papers, CUL.

[31] Seymour to Clinton, October 16, 1820, De Witt Clinton Papers, CUL.

[32] Wright to Clinton, July 10, 1821, De Witt Clinton Papers, CUL.

and in others the steepness of the banks forced the canal into the bed of the river itself. Twenty-seven locks were built in the thirty miles between Schenectady and Albany, nearly a third of those required for the entire canal. At Alexander's Mills the aqueduct carrying the canal to the north side of the Mohawk was 748 feet long and rested on sixteen piers; twelve miles below, the canal was brought back to the southern side by an aqueduct stretching 1,188 feet and resting on twenty-six piers, the longest on the canal. Although many feared that these tasks would take months, and even years, to complete, by October of 1823 the Erie Canal was opened all the way from Brockport to Albany and the entire line of the Champlain Canal was completed.

The joining of the Erie Canal with the Hudson was celebrated on the eighth in ceremonies planned by Clinton himself. The event, observed Samuel Young, was "one of the proudest in the annals of our local history."[33] William Bayard gave a glowing account of the benefits to come, and Clinton praised the canal as an "illustrious example to the world."[34] The next spring, after the canal had been opened but five days, 106 canal boats were counted in the Albany basin.[35] It is little wonder that each added link in the canal quickened heartbeats throughout the state.

One evident indication of the influence of the canal was the appearance of the suffix *port* on the names of many New York settlements, no one of which was near the shores of Lake Erie or Lake Ontario. In western New York, Weedsport, Port Byron, Port Gibson, Fairport, Spencerport, Brockport, Newport, and Middleport became

[33] New York *Evening Post,* October 11, 1823.
[34] Albany *Gazette,* October 10, 1823.
[35] *Ibid.,* May 14, 1824.

inland, water-connected villages. Other villages with less nautical names could say with the editor of the Rochester *Telegraph*, "Our basins and storehouses have assumed the appearance of an enterprising, bustling seaboard harbor."[36] The numerous basins constructed to make room for warehouses and quays, and for loading, unloading, and turning around, took the place in the new nomenclature of travel of the "corners" which were their counterpart where stages still traversed the country roads.

Wherever water filled the canal, a new leaven began to work. Even before the canal reached its full length, the line took life and boom towns appeared. Cadwallader D. Colden noted in his celebration *Memoir* in 1825 that the prophesies made for the canal were already in the act of fulfillment: "We see with astonishment, the progress already made in populating regions which only yesterday, it may be said, were uninhabited. Already the whole Canal line is occupied. Almost at every turn in its course the traveller will find a village presented to his view, about which everything indicates, by the newness of its appearance, that it is but the growth of a few months. He will frequently see, on the borders of the Canal, a large excavation for a basin, intended for the port of a town, which he will perceive by the scale on which the streets are laid out, by the preparations for public buildings, and private stores, and warehouses, is considered as the foundation of a great city."[37]

The leaven of the canal's influence did not work everywhere with equal effect. Some villages prospered; others fell behind.[38] But an inrush of new settlers, a quickening

[36] Rochester *Telegraph*, April 29, 1823.
[37] Colden, *Memoir of the New York Canals*, p. 91.
[38] Blake McKelvey, "The Erie Canal: Mother of Cities," *The New-York Historical Society Quarterly*, XXXV (January 1951), 55-71.

of the economic pulse, and phenomenal growth became a common pattern.

There was little subtlety in the process, and the excitement of growth was not dulled by repetition. "The great advantages to be derived from Canal Navigation, operates [*sic*] as a powerful stimulus in persuading me to Emigrate to the west," wrote Daniel McGlashen from Albany to Thurlow Weed in Rochester as he prepared to establish himself in business in 1823 at the junction of the canal and the Genesee River.[39] Weed, junior editor of the Rochester *Telegraph* and just turning twenty-six, had left a place of straitened circumstances in Manlius and followed the canal west to Rochester only two years before. Again, the removal of Lyman A. Spalding from Canandaigua to Lockport at the age of twenty-two was perhaps typical of the manner in which people were brought to the banks of the Erie Canal.

Spalding was born in Scipio on the shores of Lake Cayuga in 1800. When he was ten years old, his father moved to the mouth of the Genesee River, built a tavern, and joined others in sending a schooner carrying staves back and forth between Charlotte and the Montreal market. Lyman Spalding's boyhood was lived amid frontier conditions. He fished in the Genesee for catfish, and often swam his horse across the Rochester fording place. The War of 1812 drove the elder Spalding from that exposed position to Geneva in 1813 where he built a sloop for the trade of Lake Cayuga, but when the collapse of prices following the war ruined his business there, he returned with his family to a farm near Rochester.

At this point in 1816, young Lyman became a store clerk in Rochester, just as the canal question was being

[39] McGlashen to Weed, November 7, 1823, Thurlow Weed Papers, URL.

debated throughout the state. Working in the store one day, he listened while two customers engaged in a warm discussion over the canal. In the course of the argument, one said that he would not want to live any longer than it would take to construct the canal. "This boy," he said, pointing to Spalding, "may live to see it completed," but he himself did not expect to.[40]

An attractive offer as clerk and bookkeeper with the firm of Cromwell and Allen in Canandaigua took Spalding there in 1817. Within three years he assumed Allen's place as a partner, prospering well for a youth of twenty. But by 1822, western New York was alive to the construction progressing on the line of the canal. "Utica is now very busy," wrote his friend Henry G. Cole; "navigation on the 'Big Ditch' is the order of the day."[41] Another friend wrote him of the flattering prospects for Clyde with the probability of a side cut from Seneca Lake to Great Sodus Bay which would intersect the canal at that new village.[42]

Spalding wrote to a business acquaintance by the name of Douglass whom he understood to be setting up establishments for selling and forwarding merchandise on the canal. He first thought Rochester "superior to any place west of Albany," and he urged Douglass to join in the purchase of a warehouse by the new basin being formed there. He was prepared to put in all of his capital of $3,500 and move to the canal as soon as it was navigable, but this venture did not materialize.[43] Soon a personal

[40] Spalding, *Recollections*, p. 15.

[41] Cole to Spalding, April 26, 1821, Lyman A. Spalding Papers, Cornell University Library.

[42] Frederick Boogher to Spalding, February 14, 1822 (photostat copy), Lyman A. Spalding Papers, Cornell University Library.

[43] Spalding to T [?] J. Douglass, June 10, 1822, Lyman A. Spalding Papers, Cornell University Library.

friend, A. W. Howe, who had moved to Holley, wrote of the great advantages offered by that village with the extension of navigation imminent. Howe's business in "Black Salts" was thriving, and more profit, he wrote to Spalding, was to be made in a day at Holley, than in a week at Canandaigua.[44]

But Spalding turned to a place which he believed offered greater promise still. In mid-December of 1822, he left on the stage for Lockport, sending as many goods ahead by wagon as two three-horse teams could draw. At the corner of Main and Pine streets, the firm of Spalding and Cromwell set up for business.[45] Good sales followed and the store in Canandaigua was closed. His friend Howe, learning of the new establishment in Lockport, shared his enthusiasm. "I must my Dear Friend, congratulate you on leaving old Canandaigua," wrote Howe, "for I think for us young folks, we shall find a little better pickings on the confines of the Great Ditch."[46]

Business flourished. Spalding bought additional land along the canal and competed for the water privileges available from the waste water of the locks. He was part and parcel of the booming town.

Indeed, few places could offer more advantages, unless it was the juncture of canal and lake trade. But whether that prize would be held by the tiny village of Black Rock on the Niagara River, or by the citizens of Buffalo on Big Buffalo Creek, no one could then be sure.

[44] Howe to Spalding, January 29, 1823, Lyman A. Spalding Papers, Cornell University Library.

[45] Spalding, *Recollections*, p. 16.

[46] Howe to Spalding, January 29, 1823, Lyman A. Spalding Papers, Cornell University Library.

8

Black Rock or Buffalo

BLACK ROCK and Buffalo, scarcely separable today, were between 1817 and 1825 keen commercial rivals for the honor and prosperity sure to fall to the western terminus of the Erie Canal. Important in the rivalry were the twin considerations of a safe and adequate harbor and a sufficient supply of Erie water to fill the canal at least as far as the Genesee River. And the answers to these considerations would determine whether the focal point of urban expansion would center on the Niagara River or on the Lake Erie shore.

Black Rock, situated three miles down the Niagara River, had offered for two decades the only safe harbor north of Dunkirk at the eastern end of Lake Erie. Here a large black rock, 100 feet in breadth, created a quiet eddy in the seven-knot current of the river and gave the village its name.[1] Not far from the shore the reef of rocks known as Bird Island and below it the larger Squaw Island gave protection from the lake winds and created a natural harbor.

The Porter brothers, Peter B. and Augustus, dominated the shipping facilities of the Niagara River. Joining with Benjamin Barton in the firm of Porter, Barton & Co., they had controlled the portage business around Niagara Falls since 1806 and for years they had sent vessels up the lakes for trade.[2] They were engaged as early as 1809 in supplying the western military posts at Fort Wayne, Detroit, and Michilimackinac with beef, flour, whiskey, and especially salt. In 1816, Sill, Thompson and Company began to build schooners at Black Rock to add to those already operating for the earlier firm.

One major fault marred Black Rock's otherwise preeminent position. Sailing vessels could not move from the harbor up into the lake against the river current and the prevailing westerly winds. They were compelled to rely on the "horn breeze" furnished by Sheldon Thompson, who hitched fourteen oxen to a vessel by a stout hauser and drew it up the river.[3] General Porter's influence had led the national government to make Black Rock the official port of entry in 1811 during the months from April to December, and as plans for the Erie Canal matured, the commercial leadership of Black Rock seemed secure.[4] The growth of Detroit at the western extremity of Lake Erie was an example of the advantageous position held by a river location for serving the lake trade.

Only two miles through the forest to the south, Buffalo smarted under its designation as the official port of entry during the slow winter months from December until April. There Big Buffalo Creek snaked its way northward to flow into the lake in a sluggish, muddy stream. The creek flowed parallel with the lake for sixty rods before entering, and above its mouth it was from eight to fifteen feet deep

1 Richard Williams, "Black Rock Harbor, Pier, Water Power and Flouring Mills" (1865), MS, BECHS.

2 Lewis F. Allen, "Recollections of the Early Forwarding Trade on the Lakes and Canal," in *Canal Enlargement in New York State, Buffalo Historical Society Publications,* XIII (Buffalo, 1909), 377; Marvin A. Rapp, "The Port of Buffalo, 1825-1880," (unpublished doctoral thesis, Duke University, 1947), p. 13.

3 Augustus Walker, "Early Days on the Lakes," *Publications of the Buffalo Historical Society,* V (Buffalo, 1902), 303.

4 Rapp, "The Port of Buffalo," p. 14.

and sixteen rods wide.[5] Buffalo Creek thus qualified as a serviceable harbor, but it too possessed a major liability. A sand bar blocked its mouth, allowing only small boats to enter. Ships had to anchor half a mile offshore and were served by the use of lighters. This obstacle, however, could be removed, but little could be done about the wind and current which inhibited the use of the harbor at Black Rock.

In 1816 a village meeting was called at Pomeroy's Tavern in Buffalo to find aid for the improvement of Buffalo harbor, and a committee was named to take the necessary steps.[6] The men of this committee, Benjamin Caryl, Heman B. Potter, Reuben B. Heacock, Benjamin W. Hopkins, Charles Townsend, Jonas Harrison, and Samuel Wilkeson, kept the harbor project alive while the legislature in Albany struggled over the inauguration of the canal.

In spite of the sand bar, the commissioners named Buffalo as the prospective termination point of the canal in their surveys of 1816 and 1817.[7] Clinton himself rhapsodized over the day when Buffalo would be the rival of New York, thereby giving encouragement to Buffalo's hopes, and Ellicott, then serving on the Canal Board, had promoted the growth of the village ever since he had surveyed its plan as New Amsterdam in 1803. With such influential friends, the villagers of Buffalo saw the prospect of renewed growth as they sought to recover from the burning of their homes by the British during the War of 1812, but they were also mindful of the rival pretensions of Black Rock.

[5] Katherine Whittemore, "Geographic Influences in the Building of Buffalo Harbor," (unpublished doctoral thesis, Clark University, 1936), pp. 116-20.

[6] Benjamin Caryl and others to Joseph Ellicott, January 22, 1816, *HLC-WNY Canal Documents*, pp. 40-41.

[7] *Laws*, I, 198, 518-19.

At Black Rock the Porters began plans in 1815 for a steamboat to operate on Lake Erie.[8] Investors in Albany and New York took the lead, however, and organized the Lake Erie Steam Boat Company. The company elected, "much to the mortification & disappointment of the Buffalonians," to build the craft at Black Rock, and the *Walk-in-the-Water* was launched in August of 1818.[9] The steamboat still relied on Thompson's "horn breeze" for its departures every Friday to Detroit, but it made Black Rock its home port and never during its three years of service entered the mouth of Buffalo Creek.

To offset this development at Black Rock, the Buffalo harbor committee petitioned the legislature for aid in 1818. Clinton then appointed William Peacock to prepare a survey and estimate the cost of the necessary improvements. Peacock's report in January of 1819 became the basis of the first Buffalo harbor. He advised the construction of a pier which would extend a thousand feet out into the lake well south of the mouth of Buffalo Creek. Such a pier would prevent the deposits of sand and gravel, which were believed to be formed by the westerly current of the lake, and at the same time provide a safe shelter for ships at anchor. Since Peacock was in the employ of the Holland Company and the company was not disinterested, the propagandistic tone of his report is understandable. He pronounced his *"most decided"* opinion that Buffalo offered the best place for "a safe and commodious harbour" at the eastern end of Lake Erie.[10]

Armed with this report, Charles Townsend of Buffalo's

[8] Augustus Porter to Peter B. Porter, November 7, 1815, January 30, 1818, R. Wooley to Peter B. Porter, January 11, 1816, Thomas Morris to Peter B. Porter, February 7, 1816, Sill, Thompson & Co. to Peter B. Porter, January 19, 1818, Peter A. Porter Papers, BECHS.

[9] Augustus Porter to Peter B. Porter, January 2, 1818, Peter A. Porter Papers, BECHS.

[10] *HLC-WNY Canal Documents,* pp. 153-54.

harbor committee scurried to Albany for financial assistance. By this time, the Buffalo harbor appeared to be included unofficially in the Clintonian goal of the immediate construction of the western part of the canal.[11] Opposed to state aid for the harbor were those who favored the Ontario route and opposed the completion of the western section.[12] By more than coincidence, it would seem, on the day that the legislature authorized the construction of the western section (April 7, 1819), it granted an appropriation for the improvement of the Buffalo harbor. The citizens of Black Rock had sent a similar petition for aid in February without so favorable a result. A loan of $12,000 was given by the state to a group of nine Buffalonians, who were organized in effect to form a company, with the stipulation that if the canal were extended to Buffalo Creek, the debt would be canceled.[13]

David Evans considered the loan "an absolute gift," for he was confident that the commissioners would extend the canal to Buffalo the following summer.[14] But 1819 was a year of financial panic. Only Townsend and Oliver Forward were willing to provide bond for the loan and their means were not sufficient. Here Samuel Wilkeson,

[11] *Laws*, II, 518-19; David Evans to Ellicott, January 9, 1819, Letters to Joseph Ellicott, BECHS; Evans to Ellicott, February 13, 1819, *HLC-WNY Canal Documents*, p. 156; Peter B. Porter to Augustus Porter, February 19, 1819, Augustus Porter Papers, BECHS.

[12] Townsend to Ellicott, March 8, 1819, *HLC-WNY Canal Documents*, pp. 159-60; Granger, *Epaminondas*, p. 38; Niagara *Patriot*, March 2, 1819; Rochester *Telegraph*, April 18, 1820.

[13] *Laws*, I, 431-32. The following were named in this act: Jonas Harrison, Ebenezer Walden, Heman B. Potter, John G. Camp, Oliver Forward, Albert H. Tracy, Ebenezer Johnson, E. F. Norton, and Charles Townsend. The following later became members of the Buffalo Harbor Company: Samuel Wilkeson, Reuben B. Heacock, George Coit, Dr. Marshall, William Peacock, Cyrenius Chapin, Dr. Trowbridge, T. C. Love, J. A. Barker, David M. Day, W. T. Miller, and James Sheldon, Williams, "Black Rock Harbor," *MS*, *BECHS*, pp. 6-7.

[14] Evans to Ellicott, February 25, 1819, Letters to Joseph Ellicott, BECHS.

a capable, if unpolished, pioneer trader and Buffalo magistrate, came forward, joined the company, and shared the liability for the loan. He brought also the energetic spirit that when all else failed, saw the project through.

The Buffalo investors faced a dilemma. They knew that if the Erie Canal were not extended to Buffalo, the harbor would be of little value to themselves or to the state. On the other hand, they could not hope to secure the canal if they did not have a harbor. The landholders at Black Rock were striving vigorously to see that they did not get the canal.

In the summer of 1819 David Thomas, the chief engineer on the canal west of Rochester, arrived in Buffalo to survey both Buffalo Creek and the Niagara River to ascertain the best place for the termination harbor. When Thomas reached Black Rock, the Porters and others who joined together in the Black Rock Harbor Company proposed the formation of a harbor by building a 17-foot dam across the river to Squaw Island, a distance of 1,320 feet.[15] An embankment would also be constructed along the entire length of the island, and at the uppermost point a pier would be extended 5,000 feet up into Lake Erie to Bird Island, making an abutment of about a mile and a half in all. The dam would raise the water level to that of Lake Erie, and the harbor enclosed by the pier and the dam would be larger and easier to enter in time of storm than that planned at Buffalo.

With both communities wooing his favor, Thomas made his examinations and submitted his report in October. In the Thomas report the palm fell to Buffalo, but this decision was only the beginning of a prolonged contro-

---

[15] *Laws*, I, 487. The Black Rock Harbor Company included the following: Peter B. Porter, Augustus Porter, Benjamin Barton, William A. Bird, James Rough, Nathaniel Sill, James L. Barton, and Joseph G. Norton. Williams, "Black Rock Harbor," MS, BECHS, p. 7.

versy rather than its consummation. Thomas reported that
the expense of the Black Rock dam would be prohibitive.
He accepted the assertion of "credible persons" living
along the river that no pier could be made capable of
withstanding the ice for a single season. Moreover, he
believed that the Black Rock harbor would be too narrow
to allow ships to beat against the winds from down the
lake and that in time of war with the British the harbor
would be useless.[16] Despite Thomas' recommendations
no decision was made to continue the Erie Canal beyond
Tonawanda Creek, and the conditions attached to the
Buffalo Harbor Company's loan remained. Moreover, the
Holland Land Company withdrew its support from the
Buffalo group. Ellicott refused even the loan of a pile
driver after the harbor became a company venture. Busti,
in Philadelphia, had made a rule of refusing aid to all but
state enterprises and would make no exception here.

In the spring of 1820 the Buffalo Harbor Company set
to work in earnest to construct a harbor on Peacock's plan.
A professional harbor maker was engaged, but his efforts
proved ineffectual and Wilkeson himself directed the
enterprise.[17] Rain or shine, from daybreak to darkness,
Wilkeson's crew put cribs of squared timber out into the
water and filled them with brush and stone. By the end
of the season 900 feet of pier extended out into the lake.
With the force of the lake current thus checked, the
sand bar blocking the mouth of the creek could be cut.
Time was short and resources were small. Wilkeson hit
on a capital plan in May of 1821. He would use the spring
flood to gouge out the channel. The creek was dammed
near its mouth and its current turned straight across the

---

[16] *Laws,* I, 482-89.

[17] Samuel Wilkeson, "Recollections of the West and the First Building
of Buffalo Harbor," *Publications of the Buffalo Historical Society,* V
(Buffalo, 1902), pp. 188 ff.

CELEBRATING THE COMPLETION OF THE ERIE CANAL IN NEW
YORK HARBOR, 1825

*Courtesy of the Museum
of the City of New York*

THE SENECA CHIEF IN THE DEEP CUT WEST OF LOCKPORT, 1825

*Courtesy of the Canal
Society of New York State*

330-foot strip which separated the creek from the lake. Before the channel was complete, however, a great swell from the lake made a total wreck of their labors. As the swell subsided, a northeast wind threatened a freshet. Wilkeson threw his workers into the reconstruction of the dam while cold rain beat down. They worked all day and on into the night until the dam was effective again. Then they waited. In the morning a "magnificent" flood carved out a channel 5 feet deep and 90 feet wide. A harbor was made. An additional $1,800 was raised in the village, the design of the harbor was improved, and by summer's end a pier 1,300 feet long was completed. With a serviceable, if none too secure, harbor the committee could press for an answer to the all important question of the termination point of the Erie Canal.

A new memorial was sent to the legislature from Buffalo in December of 1821 which appealed for the passage of a law placing the termination of the canal at Buffalo Creek and authorizing immediate construction at that end of the route.[18] Tension mounted when it became known that the commissioners planned to decide the interlocked questions of harbor and termination point early in the 1822 spring session of the legislature,[19] and Wilkeson went off to Albany to spend the winter lobbying. To make the competition still more intense, the Mechanics Bank of Albany offered to establish a branch bank at whichever place should win the termination harbor. "Once establish such a Branch Bank at the Rock," feared the Buffalonians, "and Buffalo is virtually destroyed."[20]

Black Rock still held, in some respects, the better position, for the men at Black Rock were at least certain

[18] *HLC-WNY Canal Documents*, pp. 341-49.
[19] Oliver Forward and Samuel Wilkeson to David Evans, December 7, 1821, *HLC-WNY Canal Documents*, pp. 170-71.
[20] J. L. Barton to [?], January 9, 1822, Peter A. Porter Papers, BECHS.

of the canal. Myron Holley assured Augustus Porter in August of 1821 that no other route was feasible to supply the canal with the requisite water from Lake Erie save that along the Niagara River.[21] The stock of the Black Rock interests rose in December when James Geddes made a favorable survey of the Niagara River and lent his reputation to the merits of constructing a harbor there. Shortly thereafter, Nathan S. Roberts, an assistant engineer, appeared to survey both harbors and report had it that he too favored Black Rock. The Buffalonians accused both of laboring in the pay of the Porters, but they thought it all too likely that the Porters would succeed.[22] They felt added apprehension lest the Bucktail majority in the legislature remove Clinton and Holley from the Canal Board, a circumstance which they believed would be ruinous to their interests. "All well and in high spirits at Black Rock," James L. Barton wrote in January of 1822.[23] Just when the skies looked the brightest for Black Rock, however, the Buffalo Harbor Company was given the prize.

Since the decision was in the last analysis a technical one and political repercussions were certain, the commissioners passed the responsibility to the engineers. By happenstance the five leading engineers were present in

[21] Augustus Porter to Peter B. Porter, August 2, 1821, Augustus Porter Papers, BECHS.

[22] Wilkeson and others to William Peacock, January 9, 1822, *HLC-WNY Canal Documents*, p. 172; Oliver Forward and Samuel Wilkeson to Clinton, November 25, 1821, De Witt Clinton Papers, CUL. James L. Barton wrote in 1822, "But the true reason of his coming was, he had made a treaty offensive and defensive with a few interested individuals, that he justly dreaded this winter a Legislative censure for his . . . suffering the dam across the Hudson to be carried off—and that these individuals had promised to see him safe through the furnace of affliction if he would report in favor of B. R. which he undoubtedly would. . . ." J. L. Barton to [?], January 9, 1822, Peter A. Porter Papers, BECHS.

[23] James L. Barton to [?], January 9, 1822, Peter A. Porter Papers, BECHS.

Albany in February of 1822. Wright, Thomas, Roberts, and White gave a unanimous opinion that the canal should terminate at Buffalo Creek.[24] Geddes alone dissented and withheld his signature from their report. A pall of gloom settled on the people of Black Rock and darkened into reproach as report came back from Albany that they had been outmaneuvered. There existed, wrote Sheldon Thompson to General Porter, "a combination against our place . . . mooved [sic] by selfish motives."[25] Wilkeson was accounted the master mover. In concert with Thomas he was said to have been behind the commissioner's censure of the operations of Geddes on the Champlain Canal in 1820 in their annual report of 1822. This censure weakened Geddes' position at the parley and Thomas dominated the decision. Moreover, Wilkeson had thoughtfully stopped at Rochester where he aroused fears regarding the water supply of the canal, and he had induced Colonel Rochester to accompany him to Albany. The commissioners were accused of having brought their individual political ambitions to bear upon the decision. "It has," lamented Thompson, "become a mere speculation." The Porters and their friends had been caught completely offguard. They had been assured in Albany that nothing would be done until later in the spring. While they slept, Wilkeson had won the round.

Only a month later, however, the advantage of the Buffalo Harbor Company appeared to be temporarily neutralized. A great freshet in Buffalo Creek during the first week in March undermined the pier and created a new sand bar over which the water was less than three feet deep. Memorials were soon on the way from Black

---

[24] *Laws*, II, 519; Buffalo *Patriot*, February 26, 1822.
[25] Thompson to Peter B. Porter, March 3, 1822, Peter A. Porter Papers, BECHS.

Rock to Albany petitioning for reconsideration. With so indecisive a state of affairs, the commissioners advised financial aid to both harbors and scheduled a hearing in June of 1822, at which the vexed question would, it was hoped, be finally settled.[26]

The legislature concurred and in April reaffirmed its loan to the Buffalo Harbor Company. In addition, a contract was authorized with the citizens of Black Rock for the construction of a harbor on a plan drawn by Geddes. The legislature granted $12,000, and the harbor at Black Rock was placed on an equal footing in the patronage of the state.

Meanwhile, Wilkeson was once more feverishly directing the work of the Buffalo villagers to reclaim their harbor. Not only was the termination question at stake again, but now there was a steamboat to get out of the creek.

On her last run of the season in 1821, the *Walk-in-the-Water* had met a gale as she started up the lake and had been driven ashore just below the Buffalo pier, a total wreck. Her owners salvaged her engines and made plans to replace her with another ship. Again the rival villages vied for the privilege of building "the steamboat" and serving as her port of call.[27] Brown, the contractor, traveled to Buffalo in January to see the directors of the Buffalo Harbor Company, but arriving before the hour of business, he went on to Black Rock. There he was favorably persuaded by the carpenters who had built the *Walk-in-the-Water* to allow them to construct her successor as well. The papers were to be signed that night at Brown's hotel in Buffalo.

News of the agreement traveled quickly down the

26 *Laws*, II, 79.
27 Wilkeson, *Publications of the Buffalo Historical Society*, V, 204-208.

length of Schimmelpennick Avenue to Buffalo. When Brown returned to his hotel in Buffalo, he was quickly cornered by the harbor interests of that village. They offered him timber at a quarter less than the carpenters at Black Rock and guaranteed him $150 per day for every day that the boat was detained in Buffalo Creek by shallow water after the first of May.[28] Brown accepted and built the boat at Buffalo.

Then came the spring freshet and a closed channel. Wilkeson hurried home from Albany. A new subscription was carried in goods, cash, or labor. The villagers raced against the calendar and the progress of the boat taking shape upon the bank of the creek. Although beset by one calamity after another, they scraped barely enough channel to allow the exit on May 1 of the new steamboat *Superior,* which made Buffalo her home port.[29]

Early in June of 1822 when the Canal Board and the five principal engineers gathered at the Eagle Tavern in Buffalo to render a decision on the termination point of the canal,[30] Wilkeson related the near-miraculous accomplishments of the Buffalo Harbor Company, and General Porter presented two plans for a harbor in the Niagara River.[31] The gathering was impressed by Porter's plans, but they remained unconvinced. They stood by the decision of the preceding February and unanimously authorized placing the canal under contract from the upper end of the proposed harbor at Black Rock to Buffalo. There was still a chance for a harbor at Black Rock, however, if

[28] *Ibid.,* p. 207; Buffalo *Journal,* January 1, 1822.

[29] Wilkeson, *Publications of the Buffalo Historical Society,* V, 208-14; Buffalo *Patriot,* April 16, 1822.

[30] Wilkeson, *Publications of the Buffalo Historical Society,* V, 141-42; Whitford, *History of the Canal System,* I, 110. Bouck was the only commissioner who did not attend.

[31] Black Rock Harbor Company, *Documents,* pp. 24-26.

not for the termination point. The harbor company there was advised that if it should succeed by "fair experiment" in constructing ten or more rods of pier at a designated point in the rapids within the following year, the commissioners would then contract with them for a harbor. The commissioners candidly admitted in their report of 1823 that the effect of their Buffalo parley was "to postpone the ultimate decision of the harbor question for one year."[32] So long as construction of the deep cutting and locks at Lockport delayed the opening of the whole line they saw no reason to close the question.

The Buffalonians were overjoyed at the news that the Erie Canal would be continued to their village. On the ninth of August the contractors were ready to dig and the villagers to celebrate. The villagers assembled at the Eagle Tavern at nine in the morning and with a military band at their head they marched to the termination point of the canal. They hoisted the national flag, planted a cannon on a nearby knoll, and hitched teams of oxen to plows placed upon the canal line. Clergymen of the village made the addresses of the day, befitting their place of honor in the community. When they had finished, a salute was fired from the cannon, and with the oldest residents in the lead, the citizenry took up their shovels and began the digging. As the ox teams turned the soil, the diggers fell in behind, refreshing themselves from barrels of "pure old rye" strung alone the line.[33]

Salisbury of the *Patriot* hoped that the intervillage rivalry now would be stilled: "Political feuds and personal animosities were lost in the greatness of the scene [he reported], and nothing was heard but one universal expression of heartfelt approbation. And here we cannot

[32] *Laws*, II, 96.
[33] Buffalo *Patriot*, August 13, 1822.

but indulge the animating hope, that as this great work may be the source of our wealth and greatness, so may it prove the grave of those local feuds which have so long disturbed our repose, and impeded our prosperity."[34] But the Black Rock Harbor Company was by no means prepared to yield. With the recognition given by the commissioners to their "experiment," they launched their greatest efforts in December.

General Porter established the Black Rock *Beacon* with Lewis G. Hoffman as its able editor to give local publicity to the company's claims. The publication of a sixty-page pamphlet of documents relating to the termination question and written largely by Porter was calculated to expose the alleged falsehoods created by Thomas' reports, from which it was believed all Black Rock's troubles had stemmed.[35] "They had either to step over me, or fall at once," wrote Thomas.[36] Porter departed for Albany where he could exercise his influence prior to the submission of the annual report of the commissioners in February.

The implementation of this three-pronged offensive during the following six months brought the harbor altercation to its peak. Wilkeson and his friends gave tit for tat as they sought to deprive their rivals of the foothold they had gained. The editors of the rival presses bit and snarled at each other with no reputation sacred. In the *Beacon*, editor David M. Day of the *Journal* was a "brute," "cur," "smearer," or "blushless miscreant" possessed of a "fiend-like spirit," and his writing was "vulgar black-guardism and foul misrepresentation." The *Journal*, we may believe, returned in kind, although only a few

[34] *Ibid.*
[35] Porter to Myron Holley, December 1, 1822, Peter A. Porter Papers, BECHS.
[36] David Thomas to Clinton, November 15, 1824, De Witt Clinton Papers, CUL.

scattered issues published during the controversy are today preserved for examination.

Charge and counter-charge ensued. The Buffalonians charged that the experimental section of the Black Rock pier which was put down did not offer a "fair experiment" of the strength of the entire work. The Black Rock interests defended their experiment as a "triumphal success" in the "narrowest & swiftest" part of the river.[37] Again, the Buffalo protagonists charged that the expense of the Black Rock harbor would be a great waste of public funds, while its defendants replied that it would cost less than the length of canal it would replace.[38] The Buffalonians charged that the ice carried downstream would destroy the pier; the Black Rock interests replied that Bird Island gave sufficient protection.[39] Again, it was charged that the lake winds would be too severe at the entrance of the harbor. The harbor company produced affidavits from experienced mariners to prove the contrary.[40] To the Buffalonian charge that the entrance of their harbor was endangered by rocks and reefs, the Black Rock Harbor Company replied that their basin would offer a safe anchorage of 150 acres, six times greater than that at Buffalo.[41]

The Black Rock spokesmen, in their turn, directed their sharpest attacks upon the issue of the sand allegedly carried to the mouth of Buffalo Creek with every freshet.

[37] Samuel Wilkeson to Clinton, July 23, 1822, *HLC-WNY Canal Documents*, pp. 358-59; Porter to Clinton, July 31, 1822, *HLC-WNY Canal Documents*, p. 359; Porter to Myron Holley, December 1, 1822, Peter A. Porter Papers, BECHS.

[38] Black Rock *Beacon*, April 24, 1823; *HLC-WNY Canal Documents*, pp. 376-78.

[39] Black Rock *Beacon*, February 20, May 8, 1823; *HLC-WNY Canal Documents*, pp. 367-68, 375-78.

[40] *HLC-WNY Canal Documents*, pp. 375-81.

[41] Black Rock *Beacon*, February 20, 1823.

The Buffalonians answered that the sand came not from the creek, but from the current of the lake, easily excluded by their pier.[42] The Black Rock interests charged that Buffalo Creek was too small for a harbor; the Buffalonians replied that the creek was navigable for a mile and a quarter with an average breadth of nearly 200 feet.[43] The detractors of the Buffalo harbor made much of the grounding of the schooners *Erie, Union, Red Jacket, Beaver* and *Hannah* at the end of the Buffalo pier during the shipping season of 1822. The Buffalonians replied that the schooners had strayed from the channel.[44]

Great emphasis in the Buffalo attack was placed on the perpetuation of the "portage monopoly," charged to be the goal of the Porters.[45] The pamphlet reply of the Buffalonians to the Black Rock Harbor Company's "Documents" was primarily a personal attack against General Porter. It accused him of opposition to an overland canal and said bitter things about his personal motives in opposing the Buffalo Harbor. Porter responded to these attacks in a public letter in April of 1823. He defended the righteousness of the harbor company's cause against "the machinations of a cold-blooded conspiracy, entered into by some half a dozen men in Buffalo, to destroy my character and consideration in the community. . . ."[46] He held that the harbor project had no other object than

[42] *Ibid.*, February 20, April 23, 1823; *HLC-WNY Canal Documents*, p. 366.

[43] Black Rock *Beacon*, February 20, 1823; *HLC-WNY Canal Documents*, p. 372.

[44] Black Rock *Beacon*, January 30, February 6, 27, 1823; Buffalo *Patriot*, May 14, 1822.

[45] Niagara *Journal*, April 24, 1821; Black Rock *Beacon*, January 30, 1823.

[46] Black Rock *Beacon*, April 24, 1823. The Buffalo *Patriot* agreed and protested that "the harbor question is entirely out of view. The sole object is to destroy the political consequence of General Porter." Buffalo *Patriot*, April 29, 1823.

"merely to enlarge or widen the Erie Canal at this place into a harbor for lake vessels, without interfering in the least, with the plan of carrying the canal to Buffalo. . . ." Covertly, however, he wrote in March to a member of the legislature offering to build a private termination harbor in return for the privilege of levying port fees and observed that his offer would save the expense to the state of any canal improvements beyond Black Rock.[47]

Exclusive right or moral purity cannot be found in the record left by either of the rivals for the termination point of the canal. Either could have written with Oliver Forward in 1821 that it was "a question on which the future prosperity of this village entirely depends," and their conduct must be judged as one judges the idea of national interest.[48] Less can be said for the conduct of the engineers, and perhaps of the commissioners, who were involved.

Each of the engineers on the western section of the canal compromised his official position. Thomas identified himself openly with the Buffalo harbor committee.[49] He engaged in altercation with Porter over issues that were clearly in the exclusive purview of the commissioners. Geddes was indiscreet in his conveyance of the affairs of the commissioners to the Black Rock Harbor Company and to some degree he allowed himself to be used by them.[50] Roberts indulged in closet politics with General

[47] Porter to Seaman, March 22, 1823, *HLC-WNY Canal Documents*, pp. 361-62.

[48] Oliver Forward and Samuel Wilkeson to David Evans, December 7, 1821, *HLC-WNY Canal Documents*, p. 171.

[49] A notable example is his letter "to a gentleman in Albany," which was printed in broadside form. *HLC-WNY Canal Documents*, pp. 369-78.

[50] James Geddes to James L. Barton, February 12, 1822, Sheldon Thompson to Peter B. Porter, March 6, 1822, Peter A. Porter Papers, BECHS. "They are trying to get Gades [*sic*] down," wrote Thompson to Porter; "You must try to build him up and pull Thomas down."

Porter and other Republicans. He carried his personal animosity toward Thomas into his advocacy of the Black Rock Harbor, and he brought frequent reports of the political division among the engineers and commissioners to Porter.[51] David S. Bates, another assistant engineer, made his survey of the Niagara River with a troop of Buffalonians dogging his steps and watching his every move. Although the evidence is far from conclusive, it appears that personal political ambitions were not absent in the actions of the commissioners. Clinton was the partisan of Buffalo, planting anonymous letters in the Buffalo press and seeking information *sub rosa* from Thomas on reactions of the other commissioners.[52]

After all was said and done, however, the final decision of the commissioners must be recognized as a judicious one. They were bound by their agreement of the preceding June to enter a contract with the Black Rock Harbor Company if it was successful in its experiment. Visiting Black Rock in June of 1823, they ascertained that the experimental pier was secure and entered a contract for a harbor, Clinton alone dissenting.[53] Peter B. Porter and Sheldon Thompson agreed to construct a harbor for $83,819, which was the cost of building an independent canal (required if the Erie Canal did not pass through Black Rock harbor). The commissioners explained their 1823 decision in their annual report of the following year.

The Black Rock harbor was to be the major one of three

[51] Nathan S. Roberts to Peter B. Porter, January 20, February 17, 1823, Roberts to Alvin Bronson, March 5, 1823, Peter A. Porter Papers, BECHS.

[52] Clinton to Oliver Forward, June 25, 1824, Clinton to David Thomas, November 10, 1824, De Witt Clinton Papers, CUL.

[53] Black Rock *Beacon*, June 12, 19, 26, 1823; Monroe *Republican*, June 24, 1823; Rochester *Telegraph*, June 24, 1823; Articles of Agreement for the Construction of the Black Rock Harbor, July 24, 1823, Peter A. Porter Papers, BECHS.

harbors joining the canal to Lake Erie. The Buffalo harbor would be the smallest, "but large enough for a very extensive trade." The Niagara River itself would constitute a harbor "large enough to contain all the shipping of the Atlantic." Boats could be locked into the river at the mouth of Tonawanda Creek; a lock would carry lake vessels into the Black Rock harbor, and the Erie Canal would connect the Niagara River harbors with Buffalo.[54]

The Buffalonians were dispirited. Buffalo would have the termination point, but the center of transfer between lake and canal would be on the Niagara River. The inhabitants of Black Rock crowed over their victory, for such it appeared to every observer. Hoffman in the *Beacon* congratulated his fellow villagers as he put the controversy to rest: "The cause of the quarrel having ceased, the feelings we have enlisted in it, are at an end, and we trust that neither the 'rod' nor the pen may again interpose, to interrupt our confident anticipations of harmony and good fellowship. If there were ever a people who had reason to be satisfied with themselves, it is the people of Black Rock, and especially the editor of this paper, on a retrospect of their own conduct as regarded the harbor question."[55]

Here the story of the controversy might reasonably, and mercifully, be expected to end. "As the die is cast," said Salisbury in the Buffalo *Patriot*, "it is of very little use to us to quarrel with the commissioners or our neighbors at Black Rock on account of the decision."[56] The leading figures in the Buffalo Harbor Company, however, could not accept only partial victory. They pressed the legislature for a *new* accommodation: an alteration of the route

[54] *Laws,* II, 151-57.
[55] Black Rock *Beacon,* June 26, 1823.
[56] Buffalo *Patriot,* June 24, 1823.

of the Erie Canal by which the canal would pass parallel
to the Niagara River for two and a half miles without
entering the Black Rock harbor at all. This last of the
major objects of controversy was known as the Independent Canal, and it prolonged the harbor dispute until the
spring of 1825.

Willing to gamble even what they had won, the spokesmen for the Buffalo Harbor Company charged the commissioners with corruption and sought a reversal of the
legislature's 1823 decision.[57] Damages suffered to the
Black Rock harbor in 1824 were publicized and delegates
were sent to York (Toronto) to encourage the Canadians
to protest the construction of a dam in the Niagara River.
Articles, said to be written in Buffalo, appeared in a
Canadian paper, the Niagara *Gleaner,* threatening demoli-
tion of the harbor by powder and ball.[58]

The Buffalonians fought a last-ditch battle in the face
of events which seemed full of promise for the village of
Black Rock. Nearly $400,000 was spent in and around
Black Rock, which by February of 1825 had reached a
population of 1,031. Work progressed rapidly on the
harbor until by the opening of 1825 it was nearly completed. While Buffalo doubled in population between
1821 and 1825, Black Rock increased 150 percent in the
year 1824 alone. The Porters still carried political power
in the state, and they continued with plans to link the
steamboat traffic of the lake with the canal through their
harbor. In 1824 they proposed to certain investors in

[57] Buffalo *Emporium and General Advertiser,* February 28, 1825; Black
Rock *Beacon,* July 17, 21, August 7, 1823, March 18, 1824; David Evans
to Heman I. Redfield, March 2, 1825, Charles W. Evans Papers, BECHS.
Clinton urged them to conduct themselves with moderation so as not
to reverse public sentiment which was against the Black Rock harbor
decision. Clinton to Oliver Forward, June 28, 1823, De Witt Clinton
Papers, CUL.

[58] Black Rock *Beacon,* October 9, 1823.

Detroit and Lake Erie ports the operation of a line of
steamboats "to ply between the head of canal navigation
at Black Rock and Detroit. . . ."[59] Two years later the
Union Line Steamboat Company was organized with
stockholders in ports all around the lake. The Porter
family held forty-eight shares at $100 a share, easily a
controlling block.[60] "From a careful examination of the
two places," observed the Monroe *Republican*, "we believe that Black Rock is destined by nature to take precedence of Buffalo at no distant day."[61]

But Buffalo had grown apace. The settlement at the
mouth of Buffalo Creek contained in February of 1825
2,412 inhabitants, 232 dwelling houses, 11 inns, 5 churches,
6 schools, a court house, a library, a theater, a Masonic
hall, and over 50 shops of all kinds.[62] Seventeen attorneys
and nine physicians resided there and the villagers could
choose from four public prints. Spafford's *Pocket Guide*
noted the presence in 1824 of "about 1,000 strangers,
constantly in this village, just arrived, all in a bustle,"
and hailed the growing port as the unrivaled "Queen City
of the Lakes."[63]

The final phase of the harbor altercation between these
two prospering villages came to an anticlimactic head in
the spring of 1825. The Independent Canal Bill, spon-

[59] Peter B. Porter and others to Rufus Reed and others, July 27, 1824,
Peter A. Porter Papers, BECHS.

[60] A. Dey to Peter B. Porter, September 10, Augustus Porter to Henry
J. Hunt and others, September 25, 1824, Articles of Association forming
the Union Line Steamboat Company of Lake Erie, dated August 21,
1826, Peter A. Porter Papers, BECHS. In September of 1824 the Porters
took the leadership in organizing the Niagara River Steamboat Company
to operate between Black Rock and Niagara Falls. Copy of Articles of
Association forming the Niagara River Steamboat Company, September,
1824, Peter A. Porter Papers, BECHS.

[61] Monroe *Republican*, February 15, 1825.

[62] Buffalo *Emporium and General Advertiser*, January 22, 1825.

[63] Horatio G. Spafford, *A Pocket Guide for the Tourist and Traveller,
along the Line of the Canals* (New York, 1824), pp. 47, 49.

Black Rock or Buffalo   161

sored by the Buffalonians to prevent the Erie Canal from
passing through Black Rock harbor, was initially defeated
in the legislature in March of 1824. In January of 1825 a
new petition was sent to the legislature, supported, this
time, by merchants in Albany. The Joint Committee on
Canals now declared that the fears regarding the safety
of the Black Rock harbor were "not altogether groundless"
and introduced a bill in the assembly in February for the
construction of an independent canal which would bypass
that harbor. In spite of the protests from Black Rock, the
bill passed quickly by a vote of 71 to 31. As the bill went
to the senate it was supported by Clinton and even the
Porters were privately willing to accept it "if several
modifications favourable to Black Rock" could be added.[64]
With the Porters following a devious course, a compromise
bill passed the senate by a vote of 27 to 4 in April. By this
act the commissioners were authorized to build the independent canal along the shore of the Niagara River whenever they considered it necessary.[65] In this compromise
the matter rested. Rivalry continued for years until the
Black Rock harbor failed, and the expansion of Buffalo
ultimately necessitated the construction of the much-
disputed two and a half mile stretch of "independent"
canal.

Meanwhile, canal boats were drawn with varying success through the Black Rock harbor to Buffalo. The
harbor served the canal, but it also yielded to the ice
runs in the spring. Finally, by 1826 damages closed the

[64] *Laws*, II, 374-75; Donald Frazer to Peter B. Porter, March 23, 1824,
Sheldon Thompson to James L. Barton, February 1, 1825, Peter A. Porter Papers, BECHS; Peter B. Porter to Augustus Porter, January 7, February 17, 1825, Augustus Porter Papers, BECHS.

[65] Clinton wrote that it would be necessary for the water supply of
the canal and because of "the well formed complaints of our Canadian
neighbors." Clinton to H. R. Storrs, January 10, 1825, De Witt Clinton
Papers, CUL.

harbor and drove the forwarders to Buffalo. Clinton could not "shed a tear" over this "predicted fate." He wrote bitterly to David Thomas of the failure of the harbor: "Conceived in sin, fed by ignorance, nourished by cupidity and brought forth in iniquity, it had disappointed no observing man—as long as the Canal lasts, its ruins and history will be subjects of reproach to the projectors."[66]

The Buffalo harbor, however, was no more immune. It too was progressively weakened by storms, and in 1828 both harbors were taken over by the state. At the same time, the process began which would make Black Rock a part of Buffalo by 1853. The greater facilities developed at Buffalo led to expansion there, and the mushroom growth gradually smothered the animosities of the harbor struggle.

In June of 1825, however, all this was yet to come. All important was the announcement by Commissioner Bouck that water would be let into the Erie Canal for the nine miles between Tonawanda Creek and Black Rock. The Black Rock villagers celebrated the occasion as the "TERM- INATION OF THE GRAND CANAL." On the morning of June 3, the leading townsmen boarded the *Superior* and steamed down the river to the mouth of Tonawanda Creek. There they boarded packet boats and mingled with well-wishers from Lockport, Pendleton, and Tonawanda. Together they rode up the canal and through the crowded harbor. While the guns saluted and the people cheered, the party debarked and James L. Barton, Marshal of the Day, led the procession to the Steam Boat Hotel. It was a Black Rock festival. General Porter presided, Bouck represented the commissioners, and Roberts the engineers. Not the least incident marred the "great hilarity and good feeling" of the day.

[66] Clinton to Thomas, June 10, 1827, David Thomas Papers, NYSL.

The celebration was the culmination of a long and bitter strife which had often reached comic-opera proportions. Though local in scope, the controversy is significant in its expression of the impact of the Erie Canal on the frontier through which it passed. Moreover, before the Erie Canal could be completed throughout its entire length, its fortunes were marked by a final struggle which drove De Witt Clinton from the ranks of its builders.

9

The Politics of Removal

INCEDO SUPER IGNIS was as fitting to the diary of De Witt Clinton as to the famous diary of John Quincy Adams in the year 1824.[1] Just as the canal reached its final stages of completion, the political opponents of Clinton struck once more at its Clintonian sponsorship. These forces gained increasing control over the state government and a small group of powerful Bucktail leaders were accurately dubbed as the "Albany Regency." They were the political machine of Martin Van Buren, put together by him to dominate the state when he left New York in 1821 to serve as Senator in Washington.[2] William L. Marcy, Azariah C. Flagg, Silas Wright, Edwin Croswell, Roger Skinner, and a few others ruled the state through the power of the legislative caucus, the organ of the Albany *Argus*, and, above all, a relentless use of the patronage.

The Erie Canal, with its thousands of jobs, was tailor-made to augment the power of the patronage in New York. Starting at the top, the tenure of the canal commissioners themselves rested in Regency hands after the passage of the appropriations act of 1821. In 1824, they exercised their power without conscience and removed Clinton from his post as president of the Canal Board, a post in which he had served without pay for fourteen years. Explosive as this desperate stratagem proved to be, the calculations of the Regency which brought it to pass are nevertheless understandable.

Political fortunes of New York had been determined largely by issues entirely independent of the canal since Clinton's reelection in 1820. "Opposition to the Erie and Champlain canals had ceased," wrote Thurlow Weed of this period in his *Autobiography*. "Had it been otherwise, had the partisans of Mr. Van Buren continued their hostility to the canals, Mr. Clinton could have remained strong."[3] The contest over the constitutional revision of 1821, the question of backing the right candidate for the presidential election of 1824, and the demands for the passage of a new electoral law occupied the center of the political stage. Moreover, the New York electorate had shown no reluctance to send anti-Clintonians to the legislature in 1820, where they enjoyed a majority in both houses. Clinton's support narrowed to a personal following aided by Federalists with whom he had long acted in concert. In 1822, canal or no canal, his popularity was so slight that his backers dared not run him for reelection and they put up no opponent to Joseph C. Yates, who was elected to the governor's chair almost unanimously.[4] But Clinton himself wrote stubbornly from his home on Long Island, "If I had been a candidate, I would have been reelected governor."[5]

When Clinton left the governorship in January of 1823, there were those who wished him out of his post as canal

[1] Charles Francis Adams, ed., *Memoirs of John Quincy Adams* (Philadelphia, 1875), VI, 453.

[2] Remini, *Martin Van Buren*, pp. 8-11.

[3] Harriet A. Weed, ed., *Autobiography of Thurlow Weed* (Boston, 1883), p. 102.

[4] Hammond, *Political Parties*, II, 97-98.

[5] Clinton to Cadwallader D. Colden, January 2, 1823, De Witt Clinton Papers, CUL.

commissioner as well. Ever since the Bucktails gained control of the legislature in 1820, they had been restless to secure the removal of Clinton, Van Rensselaer, and Holley and thus to reduce the board to its Bucktail members, Bouck, Young, and Seymour.[6] Now, in January, Wilkeson advised his Buffalo friends that it was "pretty certain" that such a removal would take place.[7] Late in February, Victory Birdseye of Onondaga County moved in caucus for Clinton's removal, prompted, said Clinton, by Porter who acted with a view to his harbor at Black Rock. In March, Charles E. Dudley of Albany gave notice in the senate that he would bring in a bill to appoint canal commissioners, with the implication that the Clintonians would be replaced by men from Regency ranks. But with Van Buren's opposition to the measure and Dudley's private admission that "it would appear as a pitiful exertion of power" this effort aborted in 1823.[8] Nevertheless, it was clear that Clinton presided over the meetings of the board with a sword over his head. "Mr. Clinton has bestrode this hobby horse long enough, and since the goodly work has begun, we hope the senate destroy, root and branch, everything that savors of Clintionianism," wrote Hoffman in the Black Rock *Beacon*.[9] Hoffman's vindictiveness was heated by local bitterness, but his demand was more than prejudice. "What . . . has been the object of the last five years' struggle?" he asked; "Was it not to displace Mr. Clinton?"

While Clinton professed to be without further political

[6] Peter B. Porter to Van Buren, November 1, 1820, M. Ulshoeffer to Van Buren, January 31, 1822, Martin Van Buren Papers, LC; Wilkeson and others to William Peacock, January 9, 1822, Charles W. Evans Papers, BECHS.

[7] Samuel Wilkeson to David Evans, February 19, 1823, *HLC-WNY Canal Documents*, p. 174.

[8] Dudley to Van Buren, January 18, 1823, Martin Van Buren Papers, LC.

[9] Black Rock *Beacon*, March 6, 1823.

ambitions, he could not safely be tolerated as harmless on the Canal Board by the guardians of the Regency camp. Although he possessed little political power, he was not destitute of political support. Clintonians, quite as much as their opponents, stood for political reform. Clinton's name was toasted at every celebration from Albany to Buffalo which marked the progress of canal construction. Thurlow Weed, a rising anti-Regency power in the western part of the state, prophesied a splendid future for Clinton. As Clinton left office in 1823, Weed stood solidly behind him in the columns of the Rochester *Telegraph*: "His five years rule will be the brightest and proudest page in our history. . . . The feeble and impotent attempts of blind and stupid malevolence, to deprive him of honors he so nobly earned, serve only to confirm and strengthen his claims. When his enemies hoped to ruin him by checking the progress of the Canals their motto was *'Clinton and his canals are indissolubly connected—he must sink or swim with them.'* . . . And he does swim them! . . . When those who are strutting their brief hour upon the political stage are shuffled off and forgotten, the name of Clinton will brighten into a second life. . . ."[10]

If Clinton's friends despaired of his chances for reelection, publicly they kept alive his identification with the canal. They saw to it that the canal boat *De Witt Clinton*, with Clinton on board, was the first boat to pass through the completed eastern section of the canal into the Hudson. They made plans to purchase the boat, draw her through the streets of New York at election time, and finally to make her a public monument to Clinton's honor.[11] Clinton planned the celebration of the joining

[10] Rochester *Telegraph*, January 7, 1823.

[11] J. B. Mower to Weed, October 20, 1823, Thurlow Weed Papers, URL. A "splendid Packet Boat" called the *De Witt Clinton* was launched in 1824, "superior to any packet on the canal."

of the canal and the Hudson on October 8, 1823, with utmost care and Noah in the *National Advocate* promptly charged that the great celebration in Albany was an attempt "to revive the political complexion of the Canal."[12] At the same time, "INVESTIGATOR" wrote a series of ten "Reminiscences" in the Albany *Gazette* reviewing Clinton's canal services and the attacks made upon him as its projector.[13]

Hard-headed political realists could neither assess nor count upon the extent to which canal popularity could serve Clinton, but an immense reservoir of popular sentiment had grown with the building of the canal. Clinton had shown before that this reservoir could be tapped. The testimony of the Lyons *Advertiser* in June of 1822, that the canal "more than anything else" had come to occupy the thoughts of that community,[14] had political as well as social meaning. If the canal could be sufficiently dramatized in its relationship to Clinton, smothering suc-

[12] Quoted in the New York *Evening Post*, October 4, 1823.

[13] Albany *Gazette*, October 17, 24, 28, 1823. These articles were directed chiefly against Elkanah Watson who maintained a heated controversy in newspapers and pamphlets from 1820 to 1825 over his claims to the credit for projecting the canal policy of the state. Watson published in 1820 his *History of the Rise, Progress, and Existing Conditions of the Western Canals in the State of New York,* and began a long series of letters in the press. He was defended by Robert Troup in two pamphlets, *A Vindication of the Claim of Elkanah Watson, Esq. to the Merit of Projecting the Lake Canal Policy* . . . , (Geneva, 1821), and *A Letter to the Honorable Brockholst Livingston, Esq. . . . on the Lake Canal Policy of the State of New York* (Albany, 1822). These claims were answered in the press by a series of letters signed Tacitus and Philo-Tacitus, believed to have been written chiefly by Clinton. Clinton published a history of the origin of the canal in a pamphlet under the pseudonym, Tacitus, entitled, *The Canal Policy of the State of New York; Delineated in a Letter to Robert Troup, Esquire* (Albany, 1821). Watson's writings charged that Clinton was excluding others from credit for projecting the canal in order to serve his own political advancement. Drafts and copies of Watson's communications are found in the Elkanah Watson Papers, NYSL.

[14] See above, p. 125.

cess might again result. Thurlow Weed taunted the Regency with the potential strength of this formula when he wrote in the Rochester *Telegraph* on March 11, 1823: "If the dominant party wish to identify Mr. Clinton still closer with the Canals, let them remove him from the Presidency of the Canal Board." It would, he added, make *"assurance doubly sure."*[15]

A year, a month, and a day later, a series of events had convinced the Regency that the arguments in the formula could strike no fire. First, the Buffalo–Black Rock controversy brought the actions of the Canal Board under public suspicion. Clinton's energetic dissent from the decision to contract for a harbor at Black Rock in 1823 created mutual recriminations among the commissioners. Holley's conduct, wrote Clinton to David Thomas, "to say the least has been very reprehensible."[16] In March of 1824 the Buffalo-sponsored bill for a canal independent of Black Rock harbor led to a committee investigation in the assembly which reopened the whole question of the best termination harbor for the canal. The commissioners and engineers appeared before the committee, and Clinton took the lead in fighting for the passage of the bill in Buffalo's favor.[17] Charges of corruption ensued, and the dissension among the commissioners was publicized.[18] Although the committee found no prejudice in the majority decision of the Canal Board, the defeat of the bill was a defeat for Clinton and added to his political embarrassments. And among the charges of corruption were allegations that Myron Holley, Clintonian treasurer of the

[15] Rochester *Telegraph,* March 11, 1823.

[16] Clinton to Thomas, June 15, 1824, De Witt Clinton Papers, CUL.

[17] *Laws,* II, 196-200.

[18] Clinton to Thomas, June 15, 1824, Clinton to Oliver Forward, June 25, 1824, Stephen Bates to Clinton, December 25, 1824, De Witt Clinton Papers, CUL.

canal commissioners, had mishandled funds on the western section of the canal.

Holley had long been under attack as a Clintonian commissioner. Phocion as early as 1820 had protested in the Rochester *Gazette* at the alleged partisanship in Holley's disbursements.[19] Holley moved to Lyons in 1821 and his efforts to make that canal town the seat of a new county aroused widespread protest, so much so that in 1823 he feared removal on that account alone.[20] Although he was marked for removal as a Clintonian, the Bucktails were frank to admit that they could not well do without him; and moreover, they wished him to remain on the board to share the blame should operations exceed in cost the estimates made by the Clintonians in projecting the canal.[21] Holley's defenders relied upon his character, experience, and record of faithful service to withstand such attacks. Holley himself carefully refrained from requesting compensation for the additional responsibilities he incurred as treasurer of the board. He had personally superintended much of the early work of the canal, had made contracts at low prices to the advantage of the state, and he was known to be the author of many of the ably written reports of the canal commissioners.[22]

In February of 1824, partly as a result of the dissension over the Black Rock harbor, the commissioners were required to report on their expenditures to the assembly.

[19] See above, pp. 120-21.

[20] Myron Holley to Luther Holley, January 16, 1823, Myron Holley Papers, NYSL; Clinton to Myron Holley, April 15, 1823, De Witt Clinton Papers, CUL.

[21] Peter B. Porter to Van Buren, November 1, 1820, Martin Van Buren Papers, LC.

[22] Elizur Wright, *Myron Holley* (Boston, 1882), pp. 69-71, 74-76, 83-85. In 1823, Clinton sought arrangements for Holley, his brother-in-law Orville, and David Thomas to write a history of the New York canals, which he believed would "produce a great profit." Clinton to A. V. Goodrich, March 9, 1823, De Witt Clinton Papers, CUL.

Holley reported on the thirtieth of March and found himself unable to account for $30,000 of the funds he had received for expenditures west of the Seneca River.[23] Each of the other commissioners promptly cleared themselves of any wrongdoing.

Holley resigned from the Canal Board immediately and petitioned the legislature for aid. He admitted applying a portion of the funds "to private purposes" in the belief that he was entitled to them as "an adequate and reasonable compensation for his services and hazards as treasurer." He pleaded that over a period of eight years he had paid out $2,500,000 in small bills under conditions conducive to error without added compensation.[24] A remuneration of 1 percent of this expenditure, Holley petitioned, would enable him to clear his accounts from shortage.

Investigation revealed that careless or improper disbursements on the canal had caused a deficiency in Holley's accounts as early as 1820 and that between 1821 and 1824 he had used public money to purchase land in Lyons, Brockport, and near Rochester. Clinton came to his defense, but he found little support from the press. The Bucktail Monroe *Republican,* for example, found his excuse flimsy and was severe on him.[25] Even the pro-Clintonian Rochester *Telegraph* thought his conduct "highly reprehensible" and urged that no consideration of his public service should induce the legislature to extend to him "the least indulgence."[26]

The legislature refused any percentage of remuneration on the money Holley had expended for the state, but it did accept his personal property in discharge of the bal-

23 *Laws,* II, 212.
24 *Ibid.,* 212, 551, 556.
25 Monroe *Republican,* April 13, 1824.
26 Rochester *Telegraph,* April 6, 13, 1824.

ance against him in 1825.[27] In further censure, the legislature tightened the methods of disbursement of canal funds to prevent embezzlement. Holley's continued efforts to clear his name, however, resulted in the restoration of his property in 1828.[28] He had rendered a great service to the state, but his contribution was tarnished by party concern and his own indiscretion. The episode added to the cloud beginning to form over the Clintonian leadership in the construction of the canal.

Finally, the presidential election of 1824 came to bear upon Clinton's place as president of the Canal Board. As that dark-shadowed event approached, protest rose throughout the nation against the caucus system of electing presidential electors in the state legislatures. A movement arose in New York for a new electoral law which would place this privilege directly in the hands of the people, and in the vanguard of this attack was De Witt Clinton.[29] Bucktails and Clintonians found their positions just reversed since their conflict over the constitutional convention of 1821. The Regency was sore distracted, but stood opposed. Its leaders feared any detraction from the legislature which they controlled, and the Regency "caucus" candidate, William H. Crawford, was opposed by anti-Regency forces who favored Jackson, Adams, or Clay. The votes of New York, Van Buren believed, would make Crawford's election certain.[30] In September of 1823, the Clintonians, anti-caucus, and anti-Crawford forces joined

[27] *Laws*, II, 411.

[28] Wright, *Myron Holley*, p. 137. Holley wrote to his wife that this established "the great truth that . . . I used no money but what I had a right to use." Holley to Sally Holley, March 20, 1828, Myron Holley Papers, NYSL.

[29] C. H. Rammelkamp, "The Campaign of 1824 in New York," *Annual Report of the American Historical Association for the Year 1904* (Washington, 1905), pp. 181-82.

[30] Van Buren to Benjamin F. Butler, December 27, 1824, Martin Van Buren Papers, LC.

together in the organization of the People's party which hoped to break the control of the Regency in Albany.

The prickly measure of the electoral bill, espoused now by the People's party, fell into the lap of the Regency-dominated legislature of 1824. Regency managers could not remain deaf to the popularity of the demand for a new electoral law, but neither could Crawford's candidacy be risked. Marcy even feared the election of Clinton to the presidency if the law were passed.[31] They rejected the bill and faced the storm. To weather it they gambled all on the ancient rule of divide and conquer. Van Buren was in Washington and leadership fell to state senator Roger Skinner, whose long-festering antipathy to Clinton's position on the Canal Board matured into a neat scheme by which to undo the power of the People's party in the legislature.[32]

Minutes before the noon adjournment of the last day of the session, April 12, Thurlow Weed noted a short consultation in the assembly among the Regency leaders. Suspecting that something was up, he followed one of the members into the senate and saw him deliver a message to Silas Wright. Wright reached into the drawer of his desk, took out a slip of paper, and handed it to John Bowman of Monroe. Immediately, Bowman took the floor and read from the paper a resolution removing De Witt Clinton as canal commissioner.[33] The Regency sought to divide their opponents in the People's party. They would

[31] William L. Marcy to Van Buren, January 11, 1824, Martin Van Buren Papers, LC.

[32] Marcy had written to Van Buren, "Judge Skinner behaves quite well; now and then he indulges his spleen against *certain persons* for keeping Clinton in the board of canal commissioners—but that is seldom. These fits come to him less frequently than one would expect considering the very bad weather we have here." January 11, 1824, Martin Van Buren Papers, LC.

[33] Weed, *Autobiography*, p. 109.

send those who opposed the removal to defeat as Clintonians. Those who voted for the removal would be forever deprived of Clintonian support. The stunned senators were forced to choose, and only three dared say nay.

The resolution went quickly to the assembly, without charge against Clinton and without explanation. There, at Weed's prompting, Henry Cunningham of Montgomery sprang to Clinton's defense:

I hope there is yet a redeeming spirit in this house—that we will not be guilty of so great an outrage. If we concur in this resolution, we shall take upon ourselves an awful responsibility, one for which our constituents will call us to strict account. What, let me ask, shall we answer in excuse for ourselves, when we return to an inquisitive and watchful people? . . . The resolution may pass, but if it does, my word for it, we are disgraced in the judgment and good sense of an injured but intelligent community. Whatever the fate of this resolution may be, let it be remembered that Mr. Clinton has acquired a reputation not to be destroyed by the pitiful malice of a few leading partizans of the day.

When the contemptible party strifes of the present day shall have passed by, when the political bargainers and jugglers, who now hang round this capitol for subsistence, shall be overwhelmed and forgotten . . . —the pen of the future historian, in better days and better times, will do him justice, and erect to his memory a proud monument of fame as imperishable as the splendid works which owe their origin to his genius and perseverance.[34]

[34] Quoted in Hammond, *Political Parties*, II, 161-63. Weed wrote in his *Autobiography* (pp. 110-11) that "Van Buren's object was in part, to create a split among the anti-Crawford members, but mainly to place Messrs. Tallmadge, Wheaton, etc., etc., Tammany Hall Democrats but Adams men in a dilemma, either horn of which would prove disastrous to them. By voting for the resolution they would offend the political friends with whom they were then acting on the presidential question. By voting against the resolution, they would incur the denunciation of Tammany Hall."

Cunningham spoke for ten minutes "in eloquent and thrilling utterances," as Weed later described the scene, urging each member "to weigh and consider well the consequences" of his vote. Two others rose to oppose the resolution while not a word was spoken by the Regency followers. The assembly concurred with the senate by a vote of 64 to 34. The deed was done and the People's party legislators, "opposed to Crawford and in favor of the electoral law," as Weed put it, were caught "in the trap successfully, if not wisely, baited for them." The legislature promptly disbanded, not to meet again until November.

Public response was electric. Huge meetings were called in Albany and New York to protest the removal and draft resolutions of praise for the stricken commissioner. The latter drew more than 8,000 people; such a meeting, reported the New York *Evening Post,* "take it all in all, has never taken place in this metropolis."[35] That in Albany was reported by the Albany *Gazette* as "the largest meeting ever held in this city," and its editor judged that the removal was condemned by "nineteen-twentieths" of the state.[36] The editor of the New York *American,* who opposed Clinton politically, reported that "a more pitiful and contemptible exhibition of impotent malice was never recorded in any legislative annal."[37] The fury was even stronger in the western villages. At Canandaigua indignant villagers threatened personal attack upon the legislators who had voted for removal.[38] Thurlow Weed's paper, the Rochester *Telegraph,* called the removal "a deed which will ever blacken the annals of the State," and its editor fairly exulted at the popular

35 New York *Evening Post,* April 20, 1824.
36 Albany *Gazette,* April 19, 23, 1824.
37 Quoted in Rochester *Telegraph,* April 27, 1824.
38 Weed, *Autobiography,* p. 114.

sentiment which the act had aroused: "Every contemptible effort to rob Mr. Clinton of his well-earned fame, serves only to identify him still more indissolubly with these great national works. Clinton does 'swim' triumphantly upon his 'big ditch,' where he will continue to 'swim' long after the memory and offenses of his enemies are forgotten and forgiven."[39] He could afford the charity of forgiveness, for the Regency had given the People's party a gubernatorial candidate for the fall elections and undone much of the effect of their own part in building the canal.

Even so, the emphasis now placed upon Clinton's canal record did not alter his other disabilities, and there were many throughout the state who would not take him as a candidate for governor in 1824. Weed made two political tours of the state, and his soundings left him pessimistic over Clinton's chances for election.[40] But at bottom, the People's party could not do without him, and Clinton was eager to run. "I think our course is plain," wrote Charles G. Haines to Weed. "If *the land of the Canal turns agt* [sic] we must make up the loss elsewhere. Mr. Clinton will not decline."[41] The surest increment of support for a Clintonian ticket lay among the enthusiastic backers of James Tallmadge who had been the almost undisputed choice of the People's party for the governorship until he had cast a fateful vote for Clinton's removal. That Clinton and Tallmadge should join now was mutually distasteful but necessary. At the People's party convention at

[39] Rochester *Telegraph*, May 4, 1824.

[40] Glyndon G. Van Deusen, *Thurlow Weed* (Boston, 1947), p. 28. Weed described Clinton as "a great man with weak points." Weed, *Autobiography*, p. 205.

[41] Haines to Weed, September 4, 1824, Thurlow Weed Papers, URL. Clinton wrote in January of 1823: "Everything is in a state of chaos." Clinton to Cadwallader D. Colden, January 2, 1823, De Witt Clinton Papers, CUL.

Utica in September a compromise resulted in Clinton's nomination with Tallmadge on the ticket as lieutenant governor.

To oppose Clinton, the Regency also picked a canal candidate—Colonel Samuel Young whose record as canal commissioner was counted upon, but whose belated acceptance of the electoral law satisfied neither its friends nor its opponents. He disappointed the Regency further in November when his friends deserted the Regency in refusing to support Crawford in the legislative caucus to select electors. The Regency ticket was as much a hybrid as the Clintonian. On the slate with Young the Regency placed Erastus Root who had been conspicuous in his opposition to both electoral law and the canal. Accordingly, the Clintonian forces centered their attack on "King Caucus" and used longer range ammunition to strike at the failure of the Bucktails to keep step with the progress of internal improvements. Weed's *Telegraph* carried the combined attack: "Crawford is deserted; . . . Young, in a fit of desperation . . . committed political suicide; and Gen. Root has drowned himself in 'Clinton's big ditch!' "[42] The Buffalo *Emporium* lauded Clinton's lone dissenting vote against the Black Rock harbor.[43] Its editors, Lazell and Francis, made "CLINTON and LIBERTY" their watchword. In the election of 1824, which Alvin Kass has described as "really the acme in the battle for democracy in New York," it was the Clintonians who were "upholding the standards of democratic reform against the dogged opposition of the Bucktail Republicans."[44]

When the votes were in, the effect was a landslide. Clinton's majority over Young was 16,906 and Tallmadge

[42] Rochester *Telegraph*, October 26, November 2, 1824.
[43] Buffalo *Emporium*, October 23, 30, 1824.
[44] Kass, *Politics in New York State*, p. 90.

won an even greater victory with a majority of 32,400. The Clintonian ticket was successful in six out of eight senatorial districts, and in the assembly the ticket brought a majority of three to one. As Van Buren and Judge Skinner watched the mounting Bucktail disaster together in Van Buren's office, the Little Magician flared up: "I hope, Judge, you are now satisfied that there is such a thing in politics as *killing a man too dead!*"[45] Skinner was so affected by the entire episode that it contributed to the decline of his health and he died soon after in Van Buren's arms.

As in every election where the Erie Canal was involved, diverse elements compounded to bring victory to the People's party. Clinton was backed by canal men, Old Federalists, and moderate Republicans. Personalities, party alignments, and King Caucus carried weight, and Tallmadge ran far ahead of Clinton. But behind Clinton's election was the drama of the Erie Canal with which Clinton had been so exclusively identified that the attempts of Young's friends to claim his share in its glory were ineffectual. Hammond concluded that Clinton's removal from his office as canal commissioner was the cause of his election.[46] Mordecai Noah of the *National Advocate* lamented that "the injudicious if not unjust removal of Clinton from the Canal Board, had no small influence in producing the result." Noah explained his opposition to the costly error: "On the subject of the canal, no one opposed it originally more constantly than we did; and we opposed it from the most powerful conditions that the resources of the state were inadequate to complete a project so very extensive itself. We were in

[45] Martin Van Buren, "The Autobiography of Martin Van Buren," John C. Fitzpatrick, ed., American Historical Association, *Annual Report for the Year 1918*, II (Washington, 1920), 81.
[46] Hammond, *Political Parties*, II, 165-66.

error; and took the earliest opportunity to say so, and afford a permanent and useful support to the project. When this support became unanimous, what justification could we offer for the removal of Mr. Clinton?"[47]

The Regency, although usually astute in their quest for office, had blundered grievously. They had not followed currents of change when they opposed the electoral law, and they had undone Van Buren's remarkable recovery from earlier Bucktail fumbles on the canal. Their blunder also had far-reaching effects on the national scene.

Everyone realized in November of 1824 that no presidential candidate would have a clear majority and that the election would go to the House of Representatives. New York's thirty-six electoral votes were important. The Regency had long admitted that Crawford's chances there depended upon their success in electing a governor. News of Clinton's victory came in the midst of the balloting for electors in the legislature, where it was well known that Clinton favored Jackson. Clinton's victory shook Regency control in the assembly and gave young Thurlow Weed an opening to maneuver an agreement on a split ticket between the Adams and Clay factions.[48] "The long agony is over," wrote Stephen Van Rensselaer to Clinton; "Mr. Adams was elected on the first ballot. Mr. Clay's combination could not be resisted, and to allay the excitement we agreed to vote for Adams."[49] Moreover, Lot Clark of Buffalo reported that it was "well-known" that an understanding was entered into between Clinton and Adams that with Clinton's switch to Adams, Clinton would go to

[47] Quoted in Buffalo *Patriot*, November 23, 1824.
[48] Van Deusen, *Thurlow Weed*, p. 30. Weed wrote in his *Autobiography* (p. 109) that the Regency blunder in Clinton's removal "sealed the fate of Crawford in our State."
[49] Van Rensselaer to Clinton, March 10, 1825, De Witt Clinton Papers, CUL.

the Court of St. James.[50] New York went to Adams and
in the election which ensued in the House of Representatives, John Quincy Adams became the sixth president of
the United States. Popular support in New York for the
Erie Canal ultimately had its influence in the halls of
Congress in the selection of a president who himself
dreamed of creating a great system of national internal
improvements.

The Erie Canal was built at a period of political and
social transition. While national politics passed through
the Era of Good Feelings, the disintegration of the two
party system temporarily allowed greater emphasis on a
candidate's record.[51] Clinton's smashing victory in 1824
was perhaps one of the last instances of an achievement
like the Erie Canal operating so exclusively as a source
of political support for a single personality. The passage
of the appropriations bill of 1821 and the removal of
Clinton were evidence that the canal would come increasingly under party rather than personal sponsorship. The
growing idea that to the victor belonged the spoils
exerted a similar effect. A political revolution was taking
place in New York as the constitution of 1821 brought
all offices under direct popular control. Amid these
changing political and social patterns the canal was seen
as a shining example of the benefits of a free and democratic government.[52] At the same time, the great celebrations of the completion of the canal in 1825 were replete
with adulation of De Witt Clinton whose political record
had been so wanting in the arts of political leadership.

[50] Clark to Roger Skinner, February 28, 1825, Martin Van Buren Papers, LC. Within a year Clinton had determined to be a candidate for
president in 1828. E. Livingston to Van Buren, November 30, 1825,
Martin Van Buren Papers, LC.

[51] Charles S. Sydnor, "The One-Party Period of American History,"
American Historical Review, LI (April 1946), 450-51.

[52] See below, Chapter 19.

10

The Wedding of the Waters

ALTHOUGH the canal was not completed until the latter part of October in 1825, celebration of the event began almost with the beginning of navigation in the spring. In June, Lafayette brought his military glory to the canal. The high-spirited Revolutionary War hero had returned from France in 1824 as the "Nation's Guest." Effusive and sentimental, he was welcomed enthusiastically as he made a great circle tour of the United States that took him west to the Mississippi. On his return eastward he followed the Ohio Valley and then Lake Erie to New York, where he traveled much of the distance from Buffalo to Albany on the Grand Canal. His journey through New York became one long celebration of the canal as a blessing of the national independence which he had helped to achieve.

Arriving by boat from Erie, Pennsylvania, Lafayette entered Buffalo harbor, breakfasted with the Porter brothers at Black Rock, and embarked on the canal at Lockport, where Clinton had provided a boat for his accommodation. Work was still in progress in the deep cutting at Lockport and workmen saluted him with hundreds of small blasts which sent splinters of rock flying into the air. His secretary stood amazed at the spirited growth of Lockport and recorded the awe of the company at "that gigantic work, that grand canal, which in tightening the bonds of the American Union, spreads comfort and abundance in the wilds through which it passes."[1] As he approached Rochester on the canal he was met by a flotilla of decorated boats, which escorted him past banks and bridges thronging with handkerchief-waving spectators. At the center of the Rochester aqueduct he mounted a stage erected for the occasion where William B. Rochester presented "our magnificent *state* enterprize [*sic*], New York's grand canal."[2]

Lafayette's route took him south to the Finger Lake villages but he returned to the canal at Syracuse. The reception committee there waited up all night for his arrival, for breakfast serving him the supper kept warm since the night before. He then moved on to Rome, Utica, and Schenectady, while children showered flowers on his boat from the bridges crossing the canal. So impressed was his secretary by this evidence of "public prosperity" that he urged its study and emulation by "European politicians and economists."[3]

Lafayette saw a canal which had been in busy operation along most of its length for two years and along the middle section for nearly six. Two thousand boats, nine thousand horses, and eight thousand men were employed in the transportation of goods on the canal in October of 1825.[4] When the commissioners announced in early fall that the entire canal would be completed on October 26, most of the people along its route had already felt the heady experience of canal navigation. All could observe

[1] A. Levasseur, *Lafayette in America in 1824 and 1825* (Philadelphia, 1829), II, 192.

[2] Rochester *Telegraph*, June 14, 1825; see also Monroe *Republican*, June 14, 1825.

[3] Levasseur, *Lafayette*, p. 200.

[4] Niles' *Weekly Register*, XXIX (October 1, 1825), 66.

the fantastic changes being wrought by the boon of easy, rapid water travel. Nearly two years had passed since the Onondaga *Gazette* had noted in its columns, "The spirit of canalling is the rage of the day."[5]

New Yorkers up and down the state prepared for a time of jubilee. On September 7, a meeting in New York City headed by William Bayard and John Pintard (who had headed the original New York meeting to draft the famous petition of 1816) began to plan for a fitting commemoration. As a result of this meeting, a Committee of the Corporation of the City of New York was organized to supervise the elaborate ceremonies of the "Wedding of the Waters."[6]

The central theme of the celebration of the completion of the Erie Canal was the mixing of water carried on the canal from Lake Erie with that of the Atlantic off Sandy Hook. This brief event was almost eclipsed in the attempt by the New York committee to stage the greatest celebration in history, and by the efforts of local committees from Buffalo to New York to add embroidery to the theme.

Western New Yorkers, last to share in extensive use of the canal, entered enthusiastically into these plans. "It will be a proud day in the history of New-York," announced the editors of the Buffalo *Emporium*, "such as has not occurred since the Declaration of our country's Independence. Well may New-York rejoice in an achievement that would add glory to the most powerful nation on earth."[7] In Rochester, the *Telegraph* carried the good news of the completion to its readers and caught the mood of the state: "The work is finished! Our brightest, highest hopes, are all consummated. Let the shouts of

[5] Onondaga *Gazette*, November 26, 1823.
[6] Colden, *Memoir of the New York Canals*, Appendix, pp. 125-29.
[7] Buffalo *Emporium and General Advertiser*, October 8, 1825.

triumph be heard from Erie to the Atlantic, and from the Atlantic resound back to Erie. Let the air itself be made vocal with our paeans of exultation and gratitude."[8]

The state-wide celebration began with the entrance of the first boat into the canal at Buffalo on a through passage to New York. The *Seneca Chief* of Buffalo became the focus of attention as she was prepared for this leading role. Clinton and Tallmadge arrived to ride to Albany on her decks. With them rode Stephen Van Rensselaer, Chancellor Livingston, Samuel Wilkeson, Thurlow Weed, Joshua Forman, and the committee from New York. Her cabin was elegantly decorated with a portrait of Clinton in Roman toga done by the well-known lithographer, George Catlin. On board were two kegs of "the pure waters of Lake Erie," destined for the ceremonies off Sandy Hook, and logs of native red cedar and birdseye maple from which boxes would be fashioned for the celebration medals. Also in her cargo were pot ashes, white fish, and other products gathered from Michigan, Ohio, and Buffalo, and a canoe made by Indians on the shore of Lake Superior. Jesse Hawley of Rochester was at the Buffalo basin to send the celebration craft on its way with an address. In joining the Great Lakes with the Atlantic, he crowed, New York had "made the longest Canal—in the least time—with the least experience—for the least money—and of the greatest public utility of any other in the world."[9] At 10:00 a.m., Wednesday, October 26, the *Seneca Chief* entered the canal, eastbound for Albany.

Simultaneously, the first 32-pounder of the "Grand Salute" was fired, telegraphing the news of the canal's completion by guns spaced earshot distance apart all the

[8] Rochester *Telegraph*, October 18, 1825.
[9] Buffalo *Emporium and General Advertiser*, October 29, 1825.

way to New York City.[10] Three hours and twenty minutes later the distant rumbles in the east announced that the salute had been received at Sandy Hook and returned. In this exercise which Clinton thought a "good opportunity for some interesting experiments on the phenomena of sound," some of the guns employed were those used by Admiral Perry on Lake Erie eleven years before. Thurlow Weed had hired men to scour the forts and arsenals of western New York to locate them and distribute them along the canal.

The Buffalonians who were left behind by the *Seneca Chief* began a round of festivals which climaxed in a grand ball lasting on into the night. At one of these in the Eagle Tavern a choir sang a Celebration Ode which had been set to the tune of "Hail Columbia." In the florid style of the day its first verse told of the great work completed:

> Strike the Lyre! with joyous note,
> Let the sound through azure float;
> The task is o'er—the work complete,
> And Erie's waves, with ocean meet—
> Bearing afar their rich bequest,
> While smiling commerce greets the west.[11]

The *Seneca Chief*, meanwhile, led an ever lengthening procession down the canal. Following her, the *Noah's Ark* from Arrarat on the Niagara River, carried an assortment of birds, fish, insects, two young bears, and two Seneca boys. The elegant *Superior* carried in her cargo two sleek fawns. The *Niagara of Black Rock*, with General Porter aboard, joined the procession after participating in local

[10] Colden, *Memoir of the New York Canals*, Appendix, p. 145; Niles' *Weekly Register*, XXIX (October 8, 1825), 82. One of these guns is preserved today by the Onondaga Historical Association in Syracuse.
[11] Buffalo *Emporium and General Advertiser*, October 29, 1825.

ceremonies at Lockport and then, perhaps to enable the General to escape the eulogies of Clinton at every stop, moved out ahead to reach Albany three days sooner than the rest. At Pendleton the flotilla met a line of boats carrying the canal commissioners and the engineers who now accompanied the governor's party on their journey east.

The flotilla followed a meticulously arranged schedule which allowed a stop at every port of any consequence. Crowds gathered everywhere. Visitors in holiday spirit flocked to the canal from miles around. Horses and carriages filled the roads. People covered the towpath, crowded the bridges, and pressed forward to hear speeches of welcome, speeches of response, and speeches of farewell. Arches garlanded with evergreens and flowers spanned the canal at nearly every village and supported banners praising Clinton, republicanism, or internal improvements. Bands played and cannon thundered in salute. Local militia companies escorted the guests to feast at the best hotel; militia enough, said the Utica *Gazette*, to stand thirty feet from each other all the way.[12] After nightfall the governor's entourage was greeted by illuminations, fireworks, and transparencies. And when it had passed on, each community turned to its own local festival.

Wednesday evening the procession was lowered down the five-lock combine at Lockport, and at 3:30 the following afternoon it paused at Rochester. Here a cold October rain plagued the day, but large crowds lined the canal. Eight militia companies turned to fire salutes at successive street crossings as the boats wound through the village. The visitors stopped first at the Presbyterian church for

12 Utica *Sentinel and Gazette*, November 6, 1825.

prayer and an address, and then proceeded to Christopher's Mansion House to banquet. At seven in the evening the company was on its way east again, joined now by the canal boat *Young Lion of the West,* which was loaded with native products of the soil plus a living collection of wolves, racoons, foxes, deer, and other animals. "The citizens of most places benefitted by this great work," noted the Monroe *Republican,* ". . . seem to have truly felt that no event was so worthy of a joyous celebration, as this one, which they have gladly united to commemorate. Nay . . . all have seemed anxious to give vent by some public testimonial to the glad feelings which this event has excited."[13]

On Saturday afternoon the flotilla reached Syracuse where Joshua Forman gave the address. On Sunday the party stopped at Utica for church; on Monday it passed Little Falls. At mid-afternoon on Tuesday the "College Guards" of Union College in Schenectady fired a *feu de joie* as the long line of boats moved on to the east. Finally, at 10:30 a.m. on Wednesday, November 2, the *Seneca Chief* floated into Albany basin.

Albany was host to the grandest celebration of all on the canal. A twenty-four-gun salute welcomed the flotilla. Public speeches were made at the capitol, and in the assembly chamber were hung portraits of De Witt Clinton, George Clinton, and George Washington. A parade threaded through the town to a great double arcade at the "New Bridge." Guests and leading citizens sat down to a banquet presided over by John Taylor, Ambrose Spencer, and, among others, Martin Van Buren. Only one incident had marred the week-long journey across the state; two gunners at Weedsport had been blown to bits

13 Monroe *Republican,* November 15, 1825.

as they discharged their cannon at the approach of the governor's boat.[14]

Eight steamboats guided the official party from Albany to New York. As the squadron moved slowly down the Hudson, the banks of the river became alive with bonfires, cannon salutes, cheers, and the movement of small boats darting out from the shore. Near the state prison the squadron was met by the steamboat *Washington* bearing a deputation of welcome from New York City. Clinton's response to their fulsome greeting repeated themes touched upon by orators at nearly every ceremony enacted between Buffalo and New York. His address foretold the influence of the canal on agriculture, manufactures, and commerce, on the "duration of the Union," on the "holy cause of Republican Government," and on "social prosperity," and he was confident that it would "be recognized as such by all future times."[15]

The squadron moved into New York harbor at 7:00 a.m., Friday, November 4. It first steamed up the East River to the Navy Yard, where salutes were fired, and then returned to the Battery for the formation of the "Grand Aquatic Display." Forty-six vessels, all lavishly dressed out with flags, bunting, and flowers, took part in the maneuvers which followed.[16] Twenty-nine steamboats moved into line. Four pilot boats, seven barges, the ship *Hamlet* and the United States revenue cutter *Alert*, took their positions in preparation for departure to Sandy Hook. The four tiny canal boats from the West were almost lost in the scene.

The morning was bright and sunny and perfectly calm.

[14] Clinton to R. S. Smith and R. Merwin, November 5, 1825, De Witt Clinton Papers, CUL; Colden, *Memoir of the New York Canals*, Appendix, p. 166.

[15] Colden, *Memoir of the New York Canals*, Appendix, p. 179.

[16] *Ibid.*, p. 187.

Spectators crowded the Battery and dotted the harbor with small boats. At nine o'clock, with a salute from the Battery, the steamboats took the other vessels in tow and moved out to the ocean, bands blaring from their decks. Salutes were fired as they passed Castle William on Governor's Island and Fort Lafayette at the Narrows. Within Sandy Hook the United States schooner *Porpoise* had been moored the night before to serve as a "Deputation from Neptune." The fleet moved into a circle around the *Porpoise* and Clinton and the leading committees boarded the *Washington* for the "wedding" ceremony.

A keg of Erie water was poured slowly into the Atlantic. But not all; Clinton was careful to leave some of the now almost sacramental water to be sent to General Lafayette in a box made by Duncan Phyfe from the cedar wood on board the *Seneca Chief*. Clinton then made the address of dedication: "The solemnity, at this place on the first arrival of vessels from Lake Erie, is intended to indicate and commemorate the navigable communication, which has been accomplished between our Mediterranean seas and the Atlantic Ocean, in about eight years, to the extent of more than four hundred and twenty five miles, by the wisdom, public spirit, and energy of the people of the state of New York; and may the God of the Heavens and the Earth smile most propitiously on this work, and render it subservient to the best interests of the human race."[17] Dr. Samuel Latham Mitchill poured into the Atlantic vials of water from the Rhine, the Ganges, the Nile, and twelve other great rivers of the world, a part of the ceremony that the New York *Evening Post* called a "piece of ridicule and absurdity."[18] Cadwallader Colden

[17] *Ibid.*, pp. 320-21.
[18] New York *Evening Post*, October 25, 1825. Elkanah Watson, who was still in controversy with Clinton, was also critical of the scene: "Take it all in all it was undoubtedly the most splendid farce ever acted in any

presented his memoir of the canal celebration to the
mayor of New York. Salutes were then fired all around,
and the fleet, now in one formation, now in another,
returned to the city. As it passed the British vessels
outside the harbor, the sons of John Bull struck up
"Yankee Doodle," and the Yankee bandsmen returned the
strains of "God Save the King."

Awaiting the return of the "Grand Aquatic Display"
at the Battery was the "Grand Procession." Some five
thousand marchers lined up in fifty-nine units behind
the standard of their profession, trade, or society and
paraded through the city to the City Hall.[19] A surfeit of
processions, speeches, banquets, bell-ringing, illuminations, and fireworks continued on into the night. Some
celebrants dined on "Canal Beef," bought of Mr. Wheeler
of Fulton Market who advertised "the largest cow ever
raised in this country" which had been brought to New
York from upstate by canal.[20] New Yorkers bought canal
badges featuring Clinton's picture and a canal sketch;
they purchased "Grand Canal Turbans" for their ladies
and paid $5.00 a ticket to the Grand Canal Ball, given
"in honor of Lafayette" at the Lafayette Amphitheater.[21]

age or Country. To have celebrated on the completion of such a magnificent enterprize would have been peculiarly appropriate had it . . .
been called forth by public sentiment to commemorate an event of such
vital importance to the State—but when it is of public notoriety that the
whole object was intended to produce a political result to agrandize [sic]
a single individual to the exclusion of meritricus [sic] men, who conceived & projected the system many years before Clinton was known—&
that he contrived & managed the celebration in all its branches, from
Erie to Sandy Hook—& even the Splendid Canal ball to reflect a glow of
glory around his person—these considerations deteriorate essentially from
the real merits of the exhibition & place the whole scene with men of
sense on the level of a *splendid farce.* . . ." Elkanah Watson to John
James, draft, n.d., Elkanah Watson Papers, NYSL.

[19] Colden, *Memoir of the New York Canals,* pp. 154-59, 324.
[20] New York *Evening Post,* October 28, 1825.
[21] *Ibid.,* October 29, 1825.

Three thousand persons crowded this room, "the largest in the United States," and in the center a canal boat made of maple sugar in Utica floated in water from Lake Erie. At Castle Garden the canal boat *Noah's Ark* was displayed, animals, birds, Seneca Indians, and all. Still, one disappointment remained. Madame Johnson could not make her advertised balloon ascent from Vauxhall Garden owing to some difficulty in filling the balloon with gas. Thousands of angry people tore the balloon to pieces and made a shambles of the Garden in compensation for the loss of their fifty-cents price of admission.[22]

When it was all over, the *Seneca Chief* made her slow way up the canal to Black Rock and Buffalo, which were just recovering from a gale so severe that it had washed away seventy feet of towpath in Black Rock harbor. The *Seneca Chief* carried this time a keg of Atlantic water, upon which was printed "Neptune's Return to Pan," to be mixed with the waters of Lake Erie.

The surfeit of pageantry accompanying the celebration of the "Wedding of the Waters" was fundamentally an expression of the sense of accomplishment of the generation who built the Erie Canal. The sheer magnitude of the achievement evoked a self-conscious response from chroniclers in newspapers, pamphlets, and memoirs. A witness to Clinton's stop at Utica aboard the *Seneca Chief* was moved to send the Governor his own celebration ode:

> Fixed as a pharos midst the flood,
>   Enwheeled by glory's noontide blaze,
>   And marked by wonder's eager gaze,
> The ruling *genius* dauntless stood!
>   Who well matured the grand design
>   To change creation's ancient line;

[22] *Ibid.*, November 5, 1825.

To prostrate mountains, rend the ground,
Th' opposing streams by art to guide,
Tear up old Nature's storm-proof bound,
And blend proud Erie's waves with Ocean's tide!

.   .   .   .   .

Hark! loud the signal sounds from far—
The work's complete, the cannon roar
Along the banks from Erie's shore:
The triumph rides in thunder's car!
'Mid splendid trains in honour's cause,
With martial pride and loud applause,
Throned on a pompous barge sublime
The *patriot* comes from Erie's post,
Borne on his own invented stream,
Bound to th' emporium on the Atlantic coast.

.   .   .   .   .

Go, vassal waves, in pomp convey
Down through the state your *charge* along!
While future years revive this day,
And barges float let CLINTON's name be sung![23]

The cost of constructing the Erie Canal had been only
$7,143,789 and the potential returns from it seemed limit-
less. In their annual report of 1825, the canal commissioners noted that nearly $300,000 in tolls had been received
in 1824 and Clinton wrote to John Jacob Astor that they
would reach $600,000 for 1825.[24] With the canal com-
pleted, the commissioners calculated an annual revenue of
$1,000,000 by 1826 and $9,000,000 within fifty years. They
counted on a rapidly increasing population in the West,
which they estimated would double every ten years.

[23] Charles Giles, *The Convention of Drunkards; a Satirical Essay on
Intemperance . . . and an Ode on the Completion of the Erie Canal*
(New York, 1839), pp. 124-26.
[24] Clinton to Astor, November 10, 1825, De Witt Clinton Papers, CUL.

Thirty years hence those who had seen the completion of the Erie Canal would "see the productions and supplies of eight millions of their fellow-citizens floating upon its waters."[25]

To accommodate this increase in commerce, the commissioners proposed the construction of a second canal parallel with the eastern section and double locks along the rest of the canal line. Benjamin Wright, now employed on the Pennsylvania canals, wrote to Clinton of plans for a canal along the Susquehanna River to draw trade from southern New York and to relieve the "transportation on the Erie Canal the amount of which it is easy to see will soon be too great for that canal to pass."[26] Pamphlets published in 1825 advocated the enlargement of the Erie Canal or the substitution of sloop navigation.[27]

Cadwallader Colden's *Memoir* provided a comprehensive account of the planning and building of the canal, as well as insights into the role of the canal in the growth of New York and the nation, and it is particularly valuable as an expression of American nationalism. He congratulated his fellow New Yorkers on having completed at a cost of little more than $5.00 per person, the "longest uninterrupted canal in the world."[28] He saw the miraculous rise of towns and villages in New York and charted the beginning of an age of water travel in America. America would one day be "divided into great islands," Colden prophesied, and he mused that New York, Albany, Utica, Buffalo, Cleveland and St. Louis "may become post towns on the common high road to India."[29]

[25] *Laws*, II, 266.

[26] Wright to Clinton, July 21, 1826, De Witt Clinton Papers, CUL.

[27] *Facts and Observations in Relation to the Origin and Completion of the Erie Canal* (New York, 1825), pp. 28-29, 33; *A View of the Grand Canal from Lake Erie to the Hudson River* (New York, 1825), p. 15.

[28] Colden, *Memoir of the New York Canals*, pp. 69, 85.

[29] *Ibid.*, p. 74.

The completion of the Erie Canal was the first step in what might be called the New York miracle. It was celebrated with an awareness of the great themes of state and national development which had emerged with the planning of the canal. For the people of New York the canal era had begun.

III. *On Erie Water*

11

Packets, Freighters, and Canallers

THE ERIE CANAL brought an altogether new and
stimulating experience in effortless, quiet mobility
to the first canal generation in New York. Packet, line
boat, freighter, scow, lock, and basin became new subjects
for thought and conversation as canal travel became a
new thread in the social fabric. The canal boat was
greeted with wonder and then taken in stride. "Commending my soul to God, and asking his defense from
danger," wrote a Rochester pioneer of his first journey by
canal, "I stepped on board the canal boat, and was soon
flying towards Utica."[1]

The first packet boat company to offer canal travel to
the public was the Erie Canal Navigation Company,
which placed the *Chief Engineer* and the *Montezuma* in
operation on the middle section of the canal as soon as it
was open to navigation. The company was organized at
Rome in February of 1820 with a capital of $10,000 and
stock which was subscribed to at $100 a share.[2] Comfort
Tyler, who resided at Whitesboro, was president, and
Simon Newton Dexter, who had been engaged first in
wagoning produce between Utica and Albany and then
in digging a portion of the canal, was its treasurer. The
business of the company expanded so rapidly that by
the season of 1823 the canal boats, *Myron Holley, William*

C. Bouck, David S. Bates, Oneida Chief, Henry Seymour, Chancellor Kent, and *Benjamin Wright* had been added to the line. A superintendent managed the boats, kept them in repair, and supervised their provisioning. Each boat was manned by a captain, steward, helmsman, bowsman, cook, cabin boy, and driver.[3] One of the stockholders, Simeon Bristol, became himself captain of the *William C. Bouck,* and soon was placed in charge of operations west of Utica. What with boats at $1,000, their furnishings at $500 each, horses from $25 to $80 each, hay at $5 a ton, and bright paints of yellow, blue, red, and green to keep the boats in trim, the company found itself in an extensive operation. But the returns were rich and dividends of $86 a share were paid at the end of the navigation season of 1822.[4] The company charged $6.25 for passage from Utica to Rochester in 1823, a journey which took its boats two days and two nights to run.[5] An average trip carrying thirty to fifty passengers for various distances at four cents a mile between Utica and Rochester made a payload of from $100 to $175, one-fourth of which was profit. In a single season lasting from March to December the *David S. Bates* earned nearly $6,000.[6]

[1] Jenny M. Parker, *Rochester, A Story Historical* (Rochester, 1884), p. 113.

[2] Articles of Association of the Erie Canal Navigation Company, February 3, 1820, Simon Newton Dexter Papers, Cornell University Library. Joshua Forman and Myron Holley were among its stockholders.

[3] The captain was paid $30 a month; the helmsman, $14; the bowsman, $12; the cook, $16; the cabin boy, $5; and the driver, $7 to $10. The steward held his place as a concession, paying $125 a season for the privilege of supplying bar and table and levying a cent per mile against each "way" or boarding passenger. Receipts, Simon Newton Dexter Papers, Cornell University Library.

[4] Minutes of meetings of the directors of the Erie Canal Navigation Company, November 12, 13, 1822, Simon Newton Dexter Papers, Cornell University Library.

[5] Waybills, Simon Newton Dexter Papers, Cornell University Library. The fare was $3.84 from Utica to Montezuma, $3.92 from Syracuse to Rochester, and $2.50 from Utica to Syracuse.

As the canal was lengthened, the inevitable competition arose. In 1823 the Western Passage Boat Company placed the *Van Rensselaer, Governor Yates, Rochester, Utica,* and *Ohio* in service and advertised a through passage from Utica to Rochester in forty-five hours at four cents a mile, including meals. Still a third line of boats was inaugurated on the eastern portion of the canal by the Utica and Schenectady Packet Boat Company, which charged $3.50 for the twenty-four-hour run along the Mohawk.[7]

But competition was unwelcome to the Erie Canal Navigation Company. The first distribution of stock was made with an eye to preventing the rise of an opposition line. "Two lines cannot live," wrote Alfred Hovey, a stockholder, to Tyler, and the company took steps to squelch the opposition or to effect a merger.[8] Captains were given liberty to cut fares, an exclusive mail contract was procured, influential men were kept from buying opposition stock, and an effort was made to spruce up conditions which Tyler admitted could leave his company's boats "a dirty Set." At the same time, a powerful group of stage and canal boat proprietors set a plan afoot to drive the stock of all of the canal lines to worthlessness, after which they would gain control of canal travel in one giant combine.[9]

---

[6] Account of Erie Canal Navigation Company with James Satterlee, 1823 [?], Simon Newton Dexter Papers, Cornell University Library. See also Simeon Bristol to William Bristol, July 17, 1823, Simeon Bristol Papers, NYSL.

[7] Rochester *Telegraph*, November 11, 18, 1823.

[8] Comfort Tyler to Dexter, April 1, 15, May 23, July 17, August 18, 25, September 19, 1823, Trustees of the Utica and Schenectady Packet Boat Company to Dexter, September 9, 1823, to the Directors of the Erie Canal Navigation Company, September 16, 1823, Simon Newton Dexter Papers, Cornell University Library.

[9] Comfort Tyler to Dexter, November 18, 1823, Joseph Swan to Dexter, February 10, 1824, Simon Newton Dexter Papers, Cornell University Library.

By the close of the season of 1823, however, each of the companies was convinced that merger was more profitable than competition, and when the ice was gone from the canal the following spring, a consolidation had been achieved. Each of the three lines followed carefully integrated schedules, and fares were a uniform $6.40 from Rochester to Utica and $9.90 from Rochester to Schenectady.[10] Since the traffic between Utica and Schenectady exceeded that west of Utica by half, the companies divided the way bills. The Erie Canal Navigation Company made a net profit of $7,000 in 1824, and Tyler's goal was "only One Line anywhere on the Canal."[11] When the Albany Packet Boat Company was organized in 1824, Tyler's company made immediate overtures for an amalgamation.

The Rochester *Telegraph* protested that consolidation would "check the tide of emigration and traveling," and Horatio G. Spafford censured combination as undemocratic in his *Pocket Guide* to the New York canals. "I am sorry to see that these great Companies are making such a monopoly of the transportation business," wrote Spafford, "driving off the small capitalists, and the many hundreds of poor and industrious men, who are striving to support themselves and families, by this new species of the Carrying Trade."[12] Public sentiment refused to reserve this lucrative trade to the monopoly of the few, and as time went on, packet boats multiplied in spite of

[10] Rochester *Telegraph*, April 20, 1824; Joseph Swan to Dexter, January 29, February 10, 1824, Tyler to Dexter, February 17, 24, 1824, Erie Canal Navigation Company to Dexter, July [?], 1825, Simon Newton Dexter Papers, Cornell University Library; Simeon Bristol to William Bristol, October 10, 1824, Simeon Bristol Papers, NYSL; McKelvey, *Rochester History*, XI, 7.

[11] Erie Canal Navigation Company Report to Stockholders, November 15, 1824, Simon Newton Dexter Papers, Cornell University Library.

[12] Rochester *Telegraph*, April 12, 1825; Spafford, *A Pocket Guide*, p. 25.

attempts at combination. Freighters, which had already built up a lively trade carrying merchandise for five cents per ton per mile and produce for three cents, were fitted up with cabins to carry a few passengers at a reduced rate. Moreover, stage companies (whose co-operation was essential in a consolidation) could not be kept from lowering prices in competition.[13] By the end of the season of 1824 packet fares had been reduced as much as 70 percent. Although as late as 1827, Simeon Bristol could write that "we have no competition this season," new companies gradually appeared to grasp the growing trade in freights and passengers.[14] Smaller operators sent one or two boats plying back and forth on the canal, carrying anything available and picking up fares wherever they could.

Canal boat spaciousness, whether for passengers or freight, was limited at the outset by the 90- by 15-foot size of the locks, dimensions which boatbuilders often approached with a bare six inches of clearance on each side and enough space for the inward swing of the lock gates. Within these limits a common purpose provided the only uniformity. The first boats ran as small as forty feet in

[13] The Ontario *Repository* in Canandaigua (June 23, 1824) urged the traveler to take the older stage route from Rochester to Schenectady "for $9.24 including his regular meals and lodging, and without riding in the night, in ten hours less time than by the Canal Packets."

[14] Simeon Bristol to William Bristol, May 10, 1827, Simeon Bristol Papers, NYSL. The following are some of the companies that appeared during the next ten years: Merchant's Line, Union Line, Washington Line, Pilot Line, Troy & Erie Line, Troy & Ohio Line, Hudson & Erie Line, New York & Ohio Line, Telegraph Line, Cedar Line, Clinton Line, Transportation Line, Buffalo Line, Ithaca & Buffalo Line, New York & Michigan Line, Detroit Line, United States Line, Commercial Line, and the Pilot & Traders Line. In 1836, four daily lines of packets left Schenectady for the west. Rochester was served by three daily departures to the east and six to the west. *Badger & Porter's Stage Register*, No. LXV (Boston, 1836), p. 31; Rochester *Daily Democrat*, August 12, 1836. Hial Brockway, who toasted the arrival of the canal at Brockport, was a proprietor of a canal line between Rochester and Buffalo by 1826.

length, carried from forty to one hundred passengers, and derived their power from one, two, or three horses trotting tandem on the narrow towpath. But the most common size for packets was 80 by 14 feet. The earliest models were simple in design, pointed or snub-nosed at the bow, and sometimes had high railings enclosing a box-shaped cabin. The only deck space available was that on the cabin top, reached by a small stairway at the stern. Both sides of the packets and the living quarters on the freighters were lined with an attractive row of windows and brightly colored blinds. By the late twenties, lines had become smoother and more graceful; the sides of the boat and cabin were joined in an unbroken surface, a small lower deck was left at bow and stern, and the curves of the hull and cabin roof created a pleasing effect.

As the canallers multiplied, a new inland boat building industry developed, centered upon Rochester. Its convenient supply of logs floated down the Genesee River, its ready access to lumber brought in from Lake Ontario, and the skilled craftsmen whom it attracted gave it advantages unequalled elsewhere. Six year-round boatyards turned out a succession of packets and freighters excelling any others afloat. From the stocks of Seth C. Jones in 1829 came the packet, *Superior*, light and graceful, with a luxurious cabin seven feet high containing washrooms and a bar and decorated with fine paintings. Where the first packet boats had weighed from fifteen to twenty tons, the *Walk-in-the-Water* (hailed in 1831 as "the *lightest* and *most elegant* boat of her size ever upon the Erie Canal") weighed only a little more than ten tons. The *Triumph*, a beautiful packet built by W. W. Howell of Rochester, claimed its merit from the fact that it was constructed "without the stimulus of ardent spirits or liquid poison"; not a drop had been allowed the thirty workmen from whose hands she came. "A canal boat of the present day," noted the Rochester *Republican* in 1836, "bears little resemblance to the ill-shapen things of ten years ago." A Buffalo editor called the Rochester boats "fairy palaces in miniature." While Rochester was pre-eminent in boat building, boats were on the stocks in nearly every port of consequence. After 1842, Buffalo began to cut into Rochester's lead. Van Slyk's boat yard, its owner a former Rochester builder, began to launch vessels which rivaled Rochester productions in both elegance and economy.[15]

Although advances in packet construction claimed most attention in the public press, changes in other types of boats were equally notable. Line boats, as the company boats that carried both freight and passengers were called, improved apace. The Buffalo *Daily Sun* judged them superior even to the packets in beauty of design in 1840. "Four years ago," observed its editor, "when the Great Western Canal was crowded with splendid packet boats, which were thronged with passengers and loaded down with merchandize, we scarcely dreamed that in so short a time, the line boats, still more splendid, would take their places. But such is the fact. . . ."[16] Increasing specialization produced several types of freighters, notably "lake boats," scows, and deck scows. Scows were square at the ends and were used chiefly for carrying lumber. Freighters with rounded bows were called bull heads and had a stable in the forward end for the horses which pulled them. Iron hulls were in use on canal boats as early as

15 Rochester *Daily Advertiser*, April 16, 19, 1831; Rochester *Republican*, April 26, 1836; Buffalo *Daily Sun*, April 23, 1840. In the spring of 1846 fifty new boats, valued at $75,000, were being built at Rochester. New York *Herald*, March 24, 1846.

16 Buffalo *Daily Sun*, January 9, 1840. The collectors had frequent difficulty in distinguishing between the packets and line boats in levying tolls.

1836, but the many attempts to introduce steam on the canal met with only limited success. A variety of steam-driven craft made their debut, but none seemed able to overcome the danger to the banks of the canal incurred by rapid travel. Moreover, a four-mile-an-hour speed limit discouraged their use. A Rochester paper agreed with a Buffalo print in 1849 "in doubting the feasibility of navigating canals by steam, and that the only practical plan is a good team and a strong tow line."[17]

Canal boat construction in the interior of New York was accompanied by broad license in the assignment of nautical names. The register of boats for 1839, for example, reveals infinite and colorful variety in the titles bestowed upon these long, narrow craft.[18] Geographical names were most frequently used, with boats named for geographical features the world over. Patriotism was conspicuous in the many boats named after the Founding Fathers and those christened *Constitution, Independence,* or *Liberty.* The military glories of the young Republic were celebrated by the captains who commanded boats named after a host of generals, or after the battles of Bunker Hill, New Orleans, and Tippecanoe. Political fervor rode the canal on the *Old Hickory* and *Henry Clay,* the *Whig* and the *Democrat,* and the *Anti-Jackson,* the *Free Mason,* the *Anti-Masonic Republican* and the *Equal Rights.* That culture was not wanting was attested by the presence of boats named *Shakespeare, Archimedes, Homer, Solon, Encyclopedia* and *Science.* The strength of the moral imperative was recognized by those who conducted their business on board the *Industry, Enterprize, Endeavor, Truth, Energy, Hope, Temperance, Amity, Friendship, Civility, Assiduity, Magnum Bonum,* and the *Clergy-*

[17] Rochester *Daily Democrat,* March 29, 1849.
[18] New York (State) Comptroller's Office, *Copy of the Register of Canal Boats on the 1st of January 1839* (1839).

man. And perhaps just as frequently encountered on the canal in 1839 were the boats whose names represented a simple, sturdy society, the *Farmer, Hero, Lion, Tiger, Eagle, Frolic, Cynthia, Eliza,* and the *Betsey, Coal Pedlar, Sambo, Emigrant, Crazy John,* and *Crazy Ann.*

Traveling on these boats of varied pedigree was reported to be lazy and easy, often tedious and sometimes entertaining. But only with difficulty could we generalize here. The canal boat evoked as diverse responses as did the horseless carriage three-quarters of a century later. "I reached home last evening after all the horrors of Canal Boat traveling," wrote Francis Granger to Thurlow Weed in Albany during the fall of 1832. On the other hand, John C. Spencer of Canandaigua sent word ahead of the journey of Mrs. Giddins to Lockport in 1829, writing "as there will be a canal boat running, she will be able to go with great comfort." But whatever the disadvantages to canal travel, the hardships of stage riding were gone, as the following exchange between a tavern keeper and an Englishman outside of Trenton Falls in 1832 attests:

'But you are going west, I expect?'
'Perhaps we may.'
'Aye, you came down by the canal.'
'Yes.'
'That's fine travelling; that's what I like; you push along so slick, there's no chance of getting one's neck broke as there is aboard those stages on the rough turnpikes; if the boat sinks, one's only up to one's knees in water. . . .'[19]

The packet glided without noise save for "the merry sound of the boatman's horn," blown to signal the lock tender of the approach of the boat. The rocking motion

[19] Granger to Weed (Photostat), October [?], 1832, Spencer to James K. Livingston, April 30, 1829, Thurlow Weed Papers, URL; E. T. Coke, *A Subaltern's Furlough* (New York, 1833), I, 211.

of the boat and the warmth of the summer sun brought inevitable drowsiness. But in summertime the cabin was often warm and close, and the traveler was driven to the upper deck. There, however, the sun beat down and he must be alert to the boatman's warning—"Bridge! Passengers!—mind the low bridge." The low bridges, often ramshackle affairs connecting the farmers' fields, extended sometimes so low that passengers were required to prostrate themselves or be swept from the deck. Younger passengers found the exercise entertaining, but most, like the English visitor, Captain Basil Hall, soon tired of whatever fun there was in it. "It was rather amusing to hop down and then to hop up again," he wrote; "but by and by, this skipping about became very tiresome, and marred the tranquility of the day very much."[20] There was no alternative but to return to the close and narrow cabin.

The smaller packets in the 1820s and 1830s carried from forty to fifty passengers and larger boats sometimes accommodated a hundred. The interior of the long cabin was lined on each side with cushioned benches under the windows, and in the center were long tables for eating. A writing desk, ink stand, and small library frequently made up the remainder of the furniture. At night one end of the cabin was separated for the ladies by means of a screen or a painted drop-curtain. The benches folded out

[20] Basil Hall, *Travels in North America in the Years 1827 and 1828* (Edinburgh, 1829), I, 120. "If we get our eyes fixed and gazing with delight on anything perhaps at that moment we are loudly called to beware, the bridge, which fright scatters all our pleasures far and wide," wrote a New Jersey passenger on her way to Ohio in 1830. *Account of a Journey of Sibyl Tatum with her Parents from N. Jersey to Ohio in 1830* (Independence, Ohio [n.d.]), p. 8. A Canadian, Stewart Scott, riding on the *Oneida* in 1826, complained that from the lowness of the bridges, "people are obliged to lie flat upon the deck, (often not *too* clean) or get down below—got once knocked down by not observing one in sufficient time to take care—rec'd a severe blow, which stunned me a good deal." Diary, August 2–November 19, 1826, MS, NYSL.

into beds and above them two tiers of sacking-bottomed frames for sleeping were suspended from the ceiling by cords or chains—a precarious perch in view of the numerous collisions with other boats and in the locks.

While New Yorkers took effusive pride in their "fairy palaces," travelers from other states were more critical, and foreign visitors seldom found such accommodations inviting. The American traveler, Anne Royall, resolute in her attempt to record the American scene, thought packets "extremely pleasant" in the mid-twenties: "These packets have accommodations for thirty passengers, and very *civil* captains; the ease with which you slip along and the ever varying scenery, is very pleasing to the traveler. The only annoyance is the scraping of the boat against the locks when it is let in, the sudden rising of the boat causes it to drive from side to side, which often awakes those who are asleep; after the first night, however, one gets used to it."[21] Thomas E. Woodcock, another American tourist on the canal, was at least tolerably satisfied with his trip by packet in 1836. He ate his meals at a long table set with silver plate and "supplied with many of the luxuries of life," and conversed with a "quite Genteel" captain. But he was less happy with the tiers of "cot beds" which unfolded from each side of the boat. "The first night I tried an Upper berth," he complained, "but the air was so foul that I found myself sick when I awoke." Afterwards he chose "an under berth and found no ill effects from the air."[22]

Foreign visitors to America were particularly dissatisfied with the sleeping arrangements in the packets. Karl Frederick Bernhard, Duke of Saxe-Weimar Eisenach, drew a bench in the middle of the cabin for his berth on an

---

[21] Anne Royall, *The Black Book* (Washington, 1828), I, 37.

[22] Quoted in Warren S. Tryon, ed., *A Mirror for Americans* (Chicago, 1952), I, 113n.

overcrowded boat in 1825. Being very tall, he required
the addition of a chair at the end of the bench for his
head. With the "appearance of a hereditary sepulchre,"
as he described his situation, he endured a stiff and
uncomfortable night.[23] Carl D. Arfwedson, touring the
United States in the early thirties, found the wall-hinged
berths decidedly insecure:

A sudden thump against my side of the boat at length
spread consternation among the travellers. The shock, occasioned by another craft coming too close to ours was so
violent, that the beams cracked, and the doors flew open.
About a dozen sleeping individuals were precipitated from the
second and third tier on the unfortunate beings who were
lying on the floor. One cord gave way after another. Snoring
had ceased: lamentations filled the room. The ladies rushed
in among us. All were running, shoving against each other,
swearing, and making a noise in the dark: confusion, in short,
was at its height, until the captain made a favourable report,
which restored tranquility. The berths were soon reoccupied.
The young man who was above me did not, however, return
to his berth.[24]

Another highly critical visitor from abroad left this
account in 1843 to discourage his countrymen from
traveling by canal in America:

The night being fine, and clear moonlight, though very cold,
I remained on deck until a late hour, when getting chill and
uncomfortable, I felt inclined to go below; but such a scene
presented itself there as no one can possibly conceive! A
temporary screen was hung up at the far end of the main
cabin, and there all the female passengers were stowed away,
while the male passengers were in the after part of the cabin,

[23] Bernhard, Duke of Saxe-Weimar Eisenach, *Travels through North
America during the Years 1825 and 1826* (Philadelphia, 1828), I, 64.
[24] Carl D. Arfwedson, *The United States and Canada in 1832, 1833
and 1834* (London, 1834), II, 280.

lying on shelves about eighteen inches apart, and hung by hooks from the ceiling, and the tables were crowded in the greatest confusion with clothes, carpet bags, boots, shoes, portmanteaus, articles of merchandise, &c. With some difficulty I scrambled into the compartment allotted to me, but the stench and effluvia from such a collection of living beings can scarcely be imagined. I slept none, and early in the morning got again on deck. As soon as all were roused, and the curtain removed that divided the ladies from the gentlemen, the breakfast was laid out in the same apartment, without any attempt at ventillation [*sic*]. . . . In taking notice of this mode of conveyance, it is merely to guard my countrymen from travelling much by canal in the States.[25]

During a brief journey on the canal in the mid-thirties, Harriet Martineau and her companions were so repulsed by the appearance of the berths in the ladies' cabin that they sat on deck until the rain left them no choice but to go below. For her, none of the advantages of canalling could make up for the horrors she found in spending a night on board a packet boat:

I would never advise ladies to travel by canal, unless the boats are quite new and clean; or at least, far better kept than any that I saw or heard of on this canal. On fine days it is pleasant enough sitting outside (except for having to duck under the bridges every quarter of an hour, under penalty of having one's head crushed to atoms), and in dark evenings the approach of the boatlights on the water is a pretty sight; but the horrors of night and of wet days more than compensate for all the advantages these vehicles can boast. The heat and noise, the known vicinity of a compressed crowd, lying packed like herrings in a barrel, the bumping against the sides of the locks, and the hissing of water therein like an inundation, startling one from sleep; these things are very disagreeable.

[25] [James Lumsden], *American Memoranda, by a Mercantile Man, during a Short Tour in the Summer of 1843* (Glasgow, 1844), p. 28.

We suffered under an additional annoyance in the presence of sixteen Presbyterian clergymen, some of the most unprepossessing of their class.[26]

Line boats on the canal stowed their passengers in with their freight. These boats were sometimes divided into three compartments. The stern section was furnished with kitchen and tables, the center carried freight, and the bow offered accommodations for sleeping by night and sitting by day. Although the line boats usually traveled at three miles an hour instead of four and were less expensively furnished than the packets, they were often more comfortable and were considerably cheaper. A Pennsylvanian riding with the Clinton Line in 1829 observed with satisfaction that there was room in the cabin for "a six-footer to stand erect with his hat on" and enjoyed the "handsome promenade" on the long deck. "We really live *well* in our little house, and have an obliging captain and steward, with every convenience, but short necks, that we could ask or desire," he put down in his notes of his tour through western New York.[27]

By day the canal boat became an interesting and often convivial social unit. Frequent additions and departures from crowded wharves brought continual variety to the passenger list. Whist, draughts, and backgammon were popular diversions. The passengers joined in song, and sometimes one would read aloud for the edification of the company. The packet cabin became a ready forum for debate on any subject from temperance to politics, and there were those wits on deck who took glee in commanding at the approach to a very low bridge: "All Jackson men bow down." A traveler making the grand

[26] Harriet Martineau, *Retrospect of Western Travel* (New York, 1838), I, 77.
[27] Tryon, *A Mirror for Americans,* I, 110-11.

tour to Niagara summed up his activities on one stretch of the canal, "I walked—read—talked—sung—fiddled—eat [*sic*]—very good meals we had too—and looked upon the scenery of the Mohawk."[28] An acquaintance struck up on deck could be continued at one of the long tables below where, ladies gracing one side of the table and men the other, the captain served up the best fare that the season afforded.

The activity of the canal itself broke the tedium of traveling. "Every thing on the Canal is life and motion," wrote a Bostonian as he rode west on the Clinton Line in 1846; "every moment the boats pass loaded with western produse [*sic*]. A packet has just passed filled with passengers and a man playing the viol and Gentlemen and Ladies dancing on Deck."[29] Though there might not always be dancing on deck, some of the packets carried bands for the entertainment of the passengers. And the following poem entitled "Passing the Lock" suggests that some New Yorkers found traveling on their Grand Canal very exciting indeed:

> The Grand Canal! how proudly o'er
>   Its glorious tide we're riding now!
> The bright waves dance along the shore,
>   Or gaily kiss our fairy prow—
> The Trumpet's warning notes ring out
>   With high-tones flourish loud and brave;
> And then comes back the "tender's" shout,
>   "All ready!" up the glancing wave.

[28] Buffalo *Patriot and Commercial Advertiser*, October 25, 1837.

[29] Hamil Loring to George F. Grimm, August 5, 1846, Trumbull Carey Papers, BECHS. Travelers took frequent note of music on the canal boats. A diary of 1842 recorded, "some fair singers, a Singing Book & Bass viol aboard. Sung a Considerable." Diary of a Trip through New York State by Stage and Erie Canal, November 14–28, 1842, MS, NYSL. "We have plenty musical instruments on board," wrote a passenger at Schenectady in 1830. *Account of a Journey of Sibyl Tatum*, p. 6.

Now bear thee bold, and bear thee well,
    Thou pilot at the guiding helm!
If fail thy hand, O! who can tell
    What dangers dire our bark may whelm?
"Hold up"—the slackened traces drop,
    And down the narrowing way we run;
Till curbed and checked, at last we stop—
    Hurrah! hurrah! right bravely done!

We're in the lock! We're in the lock!
    With many a restless thump and bang!
With gurgling splash, and watery shock
    And chattering china's mingled clang!
The gates are closed, and down we sink
    Into the twilight depths below,
Where gushing streams from every chink,
    Like rich and sparkling fountains flow!

A moment now of dim repose,
    A moment's space of calm we win—
Then wide the sweeping doors unclose,
    And let the welcome daylight in.—
The "bowsman" stands upon the deck
    In his high place of power and pride,
His tin-horn dangling on his neck—
    And shouts "go on!" and forth we glide.

Then lightly o'er the waters far,
    We take our glad and devious way—
For freight we've codfish, salt and tar,
    And paving stones and potter's clay.

What soul so full as needs be told
    That to high themes my harp is strung,
Which ne'er inspired the bards of old,
    When Dante and when Milton sung.
Old Homer made what we may call,
    In liberal phrase, quite decent rhymes;

But ah! there was no grand *canawl*
To wake the muse in those dark times.[30]

When the passing of a lock became more an interruption than an adventure, many passengers welcomed a lock-side walk while the boat passed through.

The social bond which was formed with such rapidity among canal boat travelers was perhaps intensified by the long stretches of wilderness intervening between canal ports during the first half of the nineteenth century. Although a pleasant and cultivated countryside bordered the canal along the Mohawk, long stretches of swamp remained between Rome and Lyons, and in western New York the canal passed through forests thick with trees reaching as much as a hundred feet into the sky. James Boardman, passing between Rochester and Utica in 1829, found himself amidst a scene of "utter loneliness." Another traveler, Simon A. Ferrall, felt the canal pervaded by "an air of desertion and desolation" between Rome and Syracuse because of the stands of charred trees burned by accident or as a means of clearing the land. When the bustle of the canal town was reached again, even the visitor unaccustomed to American inquisitiveness might not have resented the groups that surrounded their boat "to gaze upon the passengers, and to learn their names, condition, destination and business."[31]

The ten-mile-an-hour speed of the stage could not be legitimately equalled on the canal, but packets advertised and provided "Quick Travelling." Canal travelers made frequent note of the heady sensation of speed. "We shot

[30] Signed "Hampton," quoted in Buffalo *Patriot and Commercial Advertiser*, September 13, 1837.

[31] [James Boardman], *America and the Americans* (London, 1833), p. 60; S. A. Ferrall, *A Ramble of Six Thousand Miles through the United States of America* (London, 1832), p. 24; Rochester *Telegraph*, June 28, 1825.

into Rochester through the aqueduct across the Genesee as the sun was peeping over the shoulders of the hills in Brighton," wrote Henry B. Stanton of a trip to the Flour City in 1826.[32] Packets ran regularly from Albany to Buffalo in four to six days, traveling day and night and changing horses every twelve to fifteen miles. Most passengers going west from Albany by canal, however, boarded boats at Schenectady, which was only fifteen miles by direct overland route from Albany but thirty miles (and twenty-seven locks) by canal. The substitution of this brief three-hour journey by stage saved twenty-four hours on the canal. Fast packets ran through from Schenectady to Buffalo in fifty to seventy hours, paying frequent ten dollar fines for their excessive speed.[33] More commonly the packets covered eighty miles in twenty-four hours, while the slower line boats traveled only sixty miles in the same length of time.

Best of all, travel was cheap. Packet passage in the twenties could be had for four cents a mile including board, or three cents without; such fares, noted the Monroe *Republican,* were "so low that no man who consults economy, *can afford to go on foot!*" Line boats charged at least a third less and emigrants traveled in great batches at a penny a mile. "If a man feel lazy, and wishes to lounge a day or so," calculated the editor of a Buffalo print in 1840, "to get aboard of the *Red Bird* and go to Rochester one day, and back the next, it is altogether cheaper than staying at home."[34]

[32] Henry B. Stanton, *Random Recollections* (2nd ed.; New York, 1886), p. 18.

[33] Buffalo *Commercial Advertiser and Journal,* September 30, 1839, May 25, 1842; Lockport *Democrat and Balance,* June 15, 1842.

[34] Monroe *Republican,* April 27, 1824; Buffalo *Daily Sun,* July 10, 1840. After paying one dollar for passage on the *Oneida* from Schenectady to Utica in 1826, Stewart Scott wrote in his diary, "Cheap travelling surely—just what I want." Diary, NYSL.

Fares varied widely over the years as attempts were made to gain monopolies over packet traffic on different parts of the canal. At the opening of the season of 1836, packet fare from Albany to Buffalo was fifteen dollars and line boats charged nine. During the same season, the "Old Line" and the Red Bird Line fought for control of packet travel between Rochester and Buffalo. Both hired "bullies" for their crews, and violent affrays occurred where boats of the two lines met. *"They have forfeited the good opinion and patronage of the public, and the effectual remedy is to withhold from both any patronage,"* advised a Buffalo paper. "Mr. Charles' stages are preferable to an association with a set of lawless ruffians," commented a Rochester editor.[35]

Since competitive racing endangered the banks of the canal as well as life and limb, the Canal Board increased the toll for packets from eight to twenty-five cents a mile between Rochester and Buffalo. But because the packet companies passed the increased toll on to the public in higher fares, public opinion forced the withdrawal of this measure, and the power of public censure became the deterrent to the practice of racing. The contest continued, however, and in 1840 again reached violent proportions. Again the press censured the competing companies: "Every day we expect to hear of some accident or outrage growing out of the excitement which prevails along the canal in relation to the Rochester packets. This morning the feeling was more intense than ever. Both boats left the dock together at a furious rate, and before they reached the first bridge were cheek-by-jowl striving for the lead, while the poor horses were at the top of

[35] New York (State) Canal Board, *Canal Directory, March 12, 1836,* p. 12; Buffalo *Daily Commercial Advertiser,* July 12, 1836; Rochester *Daily Democrat,* July 26, 1836.

their speed, under the lash, and the feelings of the respective crews and passengers wrought up to the highest pitch. Fair competition is laudable, but excesses of every kind should be strenuously guarded against."[36]

By August the rival lines had come to an agreement that ended fare-cutting and increased the fare of each to $2.75 for the ninety-five miles between Rochester and Buffalo. Rivalry erupted again, nevertheless, and in 1843 a new agreement was reached. This time only the Red Bird Line of five or six packets served the westernmost part of the canal and the fare was reduced to $1.50. Complete monopoly was impossible in spite of the increasing consolidation of packet lines. New lines organized east of Rochester carried through traffic to Buffalo and the omnipresent line boats carried passengers at lower rates. Packet passage from Schenectady to Buffalo could be purchased in 1846 for $7.75 with board, or $5.75 without.[37]

Consolidation was also attempted by the forwarders and shippers on the canal. In 1832 the Telegraph Line was organized as a combine of the principal millers of Rochester and several forwarding companies for the purpose of fixing the price of wheat.[38] This effort was unsuccessful, and two years later there were ten transportation lines on the Erie Canal. But in 1844 a "Canal Consolidation" appeared which was charged with holding a "complete monopoly" over canal shipping. A year later

[36] Buffalo *Commercial Advertiser and Journal,* July 18, 1840; see also Buffalo *Daily Sun,* July 13, 17, 1840.

[37] John Disturnell, *A Guide Between Washington, Baltimore, Philadelphia, New York and Boston* (New York, 1846), p. 59. A boat which operated independently of packet or line boat companies was called a "wildboat," and was as one observer noted, "the genuine democrat of the canal." Albany *Argus,* August 1, 1839.

[38] Blake McKelvey, *Rochester the Water-Power City 1812-1854* (Cambridge, 1945), pp. 170-71.

the masters of the different line boats met to try to form an association that would regulate arrivals and departures from passenger docks, set passenger rates at 1½¢ per mile with board and 1¢ without, and establish uniform freight rates at 18¾¢ per hundredweight per hundred miles. But these efforts too met general protest and the advertisements of the Merchants' and Millers' Line in the summer of 1845 emphasized that its proprietors were "free from any combination." New competition could not be kept off the canal. "Every thing that will float, and has the least place for freight, is out and doing business," wrote a correspondent from Brockport to the Buffalo *Commercial Advertiser* in 1847.[39]

It is little wonder that this variegated stream of boats brought constant excitement to the villages which bordered the banks of the Grand Canal. Each spring the public presses took note of the quickening pace of life when water was let into the canal—bustle enough, cheered a Rochester paper early one April, "to banish the blue devils engendered by a dull winter."[40] A Lockport paper carried an account of the spirited activity—typical of every canal town—as the season of navigation opened in 1839: "All is bustle and preparation. The captains and crews of the numerous boats, that were caught in the ice at this point, at the close of navigation last fall are arriving, scrubbing, painting and preparing for the opening of navigation. The horses are stationing upon the tow-path; our new superintendent . . . will have the canal in a

[39] Henry O'Reilly to Jonathan Child and others, February 12, 1834, Henry O'Reilly Papers, NYHS; Buffalo *Commercial Advertiser*, April 26, 1844, June 7, 1848; Rochester *Daily Democrat*, March 25, 1845. An example of canal boat-line consolidation is the formation of the American Transportation Company by the proprietors of the Pilot, Traders, and Erie and Ohio lines in 1838.

[40] Rochester *Republican*, April 6, 1830.

tolerable condition. All is upon tip-toe for the introduction of the water; even the rusty boat-horns, that are
wont to discourse such exhilarating sounds . . . give us
an occasional foretaste of their long pent up music."[41] A
week later a Buffalo print noted the swarm of canal boats
waiting to be off, "covered with trunks, carpet bags,
valises and merchandise."[42]

Canal life was undeniably colorful. Boatmen and canal
diggers sang songs and ballads which have been em-
broidered and varied until they have become staples of
American folklore. Most familiar have been the ballad
called "The Raging Canal," that called "the E-RI-E," and
a modern composition best known as "Low Bridge,
Everybody Down." A study of Erie Canal folklore by
Professor Lionel D. Wyld has searched out many early
canal songs and shown their later variants.[43] Professor
Wyld also relates the tall tales which have evolved to
exaggerate the virtues and the sins of the New York
canallers and which form much of the basis for a local
color literature today. If twentieth-century interest in the
Erie Canal has been stimulated, especially by the canal
fiction of Samuel Hopkins Adams and Walter D. Edmonds,
the matter of virtue and sin was a serious question in
the first half of the nineteenth century. The generations
which built and lived with the Erie Canal were not content to judge the canal only by the traffic it carried, or even
in terms of speed and comfort. The Puritan conscience of
the age insisted that the canal meet the requirements of
morality as well.

[41] Niagara *Democrat* and Lockport *Balance*, April 17, 1839; see also
Buffalo *Journal*, May 19, 1826, Rochester *Daily Advertiser*, April 20,
1831, and Buffalo *Commercial Advertiser*, April 12, 1839.

[42] Buffalo *Commercial Advertiser*, April 12, 1839.

[43] Lionel D. Wyld, *Low Bridge! Folklore and the Erie Canal* (Syracuse, 1961), chapters 5-6.

12

Pure and Wholesome Water

CANAL TOWNS in western New York belonged to a region so remarkable for its religious enthusiasms and moral crusades that it has been called the "Burned-over District." The leading student of this phenomenon, Whitney R. Cross, finds the Erie Canal itself a primary influence in making the twelve years between 1825 and 1837 "years in which a series of startling events revolutionized life in the western half of the state."[1] Difficult as it may be to show a causal relationship, the region opened and served by the Erie Canal was also a breeding-ground for revivalism, evangelism, antimasonry, abolitionism, Mormonism, millenialism, perfectionism, utopianism, and other social reforms.

"Across the entire breadth of New York State, undeviating, a hilly strip scarcely twenty-five miles wide invites the world's wonder," Carl Carmer has written to describe a path which for most of its distance ran close to the Erie Canal. "It is a broad psychic highway, a thoroughfare of the occult. . . . In no other area of the Western Hemisphere have so many evidences of an existence transcending mortal living been manifest."[2] At Watervliet had lived Mother Ann Lee and a community of Shakers remained after her. At Oneida Community, after 1848, the followers of John Humphrey Noyes sought after perfectionism through communal living and "complex marriage." At Palmyra Joseph Smith met the Angel Moroni on Cumorah Hill and founded the Mormon sect. In Rochester the followers of William Miller waited throughout the night of October 22, 1844, for the end of the world, and four years later the Fox sisters demonstrated the rappings from the spirit world that would give rise to spiritualism.

Professor Cross has contended that in the Burned-over District these movements "belong to a stage of economy either of full or closely approaching agrarian maturity," a stage of growth brought largely by the canal.[3] The canal also brought to western New York a second wave of Yankee migrants who helped to make the region "more sensitive to religious influences." Foreign-born workers settling in canal-line cities gave rise to anti-Catholic nativism and contributed to the growth of manufactures. Trade between city and country facilitated by the canal partially freed women from their work at home crafts with the cultural consequence that "the counties exhibiting the steepest decline in household production of yard goods prove to have been also the very ones most susceptible to isms."[4] With greater leisure than was enjoyed by women farther west, but less opportunity for secular pursuits than was found in the east, women in upstate New York gave themselves to revivals and social reform.

Among the canal cities it was those which served as manufacturing centers for a rural hinterland that warmed most to the enthusiasms of the Burned-over District.

[1] Whitney R. Cross, *The Burned-over District* (Ithaca, 1950), p. 55.
[2] Carl Carmer, *Listen For A Lonesome Drum* (New York, 1936), p. 115.
[3] Cross, *The Burned-over District*, pp. 55, 75-78.
[4] *Ibid.*, pp. 84-88.

Rochester, Lockport, Utica, and Rome contrasted in this respect with Buffalo, Syracuse, and Albany. These latter three cities were more concerned with the transfer of goods while the former were "exchanging ideas along with products throughout the countryside."[5] It was only to be expected, then, that the spirit of reform engendered in part by the Erie Canal should be turned against the canal itself. A censorious public watched the new waterway go into operation. "The village of Rochester contains all the materials for a very good society," admonished one keeper of the public conscience in 1824, "but it is manifestly their interest that our flourishing village should improve in respectability as it augments in size."[6]

At the outset, the canallers sought to impress the public with the sobriety and respectability of their services. The Erie Navigation Company guaranteed the services of "sober and orderly" crews and "civil and attentive" waiters, and gave assurance that "no noise or confusion is suffered to disturb or annoy passengers."[7] Each new line to enter competition gave similar notice. But in spite of their good intentions, the boatmen did not win over their detractors. A vocal segment of popular opinion was ready to write a total moral indictment against the canallers. The Rochester *Observer*, strongly moralistic in tone, contended that for the "prostitution, gambling, and all species of vice practiced on our canals," the "Big Ditch" should be called the "Big Ditch of Iniquity."[8]

Understandable reasons lay behind such charges. The waterfront of every canal town was crowded with taverns, hotels, and places of business which served a transient population. Each newcomer was fair prize to charlatans

[5] *Ibid.*, pp. 72, 75.
[6] Monroe *Republican*, July 6, 1824.
[7] Rochester *Telegraph*, November 11, 1823.
[8] Rochester *Observer*, July 7, 1831.

and panderers of every stripe. Boatmen with cash in their pockets and stopover time to spend posed a constant threat to the quiet of the rural communities which bordered the canal. The unemployed drifted to the canal and many were charged with vagrancy until work could be found for them or they could be sent elsewhere. A justice in Syracuse in 1854, for example, was asked to pass judgment on "a dozen Irishmen, without money or comfortable clothing" who were brought before him. He sent them thirty miles down the canal to Clyde where there was better prospect of employment.[9] Undeniably, canallers were a boisterous lot; their tasks demanded physical vigor, and the pugilistic inclination of the Irish who were so numerous on the canal was well known.

Scrapes might develop between rival crews or over questions of right of way at the lock gates where long lines of boats were compelled to wait their turns. Similar encouragement for conflict arose during delays at breaches in the canal. "The boys are having a good time," reported a Buffalo paper when a break near Syracuse in 1849 lined boats up for five miles on each side.[10] In 1838, a difference of opinion between Captain Frick of the Clinton Line and a passenger over payment of a fare led to a fight, a kick in the abdomen, and the death of the passenger.[11] Many altercations broke out on the towpath between canal drivers and town toughs spoiling for a fight. Such affrays quickly drew an audience of idlers and passers-by, some of whom joined in the fracas themselves. When a fight broke out at the Exchange Street bridge in Rochester in 1829, a crowd of such proportions gathered on the

[9] Syracuse *Standard*, December 9, 1854.

[10] Buffalo *Daily Courier*, June 6, 1849; see also Rochester *Republican*, July 4, 1837.

[11] Niagara *Democrat and Balance*, September 19, 1838.

bridge to watch that the structure soon gave way and plunged fifty spectators into the muddy canal.[12]

The canal was a place of combat, to be sure, and it was respectfully regarded as a place of danger, or even death. Robbery was common and piracy was not unknown. In 1854, a captain of a freighter escaped from an overtaking piratical scow by throwing oats on the towpath which the pursuers' horses stopped to eat. Fatalities to passengers most often happened when they failed to avoid the low bridges or when they fell into the canal. Although the water was shallow at most points, there were reports of even the boatmen themselves drowning as they fell into the canal or the canal basins.[13] Boats caught fire, they sank, and men and horses drowned with them. Children playing near the canal were often accidentally drowned. A brief notice in the Fonda *Herald* in 1844 expressed the danger that came with Erie water: "Drowned in the Erie Canal, near Spraker's Basin, on the afternoon of the 16th inst., Sarah Ann, daughter of Nicholas Smith, in the 10th year of her age."[14] Sometimes, too, bodies were discovered in the canal, their identities unknown, their deaths unexplained.

Moreover, none could escape the threat of sickness which the canal posed for every community along its banks. Of the more serious diseases, smallpox rode the canal, and more frequently, cholera. The series of cholera epidemics which swept over the United States in the first half of the nineteenth century could not fail to move along the route of the Erie Canal. In the early summer of 1832 cholera broke out in Canada; almost immediately it was in New York and on the canal. The *Western Barge*,

[12] Rochester *Daily Advertiser*, September 23, 1829.
[13] Albany *Argus*, November 3, 1837 (s.w.), December 6, 1853.
[14] Quoted in Albany *Argus* (s.w.), July 26, 1844.

loaded with emigrants, started west from Albany in July. Eight miles east of Utica, the captain died of cholera. At Perrinton, a woman passenger was buried after death from the disease. From that port west to Rochester, no town would allow the *Western Barge* to land. Another passenger died at Pittsford, and three new cases were discovered on board. At Rochester the boat was finally given asylum; the sick were cared for and the vessel, found to be extremely filthy, was thoroughly cleansed. A Rochester paper warned that passage on a crowded boat alone could "hardly fail of generating Cholera, though the passengers may be perfectly healthy on leaving Albany."[15] When cholera reached Utica in August, the panic produced a wholesale exodus from the city and the canal collector was hard pressed to find clerks who would inspect the boats passing through.[16] In 1849, with the "destroyer" again abroad in the land, the Buffalo *Daily Courier* urged the city fathers to prepare to meet it even before it arrived on the canal. "The emigrant travel . . . *will bring it here yet*," warned the editor.[17] The disease soon struck, first at the "Hydraulics" near the canal, and then with new cases arriving by way of the canal.

The merry sound of the boatman's horn signaled a way of life which had a less attractive side. As a consequence some felt called upon to improve the lot of the men who worked along the canal. A convention of reform met at Syracuse in 1830 to organize the Boatmen's Friend Society. Its avowed purpose was to promote "the moral and religious improvement" of the canallers.[18] The convention

[15] Rochester *Republican*, July 31, 1832; see also Buffalo *Daily Commercial Advertiser*, June 29, 1835.

[16] C. Grisswold to S. Wright, August 28, 1832, New York (State) Comptroller Papers, NYPL.

[17] Buffalo *Daily Courier*, May 18, 1849.

[18] Rochester *Daily Democrat*, August 20, 1830.

declared that gambling, drinking, profane swearing, and licentiousness were making the far-famed Erie Canal a "school of corruption," where vice was harbored and young lads brought up in degradation. The society resolved to employ a chaplain to minister on the canal, and it sought the cooperation of the forwarders and merchants in removing the vices it had found. "With you it rests to say," spoke the Reverend Joseph Penney of Rochester to the forwarders, "let these waters be pure."

The boatmen themselves replied that such charges were "rubbish" heaped upon them and declared themselves quite competent to regulate their own affairs. Moreover, they protested, among their profession, "the march of intellect has thus far been more rapid than in any other class of the community."[19] A convention of forwarders on the canal responded to the moral strictures of the society with equal indignation. "Where, we ask, are the instances of pillage or of any of the abominable vices which this immaculate society has ascribed to the people on the canal?" demanded the forwarders.[20]

But other reform movements continued to call the canal to moral account. The Sabbatarian movement censured the Sunday traveling of the stages and canal boats alike. President Eliphalet Nott of Union College appealed to Clinton in 1826 to limit canal travel on the Sabbath in the interest of religion and public morals. But this well-known defender of religious orthodoxy knew that there would be little sympathy for such a measure in the West, and he asked as well that Clinton's actions in the matter be accompanied "by an explicit avowal of the sacredness of religious liberty and the inviolability of the rights of conscience." Caught himself in the dilemma he thus

19 Rochester *Daily Advertiser*, August 28, 1830.
20 Buffalo *Journal*, September 8, 1830.

posed for the governor, he admitted that "There is no subject more difficult to treat."[21]

As early as 1825 and repeatedly thereafter, the legislature was petitioned to close the locks on Sunday.[22] The Albany legislators, believing that such prohibition would only excite resentment rather than awaken "moral feeling," refused to act. Mass meetings in Rochester and Utica in 1828 called for boycott of canal boats traveling on Sunday.[23] By 1844 the movement had grown strong enough to induce Governor Bouck to bring the question before the legislature through his annual message. In the assembly, Horatio Seymour, who was later to sit in the governor's chair himself while canals operated on the Sabbath, defended Bouck's proposal and introduced a resolution to place the matter before a special committee distinct from the canal committee. All knew, said Seymour, that the canal was not the best school of morals and the extent of the depravity originating there. He believed the boatmen entitled to a day of rest and urged the Sabbath closing of the canals on the grounds of political economy as well as of morality. In arguments with a distinctly modern ring, Seymour was answered by Allen of Buffalo who replied that no law could be passed in advance of public sentiment and that when such sentiment had grown sufficiently the public would withhold its patronage from the forwarders. Moreover, he asked, how was the state to carry out the enlargement of the canal then in progress while taking away one-

[21] Nott to Clinton, June 14, 1826, De Witt Clinton Papers, CUL.

[22] Matthew Brown to Weed, February 16, 1825, Thurlow Weed Papers, URL; Everard Peck and others to the Forwarders of the Erie Canal, November 20, 1838, Henry O'Reilly Papers, NYHS; Rochester *Daily Democrat*, July 18, 1842, March 19, 1845; Buffalo *Commercial Advertiser*, March 15, 1849.

[23] Cross, *The Burned-over District*, p. 132.

seventh of its capacity, and what of the interests of the West which depended upon the canal for a path to market? When the long debate was over, Seymour's resolution was lost.[24]

But the movement itself would not down. Pressure was exerted against individual collectors along the line to prevent them from clearing boats on the Sabbath.[25] Some boatmen themselves petitioned the legislature for a closing of the locks on Sunday, asking why they should be required to labor seven days for the same compensation which others received for laboring six. Beginning with the Hudson and Erie Six Day Line in 1827, a succession of canal boat lines, among them the Pioneer Six Day Line, the Albany and Michigan Six Day Line, and the Troy and Michigan Lake Boat Line, sought the patronage of all who thought the Sabbath violated by their competitors.

The community appeared to be of divided mind; all lines, seven-day or six-day, prospered together. A reader of the Rochester *Telegraph* spoke for the skeptical of the community, when he wrote, "I cannot see how much better these boatmen will be for stopping Sundays. Should such a law be passed I think that boatmen instead of going to church would spend their time in drinking whiskey and in short in any other way than in religious meditation."[26] Attacking from a different quarter, the "Seventh-Day Baptists" came forth in 1845 with a petition *against* closing the locks on the first day of the week and in defense of their right to travel on that day.[27] As late as 1854, Sabbatarian reformers secured the passage of a reso-

[24] Albany *Argus* (s.w.), January 14, 1844.

[25] D. P. Breis to G. W. Newell, September 2, 1842, New York (State) Comptroller Papers, NYPL.

[26] Matthew Brown to Weed, February 26, 1825, Thurlow Weed Papers, URL.

[27] Albany *Argus* (s.w.), March 28, 1845.

lution in the senate to close the locks on Sunday, but this measure died in the assembly. And with the renewal of the controversy, the press repeated arguments heard a quarter of a century before. A Buffalo print commented that boatmen idle on the Sabbath would turn to drinking, card playing, and reveling, and one in Syracuse warned that a Sabbath closing of the locks would produce such a congestion of boats that navigation would be suspended for three days out of every week.[28] For all the zeal of the Sabbatarians, and in a state which gave full measure to the reform spirit of the era, no blue law could restrict the operation of the Erie Canal.

But others besides the Sabbatarians held misgivings about the Sunday drinking habits of the boatmen, and the temperance movement also sought them out for reform. The Erie Canal Temperance Society was organized on board the boat *Patriot* in 1835 to induce boatmen, and canal passengers too, to shun strong drink. Temperance meetings such as that held on board the *Red Rover* between Rochester and Lockport in October of 1846, or that which spontaneously formed a new temperance society on board the *Hudson* in May of 1843, were frequent occurrences on the canal. Furthermore, the canal commissioners moved in 1833 to insert in canal contracts a stipulation prohibiting the use of ardent spirits by contractors and laborers. Michael Hoffman, a dissenting commissioner, protested that the prohibition was "illegal, nugatory and most mischievous," but it went into effect and applied for a time to contracts for the enlargement of the Erie Canal and the construction of the lateral canals.[29] The prohibition proved virtually impossible to enforce.

[28] Syracuse *Standard*, February 1, 1854.
[29] Hoffman to William C. Bouck, November 4, 1833, New York (State) Subjects, NYPL.

The founding of the American Bethel Society in Buffalo in 1837 was the most direct and comprehensive attempt to better the moral tone of the canal. Contributions were collected to give assistance of every kind to the men and boys on the canal, Bethel stations were established, and chaplains were sent out to work among the boatmen. One deacon, M. Eaton, who called himself a "missionary among the watermen," ministered from boat to boat in the early 1840s, preaching wherever he could be heard and helping where he could.[30]

Eaton was especially moved by the condition of the boys, numbering some five thousand in 1845, who served as drivers on the canal. Although they were paid comparatively well, they received little schooling, were often abused by the captains, and sometimes committed depredations on the canal towns through which they passed. Runaway boys took to the canal to become lost in the stream of drivers moving across the state. A proposal was made in 1845 to establish a House of Refuge in Syracuse for the reformation of "vicious drivers" and other houses at convenient places between Albany and Buffalo where canal boys could spend the winter. But apparently nothing came of this proposal. "The wretched condition of these boys cannot be exaggerated," observed a Buffalo petition for assistance in 1846, and in 1853 a correspondent of the Onondaga *Standard* urged the city of Syracuse to provide winter labor and schooling "for these poor outcasts." Perhaps the Rochester *Daily Democrat* came nearest to the truth when its editor called the canal drivers a proscribed class, "proverbially a hard set," but "not guilty of half the iniquity they are charged with." The few men who had undertaken the task of becoming acquainted with them, noted this print, found "that amid

[30] M. Eaton, *Five Years on the Erie Canal* . . . (Utica, 1845), p. 11.

all their roughness and recklessness, they possess many noble traits of character," needing only kind and gentle counsel to turn them into honorable members of society.[31]

One canal driver, Michael Moran, settled at Frankfort on the canal in 1850 as a member of a large family newly arrived from Ireland. While his father worked as a laborer pointing up the locks between Utica and Little Falls, young Michael hired out as a canal driver at fifty cents a day. He walked the eighty miles to Albany, six hours on and six hours off, for trip after trip. As an early example of the best Horatio Alger tradition, he soon became a steersman on a canal boat and saved his money. In five years he managed to buy the canal boat *Cayuga* and became a captain. He became a citizen in 1857, and by 1860 he owned a fleet of canal boats operating between Buffalo and Albany and sent in great tows down the Hudson to New York City. This led in turn to the founding of the Moran towing agency and to the fleet of Moran tugs which dominates the towing business of New York harbor and the New York canals today.[32]

The immorality of canal society has been so over-emphasized by the historical novelist portraying a robust and colorful life on the canal, that a recent study finds the fighting canaller a convention in the Erie Canal novel.[33] Foreign travelers, making the Erie Canal a major leg of their American tours, observed the amazing destruction of social barriers and disliked their accommodations, but they seldom reported anything morally amiss. Simeon Bristol, whom we have met earlier as captain of the packet *William C. Bouck* in the 1820s, wrote of his position: "We have a large share of the most genteel

[31] Rochester *Daily Democrat*, December 22, 1845.

[32] Eugene F. Moran, Sr., "The Erie Canal as I Have Known It," *Bottoming Out*, III, No. 2 (1959), 2-18.

[33] Wyld, *Low Bridge!*, p. 69.

company and I have been so fortunate as yet as to give good satisfaction to my associates & the Public in general unless they hide from me their real feelings."[34] Letters of recommendation of canal boat captains are to be found, such as that in 1844 commending J. I. Barker as "a young man of integrity & worthy of trust."[35] When sixteen irate passengers on board the packet *Ontario* published a notice to the public protesting that Captain Green had permitted card playing on board, another group of twenty-four signed a notice testifying to the good sense of the captain and noting that "we regard him a gentleman, who, from his urbanity and correct deportment [is] well qualified for the important and responsible station he occupies as the Master of a Packet Boat."[36] There were almost annual testimonies of genuine affection for the canallers as they came upon the canal each spring. In May of 1843, the editor of the Albany *Argus* noted his community waiting expectantly to "hear the grateful sound of the boatmen's horn from the other end of the line."[37] When violence or lawlessness, or even indecorum, occurred, the local constabulary were quickly upon the scene and severe punishment might be meted out. *Niles' Weekly Register* reported the following incident in 1826 with full approval: "Erastus Bearup, a steersman, has been fined and imprisoned in Rochester, on conviction of using insulting and indecorus language to ladies on another boat, as he was passing through."[38] When a dispute between two canallers in Syracuse in 1854 led to a blow from a tar swab in the face of one of the antagonists, the police intervened and

---

[34] S. Bristol to William Bristol, February 17, 1823, Simeon Bristol Papers, NYSL.

[35] George Curtiss to whom this may be presented, March 11, 1844, J. I. Barker Papers, Folder 8, NYSL.

[36] Onondaga *Standard*, August 23, 1853.

[37] Albany *Argus* (s.w.), May 5, 1843.

[38] *Niles' Weekly Register*, XXXI (October 7, 1826), 96.

the affair was settled by a four-dollar fine against "the hero of the tar bucket."[39]

Moreover, the Erie Canal connected towns and cities which became centers of culture as well as of commerce. Place names in upstate New York reveal a classical bent, and Troy and West Troy, Ilion, Utica, Rome, Syracuse, and Macedon appeared on the canal line, interspersed with the Indian names of Schenectady, Canajoharie, and Canastota. The Greek revival flowered in the first years of the canal, giving to canal towns and cities the pillars and pediments of Greek and Roman architecture. Canal structures themselves reflected the style of the period and were made beautiful by classical balance, proportion, and restraint. Aqueducts, and sometimes even the common culverts, rested upon stately romanesque arches. The weighlock building at Syracuse, built in 1853, recalls to this day the spirit of a Greek temple. Particularly on the enlargement of the 1840s and 1850s, the canal builders followed the ancients as they sought to build with such permanence that their structures would stand for eternity.

Interest in learning likewise flourished along the route of the canal. At Troy, Stephen Van Rensselaer bestowed his patronage upon the Rensselaer School for scientific education which was founded in 1824. Union College, founded earlier in Schenectady, was building an impressive new campus just as construction on the Erie Canal began. Clinton himself had always sought to mix his labors for canals with his pursuit of science and literature. It accorded well with his dreams for the Erie Canal that institutions of learning would one day be founded in Albany, Syracuse, Rochester, Brockport, and Buffalo.

The Erie Canal had actually begun to serve as a highway for education even before it was fully completed.

[39] Syracuse *Standard*, August 22, 1854.

During the season of 1824, E. E. Wilcox's Bookstore and Lottery Office floated from port to port carrying two thousand volumes of "the riches of science." During that year also, a boat fitted up as a museum and supplied with "a fair collection of natural and artificial curiosities and wax works" made its way on the canal.[40]

Amos Eaton, professor at the Rensselaer School at Troy, soon conceived the project of a traveling school of science upon the waters of the canal.[41] He had already published his geological and agricultural survey of the canal route, and he would use the canal tour for field work for his students and to extend his own lectures. In May of 1826 Professor Eaton set out with his party of twenty on board the *Lafayette*. More than two weeks later they were in Black Rock and Buffalo and were taking the tourist's view of Niagara. One of the party was Asa Fitch, who would become state entomologist in 1854, and another was George W. Clinton, son of the governor. They were joined on the return voyage across the state by Professor C. S. R. Rafinesque, the well-known botanist who was journeying east from Transylvania University in Kentucky. At stop after stop on the canal Eaton lectured, the students studied rock formations, and the party took note of the progress of settlement. At Syracuse and Lyons they left members of the company behind to lecture on chemistry and botany. When the voyage was over and Fitch was back home in Salem, New York, the young boy of eighteen recorded in his diary, "I was gone only seven weeks and yet how much I have seen! How far I have been! What new ideas I have received! and how greatly my mind has been improved!" And Fitch went west again

[40] Rochester *Telegraph*, June 15, 1824.
[41] Samuel Rezneck, "A Traveling School of Science on the Erie Canal in 1826," *New York History*, XL (July 1959), 255 ff.

on the Erie Canal with the "Rensselaer School Flotilla," in 1830 when Eaton conducted a second summer tour.

To provide a form of education for the boatmen on the canal, *The Boatmen's Magazine* was published in Buffalo in 1835. It was later named *Bethel Magazine* and *Bethel Flag*, and it contained useful information for canal navigation, pertinent statistics, a temperance department, Biblical quotations, along with sentimental accounts for moral instruction. Jacob Abbott, favorite author of stories for boys and girls, published in 1843 *Marco Paul's Travels and Adventures in the Pursuit of Knowledge: Erie Canal,* which lucidly explained the operation of the canal in children's language and was replete with moral illustrations.[42]

By 1850 the reforming zeal in the Burned-over District, which had called the canal into question, began to decline. The growth of canal cities diminished rural influences and immigration brought Europeans "seldom sympathetic with the isms of the period. . . ."[43] The Erie Canal thus contributed to the phenomenon of the Burned-over District, was itself challenged by ardent reformers, and by its influence finally helped to cool the reforming passions of the region.

By and large there is recognition of the canal as a desirable and honorable bond to society. Respect for this bond is seen in an argument advanced in 1831 by a canal enthusiast when the railroad threatened to replace it with a newer and more rapid means of transportation. "Upon the whole, sir, it is a pestilential, topsy-turvy, harum-scarum whirligig," he wrote describing the new railroad. "I go for beasts of burden; it is more primitive and

[42] Jacob Abbott, *Marco Paul's Travels and Adventures in the Pursuit of Knowledge: Erie Canal* (5th ed.; Boston, 1845).

[43] Cross, *The Burned-over District*, p. 355.

scriptural, and suits a moral and religious people better."[44] If the Erie Canal had come to be accepted by a moral and religious people over the charges of iniquity leveled against it, the achievement belonged in good measure to the state officers who brought order and system to the variegated stream of goods and humanity constantly afloat on the new waterways of the Empire State.

[44] Rochester *Daily Advertiser*, May 29, 1831.

13

The State Runs a Canal

THE OPERATION of this new water highway became a complex process. Down canal traffic was given right of way over boats going west. When one boat passed another, the team of the first boat was checked, and its long towrope fell slack in the water and across the towpath. The overtaking boat then passed over the rope and on ahead. By the 1840s every boat was required to have a knife on its bow to cut any tow rope with which it might become fouled, and a semicircular bow was specified to lessen the damages from collision.

Packets took precedence over freighters at the locks. When boats waited at each side of a lock they entered alternately, so that each lock-full of water served one boat up and one down. A boat traveling from a higher level to a lower level entered the lock as soon as its forward gates had been swung closed. The lock gates behind the boat were then closed and water was let out of the lock through sluices. As the water level fell, the boat was lowered rapidly, the forward gates were then opened, and the boat was drawn out at the lower level. A boat could pass a lock in as little as three minutes, and in the busiest season it was common for 250 boats to pass a lock each day.[1]

Cleverly devised "change-over" bridges made it possible

for the team to follow the towpath as it changed from one side of the canal to the other. They were not unlike the modern cloverleaf highways. The team was unhitched from the boat, it moved up and over the bridge, and then turned down and under the bridge to walk parallel with the boat as it floated under the bridge and alongside.

Feeders maintained the supply of water in the canal and waste weirs carried off the surplus, no easy matter when freshets made a "raging canal." Guard gates could be closed to protect the canal from high water. At many locations the surplus waters of the canal were leased to private individuals and became a valuable source of power for milling or other manufactures. These leases, however, were subject to gross abuses. More often than not, water was taken by the leaseholder that was needed for the canal. "The code of morals seems to prevail," wrote Commissioner Frederick Follett of the leasing of the surplus waters in the early 1850s, "that the State is a public goose, and he who will has the right to pluck him."[2] A particularly prominent controversy arose in the 1830s over the water privileges held by Lyman A. Spalding, the young man whom we have earlier followed to the banks of the canal at Lockport. Charges of misappropriation of canal water led finally to a sheriff's sale of his property in 1846.

Although the canal operated from seven to nine months of the year, the care of this 363-mile-long "artificial river"

[1] *Report of the Select Committee of the Assembly of 1846 upon the Investigation of Frauds . . . upon the Canals of the State of New York* (Albany, 1847), p. 350. In November of 1843 the tender at the Fultonville lock recorded the passage of ninety-two boats in seven hours and fifteen minutes. At lock number 16 during the same month there were 204 lockages in a period of twenty-two and a half hours. Albany *Argus* (s.w.), February 1, 1842, November 11, 24, 1843.

[2] Frederick Follett to Henry O'Reilly, n.d., Henry O'Reilly Papers, NYHS.

was a year-round task. Early every spring the canal had to be "bottomed out" to remove the deposits which accumulated in it and the grass which grew thick and matted beneath the water. Sand bars formed, debris cluttered the channel, and banks needed raising to maintain a canal of full depth. New inventions resulted in continual improvement of the hydraulic machinery used on the canal. Of the forty-two patents taken out in Rochester before 1836, a majority dealt with the operation of the Erie Canal.[3] Superintendents of repairs stationed along the canal were charged with keeping the canal navigable and assisting boats meeting with ice or with other obstructions. The 66 percent increase in the average weight of cargoes reaching tidewater in the decade between 1835 and 1846 was due in part to the use of larger boats on the canal, but it was equally the result of the improved condition of the canal.[4]

During the season of navigation constant vigilance was required of the superintendents to guard against breaks. Breaches occurred several times every year, washed out from a few feet to many rods of earth, and often cost several thousand dollars to repair. When a breach occurred, the cry of "break" went out, and the state scow carrying from five to ten "State hands" was dispatched to the spot to make immediate repairs. If the breach were large, the canal was dammed and wagons carried goods and passengers to points where it was again navigable. To the forwarders and boatmen breaches were costly delays. A breach at Schenectady in 1846 was estimated to have cost the 300 boats which were detained there five dollars each for every day of delay.[5] Moreover, the

[3] McKelvey, *Rochester History*, XI, 18.
[4] *Report of the Select Committee*, p. 348.
[5] Albany *Argus* (s.w.), April 24, 1846.

delay in clearing the boats lined up at a breach was sometimes as long as that occasioned by the repairs themselves. The forwarders accordingly urged the canal commissioners to hold up the opening of the canal in the spring, when most breaches occurred, until the banks were settled and the frost was well out of the ground. "We care not how early the canal is open, if it be but in good order," petitioned a group of forwarders to the commissioners in 1841.[6]

Each year the facilities of the canal were strained more heavily. The volume of traffic swelled until it choked the tiny 40- by 4-foot channel. There were 3,000 boats on the canal by 1836. Albany saw the arrival of 1,329 boats from the West in 1823; by 1826 the number had multiplied to nearly 7,000. Buffalo registered 5,126 clearances on the canal in 1835, 6,875 in 1844, and 8,107 in 1846. Rochester issued a peak number of 8,630 clearances in 1847. Lockages at Fort Plain, thirty-eight miles east of Utica, climbed to 34,942 in 1846.[7]

Soon, the operation of the Erie Canal was made part of a greatly expanded New York canal system. The canal fever spread rapidly over the state. Even before the Erie and Champlain canals were completed, the legislature was besieged with petitions for the construction of other waterways. Many of these appeals found their way into bills and in April of 1825 an act known as the "great canal law" authorized surveys for seventeen new canals.[8] The long-contested "Ontario route" came into being with

6 *Ibid.*, May 28, 1841.
7 Oliver G. Steele, *Steele's Western Guide Book* . . . (Buffalo, 1836), p. 10; Buffalo *Journal and Commercial Advertiser*, September 19, 1826; Buffalo *Patriot and Commercial Advertiser*, April 6, 1836; Buffalo *Commercial Advertiser*, December 3, 1844; Buffalo *Daily Courier and Patriot*, November 28, 1846; McKelvey, *Rochester History*, XI, 13; Buffalo *Daily Courier*, February 8, 1847.
8 *Laws*, II, 279-85, 397-98, 578-79.

the completion of the Oswego Canal from Syracuse to Oswego in 1828. Jesse Hawley's earlier prophecy that the Finger Lake region would be "laced with canals" soon came to pass. The Cayuga and Seneca Canal was completed in 1829; the Chemung Canal, extending from Seneca Lake to Elmira and supplied by a feeder from the Chemung River, was finished in 1833; and Seneca Lake was linked with Crooked (Keuka) Lake in the same year. The Erie Canal was joined with Oneida Lake by five miles of canal in 1835, and with the Susquehanna River through the Chenango Canal in 1837. In a miracle of engineering skill the Black River Canal was constructed from Rome to the Black River in the foothills of the Adirondacks. The commissioners wisely abandoned a plan to use the system of inclined planes employed on the Pennsylvania canals and the work was completed in 1851.

Western New York demanded a waterway to connect the Erie Canal with the Allegheny River. Three routes emerged out of local rivalries and the contest among them continued for a decade until the passage of the bill for the Genesee Valley Canal in May of 1836.[9] The victory was celebrated from Olean on the Allegheny to Rochester at the falls of the Genesee. The editor of the *Daily Democrat* in Rochester predicted that Rochester would be made "rich as Croesus" and added: "We are glad the good people of the Genesee Valley did throw up their caps, ring their bells and fire their cannon, for it gives evidence that they are alive to their interests. They

[9] The people of Rochester and the Genesee Valley petitioned for a canal along the Genesee River to the Allegheny River at Olean; Batavia landholders worked for a canal which would follow the path of the Tonawanda Creek and join the Allegheny at Olean; and Buffalo interests fought for a canal through the Conewango Valley to the Allegheny at Warren. Buffalo *Emporium and General Advertiser*, December 9, 1826; Monroe *Republican*, March 28, 1826.

know that the construction of the Canal will make them rich, and they are not afraid to own to it. . . . As soon as our citizens get over their first impulse of joy, we will shout louder, ring harder, and fire longer, than any other place on the whole line of the canal."[10] Although construction stopped short at Mt. Morris in 1841 and the canal never reached Olean until 1856, its commerce, like that of the other lateral canals, swelled the traffic on Erie water.

The press of traffic and the extension of the lateral canals led to the decision to rebuild the Erie Canal in 1835. Benjamin Wright wrote to William C. Bouck in 1834, "we see in the size of our Canal that we have made great errors, very great indeed," and he warned the canal commissioners not to err again.[11] The legislature authorized an enlargement of the Erie Canal to new dimensions of 70 feet wide and 7 feet deep, with double locks of 110 by 18 feet, on which construction began in 1836.

The New York canal system was operated by the Canal Board, which was composed of the canal commissioners and the commissioners of the Canal Fund. The former supervised the improvement, repairs, and management of the canal, while the latter collected the tolls and were responsible for canal finances.[12] Three major divisions of the canals were marked out and each was placed under

[10] Rochester *Daily Democrat*, May 19, 1836.

[11] Wright to Bouck, December 23, 1834, William C. Bouck Papers, Cornell University Library.

[12] *Laws*, I, 518-29. After Clinton's removal, Van Rensselaer, Young, Seymour, and Bouck continued to serve as commissioners. In 1830, the number of canal commissioners was increased to five. The commissioners of the Canal Fund remained as constituted in 1817. The office of the State Engineer and Surveyor was established in 1846 and this official became a member of the Canal Board. The names of the members of the Canal Board can be found in Whitford, *History of the Canal System*, II, 1131-34.

an "Acting Commissioner." In 1848, Division No. 1 embraced the Erie Canal from Albany west to the Oneida Creek Feeder, the Champlain Canal, and the Black River Canal, making 271 miles in all. Division No. 2 included the Erie Canal from Oneida Creek to the eastern boundary of Wayne County, the Oswego Canal, and the Chenango Canal, an extent of 305 miles. Division No. 3 was made up of the Erie Canal from Wayne County to Buffalo and the Genesee Valley Canal, totaling 272 miles.

Together the members of the Canal Board appointed the holders of the canal offices, fixed the rates of toll, and granted the water privileges along the canal. Although the board was responsible to the legislature, great economic powers were placed in the hands of a small body of men, the full extent of which the commissioners were often reluctant to exercise. At the outset, these powers seemed so far-reaching that a correspondent to a Utica paper in 1826 believed them "both dangerous in nature, and without . . . a single other precedent in practice in any other free government."[13] The paper itself urged more direct supervision of the canal by the comptroller and the legislature. On occasion, the legislature did suspend increases in tolls which had been established by the board.

The Canal Board issued regulations requiring each boat to be registered and to carry a bill of lading and a clearance. The bill of lading listed every article transported, where it had been taken on board and where it was to be landed, along with its weight, quantity, or length, depending upon the method by which it was assessed for toll. The master of the boat was required to know the contents of his cargo and to be able to verify

[13] Utica *Sentinel and Gazette*, January 31, 1826.

Side cut of the Erie Canal into the Hudson River at West
Troy, about 1830

*Courtesy of The New-York
Historical Society, New York City*

JUNCTION OF THE ERIE AND THE CHAMPLAIN CANALS, ABOUT 1830

*Courtesy of The New-York
Historical Society, New York City*

his bill of lading by an oath, under penalty of a triple toll. An Inspector of Boats checked the cargo and upon his certificate, a clearance was given by the Collector of Tolls. No boat could proceed without a clearance, or proceed beyond the place to which it was cleared.[14] Some seventeen collectors were established at principal canal ports.[15] Toll was paid to the first collector met by the boat and his receipt was exhibited to subsequent collectors on the canal until additions to the cargo were made and a new toll was paid. The tolls were most often based on the weight of the cargo which was determined by hydraulic weighlocks located at Albany, West Troy, Utica, Syracuse, and Rochester, and by calibrated metal scales placed at the waterline of the boat.[16] Each year at the opening of the season, canal boats were weighed light, in order to establish the toll to be paid on the boat for the season and to make possible the weighing of the cargo in the weighlock. Captains could enter more than one weighlock to verify the weight of their cargoes, and an elaborate experiment was carried out each spring to keep the weighlocks in uniform accuracy.

New schedules of tolls were published each year. In 1836, for example, the toll on flour and wheat was four and a half mills per thousand pounds per mile, while double that amount was assessed on merchandise. Packet

[14] The clearance showed the name of the boat, its captain, the items on the bill of lading with places of origin and destination, the number of miles to be traveled, and the amount of toll paid.

[15] Toll collectors were stationed in the 1830s at Albany, West Troy, Schenectady, Fultonville, Little Falls, Utica, Rome, Syracuse, Montezuma, Lyons, Palmyra, Rochester, Brockport, Albion, Lockport, Black Rock, and Buffalo. After 1842 canal craft navigating the Hudson were required to take out papers at the Custom House and in 1846 a collector was appointed in New York City.

[16] The weighlock building in Syracuse, built in 1850 and notable for its Greek revival style of architecture, has been preserved as a canal museum.

boats paid fifteen cents a mile between Schenectady and Utica and eight cents a mile west of Utica, plus an additional two mills per passenger.[17]

Hundreds of bills of lading and clearances are preserved so that journey after journey on the Erie Canal or the lateral branches can be followed. In 1836, the boat *Venice* of Rochester, Captain L. Daggett, carried 38,000 pounds of merchandise to canal ports between Troy and Buffalo and paid a toll of $12.50 on the boat and $124.84 on the cargo. In 1842, the boat *Massachusetts* of Elmira, Captain W. Chase, carried seven passengers, 100,000 pounds of flour, and smaller amounts of tallow, cheese, apples, lard, ashes, peaches, and High Wines from Buffalo to Troy, paying a toll of $200.28. In 1833, the boat *Equity* of Rochester, Captain S. Van Schuyver, carried 13,322 pounds of furniture from Albany to Buffalo and paid a toll of $24.20 for the cargo and $11.98 for the boat. On the clearance we note that at Holley the boat picked up two dozen eggs and half a barrel of molasses, and, at Rochester, five and a half barrels of fish, a cask of oil, and a cask of butter. Along the way we find notation of first six passengers, then ten passengers, then four and a half passengers, then three and a half passengers, and finally two and a half passengers picked up for trips of varying lengths. Altogether the boat carried 15,900 pounds and paid a toll of $44.06. It bore the signatures of collectors at Holley, Rochester, and Buffalo, and the interesting addition to the clearance, "30 Dutchmen Emigrating."[18] One of the largest tolls paid by a single boat before 1854 was that of the *Toledo* of the Fulton

<hr>

[17] New York (State) Canal Board, *Canal Directory March 12, 1836,* pp. 2-6.

[18] Clearance of Boat *Equity,* Collector's Office, Albany, October 24, 1833, New York (State) Comptroller Papers, NYPL.

Line, which paid $401.45 on a cargo weighing 121,600 pounds.[19]

Until 1841 the business of the canal was done in the office of the comptroller in Albany, who was a member of the Canal Board. In that year a Canal Department was set up and administered by a chief clerk and four assistants appointed by the commissioners of the Canal Fund, of which body the comptroller was the nominal head. Collectors, weigh masters, and inspectors of boats notified the comptroller or the Canal Department in detail of the affairs of their posts and kept them informed of breaks in the canal, the progress of repairs, the balances of canal deposits in local banks, conflicts with local authorities, and infractions of the rules and penalties imposed. From the reports of John F. Kittle, weigh master at Utica, to Comptroller Flagg in 1837 we learn of the captain of the boat *Perry* being fined $25 for failure to pay toll on seventeen boxes of herring, eight boxes of raisins, and four of codfish which were "secreted under his stern deck."[20] The captain of the boat *Francis Marion* paid the usual fine of $25 in 1834 for four barrels of nuts "not cleared or reported." To avoid paying full toll captains most frequently reported cargo as taken on board short of the actual distance it had traveled on the canal. Tolls were often paid only to the next village beyond the collector's office, under pretence of depositing the goods there when the actual intention was to unload them much nearer to the next collector on the line. "Every expedient is resorted to, to get rid of paying tolls," complained Michael Hoffman to Flagg in 1833, "and if they must be paid, to pay them after instead of before

19 Albany *Argus* (s.w.), August 25, 1843.
20 Kittle to A. C. Flagg, August 31, 1837, New York (State) Comptroller Papers, NYPL.

transportation and the means by which the last is attained are well calculated to effect the first."[21] No satisfactory system was ever found for collecting tolls on cargo loaded or unloaded between collectors' offices, or on boats carrying cargo destined for an unspecified port depending upon where the cargo could be sold.[22]

In spite of law to the contrary, clearances were often issued on the basis of abstracts furnished by the shippers rather than on bills of lading. At the close of the season of 1836, Thomas M. Francis, collector at Utica, wrote to Flagg of the frequent discrepancies between the bill of lading and the clearance, finding articles entered at half their weight, cargoes of lumber cleared by "mere estimation" instead of actual measurement, or boatloads of flour shipped with no accurate weight until the boat was forced into a weighlock. "The business done on the canal is a matter of no small amount," he wrote, "and that it should be correctly done is equally important."[23] Francis put part of the blame on the fact that in the face of a steady increase in canal commerce, no increase had been made in the number of clerks in the offices of the collectors.

Francis reported that the two clerks in his office at Utica began their day at 6 in the morning and remained until nine or ten at night seven days a week. In addition, one remained on duty every night, while the collector himself was on duty around the clock. "But few active and well qualified young men can be procured, to accept of conditions in Collector's offices; and this, plainly for the reason that for less arduous services they can procure

[21] Hoffman to Flagg, June 25, 1833, New York (State) Comptroller Papers, NYPL.

[22] See C. S. McConnell to Flagg, August 14, 1833, New York (State) Comptroller Papers, NYPL.

[23] Francis to Flagg, December 26, 1836, New York (State) Comptroller Papers, NYPL.

a much larger compensation in other business," he complained. As a result clerks were often poorly qualified for their tasks, and turnover was high.

Lock tenders were appointed, one to a lock, even though twenty-four-hour service was required. They were paid from $20 to $60 a month depending upon the average number of boats passing each day. With this salary the lock tender was expected to hire an assistant to serve during the hours when he wished to be off duty, a practice which often left the locks poorly manned for part of the day or night.

After 1840, inspectors of boats received from $50 to $65 a month, but at the opening of the season of 1831, J. Davenport, inspector at Buffalo, wrote Comptroller Silas Wright for an increase in pay. He had been serving as inspector for three years at $38 per month. He worked from six in the morning until nine, ten, or eleven o'clock at night. Buffalo, he noted, received more "way freight" than any other place on the canal, including household goods, machinery, and sundries, "of which there is scarce ever a regular Bill in the possession of the Captain." His board and washing came to $17 a month leaving him $21 a month balance and the prospect of four months of each year without employment. Davenport reminded the comptroller that he had exposed the frauds of the New York and Ohio Line and argued that an increase in pay for inspectors would help to check "those schemes of fraud which would otherwise be entered into, it is to be feared, by a large portion of those who navigate the canals."[24]

Understandably, there was much room for complaint about the operation of the system. Canal clerks found themselves dealing with "habitual grumblers" and boat-

[24] Davenport to Wright, February 20, 1831, New York (State) Comptroller Papers, NYPL.

men complained of a too rigid compliance with the law. The Troy and Erie Line protested to the comptroller in 1827 that the weighlock in Syracuse was known to the canallers as *"the guess pond,"* that the suspension of the loaded boats in the weighlocks strained their timbers and caused them to leak, and that the weigh master at Syracuse was capricious and overbearing in the exercise of his authority. "But why," asked the spokesman for the line, "are we . . . to be treated all as knaves, and every errour magnified against us while none are permitted to operate in our favour?"[25] On the other hand, one collector wrote that "no class of citizens are less tame under real or supposed injuries" than the boatmen.[26] Horatio Cheney, clerk in the canal office in Syracuse in 1831, wrote that the masters "considered it a *virtue* to complain of the collectors."

Needless to say, shippers considered the tolls too high and, like the price of public lands under similar pressure, the direction of the tolls was steadily downward until they were abolished altogether in 1883. The amount of toll exacted was often a critical factor in what traversed the canal and what did not. In 1827 a petition from residents of New York City sought removal of the double toll on rafts of lumber which they believed cut off lumber "essentially requisite for the growth and prosperity of our City."[27] An increase in the tolls on the red cedar shipped from Oswego, used for railroad ties and fence posts, was reported by an Oswego paper in 1843 as "a perfect

[25] John H. Redington to William L. Marcy, June 7, 1827, New York (State) Comptroller Papers, NYPL.

[26] Matthew W. Davis to Silas Wright, February 21, 1831, New York (State) Comptroller Papers, NYPL.

[27] Peter Sharpe and others to the Honorable the Legislature of the State of New York in Senate and Assembly convened, February 26, 1827, New York (State) Miscellaneous Manuscripts, NYHS.

interdict, an absolute prohibition on the red cedar trade."[28]
A long campaign was waged to lower the tolls on imported
salt, levied in favor of the Onondaga salt works and raised
in 1830 to counter the effect of the reduction of duty by
Congress. In 1850, ten thousand persons petitioned the
Canal Board and the legislature for relief, showing that
pork, beef, and butter would all bring substantially
higher prices in eastern markets if packed in foreign salt
rather than in the domestic variety.[29] Buffalo forwarders
sought to induce the Canal Board to lower the toll on
"High Wines," made from grapes grown largely in central
and southern Ohio and marketed in Cincinnati. With the
opening of the Ohio canals and railroads, the Ohio vint-
ners were willing to try Eastern markets and by 1850 the
forwarders were eager to accommodate them. The decline
in the market for ashes had reduced their chief deck
cargo, needed for the trim of their boats, and High Wines
being equally impervious to exposure were just the
substitute needed. They saw this trade within their grasp
and needed only a reduction of tolls to secure it.[30] As
railroad competition arose in the late forties and early
fifties, packet boats found their very survival dependent
upon reduction of canal tolls.[31]

[28] Quoted in Albany *Argus* (s.w.), July 21, 1843.

[29] New York *Journal of Commerce*, March 11, 1851.

[30] E. Ruden and others to the Honorable Canal Board of the State of
New York, February 18, 1850, New York (State) Comptroller Papers,
NYPL.

[31] Hiram Greenman to J. Hinds, February 22, 1850, Thomas Wheeler
and others to the Honorable Canal Commissioners of the State of New
York, [1851?], New York (State) Comptroller Papers, NYPL. In 1850,
the New York State Agricultural Society petitioned the canal commissioners to lower tolls on agricultural machinery which was subject to the
highest rate of toll. "When we consider the character of the Implements
in use throughout the Country generally," wrote the petitioners,
"we cannot but feel the necessity of the introduction of more and better
implements and as the agricultural public is waking up to a sense of
their situation, and becoming more willing to supply themselves with bet-

In the course of time the administration of canal affairs became increasingly centralized and bureaucratic. At the outset, emphasis was placed on personal responsibility and personal relationships, as befitted a small and agrarian society. A circular to weigh masters from the comptroller's office in 1835 enjoined the weigh master to "exercise the same care and economy which would guide his conduct, if his own personal interest were involved."[32] Minutes of the proceedings of the Canal Board from 1822 until 1828 were never transcribed in the official records of the board and were lost. Until 1836 no complete records were kept of the trade of the canal; instead, record was made only of property passing Utica and of certain leading products arriving at tidewater. In 1836 forms were prepared and sent to all collectors on which they were instructed to list all property cleared or left at their offices so that a full statistical record could be kept of canal trade. In an effort to improve the procedures for disbursement of canal funds for repairs and other expenses, Michael Hoffman recommended in 1833 the fuller use of estimates and reports. "In the history of public expenditures I do not believe there is such an instance of want of system and accountability," he complained to Flagg. "Expenditures of near half a million a year cannot be left in their present irresponsible condition."[33]

Canal repairs and new canal construction soon became notorious for their frauds practiced against the state. The

---

ter if not the best of Implements, we deem it of the greatest importance, that they be enabled to procure them at . . . reasonable rates. . . ."
B. P. Johnson and others to The Honorable The Board of Canal Commissioners, January 18, 1850, New York (State) Comptroller Papers, NYPL.

[32] *Circular to Weigh Masters,* April 6, 1835, New York (State) Comptroller Papers, NYPL.

[33] Hoffman to A. C. Flagg, August 4, 1833, New York (State) Comptroller Papers, NYPL.

cost of repairs on the Erie Canal climbed rapidly from
$493 per mile in 1829 to $883 per mile in 1834.[34] "No part
of the public service furnished greater opportunity for
infidelity to the public interest than the present system of
canal repairing," wrote a correspondent to an Albany
paper in 1846.[35] That year the legislature appointed a
committee to investigate frauds on the canals which
resulted in publication of a fat volume which made it
clear that deception and corruption had become common
in the management, repair, and construction of the
canals.[36] The committee found that acting commissioners
charged with a division of the canal were on the canal line
only two or three times a season and that the management
of the canal was left largely to the superintendents.
Materials for the canal were purchased at private sale
rather than by competitive bids. Severest censure went
to the canal engineers and to the passing of responsibility
from the chief engineer to resident engineers to assistants,
the latter of whom were usually "mere boys." "It has
become proverbial that an engineer's estimate is nearly
worthless," said the committee, "and our canal history
would appear to justify such a conclusion."[37] In one
example of fraud or inefficiency reported by the committee, the digging of two drainage ditches of three miles
each on level land along the Tonawanda Creek was supervised and completed by seven engineers working in the
seasons of 1837, 1838, and 1839 at a cost of nearly
$100,000. Investigation revealed that one engineer could
have done the job in two to three weeks.[38]

To curb excessive expenditures, a movement began
in the legislature in 1846 that all repairs would be made

[34] Albany *Argus* (s.w.), May 4, 1838.
[35] *Ibid.*, March 27, 1846.
[36] *Report of the Select Committee*, pp. 351-52.
[37] *Ibid.*, p. 342.   [38] *Ibid.*, pp. 149-51.

under contract to the lowest bidder, supervised by the canal engineers. A system gradually evolved whereby the Canal Board shared responsibility with the state engineer and surveyor for the care of the canals and the Erie Canal was divided into twelve sections each under a Superintendent of Repairs. An elaborate procedure of accountability was put into effect for the letting of contracts requiring maps, profiles, estimates, surveys, field books, bonding, and affidavits. Moreover, since the enlargement of the Erie Canal was authorized only ten years after its first completion, most of the problems of maintenance and repairs were interlocked with the progress of new construction.

When the contract system went into effect, much was hoped for, but the results were disappointing. Although contractors were compelled to give security for the completion of their work in the manner and time specified, few were ever prosecuted for failure to do so. Commonly they did the easier part, were paid for what they had done, and left it to the state to relet their contracts a second, or even a third time at great expense and delay. Where political influence was in effect, unsatisfactory work was certified as satisfactorily performed and deterioration of the canal resulted. Canal Commissioner Frederick Follett found his estimate of repairs for the eastern division in 1850 swelled by political pressure from $38,000 to $50,000 against his recommendations, and by 1854 his successor on that section, Commissioner Mather, was spending $122,000 for repairs. Follett concluded that a "Canal Ring" had been "silently, stealthily, and for years, undermining and sapping the foundations of our Canal System."[39]

Since the canal officers were appointed by the Canal

[39] Follett to Henry O'Reilly, n.d., Henry O'Reilly Papers, NYHS.

Board they early became part of the patronage of the party in power. Every shift in political power in the state brought new engineers, collectors, weigh masters, boat inspectors, superintendents, and lock tenders to the entire line of the canal. There were exceptions to be sure, as when the distinquished engineer William Jarvis McAlpine was appointed by a Democratic administration in 1834, served under the Whigs from 1839 until 1841, and was retained by the Democrats when they regained control of the canal in 1842. Working under the direction of the engineers were the contractors, whose political loyalties were also weighed on a partisan scale. As William C. Bouck gathered his forces in a bid for the governorship in 1842 the engineer Edward Broadhead assured him from Utica, "Among the Contractors you have many strong and in fact influential supporters. The influence of the Contractors is much more extensive then I had any idea of, it extends in some way or other from the laborer, through all classes of business men."[40] Party leaders were besieged with applicants, worthy and unworthy, for places on the canal. In 1854 there were 150 applicants for the twelve berths on the state scow operating on the middle section.[41] After every election the press took note of the displacement of the incumbents and printed the list of the new appointees.

Once appointed, the new officers were expected to do their duty by their party. The Oneida *Morning Herald* expressed its satisfaction that the Whig canal appointees in Oneida County in 1848 were "men who, while they will most faithfully perform their duties to the State, will not forget the obligation they owe to party. They are emphatically, 'tap of the drum Whigs'—Whigs whose zeal

[40] Broadhead to Bouck, July 18, 1842, William C. Bouck Papers, Cornell University Library.
[41] Syracuse *Standard,* January 28, 1854.

is not dampened by adversity, but who, in foul as well as in fair weather, may be found at the Whig Council fires, with their armor on, ready for the hard services of the contest."[42] Although there was some revulsion at the graft and inefficiency which accompanied the exploitation of the canal patronage, the party administration of the canals was fair game in every political contest. The increase in toll receipts over the year before was heralded as a sign of the good management of the party in power. A succession of breaks or delays in navigation were found to be political in origin. Statistics of receipts or expenditures were made to support any charge or countercharge in the hands of jousting editors. When the Whigs removed every superintendent save one after they took control of the state in 1839 and an unusual number of breaks delayed the opening of navigation, the opposition press immediately found cause and effect. "The new superintendents are generally without skill or experience, mere green hands, in a business requiring skill, experience, watchful observation and energy, as much as the management of a ship at sea," noted the Oswego *Palladium*.[43] "Such is the unavoidable result of removing capable and effective officers from the canals, and substituting a set of clamorous brawlers, who are probably as ignorant of their duties as they are neglectful of them," concluded the Rochester *Daily Advertiser*.[44] But on the other hand, when a thaw opened the canal at the end of the season of 1839 after it had already been frozen shut, the Whigs were quick to attribute the boon of prolonged navigation to the "Whig management of the canals."[45]

The management of the canal was equally embroiled in

[42] Oneida *Morning Herald*, February 9, 1854.
[43] Oswego *Palladium*, May 1, 1839.
[44] Rochester *Daily Advertiser*, May 13, 1839.
[45] Albany *Daily Advertiser*, December 1, 1839.

the factional fight that split the Democrats in the 1840s and early 1850s. As the party divided into a radical wing called the "Barnburners" or "Locofocos" and a conservative or "Hunker" wing, Democratic office seekers on the canals were caught in the conflict. John Staats of Geneva, for example, sought an office as collector in 1845 and wrote William C. Bouck for help. He inquired whether the "old Hunkers" held a majority on the Canal Board. "If they have not," he added, "it would be useless for me to apply."[46]

But the more fundamental question of the party administration of the New York canals was that of the management of the Canal Fund by the commissioners charged with responsibility for canal finances. The commissioners of the Canal Fund were made up of the lieutenant governor, secretary of state, comptroller, attorney general and surveyor general. Their annual reports were separate from those of the canal commissioners and accounted for all money received and expended on the canals. More than this, they provided a summary of the trade, tonnage, value, and indebtedness of the New York canal system.

Toll receipts became part of the "Erie and Champlain Canal Fund" to be applied to the reduction of the canal debt, the repairs of the canal, the construction of the lateral canals, the enlargement of the Erie Canal, and to the revenues of the state. But almost from the beginning of the history of the Erie Canal, the Canal Fund had been the most dominant influence in the economic development of the state.[47]

In the administration of the revenues making up the Canal Fund, some were invested in loans to banks earning interest, some were invested in stocks and bonds, and some were loaned to the treasury of the state. Stock issued

[46] Staats to Bouck, February 10, 1845, William C. Bouck Papers, Cornell University Library.

[47] Miller, *Enterprise of a Free People,* chapters 7-8, pp. 262-66.

for the initial construction of the canal was gradually redeemed until the last payment on the principal was made in 1845, a feat the more remarkable since payments during the depression of 1837 were made in specie and therefore at a considerable premium.

From 1826 on, the commissioners deposited surplus revenues in state banks, first in Albany and then in cities throughout the state, where they earned up to 5 percent interest for the Canal Fund and served as a credit source in local banking operations. After 1831, the commissioners loaned surplus funds to monied institutions on terms which required sixty days notice for withdrawal, thus adding still more to available credit reserves and in a form allowing longer term operations by the banks. It was the first wish of the commissioners to redeem outstanding canal stock rather than to secure interest from loans, but since the stock remained at prices well above par, the commissioners increased their loans to banks until the total reached $3,600,000 by 1836. Loans were made to some fifty-two institutions throughout the state.[48]

Canal Fund loans became critically important to the banks. In times of credit stringency, as most of the period was and especially in western New York, these loans served as credit for business which in turn created commerce for the canal. For example, Lot Clark of Lockport (now removed there from Buffalo) requested the commissioners in 1835 to maintain at least $60,000 in the Lockport bank. "Nearly every dollar of canal tolls paid here are by loans from us," he wrote to Comptroller Flagg as he sought to link his bank, the growth of Lockport, and the canal revenues by bonds of common interest.[49] As Nathan Miller has shown in his seminal study

[48] *Ibid.*, pp. 125, 136.
[49] Clark to A. C. Flagg, July 22, 1835, New York (State) Comptroller Papers, NYPL.

of the New York canals in the economic development of the state, the Canal Fund was made by the commissioners into "a development bank."[50]

The preponderant influence of the Canal Fund in the banking operations of the state immediately subjected the commissioners to the charge of political favoritism. The charge became more acute as Jacksonians and Whigs went to war over the power of the Second United States Bank and Nicholas Biddle sought to force the recharter of his institution in 1834 by tightening the credit resources of the entire nation. In the panic which ensued, the Democratic commissioners of the Canal Fund reversed their long established policy of redeeming the outstanding canal stock and now sought to aid the state banks in their struggle against the "monster" of Chestnut Street. It suited the Jacksonian politics of the commissioners to come to the aid of the banks, but at the same time, they came to the aid of both Democratic and Whig banks alike.

The Commissioners of the Canal Fund made common cause with the bankers again when the impact of the panic of 1837 forced the banks to suspend specie payment. They sought to assist the banks with canal loans and at the same time to preserve the credit of the state. They determined to pay the interest on the canal debt in specie at a time when most other states of the Union were compelled to stop interest payments or repudiated their debts for internal improvements. Comptroller Flagg issued a "little specie circular" to induce the banks to repay their loans partly in specie, and the commissioners successfully raised the required specie for interest payments in 1837.[51] As the depression worsened, the commissioners

[50] Miller, *Enterprise of a Free People*, p. 265.
[51] *Ibid.*, pp. 213-15.

sought to help the bankers resume specie payments by issuing stock before it was needed for construction and loaning it to banks so that it could be used by them to secure specie. Not only did they wish to support the banks of New York, but they wished to restore the confidence of the London money market in New York investments in general and in the Canal Fund in particular.[52] More than two and a half millions in canal stock were loaned in 1837 to seven New York banks to help them obtain specie.[53] The bankers, in turn, agreed to pay interest on the stock in specie, and to repay the principal in specie.

To speed resumption, Governor Marcy proposed in 1838 a new loan of state stocks to the banks. But a national banking convention held in New York City bent under the influence of Biddle's successor to the Second Bank of the United States, the United States Bank of Pennsylvania, which opposed resumption, and Marcy's program for resumption met its demise in the New York legislature. The Regency-dominated senate passed a bill which included Marcy's proposed stock loan but which was doomed by its inclusion of an attack on Biddle's bank. For its part, the Whig-controlled assembly opposed Marcy's loan and passed a measure which allowed specie-paying banks to issue small bills in denominations of less than $100 along with permission to borrow and dispose of canal stock. The legislature remained divided; the issue went into the election of 1838, and neither bill could be passed.

The Whigs emerged victorious from the election of 1838 and ended ten years of remarkably successful Democratic management of the Canal Fund. But for all their

[52] *Ibid.*, p. 220.
[53] *Ibid.*, p. 221.

LOCKPORT, THE UPPER VILLAGE, 1836

LINE BOAT AND PACKET IN CHILD'S SLIP, ROCHESTER, 1838

opposition to Regency financial policies, the Whigs outdid their predecessors in the application of the Canal Fund to the economic growth of the state. They continued to lend canal funds to banks most in need of them; they worked gradually for the resumption of specie payments, and most important of all, they launched a vast new program of canal construction which made the canal debt one of the most important economic and political issues in New York in the decade to follow.

14

The Trade of the "Teeming West"

THE PRIMARY FUNCTION of the Erie Canal was carrying freight rather than passengers, and the tonnage carried on Erie water—first drawn from the trade of New York state and then increasingly from the greater West—increased each year by geometric bounds. As early as 1825 the canal commissioners considered the total exclusion of packet boats from the portions of the canal where the press of business was heaviest.

During the first years of navigation on the Erie Canal, the bulk of the goods carried came from New York state itself. Emigrants and tools had first to be delivered to the shores of the Great Lakes before western products could pass through New York in significant volume. Until about 1830, Buffalo forwarding houses could not find goods enough to fill the canal boats and sent them more than half empty to Rochester where a full cargo was gathered for shipment east.[1] Most of the comparatively small amount of grain shipped east from the Old Northwest in the early 1830s came from northern Ohio, while the products of the Ohio Valley and the southern part of the Old Northwest went south to New Orleans.[2] Michigan did not begin to add wheat to the agricultural surplus moving northeast until 1835. The first shipment of wheat from Chicago to Buffalo arrived in 1838, and grain did not come east from Wisconsin until 1841.[3] Tonnage from Western states nearly equalled that from New York on the canal in 1842, but it was not until 1847 that the former exceeded the latter.

Little distinction in kind could be made, however, between the goods of New York and the products of Western states which filled the long snub-nosed freighters on the Erie Canal. Western New York exported essentially the same products as those beginning to be transshipped at Buffalo from the holds of Lake Erie schooners and steamers. Furs, lumber, staves, pot and pearl ashes, wheat, flour, barley, beef, pork, butter, cheese, and whiskey,—all staples of Western trade—were carried east on the canal in volume. Merchandise, furniture, and salt comprised the principal cargoes carried west, whether destined for a port in western New York or for the Old Northwest.

The tonnage of Western staples rose from 302,170 in 1826 to 735,191 in 1835.[4] Goods going west from tidewater on the canal increased correspondingly from 35,435 tons to 128,910 tons. Six years later, in 1841, in spite of the panic of 1837 and the fluctuations in the foreign grain markets, down commerce totaled 774,334 tons and up commerce increased less rapidly to 162,715 tons.[5] By this time, to be sure, Western produce was supplementing

[1] James L. Barton, "Early Reminiscences of Buffalo and Vicinity," *Publications of the Buffalo Historical Society*, I (Buffalo, 1879), 171.

[2] A. L. Kohlmeier, *The Old Northwest as the Keystone of the Arch of American Federal Union* (Bloomington, 1938), pp. 19-20; R. Carlyle Buley, *The Old Northwest Pioneer Period 1815-1840* (Indianapolis, 1950), I, 537.

[3] Rapp, "The Port of Buffalo," pp. 27, 29.

[4] Buffalo *Daily Commercial Advertiser*, March 14, 1836.

[5] Freeman Hunt, *The Merchants' Magazine and Commercial Review*, VII (October 1842), 366, (cited hereafter as *Hunt's Merchants' Magazine*). The total value of property moving on the canal in 1841 was $92,202,939. J. D. B. De Bow, *The Commercial Review of the South and West*, VIII (May, 1850), 486 (cited hereafter as *De Bow's Review*).

that of New York, but as late as 1847 when the volume of Western products on the canal exceeded those of New York, New York contributed nearly a third of the two million tons going to tidewater.[6]

Wheat and flour were by far the most important articles of down canal trade. In 1834 they made up one-fourth of the property carried to tidewater, and by 1840 the proportion had risen to one-third of the property reaching the Hudson.[7] Even more strikingly, they constituted 40 percent of the total valuation of thirteen millions estimated for the goods going to tidewater that year, and they continued to lead in value all other agricultural produce shipped on the canal.[8] Nearly two million barrels of flour and more than one and a half million bushels of wheat reached tidewater by canal in 1840. Seven years later these figures had more than doubled.[9]

The development of western New York went hand in hand with this rising water-borne commerce. Only lightly settled before 1820, the counties bordering the canal west of the Mohawk afterward became the most rapidly growing part of the state.[10] Between 1810 and 1835 the region trebled in population, becoming even more populous than the longer-settled sections of eastern New York

[6] Whitford, *History of the Canal System*, I, 910.

[7] Buffalo *Commercial Advertiser and Journal*, December 18, 1844; *Hunt's Merchants' Magazine*, X (January 1844), 74, XI (August 1844), 140; Buffalo *Commercial Advertiser*, November 29, 1845.

[8] *Hunt's Merchants' Magazine*, XIII (July 1845), 61.

[9] *Ibid.;* see also Albany *Argus* (s.w.), December 5, 1848.

[10] An excellent analysis of the influence of the Erie Canal can be found in Chapter XXV of Whitford's *History of the Canal System*. The author delineates a western section of the canal 232 miles long and includes within its immediate influence the counties of Madison, Onondaga, Cayuga, Seneca, Wayne, Ontario, Orleans, Niagara, Erie, and Chautauqua. Unless otherwise designated, reference to the western part of the canal is based on these counties. Another valuable study of the canal's influence is found in an unpublished doctoral thesis by Julius Winden, "The Influence of the Erie Canal upon the Population along its Course," (University of Wisconsin, 1900).

outside of New York City.[11] Moreover, where the population pattern along the Hudson River and along the eastern section of the Erie Canal was not basically altered as population increased, the belt of land bordering the western section of the canal became five times as densely settled in 1835 as it had been in 1817 and increased in population far more rapidly than areas farther from the canal.[12] Between 1820 and 1840 the population of Onondaga County increased by 63 percent, that of Monroe County by 43 percent, and that of Erie County by 145 percent.[13] It is not surprising that a campaign was waged in the 1840s to move the capital westward from Albany to Utica or Syracuse. The latter city sprouted in population from 1,814 in 1820 to 22,271 in 1850.

Many of the cities mothered by the canal in western New York took places near the top of the list of the most rapidly growing urban centers in the nation. Every city in the state which could be judged a city was located along the route of the canal or that of a connected waterway. In western New York, Rochester increased in population from 1,502 to 36,403 between 1820 and 1850; Buffalo from 2,095 to 42,261; and the new settlement at Lockport increased from 3,007 in 1825 to 12,323 in 1850.[14]

[11] Whitford, *History of the Canal System*, I, 852, 855.

[12] *Ibid.*, p. 856. Winden shows that the area in the western counties six miles from the canal increased in population between 1820 and 1835 by 44.8 persons per square mile, the area between six and twelve miles from the canal by 16.7 persons per square mile, and the area more than twelve miles from the canal, but influenced by it, by 19.5 persons per square miles. Winden, "Influence of the Erie Canal upon Population," p. 32. But Lee Benson holds that the Erie Canal "did not signal the beginning of general prosperity throughout central and western New York" and illustrates his thesis with particular reference to Chautauqua County. Lee Benson, *The Concept of Jacksonian Democracy: New York as a Test Case* (Princeton, 1961), pp. 150-55.

[13] Whitford, *History of the Canal System*, I, 918.

[14] *Ibid.*, p. 914; see also Winden, "Influence of the Erie Canal upon Population," pp. 33-38.

Largely because of the influence of the Erie Canal and of the changes wrought west of the Mohawk, the state of New York reached a population of more than three millions in 1850 and by almost every measurement showed phenomenal growth.[15]

The predominance of agricultural staples in canal commerce reflected the 22 percent increase in the area placed under cultivation between 1821 and 1835 and the increase in the average number of improved acres per individual engaged in agriculture from sixteen to twenty-three.[16] At the same time, the canal spurred the diversification of the economy in western New York. The number of people engaged in manufacturing in the western part of the state increased by 262 percent between 1820 and 1840 and the number of those employed in commerce and navigation increased tenfold.[17]

Western New York became a rich farming region whose wheat fields yielded from twenty to forty bushels per acre.[18] The wheat district reached westward for 150 miles in a belt 40 miles deep from Cayuga County to Lake Erie. The annual exports of wheat and flour from this comparatively small region amounted to more than six million dollars and "Genesee" flour earned a reputation for "sweetness and fineness" second to none throughout the East. It brought from $4.00 to $10.00 a barrel and it was

[15] *Census of 1850* (Washington, 1853), p. xxxiii.

[16] Whitford, *History of the Canal System*, I, 920-21, 946. Winden shows that the percentage of improved land within six miles of the canal increased from 19 percent in 1820 to 48 percent in 1840; in the area from six to twelve miles from the canal, from 25 percent to 53 percent; and in the area more than twelve miles from the canal but influenced by it, from 15 percent to 22 percent. Winden, "Influence of the Erie Canal upon Population," pp. 49-51.

[17] There were 6,938 employed in commerce and navigation in the eleven western counties referred to above in 1840. Whitford, *History of the Canal System*, I, 883, 922-23.

[18] McNall, *History of the Genesee Valley*, pp. 118-19.

first in value on any list of products shipped to tidewater until about 1844.[19] Using figures for the year 1840, the largest volume of agricultural surplus for canal commerce in western New York was produced in Monroe, Genesee, Livingston, Orleans, Ontario, Cayuga, Onondaga, Wayne, and Seneca counties.[20] More than a million bushels of wheat were produced in Monroe County in 1840 and in Genesee, Livingston, Ontario, and Orleans counties production was nearly as great. Barley was grown in largest volume for canal commerce in Onondaga County where 384,000 bushels were produced, but Madison County produced nearly half as much and other counties grew lesser amounts. Almost every canal county in western New York grew large quantities of oats, the volume varying from 200,000 to 700,000 bushels each. Corn also ranked high among the staples grown in western New York. Cayuga County produced nearly 600,000 bushels, Monroe and Onondaga more than two-thirds that amount, Wayne and Oneida more than half, and Genesee and Orleans more than 200,000 bushels. Although only those counties producing large amounts of cereal grains are mentioned here, each of the counties near the canal added to the surplus of these crops which found its way to market as part of the commerce of the canal.

The first commercial center of much of this vast granary was Rochester. Situated in the leading wheat-growing county in the state and possessor of the water-power of the Genesee River, Rochester held natural advantages over any other canal town in western New York save

---

[19] Genesee flour reached a low value of $4.56 in 1843 and a high value of $10.12 in 1837. Tables of its yearly value in New York City from 1823 to 1848 can be found in the Buffalo *Commercial Advertiser Directory, 1849-1850* (Buffalo, 1849), p. 80, and in *Hunt's Merchants' Magazine*, XV (November 1846), 520.

[20] *Hunt's Merchants' Magazine*, V (July 1841), 90-91.

Buffalo. But Buffalo's growth awaited the increase of the lake trade and no milling facilities of any size were available west of Rochester in the state until the 1840s.[21] Thus grain came to Rochester for flouring by wagon and river boat from the south and by canal boat from the west. Some wheat arrived from the western lakes by way of the Welland Canal and Lake Ontario, sent by that route to avoid unloading and loading at Buffalo, or as a stop on the way to Montreal. "Wheat is coming in from the west, and flour going east and north," noted a Rochester print as the canal season opened in 1835. "Our prospects are full of high and cheering promise for the present and future."[22]

Flour shipments from Rochester climbed to 300,000 barrels in 1833, representing a third of the flour carried down to the Hudson that season.[23] Flouring was done in 1835 by twenty-one mills, equipped with ninety-six run of stone. As wheat cargoes arrived from the west on the canal, awesome machinery reached into the holds of the boats, carried the grain into the mills, ground it into flour, and packed the flour into barrels ready to go into boats again for transshipment east. In 1836, 365,000 bushels of western wheat came to Rochester by canal and was exported as part of 369,000 barrels of flour.[24]

The Erie Canal also served a prospering lumber industry in Rochester. Rafts and logs were floated down the

[21] Lockport possessed two flouring mills with fifteen run of stone in 1829. Buffalo *Republican,* April 4, 1829. Of the $795,042 in tolls collected in 1829, $98,000 was collected at Rochester, $25,000 at Buffalo, $12,000 at both Lockport and Albion, and $10,000 at Brockport. Rochester shipped 173,185 barrels of flour east in 1829 on the canal, and only 15,019 barrels shipped that year originated further west. Rochester *Republican,* December 28, 1829, February 9, 1830; Rochester *Daily Advertiser,* February 3, 1830.

[22] Rochester *Daily Democrat,* April 20, 1835.

[23] McKelvey, *Rochester,* p. 171.

[24] Rochester *Republican,* December 20, 1836.

Genesee River to the sawmills and factories of the "Water-Power City." After processing, they went on board canal boats in Rochester as part of 753,000 feet of boards, 585,000 pounds of staves, and 2,000,000 pounds of furniture also exported by canal in 1836. And like other canal towns in western New York, Rochester contributed beef, pork, potatoes, peas, beans, ashes, wool, dried fruit, whiskey, cheese, butter, lard, and other goods in lesser, but still considerable, volume to the commerce of the canal. Up-canal trade unloaded more than five million tons of merchandise at Rochester's eight canal basins.

Rochester's canal shipments came to exceed those of any other port west of Albany and only the capital with its position at the starting point of up-canal traffic collected more tolls. In the 1830s, for example, the tolls collected at Rochester amounted to as much as 13 percent of the total for the entire canal.[25] As canal business increased, the city claimed full share of the nation-wide prosperity which was finally cut short by the panic of 1837. Rochester's flour production was valued at from three to four millions annually, and its citizens held $300,000 worth of stock in nineteen different canal boat lines. Property values rose with the boom times. The Eagle Tavern was sold in 1836 for $80,000, the famous Arcade brought $75,000, and the Rochester House changed hands for the consideration of $46,000. Joseph Strong sold recently purchased ground in the Third Ward for $36,000 and pocketed $16,000 in profit. Adamson Palmer held the building which housed the United States Branch Bank from August through December in 1835 and sold it to David E. Evans of Batavia at 50 percent clear profit.

For better or worse, Rochester's future clearly flowed with the Erie Canal. Chafing at the maintenance of the

25 *Ibid.*

stage route through the older cities of Canandaigua and Geneva to the South in 1830, a Rochester editor invited the establishment of a new stage line along the route of the canal and added, "Our business must hereafter be almost wholly upon and along the Canal, and there is no reason why we should put ourselves to so much inconvenience to benefit our neighbors."[26] Rochester's canal trade continued to grow until tolls collected in the "Flour City" reached their peak in 1840. After that year more and more through traffic was passing Rochester's door. The infant village of Buffalo on Lake Erie was coming of age.

Buffalo bridged the Erie Canal and the greater West. Its early commerce, however, reflected the primary place of western New York in the trade of the canal. Shipments from Buffalo on the canal reached nearly 900,000 tons by 1835, but Western states contributed only 12,000 tons to this commerce in 1830 and 22,000 tons in 1835. Out of the 18,000 tons of merchandise which arrived at Buffalo by canal in 1835, only 7,000 tons left the state. Nevertheless, the rise of the port of Buffalo is more truly the measure of increasing Western products on the Erie Canal than of the development of western New York.

The transfer of wheat marked most conspicuously the growth of the lake-canal trade. Cargoes loaded into eastbound canal boats increased from only 3,640 bushels in 1829 to nearly 500,000 bushels in 1837, and to more than 1,000,000 bushels in 1841. But by 1841 the nearly 6,000 clearances on the canal at Buffalo included 67,000 barrels of pork, more than 1,000,000 pounds of cheese, 5,000,000 pounds of butter and lard, 300,000 pounds of wool, 700,000 barrels of spirits, and sizable amounts of lumber, furs and corn. To fill the Western market created by the

[26] Rochester *Republican*, February 2, 1830.

sale of this surplus, 78,000,000 pounds of merchandise arrived at the Queen City of the Lakes, in addition to 4,000,000 pounds of furniture, and almost 2,000,000 pounds of iron ware. Buffalo passed Rochester in toll collections in 1838 and tolls rose to $602,423 in 1841. On a single day in June of 1846, tolls of more than $20,000 were received for clearances of 126 boats carrying 27,000 barrels of flour, 80,000 bushels of wheat, and 41,000 bushels of corn.[27]

This commercial expansion required vastly greater harbor facilities than those provided by the exertions of Samuel Wilkeson and his fellow laborers in 1821 and 1822. The harbor was gradually enlarged, slips were built to accommodate the ever greater number of canal boats, and warehouses and mercantile buildings crowded around the waterfront. Still, the failure of Buffalo harbor facilities to keep pace with the expansion of trade made the situation "desperate" by 1845. Two years later a Buffalo paper reported that so great was the influx of goods that business was brought "almost to a stand-still" for want of canal boats and accommodations for storage.[28] It was not until 1852 that improvements were completed which relieved harbor congestion. Witnessing the press of business at the western extremity of the Erie Canal, the Albany *Argus* observed with wonder, "Verily! Buffalo is a great and growing place."[29]

Perhaps the greatest improvement for the accommodation of canal trade came in 1842 when Dart's elevator was constructed, the first vertical storage elevator ever built for the handling of grain. Prior to its use, grain was stored in warehouses or left in mountainous piles upon the docks.

The key figure in the transfer of goods from lake to

[27] Albany *Argus* (s.w.), June 4, 1846.
[28] Albany *Argus* (s.w.), May 25, 1847.
[29] *Ibid.*

canal was the commission merchant. It was his function to contract for goods from western grain dealers, ship captains, and New York merchants, to store and handle the goods, and then to ship them by canal or otherwise conduct their sale.[30] Commission merchants often owned lake vessels and canal boat lines, and they owned or established connections with steamboats on the Hudson River which towed the canal boats to New York. They also helped to set freight rates on the canal, which in the 1830s averaged $7.15 per ton including toll for down freight from Buffalo to Albany and $18 per ton for freight carried up the canal from Albany to Buffalo.[31]

Charles Townsend and George Coit, who were in the thick of the Buffalo–Black Rock harbor controversy, established the first commission firm in Buffalo in 1816. When the canal was completed to Buffalo in 1825, they joined with Griffith and Co., of Troy, to organize the Troy and Erie Line of canal boats, the first forwarding company to operate throughout the entire canal. Moreover, many Black Rock merchants soon entered the commission business in Buffalo. After the destruction of the Black Rock pier in 1826, James L. Barton joined the Buffalo firm of his erstwhile enemy, Samuel Wilkeson. Sheldon Thompson, who combined with Townsend and Coit in 1827, lived to become mayor of Buffalo in 1840.

Like Rochester, ninety miles to the east, Buffalo entered a period of frenzied prosperity in the 1830s. Buffalo was both lake port and canal town and was styled by a local editor as "the capital of the west."[32] In 1829 it attracted a branch of the United States Bank and in 1831 the

[30] Rapp, "The Port of Buffalo," pp. 154-57.
[31] *Ibid.,* pp. 132-39; J. B. Mansfield, *History of the Great Lakes* (Chicago, 1899), I, 186.
[32] Buffalo *Republican,* December 6, 1828.

legislature incorporated it as a city. During the 1830s, its lake tonnage increased fivefold.[33] In the year 1835, when population had grown to nearly 20,000, Buffalonians invested two-thirds of a million dollars in lake and canal boats, made advances of nearly two millions for merchandise, produce and other freight, manufactured an equal value of goods themselves, and made merchant sales of nearly seven millions.[34] As a tangible result of all this transfer of the world's store, more than a million dollars were spent that year in the erection of new buildings.

An ebullient correspondent wrote from Buffalo in 1836 that real estate could not "be depressed by anything short of draining the Lake, or closing the Canal."[35] Property advanced in value beyond the wildest dreams of those who had struggled to build a harbor or gain the terminus point of the canal a decade earlier. James L. Barton had purchased two lots in Black Rock along the Niagara River in 1815 for $250. In the fall of 1835, while walking down the streets of Buffalo, he was offered $6,000 for the lots. He took the offer under consideration, and continuing down the street, he met another man who offered $7,500. A little further on he was hailed by still another buyer who asked him his price and his terms. "Twenty thousand dollars; ten per cent down, the balance in four annual payments with interest," replied Barton. "Say six annual payments, and I will take it," answered the buyer. Barton assented, walked to his office, received $2,000, took a bond and a mortgage for the balance, and the property was sold.[36]

The commercial activities of Buffalo and Black Rock

[33] New York *Daily Express*, August 15, 1838.
[34] Buffalo *Patriot and Commercial Advertiser*, April 6, 1836.
[35] New York *Daily Express*, November 10, 1836.
[36] Barton, *Publications of the Buffalo Historical Society*, I, 172-73.

were closely integrated although the two communities were not joined until 1853. A group of Buffalonians purchased in 1836 virtually all of the lands held by Peter B. Porter, the general reserving only a residence near the Niagara River.[37] In the later thirties and early forties Black Rock millers began to expand their establishments, and they ground increasing amounts of the flour purchased by Buffalo commission merchants.[38] "Much of the property there is owned by our citizens," observed a Buffalo paper with regard to Black Rock in 1840, "and many, whose business is in this city, reside within the limits of Black Rock."[39]

By 1845 Buffalo carried on a volume of trade in grain, flour, and livestock, greater than that of any other city in the United States. The consequent growth of the city was viewed by Buffalo residents as the very essence of progress. But not all visitors who witnessed the changes taking place were equally impressed. The well-known Englishwoman, Mrs. Frances Trollope, who visited Buffalo in the early thirties, left this critical account: "Of all the thousand and one towns I saw in America, I think Buffalo is the queerest looking; it is not quite so wild as Lockport, but all the buildings have the appearance of having been run up in a hurry, though every thing has an air of great pretension; there are porticos, columns, domes, and colonnades, but all in wood. Every body tells you there as in all their other new-born towns, and every body believes, that their improvement, their progression, are more rapid, more wonderful, than the earth ever before witnessed;

[37] Black Rock *Advocate*, April 21, 1836.
[38] Buffalo *Commercial Advertiser and Journal*, October 23, 1839, December 29, 1840, August 31, 1841; Buffalo *Commercial Advertiser*, August 16, 1845. There were four flour mills with twenty-six run of stone in Black Rock in 1845.
[39] Buffalo *Commercial Advertiser and Journal*, December 29, 1840.

while to me, the only wonder is, how so many thousands, nay millions of persons, can be found, in the nineteenth century, who can be content so to live."[40]

A major factor in Buffalo's bustling growth was the travel of emigrants across Buffalo wharves in search of new homes in the West. Three days after the first canal boat arrived in Buffalo from the East in October of 1825, the *Hiram* arrived by canal to deposit fifty emigrants "bound for Michigan."[41] A year later, 1,200 arrived in a single day, all seeking "the west." They crowded Buffalo hotels and thronged the streets as they prepared to embark upon the lake. The following description, written in 1832, suggests the transformation they brought to Buffalo each spring once the ice was gone and the canal was open:

Canal boats filled with emigrants, and covered with goods and furniture, are almost hourly arriving. The boats are discharged of their motley freight, and for the time being, natives of all climates and countries patrol our streets, either to gratify curiosity, purchase necessaries, or to inquire the most favorable points for their future location. Several steamboats and vessels daily depart for the far west, literally crammed with masses of living beings to people those regions. Some days, near a thousand thus depart. As I have stood upon the wharves and seen the departure of these floating taverns, with their decks piled up in huge heaps with furniture and chattels of all descriptions, and even hoisted up and hung on to the rigging; while the whole upper deck, and benches, and railing, sustained a mass of human bodies clustering all over them like a swarming hive—and to witness this spectacle year after year, for many months of the season, I have almost wondered at the amazing increase of our population, and the

[40] Frances Trollope, *Domestic Manners of the Americans*, Donald Smalley, ed. (New York, 1949), p. 389.

[41] Buffalo *Emporium and General Advertiser*, October 20, November 5, 1825.

inexhaustible enterprise and energy of the people! What a country must the vast border of these lakes become! And Buffalo must be the great emporium, and place of transit for their products and supplies.[42]

Although the residents of Buffalo shared in the more dramatic transfer of emigrants from canal to lake, every canal community across the state beheld the unending succession of emigrant-laden boats moving westward. "Those who reside upon the Erie Canal must have frequently thought that Europe was moving to this country, or at least the German states," observed a Lockport editor in the summer of 1847.[43]

The best measure of the press of emigrants to the West might be found in the ever-growing numbers entering the port of New York. New York City, with its cosmopolitan population and easy access to the interior, attracted by far the largest share of foreigners moving to America. Nearly 9,000 emigrants entered the port of New York in 1825; in 1830 their number rose to 30,000; in 1840, it reached nearly 63,000; in 1848, nearly 192,000; and in 1852, nearly 300,000.[44] Altogether more than a million and a half newcomers from abroad landed at New York in the three decades from 1820 to 1850. Many of them moved west on the Erie Canal. For example, more than 300,000 emigrants landed in New York between 1840 and 1845, but the population of the city increased only 80,000 during those years. Emigrants traveled up the Hudson River to Albany, and either there or at Schenectady chose

[42] Quoted from the *Genesee Farmer* in the Rochester *Daily Advertiser*, June 9, 1832. Other descriptions of the arrival of canal-borne emigrants at Buffalo can be found in the Buffalo *Journal*, June 8, 1831; Buffalo *Republican*, May 24, 1834; Buffalo *Daily Commercial Advertiser*, October 24, 1836; Buffalo *Whig and Journal*, June 10, 1835; and Buffalo *Commercial Advertiser*, May 1, 1839, November 9, 1847.

[43] Niagara *Democrat*, July 22, 1847.

[44] Albany *Argus*, December 2, 1853.

between the importunate "runners" who sought to arrange their passage on the different canal lines to Buffalo. The manner of their arrival, their ignorance of the English language, and their meager finances often made them easy prey to captains who fleeced them of their savings or transported them in crowded or unsanitary boats.[45] Sometimes the journey across New York state by canal proved to be a greater ordeal than the long sea voyage to America. One Norwegian emigrant complained of the "ten hard long days" it took him to make the trip by canal during which he and his friends were "treated like swine."[46] But once the emigrants had arrived at their destination in the Old Northwest and beyond, much of their agricultural surplus moved to market on the Erie Canal.

By the mid-forties, as we have already noted, the swelling tide of staples sent back from Western states far outweighed the productions of New York upon the canal. Public attention focused increasingly on the "teeming West" whose agricultural production appeared "absolutely illimitable."[47] Wheat alone sent from the Lake Erie basin to the Erie Canal increased from 14,000 bushels in 1826 to nearly 8,000,000 bushels in 1840. New York still produced more wheat in 1846 (16,000,000 bushels) than any one of the states of the Old Northwest, but their aggregate production of wheat was double that of the Empire State and this productivity was quickly reflected in the western shipments on the Erie Canal.[48] The same or greater productivity in the Old Northwest was true for barley, oats, buckwheat, and corn. In 1836, 48,000 tons of agricultural goods came to tidewater from Western

[45] Rochester *Daily Democrat*, May 3, 1849.

[46] Theodore C. Blegen, *Norwegian Migration to America* (Northfield, 1940), p. 31.

[47] Albany *Argus* (s.w.), November 27, 1845.

[48] *De Bow's Review*, IV (September 1847), 67.

states and Canada on the Erie Canal while 117,000 tons
originated in New York. A decade later, in 1846, the
tonnage from Western states had grown to 410,111 and
was more than double that from New York.[49] A study
undertaken by the New York canal commissioners in 1844
revealed that during the second half of the decade between 1834 and 1844, Erie Canal tolls on western products
had increased by more than $2,000,000 while tolls on
commerce originating in New York had decreased by
nearly $77,000.[50]

Indeed, many New York farmers had already moved to
richer fields in Ohio, Illinois, Indiana, Michigan, and Wisconsin. The state census of 1845 actually showed a five-
year decrease of 15,000 in the population of nine counties
in western New York.[51] With the money that landowners
could obtain for one acre near the Erie Canal in New
York, they could purchase five or six acres of better
quality in the West. And with transportation made easy
by the canal, they could get nearly as much for their
goods in the West as they had received at their former
locations in New York.

Thirty percent less wheat was grown in New York by
the early forties than had been produced a decade
earlier.[52] The Buffalo *Commercial Advertiser* noted in
1845 that wheat could be brought from the interior for
five cents a bushel and concluded that "without the aid
of Agricultural science, the wheat growers of Western
New York must give up this unequal contest." The only
hope for the continued prosperity of New York farmers,
said the *Advertiser*, lay in adopting "the dictates of modern science: . . . If our farmers generally instead of selling

[49] New York, *Senate Documents*, 70th Sess., III, Doc. 90, Statement 42.
[50] *Hunt's Merchants' Magazine*, XI (August 1844), 141.
[51] Albany *Argus* (s.w.), November 25, 1845.
[52] Buffalo *Commercial Advertiser and Journal*, September 13, 1843.

off their farms and going west, or giving way to despondency, would inform themselves in regard to the laws governing life and growth, their condition would soon be as prosperous as it ever was. . . . More attention should be paid to fruits, choice stock &c., which would afford a pleasing diversity of employment and secure the farmer against seeing his hopes blasted by the failure of a single crop to which his attention has been exclusively directed."[53] A Rochester correspondent attributed the hard times experienced by Rochester millers in 1844 to the fact that considerable milling was now being done in the West where the wheat was grown. "Indeed, I am satisfied," he despaired, "that the course of business heretofore pursued can never be renewed with any profit."[54] The creation of the Erie Canal had thrown New York into competition with richer lands farther west, and the sight of thousands of emigrants moving westward was living proof that the West had passed western New York by.

Still, in the eyes of its inhabitants, western New York had become "the pride and boast of the Empire State."[55] In the place of a frontier they saw growing communities, cultivated fields, and the beginnings of a diversified economy. "Ours is no longer a *western* settlement," observed the editor of the Buffalo *Journal* as early as 1830; "our children are surrounded by the comforts, the blessings and the elegances of life, where their fathers found only hardship, privation and want."[56] The Erie Canal provided easy, rapid, and economical transportation to markets in New York City and abroad, and most important of all, western New Yorkers lived close by the most-traveled highway to and from the Old Northwest. A poem written

[53] Buffalo *Commercial Advertiser*, August 19, 1845.
[54] Rochester *Daily Democrat*, June 15, 1844.
[55] Buffalo *Commercial Advertiser*, November 14, 1848.
[56] Buffalo *Journal*, March 17, 1830.

in 1843 as a panegyric to the rise of the village of Lockport could as well have been written in any canal community west of the Mohawk which had watched this miracle of growth come to pass:

> Oh! rock enthroned! fair daughter of the West,
> The wilderness is gone, and thou are here;
> So full of commerce, busy, bustling, gay;
> The splashing of a hundred water wheels;
> The hum of industry, of a thousand hammers;
> The sharp clink, and all the varied forms
> Of manly, wealth-producing industry—that one
> May almost turn the ear incredulous
> At the great changes. Thy fathers even, they
> Who cut the proud old forest down, are here,
> Stand proudly up, almost unbent with years;
> See! through thy streets, how Erie's waters come,
> Wafting the golden wealth of the great west,
> And dashing down thy mountain, bear away
> A tide of plenty on to Hudson's tide.
>
> .   .   .   .   .
>
> Fair daughter of the West,
> Thy circumjacent forest still retires,
> And o'er the golden fields which mark the toil
> Of husbandmen, rings merrily the harvest home;
> Increasing plenty pours along thy streets;
> The wilderness is gone, and *thou* art here.[57]

During the second quarter of the nineteenth century the commerce of the Erie Canal was respected as the very base of society in New York. New Yorkers of these years might have joined with Carlyle in his famous dictum that "Commerce is King."

[57] Niagara *Democrat*, November 1, 1843.

15

"Commerce Is King"

For all the phenomenal changes produced by the trade of the Erie Canal in western New York, the press of western goods was greatest as traffic approached the eastern terminus at the Hudson. Congestion here made the eastern section of the canal the first to be enlarged and fitted with double locks. The descent of the Erie Canal through the Mohawk Valley was dramatic. At Little Falls, nearly 400 feet above the Hudson, the valley narrowed to a gorge; steep escarpments rose on either side, and the canal followed the descending valley plain through the villages of Fort Plain, Canajoharie, Yatesville, and Fultonville. When Schoharie Creek was reached, canal boats first crossed the stream using ropes and windlasses behind a dam, but after 1845, they used a beautiful aqueduct of 624 feet, supported by fourteen majestic Romanesque arches. Twenty miles farther, the canal passed through the city of Schenectady, long the lower terminus of river trade on the Mohawk. Just below Schenectady, an aqueduct led the canal across the Mohawk to the north side of the river, which it followed for twelve miles until it turned south across the river again on a second aqueduct at Crescent, immediately above Cohoes Falls. The canal then began its descent through the famous nineteen locks, past Cohoes Falls, through "Juncta," where the Erie Canal and the Champlain Canal joined, to West Troy or Watervliet on the Hudson. At West Troy the captain of a canal boat could lock into the Hudson and terminate his journey at the canal basin at Troy, which received about one-third of the commerce of the canal. Otherwise, the captain turned south with the canal, passed under the shadow of the United States Arsenal, and continued with the Hudson close on his left five miles farther to the Albany basin.

Schenectady, Troy, and Albany each served as a terminus for canal commerce. Most passengers left the canal at Schenectady where they boarded the stage or the Mohawk and Hudson Railroad and saved a day's travel by canal. Troy and Albany shared also in the trade of the Champlain Canal as boats from the north crossed the Mohawk behind a dam in the river below Cohoes Falls to enter the Erie Canal at Juncta.

By 1843, arrivals and clearances at Albany on the canal averaged eighty per day. They entered or departed from the Albany basin in the Hudson, which was advertised in a contemporary pocket guide as "one of the greatest works connected with the canal."[1] The basin extended for 4,000 feet at the river's edge and received sailing vessels and steamboats as well as canal boats. On the river side, the state constructed a great pier, wide enough for a spacious street and the privately owned warehouses which handled the vast quantities of goods arriving at the Hudson. For the traveler about to go north and west on the Erie Canal, here was the first introduction to the swarms of canal boats crowded against each other, the teams moving back and forth on the towpath, and to all the bustle and business of canal trade.

[1] *The Northern Traveller, and Northern Tour* . . . (New York, 1831), p. 46.

Shipments up the Erie Canal from the Albany basin reached 82,000 tons in 1836 and more than doubled again by 1852.[2] Tolls collected at the first lock climbed to $385,000 in 1836 to make collections there the largest on the canal. By 1852, down-canal traffic annually brought to the Albany basin more than a million tons of property, valued at more than twenty-seven millions.

Under the stimulus of this commerce, the population of the capital quadrupled between 1824 and 1850, numbering more than 50,000 persons in the latter year. Early rivalry between the canal and the railroad in Albany, after the Mohawk and Hudson began to operate in 1831, left the capital a divided town. The company impudently named its first locomotive the *De Witt Clinton* and the railroad itself was built by John B. Jervis, who had served as an engineer on the middle section of the Erie Canal. Life in the northern part of the city centered on the basin and the canal, while the southern part became known as "the railroad quarter."

Some goods arriving at the Albany basin were transferred directly from canal boat to sloop, schooner, or steamboat for overseas trade. But most remained in canal boat holds as the boats themselves were towed by steamers, from 50 to 100 lashed together, down the Hudson to New York City. In the season of 1843, for example, river arrivals and departures from Albany included 33 steamboats, 64 steam towboats, and 2,470 sloops and schooners. In a single day in November of 1844, an Albany paper recorded 120 sailing vessels moored to Albany wharves, "besides the usual number of steam and tow-boats."[3]

Some fifteen towboats drew the canal boats in great flotillas down the river in 1846, but they were only part

[2] *Morning Courier and New York Enquirer*, May 10, 1841; Albany *Argus*, December 25, 1852.
[3] Albany *Argus* (s.w.), November 22, 1844.

of a larger river trade between New York and the Erie
Canal. It was estimated that nearly a million passengers
were carried annually up and down the Hudson.[4] Over
100 steamboats carried freight and passengers on the river
in the 1840s, some of them "unequalled in any part of the
world" for speed and accommodations.[5] One, the *South
American,* made a flying trip between Albany and New
York in 1846 in only seven hours. Like the early packet
lines on the canal, the steamboats had entered an intense
competition which had driven passenger fares as low as a
shilling a passage; but in 1833, the Hudson River Steamboat Association was organized to "produce a fair remuneration for the large amount of capital employed . . . as
well as to ensure the public a safe, regular, and expeditious
conveyance."[6] In addition to the steamboats, sloops and
schooners, in numbers beyond counting, plied the river,
doing business on their own.

The influence of this commerce on the rise of the port
of New York is as important to the history of the Erie
Canal as it is difficult to assess. There can be little doubt
that canal trade stimulated the growth of the city and
that it contributed to the supremacy of New York over
rival Atlantic seaports. But it has been tempting to claim
too much. A distinguished authority, Robert Greenhalgh
Albion, finds greater stimulus for the rise of New York
as a port in the "cotton triangle" and New York's "capital-
ization of its sea routes" in world trade. Albion attributes
less influence to the "flour and other articles brought
eastward" by the canal because of the greater importance
of imports over exports in the trade of the city. His more
restrained appraisal of the influence of the Erie Canal on

[4] Robert Greenhalgh Albion, *The Rise of New York Port 1815-1860*
(New York, 1939), p. 164.
[5] New York *Herald,* March 27, 1846.
[6] New York *Journal of Commerce,* April 17, 1835.

the growth of New York emphasizes the "opportunity which it gave to the westerners to send to the seaboard the 'cash crops' wherewith to pay for the imports they desired" and the increase it brought in the number of Western country stores drawing their supplies from New York.[7]

In the literature of the Erie Canal, however, we find a more pervasive influence on New York City anticipated; and as the city grew, a greater influence attributed to the effects of the Erie Canal. Contemporary observers in New York, perhaps overawed by their achievement in building the canal, credited it as the chief source of the supremacy of New York over her rivals on the Atlantic Coast and over New Orleans in the Southwest. Typical is the 1832 comment of Samuel B. Ruggles, whose personal speculations in New York real estate made him intimately concerned with the growth of the city: "The flourishing growth of this city must be attributed almost entirely to the Erie Canal, which has opened our internal Commerce with the West, and poured in upon us a rare, steady, and rapidly increasing stream of wealth."[8] A decade later, the editor of the Albany *Argus* traced the growth of New York City as "the Commercial Emporium of America" and was equally explicit in the reasons for it:

To what may this change be attributed? Is it not clearly to the influence of the western trade, which seems to be a mine

[7] Albion, *Rise of New York*, pp. 92-94. More recently, Lee Benson has written that the contribution of the Erie Canal was to capitalize on the natural advantages of New York State. Noting that the port of New York led the nation in foreign trade by 1797, he wrote that the Erie Canal made "New York's bid firm" and not until the canal enlargement after 1835 "did the port's primacy become overwhelming." Lee Benson, *Merchants, Farmers, & Railroads: Railroad Regulation and New York Politics 1850-1887* (Cambridge, 1955), pp. 30-31.

[8] Ruggles to N. P. Tallmadge, January 23, 1832, Samuel B. Ruggles Papers, NYPL.

of wealth and power and population beyond human calcula-
tion. . . . The settlement of Western New-York and Ohio
forced the construction of the Erie Canal, which literally
united the waters of the western seas with the Atlantic ocean.
For only twenty years, the wealth of the teeming West has
poured down that avenue, and already it has placed New-York
on an eminence as the Commercial Emporium of America. . . .
So long as New-York remains at the head of the western trade,
. . . it must irresistably advance in wealth, influence and
population, until she will be known not only as the great city
of America, but as the *great city of the world*.[9]

Although diverse sources of trade created the metropolis
at the mouth of the Hudson, the Erie Canal brought
staggering quantities of goods from the fertile west, and
New York in turn contributed much of the merchandise
which moved west on the canal, smaller in tonnage but
equal in value.

Most important among the articles of canal trade reaching the New York harbor was, of course, flour. The
accounts of the state flour inspector revealed that New
York surpassed all other American ports in the export of
this staple by 1827.[10] In 1833, more than a million barrels
of flour were inspected in New York, double the amount
of the nearest competitor, Baltimore, and nearly four
times that of New Orleans. Crop failures in 1836 and
1837 temporarily reversed the current of trade and led to
the import of flour and wheat from abroad, but the repeal
of the English Corn Laws in 1846 drew still greater
quantities of American grain to New York for export.
Exports of flour from New York in 1846 were double those
of 1845, and the amount of wheat sent abroad more than
quadrupled in volume.[11] Changes in the New York flour
market were felt wherever wheat and flour were handled,

9 Albany *Argus* (s.w.), August 12, 1845.
10 Albion, *Rise of New York*, p. 92.　　　　　11 *Ibid.*, p. 93.

along the Erie Canal in New York, and in the greater West. A rise in the price of flour, commented an Albany paper in 1845, "acts electrically upon the business of the western country. . . ."[12] Prices for flour in New York varied widely, ranging from five dollars a barrel in 1825, to eight a barrel in 1829, to thirteen a barrel during the bad crop year of 1836. New York City itself consumed 1,000 barrels a day in the 1830s, and the balance of Erie Canal flour was shipped in the coastal trade to New England or in exports abroad.

The financial role of New York merchants was as important as the marketing facilities of the port of New York in the wheat and flour trade of the Erie Canal. Millers in western New York often selected an agent in New York with whom they arranged the raising of the funds needed to purchase wheat arriving at their mills. By mortgaging their mills and giving personal security they established a credit in New York City payable in drafts at local banks. Wheat was then purchased, in New York state and in western states as well, brought to the mills and ground into flour, and sent upon its way to commission merchants in New York who completed the operation. In 1838 a few merchants, not more than ten in number, dominated the flour trade and gave credit of eight to ten million a year.[13] Doggett's *New York Business Directory* for 1846 listed some eighty-six commission merchants for flour and other produce.[14]

Samuel B. Ruggles, noting in 1832 that the population of New York City had been for years roughly a tenth that of New York, calculated that the interests of the state required that "every tenth man be placed on this island to do the business of the other nine." But, he added,

12 Albany *Argus* (s.w.), October 10, 1845.
13 New York *Daily Express*, October 25, 1838.
14 Albion, *Rise of New York*, p. 275.

"now that Our Statesmen have yoked together the Atlantic and Mississippi Valley by the Erie and Ohio Canals, . . . we must forthwith get more hands here to do the work."[15] The mushroom growth of the city more than fulfilled his expectations, as population increased from 125,706 in 1820 to 515,547 in 1850, the latter figure equaling one-sixth of the state's population. The city of New York looked out to the sea and saw its fortunes in trade with near and distant ports, never more than when the *Sirius* and *Great Western* arrived in April of 1838 to open trans-Atlantic steam navigation. But the city looked inland as well and saw constant reminders of the place of the Erie Canal in the life of its trade.

The celebration of the completion of the canal was held in the city, and few pageants thereafter outshone the day-long festival of the "Wedding of the Waters." In the season of navigation the long tows of canal boats were carried to the East River where they were broken up and distributed to their piers. During the winter months, canal boats by the hundred huddled close together in Brooklyn's Atlantic basin, the boatmen and their families living on board in a floating community. When calamity struck the city in the great fire of 1835, which burned out fifty-two acres of the business district, the commissioners of the Canal Fund came forward with loans to the New York banks for the relief of the prostrate business community.[16] What was more, when the railroad came to the Empire State, the through connection from New York to Chicago and the West followed the water-level route along the Hudson and the Erie Canal.

Paradoxically, the years of greatest expansion of canal transportation saw also the rise of the competitor which

[15] Ruggles to N. P. Tallmadge, January 23, 1832, Samuel B. Ruggles Papers, NYPL.
[16] Miller, *Enterprise of a Free People*, pp. 172ff.

would ultimately bring an end to the canal era. In April of 1825, when all of western New York awaited the opening of the Erie Canal, the Buffalo *Emporium* reported that "a proposition has already been made in New-York for an experiment to ascertain the value of the invention of rail roads and steam carriages."[17] The experiment was to prove a remarkable success, but the rise of the railroad did not soon shake the loyalty of New Yorkers to the Erie Canal; and in the period before 1854, the Iron Horse was only beginning to challenge the New York waterways in the movement of freight.

The first railroads in New York were in fact built as feeders to the canal. The construction of the thirties, which began with the Mohawk and Hudson Railroad from Albany to Schenectady in 1831 and which pushed track upward through the Mohawk Valley and westward across the state, was viewed as complementary to the service of the canal.[18] It was thought that the railroad could serve best for passengers but that the canal could not be surpassed for the conveyance of freight. The Buffalo *Journal*, for example, assured its readers in 1831 that the railroads could not become a successful competitor of canals for carrying goods. "They can reach no such point of supremacy," said the *Journal*, "but where canals *cannot* be had they may be substituted, and prove, indeed, superiour to any other *land* conveyance."[19] A Lockport paper a few years later saw the inevitable tendency of railroad travel to force the lowering of canal tolls as a positive boon to canal commerce, one which would be "the means of securing to the Erie Canal, the transporta-

[17] Buffalo *Emporium and General Advertiser*, April 16, 1825.
[18] Ontario *Repository*, June 9, 1830; Buffalo *Journal*, August 31, 1831; Rochester *Daily Advertiser*, March 27, 1832; Black Rock *Advocate*, August 4, 1836; Niagara *Democrat*, September 9, 1836; *Hunt's Merchants' Magazine*, III (October 1840), 280.
[19] Buffalo *Journal*, September 28, 1831.

tion of nearly all the surplus of the west, with vastly increased amounts of merchandise."[20]

The population which had been drawn to the banks of the Erie Canal, however, was eager that the canal villages should be linked by rail as well as by the canal. A convention of delegates from canal villages between Syracuse and Rochester met at the canal town of Lyons in the fall of 1836 to promote the incorporation of a company to build a railroad between the two canal ports. Subscriptions for railroad stock were taken up along the canal in 1838 with such universal haste that one George H. Boughton of Lockport wrote to Thurlow Weed in Albany, "What has become of the Erie Canal? Lost in the fog of Rail Roads and Ship Canals."[21] Albany and Troy, while sharing in the terminus trade of the Erie Canal, began a spirited rivalry for railroad connections to the west, north, east and south.[22]

By 1842, the junction of the Attica and Buffalo Railroad with the Tonawanda Railroad and six other lines completed the process of linking Albany and Lake Erie by rail.[23] After the Attica and Buffalo line was completed, the event was celebrated in Buffalo by the very men we have seen caught up first in the movement for a canal. With Samuel Wilkeson in the chair and James L. Barton serving as secretary, a celebration meeting resolved that the railroad connection between Buffalo and Boston, which completed a through railroad connection with

[20] Lockport *Balance*, August 27, 1833. The Rochester *Daily Advertiser* assured its readers on April 3, 1833: "Our Canals have nothing to fear from the competition of Rail Roads, in the transportation of Property."

[21] Boughton to Weed, April 6, 1838, Thurlow Weed Papers, URL.

[22] David Maldwyn Ellis, "Albany and Troy—Commercial Rivals," *New York History*, XXXIV (October 1943), 484-511.

[23] Buffalo *Commercial Advertiser and Journal*, March 18, 1842. The other railroads in the chain were the Mohawk and Hudson, Saratoga and Schenectady, Utica and Schenectady, Auburn and Syracuse, and the Auburn and Rochester.

Albany in 1842, was "an event in the history of the enterprize of this country, second only in importance to the completion of the Erie Canal."[24] Perhaps the following comment by a Lockport editor in 1835 best illustrates the capacity of the first canal generation in New York to welcome the railroad as they had the canal:

We know full well that the canal has added more blessings to the country than any improvement of the same cost ever did to any country. We know that Lockport sprung up out of the canal, and would be nothing without it. No one appreciates its advantages more than we do. The canal is a fixed fact, we have it, and it cannot be taken from us. We have the advantages which have grown out of this great work, and that we may hold these advantages and keep our relative position, since the world has found out a way of travelling which they seem determined to adopt, in the use of steam locomotives; we think it wise to adjust ourselves to the new state of things, and furnish them accommodations to come along this way, instead of quarrelling with their taste, till we are left alone, and stripped of our advantages, by the greater enterprise, and superior activity of our rival neighbors.[25]

The "strong desire of the travelling public to be whisked through the country at the quickest possible rate," as a Rochester paper put it in 1842, insured the ultimate replacement of the packet by the locomotive in the conveyance of passengers.[26] Three daily trains ran each way across the state in 1843, charging an average fare of three cents a mile.[27] By 1849 six trains left Albany daily, four of which ran through to Buffalo. The fastest of them completed the journey in only fifteen hours.

[24] Buffalo *Commercial Advertiser and Journal*, June 28, 1843.
[25] Niagara *Democrat*, October 15, 1845.
[26] Rochester *Daily Democrat*, May 17, 1842.
[27] *Ibid.*, July 11, 1843; Buffalo *Daily Courier*, September 19, 1840; Buffalo *Daily Courier and Pilot*, April 28, 1843.

Although it was initially believed that railroads could carry only passengers, freight began to be transported on the cars in the early 1840s. "It is found that this freight will pay," noted a Rochester paper in 1843 after 300 pounds of flour and 100 barrels of pork were forwarded to Utica via the Auburn and Rochester railroad.[28] The various railroads carrying east-west freight in New York soon agreed upon rates of five cents per ton-mile for merchandise and three cents for produce. They were hampered, however, by the refusal of the legislature to allow them to carry freight except during the suspension of canal navigation, and even then they were required to pay canal tolls. Not until 1851 did the state remove the tolls from the railroads altogether and leave them free to compete with the Erie Canal for the trade of the West. At mid-century there were some twenty-two railroads operating in New York, carrying both passengers and freight and earning hundreds of thousands of dollars a year.[29]

Indeed, the future demise of the canal era was written in an announcement of the arrival of the canal boat *Experiment* at Albany in 1840 with the first cargo of Blossburg coal. It marked, said a Rochester paper, "an era in the history of fire; since it denotes the 'turning of the tables' and the introduction of coal, both for mechanical and family uses."[30] Eight years later the railroad age was heralded in a Buffalo print as part of the "Triumph of Steam." It may now be fairly assumed, we find this Buffalo editor announcing to his readers, that "the commercial and personal intercourse between nations, will henceforth be maintained by the agency of steam applied to the propulsion of vessels on the oceans and water

28 Rochester *Daily Democrat,* December 21, 1843.
29 Buffalo *Commercial Advertiser,* July 31, 1849.
30 Rochester *Daily Advertiser,* July 30, 1840.

courses, or of railroad cars on land. In fact, steam has become one of the mightiest agents of civilization, and its use is indispensable."[31]

Even as these words were being written the New York and Erie Railroad was striking out across the "southern tier" to connect Lake Erie at Dunkirk with New York City by a route through the Susquehanna Valley. The Erie Canal had helped to create its newest rival, for the southern railroad had been chartered in 1832 and aided liberally with state funds as compensation for the millions spent earlier in the canal counties to the north. Construction had been fraught with mismanagement, disappointment, and delay, but in the spring of 1851 the work was finally done. Moreover, in the fall of 1851 the first train ran over the Hudson River Railroad from New York up to Albany to give New York City a second connection with Lake Erie by rail. Within two years more, in 1853, the ten little lines of railroad paralleling the Erie Canal from Albany west would consolidate and form a new company, the New York Central Railroad, with its unbeatable connections to Chicago.

Not a year too soon had New York moved to complete its two major rail routes from Lake Erie to New York City. Rival states with rival Atlantic ports came within an eyelash of wresting from New York the Western trade first garnered by the Erie Canal.[32] The Baltimore & Ohio reached across the mountains to Wheeling in 1852, and in the same year, the Pennsylvania Railroad was completed from Philadelphia to Pittsburgh. Boston had moved more rapidly than her rivals in railroad construction and had enjoyed a through railroad connection to Albany since 1842. In the contest for Western trade, New York had

[31] Buffalo *Commercial Advertiser*, September 9, 1848.
[32] Albion, *Rise of New York*, pp. 384-86.

parlayed her winnings from the Erie Canal and the financial services of the New York commission merchants into a triumph in the Railroad Era as well. On the eve of the Civil War, the two New York railroads together carried nearly three times as much Western freight to tidewater as the Pennsylvania and more than twice that of the Baltimore & Ohio. Even so, we must return our attention to the Erie Canal, for the volume of western freight carried to the Hudson on that waterway was still greater than that of all four railroads combined.[33]

Just as the American clipper ship reached the pinnacle of its success after its doom had been sealed by the steamships of England, so the Erie Canal entered a golden age while the coming of the railroad foreshadowed its eventual decline. The creation of a through route from Albany to Buffalo by rail coincided with the progress of the enlargement program of the Erie Canal. The new Rochester aqueduct, for example, was completed in 1841 at a cost of $430,000. Seven arches of fifty-two-foot span rested on six piers and two abutments. The structure was now forty-five feet wide, and it could take both up and down traffic at the same time. At Lockport a new series of locks were constructed at a cost of $600,000. They were guarded by iron railings and broad platforms were built between each pair of locks, connected by successive flights of steps. Brightly lighted by night, the locks took on an appearance "like the ascent to a gigantic temple." The great thirty-one-span Richmond aqueduct at the Seneca River was not brought into use until 1856, but the Schoharie Creek aqueduct was completed in 1841, and the enlarged upper and lower aqueducts across the Mohawk were finished in 1842. The rebuilding of the canal proceeded slowly during the forties, but as it was completed

[33] *Ibid.,* p. 385.

it allowed the use of larger freighters and packet boats boasting new standards of comfort.

The Red Bird Line, managed by Hial Brockway of Brockport, introduced the *Rochester* and the *Empire* in 1843. They were cedar built, 100 feet long and 12 feet wide, and berthed 100 passengers. Packets such as the *Niagara, Sultana, Louisiana,* and *North America* were acclaimed all along the canal for their beauty, comfort, and style. "These commodious traveling palaces," noted a Rochester paper, "run full both ways. Capt. Dan Bromley came out of Utica the other day with 170 on board. . . . The old ditch can't be run off."[34] Captains such as Dan Bromley became great favorites and won affection in every canal port. They often received public praise such as that which appeared in a Lockport paper at the opening of the navigation season in 1845: "Capt. Bromley is on the canal of course; he would be very much missed if he was not. A noisy whig as he is, he makes a first rate Packet Captain. The Packets should do a good summer's business; for their owners and managers are indefatigable in deserving business."[35] Passenger fares moved steadily downward until in 1849 the fare from Buffalo to Schenectady was only $6.50 including board.[36] A year after a Buffalo editor had castigated the Tonawanda Railroad as a "rickety, jolting, breakneck road," he published this praise for packet travel:

The superior cheapness of the packets unquestionably is the principal inducement with some travelers to take that mode of conveyance; but so excellent are the accommodations now

[34] Rochester *Daily Democrat*, July 6, 1842.
[35] Niagara *Democrat*, April 24, 1844.
[36] Rochester *Daily Democrat*, October 4, 1841; Niagara *Democrat*, April 24, 1844; Buffalo *Daily Courier*, April 14, 1849. In 1842, passage could be had from Utica to Syracuse for $1.00, just half the fare of the railroad. Buffalo *Commercial Advertiser and Journal*, April 13, 1842.

offered by the packets, and so infinitely more attractive are they to all who travel merely for pleasure, or who wish to travel in the greatest ease and security, they would do a good business were their prices as high as charged on the railroads. The boats that ply between this city and Rochester and Syracuse and Utica, are comfortable and roomy as the cabin of a steamboat. . . . we can conceive of nothing more agreeable than floating tranquilly through beautiful country, such as the canal route has become, with ability to read, write, or talk as the inclination prompts, and with every thing at command that a good hotel can furnish.[37]

Tolls assessed on packet boats were lowered from 8¢ a mile in 1837 to 5¢ in 1841. Collections from packet tolls fell from a high of $41,116 in 1839 to $16,500 in 1847, although packet mileage on all the New York canals rose slightly from 405,050 in 1837 to 443,080 in 1847. Freighters, meanwhile, increased their mileage in the same decade from 5,556,950 to 11,733,250.[38]

Although the competition of the railroad cut heavily into passenger travel on the Erie Canal during the 1840s, nearly every type of canal boat increased in number. The greatest increases, of course, were in those which carried freight alone. A decade earlier half of the boats on the canal had either served as packets or carried passengers along with their freight, but by 1842 only one-fifth of them were equipped for passenger travel.[39] The number of canal boats in service on the New York canals doubled between 1843 and 1847. Of the 4,191 boats in service in 1847, only 62 were packets and 621 were line boats carrying freight and passengers. All the rest were

[37] Buffalo *Commercial Advertiser*, June 25, 1845.
[38] New York, *Senate Documents*, 71st Sess., II, Doc. 50, Statement 51, p. 191.
[39] *Hunt's Merchants, Magazine*, XI (August 1844), 138.

freighters. In the years between 1843 and 1847 the total
tonnage capacity increased from 117,453 to 279,260 and
98 percent of this increase came in the year 1847 alone.[40]
Now Seth Jones of Rochester, for example, began to turn
out giants 97 feet long and 17 feet wide, with a capacity
of 1,000 barrels of flour or 4,000 bushels of wheat. Forty-
two of these new freighters were launched at Rochester
in the spring of 1844, and one of them set a record in
April for the largest load carried on the canal until that
time, seventy-five and a half tons of flour and ashes. In
1849, the *Boston* set a new record at the Rochester weighlock with a load only 400 pounds short of ninety-one tons.
Some thirty-seven transportation companies were operating on the canals in the 1840s, and more than ten
thousand people were employed in the internal navigation
of the state.[41]

Meanwhile, the Canal Board lowered the tolls on
freight about 50 percent between 1832 and 1846, and by
the latter year, wheat, flour, beef, pork, and most other
agricultural products paid a toll of four mills per 1,000
pounds per mile.[42] A cargo of fifty tons of flour passing
from Buffalo to Albany paid a toll of $254 in 1832, $163
in 1834, and of $145 in 1846. This reduction of tolls, along
with the greater efficiency of larger boats, lowered the
cost of transportation. The average down-freight charge
per barrel of flour weighing 216 pounds was $1.00 in
1832; in 1846 it was 64¢. The average up-freight charge

[40] New York, *Senate Documents,* 71st Sess., II, Doc. 50, pp. 15-16.
The twelve heaviest laden boats of the Buffalo lines carried an average
of 65 tons down the canal and 60 tons up the canal in 1842.

[41] Buffalo *Courier,* December 17, 1845; *Hunt's Merchants' Magazine,*
VI (March 1842), 278.

[42] Rochester *Daily Democrat,* July 19, 1845. In 1832 these products
paid seven mills per 1,000 pounds per mile. Rochester *Daily Advertiser,*
March 14, 1833.

per hundred pounds was $1.00 in 1832; in 1846 it had dropped to 40¢.[43]

Vastly greater carrying capacity was needed on the Erie Canal in the 1840s and early 1850s as the full impact of Western settlement began to be felt in New York. The Old Northwest continued its rapid development and sent larger and larger surpluses to the East by water.[44] Moreover, these exports were expedited by the new waterways and railroads either being completed or under construction throughout the West. The dream of Washington, Gallatin, Clinton, and John Quincy Adams of a nation-wide system of internal improvements had moved far towards fulfillment. New Yorkers watched with keen interest, and often invested in the network of canals that wound through the mountains of Pennsylvania, connected the Ohio River to Lake Erie, and extended to Terre Haute, Indiana, on the Wabash River by 1849. A New York print noted that with the completion of the Wabash and Erie Canal, "the chain, by artificial water route, from New York through the Great West to New Orleans, will then be perfect in all its links."[45] Attempts were made to integrate Erie Canal boat lines with those of the Western waterways and to transform them into "tributaries" of the New York canals.[46]

Largely as a result of increasing Western production, the amount of wheat shipped east from Buffalo in the first two weeks of 1844 was only 25 percent less than

[43] New York, *Senate Documents*, 71st Sess., II, Doc. 50, p. 190.

[44] Kohlmeier, *The Old Northwest*, Chapter 3.

[45] New York *Evening Star*, April 2, 1835.

[46] Buffalo *Emporium and General Advertiser*, March 26, July 9, December 31, 1825; Rochester *Daily Advertiser*, May 15, 1833; Rochester *Daily Democrat*, March 7, 1835, April 12, 1843, July 30, December 31, 1845. In 1839, the Buffalo *Commercial Advertiser* of March 11 anticipated the day when the agricultural produce of ninety million people would be sent to New York via the western waterways and the Erie Canal.

that shipped in the entire season of 1834, a decade earlier. When the season of 1845 had shattered all previous records in tonnage, volume, or value, a Buffalo paper took note that canal business "keeps fully up to the expectations that have been formed on the effect of the western trade upon this great thoroughfare."[47] The tally of products entering the canal at Buffalo reported by this print totaled 1,330,000 bushels of wheat, 700,000 barrels of flour, 3,500,000 pounds each of wool and butter, and nearly 3,000,000 pounds each of lard and cheese. Western forests that year sent to the canal 20,000,000 feet of boards, more than 40,000 tons of staves, and almost 40,000 casks of ashes. To these figures must be added the Western goods entering the Erie Canal at Black Rock on the Niagara River and those reaching the Erie Canal at Syracuse by way of the Welland Canal, Lake Ontario, and the Oswego Canal. Moreover, New York itself, with its growing system of lateral canals, still contributed to canal commerce. Altogether the total traffic arriving at the Hudson in 1845 thus included nearly 2,000,000 bushels of wheat, 2,500,000 barrels of flour, 20,000,000 pounds of butter, and nearly 30,000,000 pounds of cheese. Forest products arriving at tidewater were swelled to include 237,000,000 feet of boards and 70,000 tons of staves.[48] Trade arriving at tidewater on the New York canals in 1845 reached a total tonnage of 1,204,000 valued at $45,452,361.

At the end of the decade a steady advance is seen in the volume of nearly every product arriving at tidewater on the New York canals. The long rows of figures in the statistical tables published by the auditors of the Canal Department only imperfectly impress upon our minds the

[47] Buffalo *Courier*, January 2, 1846.
[48] New York, *Senate Documents*, 69th Sess., II, Doc. 50, Statement 8.

immense quantities of goods moving through this commercial artery. Although being steadily widened, parts
of the channel which carried this commerce were still but
40 feet wide and 4 feet deep and employed the original
locks only 90 feet long and 15 feet wide. In 1849 the
volume of wheat carried to tidewater approached 3,000,000
bushels, and flour mounted to more than 3,250,000 barrels. With these went also 21,000,000 pounds of butter,
42,000,000 of cheese, and 8,500,000 pounds of bacon.
From the forest now came nearly 300,000,000 feet of
boards and 77,000 tons of staves. In all, 665,547 tons of
forest products were carried to tidewater in 1849, valued
at seven millions; 769,000 tons of agricultural products, at
thirty-eight millions; 44,286 tons of manufactured products, at four millions; 5,872 tons of merchandise, at half
a million dollars; and 95,000 tons of other articles, at more
than two millions. These products made up a total down-
canal tonnage of 1,580,072, valued at $52,375,521. Since
up-canal traffic moving west from the Hudson was largely
merchandise, its total tonnage was only 315,550 in 1849,
but its value was nearly $70,000,000.[49]

A final tally of canal commerce for the period under
study in this volume shows 2,491,497 tons carried to tidewater on all New York canals in 1853. Forest products
accounted for 1,343,903 tons; agricultural products, 921,321
tons; and manufactured goods, merchandise and other
articles reaching the Hudson totaled 226,273 tons. The
total valuation of these products was $74,443,061. Ton-
nage moved from tidewater reached 560,754 tons in 1853,
valued at $114,090,801.[50]

The earnings of the Erie Canal rose rapidly until 1847,

[49] New York, *Assembly Documents*, 73d Sess., VI, Doc. 140, Statement 9, pp. 104-106.
[50] *Ibid.*, 77th Sess., II, Doc. 65, pp. 7-10.

then declined until they reached their peak during the Civil War. The $687,976 collected in 1826, the year after completion, was almost exactly doubled in the $1,375,673 collected in 1835. In 1847, the high point of toll receipts before the Civil War was reached with collections of $3,333,347, and in 1853 they had declined to $2,833,970. When tolls were abolished completely in 1883 the Erie Canal had earned total revenues of $121,461,871.[51] By the latter year the cost of the construction and enlargement of the canal totaled nearly fifty millions and the cost of collection, superintendence and repairs amounted to nearly thirty millions. The Erie Canal had earned a handsome surplus over its cost, but its value can be judged in no such limited terms.[52]

The lateral canals in New York also contributed to the earnings of the Erie Canal, and the Champlain and Oswego canals proved to be profitable investments. Other laterals such as the Chenango, Genesee Valley, and Black River canals, however, were less successful. Built as they were when Western lands were more attractive than lands in New York and when they faced growing railroad competition, they yielded only fractions of their total cost.

But for those who operated the Erie Canal and the laterals, such sanguine calculations of its commerce and its tolls lay always in the future. If the commerce of the canal was to grow, if it was to maintain its hold on Western trade, or if it was to survive the competition of

[51] Whitford, *History of the Canal System*, II, 1064-68.

[52] Harvey H. Segal has calculated that the Erie Canal earned a surplus over costs, including interest, by 1826, but he believes its most important contribution "is the one most difficult to measure. By accelerating the growth of interregional trade between the northern Atlantic seaboard and the territory of the old northwest, the Erie Canal and its tributaries played a vital role in extending and integrating spatially separated markets." Segal, "Canals and Economic Development," in Carter Goodrich, ed., *Canals and American Economic Development*, pp. 240, 247.

the railroad, right and timely decisions needed to be made. To make matters more difficult still, they needed to be made by the ultimate owners of the New York canals, the people of the state. They were made by a people who enjoyed no such hindsight as the statistics of this chapter allow, but who, instead, arrived at their decisions through a process where all was subject to partisan purpose, the process of political debate.

IV. *Politics & Nationalism*

16

The "Forty Million Debt," 1835-1841

THE COMPLETION of the Erie Canal in 1825 by no means ended the political struggles over the fortunes of this successful waterway. For a period far beyond the scope of this volume, rival attitudes toward internal improvements and conflicts over canal patronage kept the canal embroiled in state and local politics. Samuel B. Ruggles, himself a leading figure in these contests, wrote in 1849 that the history of the Erie Canal since its completion "would constitute in good degree, the political history of the state."[1] Indeed, political controversy over the canal can be found in nearly every issue of leading newspapers from Buffalo to Albany, and in New York City as well.

Clinton's political future continued to be identified with the Erie Canal as he was reelected to the governorship in 1826. He enjoyed the acquiescence of the Bucktails who wanted the renewal of his pledge to Jackson for the presidency, and his support for a state road through the "southern tier" gave him the election. But anti-Clintonians dominated the legislature and representatives from the canal counties killed the bill for the state road Clinton had backed.

Just as New York had exercised a critical influence in the national election of 1824, so all expected the Empire

State to hold the key to the coming contest between Adams and Jackson in 1828. Van Buren was firmly convinced in 1827 that Clinton aspired to the presidency himself, although he was assured that Clinton was willing to take the second place on the ticket with Jackson.[2] Clinton's name was actually placed in nomination in New York and his correspondence became increasingly more national. He gave patient and detailed attention to the requests for canal information that flooded in from other states. He journeyed to turn the first spadeful of earth for the Ohio canals in 1825 and induced John Jacob Astor to loan a million dollars for their construction. Returning from Ohio by way of Pennsylvania, he warmed to effusive plaudits offered him everywhere as New York's great canal builder. But Clinton's chances for a place on the national ticket in 1828 were, in cold reality, hopeless. As the election approached, he disavowed his candidacy and gave his support to Jackson. The outcome of that election Clinton was never to know for he was suddenly stricken and died in February of 1828.

Clinton died with a judgment of $6,000 against his estate which only the auction of his property could meet. In recognition of his years of service for the canal without compensation, the legislature granted $10,000 to his wife and four minor children who were otherwise without support. Clinton's unexpected death ended the era of the

[1] Samuel B. Ruggles, *Vindication in 1849 of the Canal Policy of the State of New York* . . . (Rochester, 1849), p. 4. See Lee Benson for a concept of voting cycles in New York history in which the period 1832-1853 shows "comparatively little change" in most counties and "the relative strength of parties remains fairly constant." Benson argues that "traditional claims about New York voting behavior" erred in part because of "the time-honored but fallacious assumption concerning the impact of the Erie Canal on rural prosperity in central and western New York. . . ." Benson, *Concept of Jacksonian Democracy*, pp. 125-31, 150.

[2] Van Buren to Thomas Ritchie, January 13, 1827, Van Buren to C. P. Van Ness, February 22, 1827, Martin Van Buren Papers, LC.

canal as a political hobby and speeded the reorientation of New York politics around the new issues of Jacksonian democracy.

After the death of Clinton, the Democratic banner of the Albany Regency flew over the state for a decade. Testimony to the nature and power of this political clique is found in the first report of a correspondent for the New York *Commercial Advertiser* from Albany. Newly arrived and knowing not a soul in the legislature, he soon discovered "a secret superintending spirit . . . called here the Albany Regency—consisting of a small squad that are said to meet, and consult, and determine, for or against such measures, as they conceive will help to strengthen their power."[3] Van Buren, Marcy, and other Regency leaders controlled the state and, from their offices, operated the canals. But absolute as was their power, their canal policies were stated with such ambivalence that they furnished substance for unending editorial skirmishing in the party presses and created the divisions over internal improvements which were to wrack the Democratic Party with dissension in the 1840s.

As Van Buren assumed the governor's chair in 1829, his recommendations on canals called for "judicious" use of state credit for their expansion in such ambiguous fashion as to be reminiscent of his speeches on the tariff. "The Delphic Oracle never spoke more enigmatically," commented Jabez Hammond.[4] When Van Buren resigned shortly to join Jackson's cabinet, his successor, Enos Throop, was almost equally noncommittal. Yet the Regency exulted with their Whig opponents at the growth of trade and tolls upon the Erie Canal. Regency politicians serving as commissioners of the Canal Fund husbanded the revenues entrusted to their care, sought to

[3] New York *Commercial Advertiser*, March 31, 1835.
[4] Hammond, *Political Parties*, II, 294.

make advantageous investments for the Canal Fund, and used their financial power for the economic development of the state.[5] They yielded, albeit reluctantly, to the demands for the lateral canals; during their sway the Chenango, Cayuga and Seneca, Oswego, Black River, Genesee Valley, and Crooked Lake canals were all inaugurated. Even Michael Hoffman, a Regency leader soon to be charged with the bitterest enmity to the Erie Canal, wrote in 1826 that the completion of the Erie and Champlain canals was a pledge that the system should be extended for the equal accommodation of all: "To stop where we are will be a robbery of those who have aided and have not yet been served."[6]

More important still, the enlargement of the Erie Canal was begun under Regency auspices. The Democratic editor of the Rochester *Daily Advertiser,* Henry O'Reilly, wrote the memorial sent by the Rochester canal committee which was the first to petition the legislature for rebuilding the Erie Canal.[7] It was a Regency-dominated legislature which enacted in 1835, after little debate, the law bearing the cautious title, "An act in relation to the Erie Canal," which authorized the enlargement of the canal and construction of double locks "as soon as the canal board may be of opinion that the public interest requires such improvement." The following year, in 1836, Governor Marcy recommended to the legislature the completion of the enlargement "at the earliest practicable period," and contracts were let for double locks along the eastern section and for enlargement of the first level west of Albany.

A spirited controversy arose over the best dimensions

[5] Miller, *Enterprise of a Free People,* pp. 115-22, 137.
[6] Hoffman to H. I. Redfield, July 31, 1826, William L. Marcy Papers, LC.
[7] MS, Henry O'Reilly Papers, NYHS.

for the new canal at the conclusion of which the Canal Board, composed entirely of Democratic officers, settled upon a width of 70 feet and a depth of 7 feet. Such a canal, it was confidently believed, would allow the use of boats which would carry three times the volume of those currently in use, and result in halving the cost of transportation. In 1838, with only $600,000 expended on the enlargement, Governor Marcy made an even stronger plea to the legislature that "the best interests of the State appeal to you with great earnestness to provide for the early completion of this important improvement."

But the degree of sincerity in these acts of Regency canal building remained an open question during years of acrimonious debate. The Whigs in New York saw themselves as the true inheritors of the mantle of De Witt Clinton, and on every serviceable occasion they cast the Democrats as reluctant advocates of a program they could not defeat. This view gained credence from outspoken leaders of the Democracy whose attitudes toward state expenditures or indebtedness for canal building were essentially negative. In 1827 Silas Wright, then chairman of the canal committee in the senate, made his celebrated report minimizing anticipated canal revenues and opposing the extension of the New York canal system without taxation to pay the costs of construction. Wright was not opposed to internal improvements, but it became a cardinal principle of Regency policy that further expenditures for canals must be made only out of the surplus revenues of the canals or by taxation.[8]

At bottom Regency canal policy reflected the Jeffer-

[8] John Arthur Garraty, *Silas Wright* (New York, 1949), p. 48. Analyzing the election of 1844 in New York, Lee Benson concludes that differences between Democrats and Whigs "were relatively narrow in scope," and that socioeconomic issues did not influence voting behavior as much as ethnocultural and religious conflicts and localistic factors. Benson, *Concept of Jacksonian Democracy*, pp. 292-93.

sonian-Jacksonian conscience for the preservation of small government and fear of public debt, as well as many of the *laissez faire* ideas of the European classical economists. The latter influence, said Ruggles, led them to believe that "Nature is to be let alone—especially by Government; that without its aid all things will find their level, Canals with everything else."[9] Private enterprise, minimal government, and decentralized agrarian society became essential tenets of their philosophy. They reflected the spirit, if not the politics, of Jackson's famous Maysville Road veto of 1829. One of the most prominent Regency canal commissioners, Samuel Young, first supported the construction of the Erie Canal by the state as a venture too great for individual enterprise but then became one of the most austere expositors of *laissez faire* philosophy. He served on the commission from 1816 until 1839 and argued with a voice increasingly shrill that state indebtedness for internal improvements was but a tax on posterity. Some Jacksonians in New York, among them William Cullen Bryant of the New York *Evening Post*, Gerrit Smith, and even for a time Henry O'Reilly, urged the sale of the New York canals to private business, so fearful were they of the corrupting influence of public internal improvements. Gerrit Smith's broadside, *Keep Government Within Its Limits*, attacked ownership of the New York canals by the state with the warning: "Better that she should give them away, if, by so doing, her government would thereafter be confined to its appropriate duties. . . ."[10] The *Evening Post* put it still more flatly in 1841: "Legislation has nothing to do with building rail roads and canals."[11]

With the rise of the Whigs in New York, the Regency

[9] Ruggles, *Vindication*, p. 6.
[10] Broadside, April 4, 1842, Henry O'Reilly Papers, RPL.
[11] New York *Evening Post*, March 8, 1841.

faced an opposition whose canal policy drew upon a more nationalistic philosophy and reflected their party's stress on internal improvements. The Whigs harked back to Federalist concepts of the powers of government and endorsed the "American System" of Henry Clay. They welcomed the opportunity to portray themselves as the exclusive friends of the Erie Canal, much as the Clintonians had done a decade earlier. There were votes and endless log-rolling possibilities in canals and other internal improvements, a point not lost on Whig leaders such as Thurlow Weed who voted for almost every canal proposal while he was a member of the legislature and continued to support the canals when he became his party's most influential editor.[12] It was the Whigs who dwelt upon the growth of the Empire State and the West, anticipated the trade that would seek an Eastern market, kept jealous watch on the projects of rival states, and made free use of the credit of the state to expand the New York canal system. All that was required was that canal revenues pay the interest on the necessary loans, gradually reduce the principal, and meet the costs of maintenance and repairs. "The western trade is a subject of fair competition," said the editor of the Whig New York *Daily Advertiser* in 1835, "and if we have the means of securing it, and neglect to do so, we have only to blame ourselves."[13] Even as the Regency-sponsored Erie enlargement bill passed the assembly and went to the senate, that print warned that the views of the Regency were "too narrow to embrace the large and liberal plans that are now in progress by the people."[14]

The Whig victories in the elections of 1837, which swept their party into control of the New York legislature,

12 Van Deusen, *Thurlow Weed*, pp. 32, 116-17.
13 New York *Daily Advertiser*, January 8, 1835.
14 *Ibid.*, May 7, 1835.

presented the Whigs with an opportunity to give full scope to these large and liberal plans. Their challenge to the Regency canal program was made in March of 1838 with the masterful report of Samuel B. Ruggles, now chairman of the Committee of Ways and Means in the assembly. Ruggles was by temperament an optimist and a projector, ebullient in his dreams of national growth through internal improvements. It was typical of the man that he should propose a bold, and even extravagant, program of canal and railroad construction, in the midst of the depression following the panic of 1837. He had laid out Union Square in New York and owned many lots around it. He was a lobbyist for the New York and Erie Railroad and stood on the threshhold of a career of canal and railroad building.

The Ruggles report gave a glowing account of Western trade and calculated the rising tolls certain to be poured into the coffers of the state from the Erie Canal. Ruggles alluded to the struggle going on "between the friends of a vigorous system of internal improvements, and those who deny its expediency or safety." Although the rate of tolls had been reduced by one-third since 1833, the annual revenue had reached nearly one and a half millions in 1835, and in 1836 totaled enough to redeem the entire canal debt. Calculating that a revenue of half a million dollars would sustain the interest on a debt of ten millions and anticipating the increase of tolls to three millions annually after the canal was enlarged, Ruggles estimated that the state might safely borrow four millions each year for ten years to be expended on canals and railroads. Such a debt, he predicted, could be redeemed in 1865. Although Ruggles and his committee disclaimed any recommendation that this amount should actually be borrowed and spent upon the public works, his report was made out by his opponents to advocate a "Forty Million Debt."

The Ruggles report was immediately acclaimed by the Whig press as authentic Whig doctrine. The New York *American* likened it to the reports of Gouverneur Morris and became almost lyrical as it portrayed the "beneficent career" of New York in developing the West: "we have a wilderness blossoming like the rose, cities, towns, and villages, a comparatively dense population, the industry that enriches, and the arts that adorn life, exemption from debt, and an overflowing revenue—all under the aegis of freedom and law, and all due to the construction of the Erie Canal."[15] But nowhere were such paeans more popular than in western New York.

Western New York had been alive with meetings and demands for more rapid progress on the enlargement of the Erie Canal since 1835. A visiting correspondent from New York City reported that that region had never been more united on any subject.[16] The canal movement here was nonpartisan. The Democratic editor in Rochester, Henry O'Reilly, placed his canal enthusiasms ahead of his party's doctrines and proposed a plan for "an immediate enlargement" of the Erie Canal by means of a "Loan anticipating Canal Revenue." A Rochester canal meeting endorsed his proposal and called for a state convention to support it. Thus the Western Canal Convention met in Rochester in 1837 with delegates from fourteen counties and petitioned the legislature to speed the enlargement by loans based upon "the faith of the Canal Revenue."[17] Nonpartisan as the convention was, the political pressures to be exerted by its members were bluntly stated. "Let the voice go forth from this convention," spoke Seth C. Hawley of Erie County to the delegates,

---

[15] Quoted in Albany *Evening Journal*, March 22, 1838.

[16] New York *Daily Express*, March 14, 1838.

[17] *Proceedings of the Convention upon the subject of an immediate enlargement of the Erie Canal; held at the Court-House in Rochester on the 18th and 19th days of January, 1837* (Buffalo, 1837).

"that we will stand by those, and those alone, who will perform this work in the shortest time, and be their backers."

With this and a host of other appeals before it, and the Ruggles report at hand, the legislature of 1838 enacted perhaps the most critical measure in the history of the Erie Canal enlargement. The bill was entitled "An act for the more speedy enlargement of the Erie Canal," and it directed that construction be speeded to completion within only five years. It appropriated four millions to be borrowed, not on the credit of the canal revenue as the Western Canal Convention had proposed, but on the credit of the state.[18] Aided by this loan, the canal commissioners were directed to put under contract immediately work totaling some eight millions.

The enactment of the enlargement law of 1838 was the result of a fortuitous combination of circumstances. Ruggles' optimistic calculations as to future revenues took some of the sting from the debt to be incurred. Pressure from western New York, what the Rochester *Daily Advertiser* called "the imperious voice of the people," prodded the lawmakers.[19] Governor Marcy was committed to a vigorous prosecution of the enlargement and the able Democratic Canal Commissioner, William C. Bouck, was for it. The chairman of the canal committee in the assembly was George W. Patterson of Livingston County who worked for the bill because his pet, the Genesee Valley Canal, was also provided for. And on the canal committee as well was S. F. Allen, a Whig from Black

---

[18] O'Reilly later wrote that this was a disastrous departure from the "Rochester plan" based on the credit of the canal revenues. He believed that the creation of a state debt allowed the "Lobby" to squander funds on the lateral canals which "proved a dead-weight on the Erie Canal" and led to the "Stop & pay" policy of 1841. MS, Henry O'Reilly Papers, NYHS.

[19] Rochester *Daily Advertiser*, March 26, 1838.

Rock, who wrote later, "I had the thing pretty much my own way with the Erie Canal."[20] In spite of "strong doubts existing in the minds of many sensible men in all parts of the State," the measure was passed, said Allen, "by a harmonious intercourse, & a full understanding between the right parties, . . . so happily arranged, that only three dissentient voices were heard" in the assembly. In the senate enough influential Democrats voted with the Whigs to pass the bill, and Governor Marcy signed it into law.

But in the newspaper wars over the New York canals, the Whigs were never to let the Regency forget that only Democratic votes had opposed the measure. The Regency and their followers, for their part, were never to desist from their charge that here was the opening of a Pandora's box of troubles with construction financed by a state debt rather than from the surplus revenues of the canals. The enlargement of the Erie Canal was by this act thrust into the political cauldron, there to boil for a quarter of a century until the work was done in 1862. Sufficient to the day for the Whigs in the spring of 1838 was the declaration of Thurlow Weed's Albany *Evening Journal* that "a new impulse has been given to the cause of Internal Improvement—an impulse quickened and invigorated by the triumphant Report of Mr. RUGGLES."[21]

The events of the spring were prelude to the fall elections which made William Henry Seward the first Whig governor of New York, carried Marcy to defeat, and left only the senate under Regency control. The root of this victory lay in the impact of the deepening depression in New York, but the campaign debates turned also on the issue of the enlargement of the Erie Canal.

[20] S. F. Allen to O'Reilly, December 30, 1840, Henry O'Reilly Papers, NYHS.
[21] Albany *Evening Journal*, April 19, 1838.

The Whig Young Men's Convention had met at Utica in July, where they hailed "with gladness and hope" the work of the legislature in supporting internal improvements and resolved that "the public interest requires an early completion of the Erie Canal." In October the Whig majority in the legislature accused the Democrats of "ABSOLUTE HOSTILITY" to the cause of internal improvements and charged the Regency with making canal expenditures "a mighty engine of favoritism and patronage." Weed's *Journal* focused censure upon Marcy's land speculation at Lockport and Oswego and alleged that "a band of Regency speculators" had used the canal to build a rival to the village of Lockport.[22]

In defense, the Democracy reminded the electorate that they had collected fifteen millions in tolls since the completion of the canals "without the loss of a single dollar," and that Marcy himself had served as comptroller responsible for collecting the tolls. They pointed to their own expenditures, made or authorized, of twenty-seven millions on seven canals, and to Seward's embarrassing vote against the Chenango Canal when he was in the senate.[23] The Democratic Albany *Argus* was quick with counterthrust to make out Seward as "the agent of the Holland Land Co. speculators" because he had been appointed to adjudicate land titles on the Holland Purchase in Chautauqua County.[24] On election day the Whig press called "Canal Men! Ahoy" to keep the canallers mindful of "REGENCY PERSECUTION OF SAILORS AND BOATMEN."[25] But Marcy complained that "every man on board of a . . . canal boat is advised [by the Whigs] that his place of residence is where the boat lies."[26]

[22] *Ibid.,* October 27, 1838.
[23] Albany *Argus,* October 12, 1838.
[24] *Ibid.,* November 16, 1838.
[25] Albany *Evening Journal,* November 5, 8, 1838.

When the canal issue and a complex of other causes had carried the Whigs to victory, Seward prepared to implement the Ruggles report. The new governor should, said Ruggles, "march boldly & fearlessly forward like his great prototype & exemplar DeWitt Clinton, and manfully create the public opinion which is to sustain him."[27] Seward marched fearlessly indeed. His first message to the legislature urged the speedy enlargement of the Erie Canal, the construction of the lateral canals, aid to railroads, and the creation of a new "board of internal improvements." He paid lavish tribute to Clinton and recommended that a monument be raised to his memory. All of this while the depression worsened in the state. The defeated Marcy chided that the message "out clinton's Clinton," and G. A. Worth, puckish friend to the Regency, wrote that the message was "another history *of the creation!*"[28] A critic from Herkimer thought that Seward's program should be called "eternal improvements." The *Argus* once more declared its support for a "liberal" system of internal improvements, but shrank at the prospect of "engaging at once in every thing that the wit of man ever suggested."[29]

Seward's program was predicated upon the growth of the West, the tolls to be collected from Western trade, and his confident conviction that canals and railroads built on borrowed money would redeem themselves without requiring recourse to taxation. The vision was broad. The spirit was liberal. The growth of the West was certain. But the calculations of future trade were also

---

[26] Marcy to P. M. Wetmore, November 7, 1838, William L. Marcy Papers, LC.

[27] Ruggles to William Henry Seward, December 17, 1838, Samuel B. Ruggles Papers, LC.

[28] Marcy to P. M. Wetmore, Worth to Marcy, January 21, 1839, William L. Marcy Papers, LC.

[29] Albany *Argus,* January 7, 1839.

conjectural, the means were costly, and the prospect of Western growth was clouded by hard times. So evenly are these points in balance that the reader who follows the partisan debate in the Whig and Democratic presses of the time is tempted to agree always with the argument read last. In the final weighing, however, the Whig program was too extravagant for the times. The verdict goes to the Democratic opposition as it did when the supporters of the Seward program were roundly defeated in the election of 1841. After this defeat the Democrats regained control of the state and brought to a halt the internal improvements so bravely launched by Seward in 1839.

In this long debate several questions were continually, almost monotonously, at issue. First was the technical question of the physical necessity for the expansion of the New York canal system. That double locks on the Erie Canal should be constructed all agreed, but that traffic would require an enlarged channel or enlarged locks throughout was strongly contested. Neither the slight increase in the number of lockages at Alexander's Lock between 1835 and 1840, nor the increase in the number of arrivals and clearances at Albany and Troy during these years seemed to justify a rush program of construction.[30] Since 30,000 fewer tons arrived at tidewater by canal in 1840 than in 1835, it is understandable that many should be skeptical of the notion that the canal would be unable to accommodate the future demands placed upon it.

Moreover, the change from the predominance of forest products to agricultural products in canal trade that took place during the 1830s reinforced the view that enlargement was unnecessary throughout. The 26 percent de-

[30] *Ibid.* (s.w.), February 2, May 7, 1841.

crease in forest products arriving at tidewater between 1835 and 1839 was accompanied by an increase of only 12 percent in all other products. Since the products of the forest decreased faster than those of agriculture increased, it was believed that down freight would at best remain constant or take some thirty to sixty years before it showed significant increase.[31]

It proved exceedingly difficult to calculate the rate at which Western trade would grow, the amounts of Western trade that would be siphoned off by rival routes to the Atlantic, or the tolls which might be collected. While the canal might carry emigrants to the Great Lakes and the West beyond, weather, credit, machinery, and markets must determine the period to elapse before surplus agricultural products could flow towards the Atlantic. Meanwhile other states pushed forward to tap the Western trade and New York itself was busily aiding the New York and Erie Railroad to create a rival to the Erie Canal. Little wonder, then, that the speculations of Seward and Ruggles were highly vulnerable to the barbs of the *Argus* when its editor, Edwin Croswell, parodied their calculations: "There are so many miles of territory in certain western states, which it is *supposed* will seek a market through the Erie Canal, for their surplus products. It is *estimated* that so many square miles will furnish so many bushels of wheat, and corn or what not, and of so much amount, it is *estimated* that so many bushels will go to market through the Erie Canal, and pay so much toll to this state."[32] By such multiplication, the Whig *Morning Courier and New York Enquirer* estimated future canal tolls sufficient to support a debt of 100 millions.[33] Experience did not bear out even Ruggles' predictions for the

[31] *Ibid.*, October 3, 7, 1839.
[32] *Ibid* (s.w.), June 21, 1838.
[33] *Ibid.*, August 20, 1839.

first years after the publication of his famous report. Where he had calculated a surplus at the close of the season of 1840 of nearly two millions, there was not a dollar of surplus, and a debt of fifteen millions for internal improvements remained to be met.

The most immediate problem in the debate over the Seward program hinged on the ability of the state to carry it out in the midst of a financial depression. Ruggles and Seward remained blithely confident that the revenues from the public works would "continue to reimburse the principal and the interest of such monies as may be required for their further extension."[34] The commissioners of the Canal Fund, however, were faced with the constant problem of maintaining specie payments, preserving the credit of the state in the London money markets, and selling stock that had fallen to 22 percent below par by 1839.[35] In October of that year, the *Argus* reported New York stocks "a perfect drug on the foreign markets."[36]

Yet the strength of the Whig arguments lay in their view of economic growth and in a broader concept than the Jacksonians of the profitability of the canals to the state. In this they were closer to the economic thought of our own day. The Seward program of deficit financing for public works in a time of depression finds a ready parallel in the New Deal policies of the 1930s. The Whigs were real innovators and saw the important role that government must play in the formation of the "social overhead capital" which W. W. Rostow today has described as one of the preconditions for the "take-off" stage of economic growth.[37] Recent economic history has gone

[34] Ruggles to Wynham Roberts, January 21, 1839, Samuel B. Ruggles Papers, LC.

[35] Miller, *Enterprise of a Free People*, pp. 217-27.

[36] Albany *Argus*, October 1, 31, 1839.

[37] W. W. Rostow, *The Stages of Economic Growth; a Non-Communist Manifesto* (Cambridge, 1960), pp. 24-25.

far beyond the financial criterion in judging the profitability of the canals to the state set forth by Silas Wright
in 1827. By stimulating commercial agriculture, providing
the basis for cities, and connecting the Atlantic seaboard
with the Old Northwest, the Erie Canal, according to
Harvey S. Segal, helped to promote a rapid rate of growth
in the overall economy of New York.[38]

The Whigs of Seward's time were less scholarly in
their analysis of economic change, but they believed
fervently in the benefits to be derived from New York
canals. They found ample security for the debts they
would create in the increase in the assessed valuation of
the property of the state (from 150 millions to 200
millions between 1833 and 1841) and took a long-range
view of profit and loss. As the Albany *Evening Journal*
put it in 1839:

> The Erie Canal, by developing and increasing our resources,
> coined money for the payment of its construction. And having
> thus paid for itself, the Canal is constantly enriching the
> People and the State.
>
> That the Canals may be 'profitless,' in many instances,
> to those who construct them, we admit. But that the spirit
> of Improvements should, for this reason, be repressed, we
> deny. These works greatly benefit the community. The lateral
> Canals of our own State have been 'profitless' to the Treasury,
> but they have enriched the portions of the State through
> which they pass, and greatly enhance the wealth and blessings
> of the People for whose use and accommodation they were
> constructed.[39]

The legislature of 1839 took up the grandiose recommendations of Seward's message in the face of these
imponderables. Henry O'Reilly, leading the canal forces

[38] Segal, "Canals and Economic Development," p. 247.
[39] Albany *Evening Journal,* December 30, 1839.

of western New York, was soon warned that "a desperate effort will be made to arrest the enlargement, during the present session . . . unless the friends of the measure shall consent to tack to it a host of wild and impracticable undertakings. . . ."[40] Notwithstanding a parting shot from the Regency comptroller showing that the canal revenues would never sustain the Ruggles estimates, the Whigs in the assembly pushed through bills appropriating five millions to the Erie Canal and ten other works of internal improvement. But the Regency-dominated senate could still block any major appropriation. A battle royal over the enlargement of the canal ensued. A bill was brought into the senate to build a ship canal around the falls of Niagara, which William A. Mosely advised O'Reilly was "of no moment save as it is one of the many antagonist projects of the Erie Canal Enlargement."[41] The Whigs produced a report in the senate showing the ability of the canal tolls to support a debt of forty-five millions, and the Democrats countered with a report which held that the annual tolls of three millions anticipated by the Whigs from the completed enlargement in 1846 would not actually be realized until forty years later.

For the first time it became clear that the twelve millions estimated by the Regency Canal Board in 1835 for the enlargement was too low by half. The consequence was a Democratic bill to reduce the dimensions of

[40] M. Cadwallader to O'Reilly, January 6, 1839, Henry O'Reilly Papers, NYHS.

[41] Mosely to O'Reilly, April 12, 1839, Henry O'Reilly Papers, NYHS. Levi Chatfield, Democratic assemblyman from Otsego, brought in a bill to limit the Erie enlargement to that part of the canal east of Utica. This led "Hercules" of Lockport to propose that if such was to be done, the canal should be sold to a joint-stock company, owned in western New York. The Niagara *Courier*, March 13, 1839; Lockport *Democrat and Balance*, March 13, 1839.

the enlargement to 60 feet in width and 6 feet in depth, which in turn brought protest meetings in western New York. Canal meetings were held in Buffalo, Rochester, Palmyra, and Lockport, the latter presided over by Jesse Hawley himself.[42] The upshot of it all was the defeat of the Democratic bill to reduce the size of the canal, but the Whig appropriations went down as well.

To dramatize their endorsement of the Ruggles report, the Whigs appointed Ruggles to the Canal Board. But the board, dominated by Democrats, promptly made him an acting commissioner and assigned him to the western section of the Erie Canal and the Genesee Valley Canal. That post, chuckled Marcy, would cause Ruggles "to have the *bitter* as well as the *sweet* of office."[43] As the session of 1839 came to a close, the Whigs had ridden hard for the enlargement of the Erie Canal and for the Seward program. "The fate of the Whig party, so far as the Legislature is concerned," reported a Whig print in New York, "hangs on its sincere and determined devotion to the great Clinton policy of internal improvement. . . ."[44] The Regency, on the other hand, had succeeded in checking a program in which, to use the words of the *Argus*, "extravagance was dignified by the name of public spirit, and visionary theories were called statesmanship."[45]

As the parties of New York gathered forces for the fall

[42] The meeting at Rochester resolved that the enlargement "should be accomplished, and speedily accomplished, be the expense what it may" and declared that "differing much as we may do respecting political measures and political men, we will present a united front in favor of that essential branch of Internal Improvement. . . ." *Internal Improvement; Enlargement of the Erie Canal; Meeting at Rochester* [March 23, 1839], Broadside, Henry O'Reilly Papers, NYHS.

[43] Marcy to P. M. Wetmore, March 7, 1839, William L. Marcy Papers, LC.

[44] New York *Evening Star*, May 1, 1839.

[45] Albany *Argus*, February 5, 1839.

campaign of 1839 and the Whigs saw a prospect of adding the senate to their domains of the assembly and the governorship, the canal was placed once more in the stakes. In Whig journals, the Democracy had demonstrated beyond all doubt its hostility to the enlargement and the Whigs alone remained its friends. They ingeniously answered the charge of extravagant indebtedness with the countercharge that they were only completing improvements begun by the Regency at deceitfully low estimates. The *Evening Journal* lamented the "hoarse raven cry of the 'Forty Million Debt'" as want of faith in the state, the West, and the future.[46] Whig logic made the canals and railroads of New York the foundation of the Empire State. "He who makes war upon them, makes war upon her prosperity and the happiness of her people," warned the *Evening Journal* on the eve of the election.[47] With a Democratic victory would come, as surely as night followed day, ruin, bankruptcy, and the decline of the state.

At his masthead in the *Argus*, Edwin Croswell put the slogan, "For a Prudent and Impartial System of Internal Improvement, Against a 40,000,000 State Debt." Day after day the Democratic presses, on and off the canal, deplored the reckless building program of the Whigs and saw ruin and bankruptcy equally certain in their victory. With the credit of the state far below par, with lateral canals which could not support themselves, and with workers being paid in uncurrent funds, the Democrats found it the sheerest madness to borrow, spend, and tax. When the votes were counted, the Whigs had won control of the state. For the first time since 1818 the Democrats were without a majority in the senate. As always, the victory was compound. Marcy

[46] Albany *Evening Journal*, April 20, 1839.
[47] *Ibid.*, October 25, 1839.

attributed the Democratic defeat to the issue of small bills in New York. But the *Courier and Enquirer* in New York used the victory to cement the alliance of the Whigs with the fortunes of the Erie Canal: "*The whig party is now identified with the great cause of improvement, and with it must stand or fall.*"[48]

Seward's annual message of 1840 displayed, said Marcy, "the enthusiasm of a votary and the eloquence of a patriot" on the subject of internal improvements, though Marcy judged that "our little *Icarus* has not flown so high as he did last year."[49] The new regime took advantage of its power in the senate for the wholesale removal of the Democratic canal commissioners, including Samuel Young and William C. Bouck, and appointed Whigs to their places. One of the new appointees was Simon Newton Dexter whom we first met as president of the Erie Navigation Company in 1819. The new Canal Board plunged ahead with plans to finish the enlargement within five years. Against dogged Democratic opposition, the legislature appropriated two and a half millions more to the enlargement and four millions to the lateral canals and railroad companies. This raised to seven and a half millions the amount spent or appropriated for the enlargement of the canal by 1840. Party lines and canal pressures were mixed in this as in every appropriation that aided the New York canals. Abijah Mann, Regency senator from Syracuse, led the Democratic opposition while Jesse Hawley, life-long Democrat of Rochester and Lockport, petitioned the legislature to maintain the 70- by 7-foot dimensions of the enlargement agreed upon in 1836.[50]

[48] Quoted in Albany *Argus,* November 21, 1839.

[49] Marcy to P. M. Wetmore, January 9, 1840, William L. Marcy Papers, LC.

[50] Jesse Hawley to the Honorable the Legislature of the State of New York, January 11, 1840, Henry O'Reilly Papers, NYHS. See also Jesse Hawley, *An Essay on the Enlargement of the Erie Canal . . .* (Lockport, 1840).

Much had been accomplished on the enlargement of the Erie Canal after nearly five years of labor under both Democratic and Whig administrations. Portions of new canal were opened to use on the West Troy level and at Schenectady in April of 1840. The new upper and lower aqueducts on the Mohawk and the new aqueduct over Schoharie Creek were advanced sufficiently that their completion was expected within another year. The line between Amsterdam and Sprakers Basin was being dug and work had begun at Little Falls. The arches of the new Rochester aqueduct were closed and the parapet walls nearly completed. At the five-lock combine at Lockport the lockpits were in and the walls of the lower lock had risen with three courses of stone. A new dam was in to deepen Tonawanda Creek. Alfred Barrett, the Democratic engineer in charge of the work at Lockport, worried that the appropriation for 1840 had not been larger so as "to weaken the inducement for stopping the Enlargement west of Montezuma."[51]

When Seward's term expired in 1840, the Regency sought to parry his strength on the canal issue by the selection of William C. Bouck, the ablest canal commissioner of their party, to oppose him in his bid for reelection. Bouck had been a hard-working farmer in Schoharie County and for nineteen years had served as an acting canal commissioner. He had supervised construction on the original Erie Canal, the Erie enlargement, and the lateral canals, winning the respect and the affection of the engineers. His old Dutch wagon and white horse had become a familiar sight on the canals and from his trunk some eight millions had been dispensed to contractors without the slightest damage to his reputation for honesty.

[51] Barrett to William C. Bouck, May 20, 1840, William C. Bouck Papers, Cornell University Library.

What was more he had been a staunch advocate of the enlargement and had voted in the Canal Board for the largest dimensions, 80 by 8 feet. His removal from office by the Whigs during the preceding spring lent him a touch of martyrdom (as a similar removal had done for Clinton in 1824), and, most important of all for Democratic orthodoxy, Bouck had signed the reports of the Canal Board declaring that the enlargement should proceed only out of the surplus canal revenues.

Unhappily for Bouck, his challenge to Seward and the "Forty Million Debt" was made in a year of national victory for the Whigs, when the Log Cabin campaign of Harrison and Tyler swept Van Buren out of office. In New York, the Democrats assailed Seward's spending which had already cost six millions and authorized in addition the expenditure of five millions more to "carry a railroad or canal to every man's door."[52] They did not allow it to be forgotten that Bouck had sought to protect the wives and children of laborers on the canal by personally seeing to it that money paid to contractors went to the laborers with a minimum of delay. And they nearly won. Seward and the "Forty Million Debt" were sustained, but this time by a margin of only 5,000 votes. Bouck carried four canal counties and Seward badly trailed the Whig vote for Harrison in the state. The Whig majority in the assembly was cut to the slim margin of four.

Once more the Whigs prepared to press forward with a new enlargement appropriation for 1841. In western New York some Whigs still hoped for bipartisan cooperation on the canal issue. S. F. Allen, a Whig of Black Rock, assured Democrat O'Reilly in Rochester that he was "certain that on a subject of such vital interest to the

52 Albany *Argus* (s.w.), September 18, 22, 1840.

welfare of our State, there can be no *real* political question connected with it, & if it be entangled with politics on either side, it will be only incidental, & temporary."[53] Despite such sanguine predictions, the decade of the 1840s saw the most critical embroilment of the canal in the politics of the state in its long and troubled history.

With a tiger by the tail, Seward showed increasing dismay over the alarming cost of the enlargement, but he did not flinch at the prospect of going on to its completion. He proposed a somewhat delayed timetable of construction which would complete the portion of the canal between Albany and Rome in 1843, that between Rome and Rochester by 1845, and the remainder, from Rochester to Buffalo, in 1847. The legislature, like its predecessor, supported his program with an appropriation of nearly four millions, almost three millions of which were for the enlargement of the Erie Canal.

But this too was enacted over the continued opposition of the Regency. "Most of the other phantoms of the great year of phantoms, 1836, are gone, but this phantom of the enlargement of the Erie Canal walks most perseveringly yet," chided the New York *Evening Post* as it reported on the Seward program.[54] Democratic opposition in the legislature sought to limit the enlargement at least to the portion east of Syracuse, which left western New Yorkers fuming at the prospect of the increasing rivalry

[53] Allen to O'Reilly, December 30, 1840, Henry O'Reilly Papers, NYHS. The following spring, S. G. Andrews wrote from the senate chamber to O'Reilly that "Western New York has no interests political or otherwise which are not subservient to this great question—and she knows no party obligations which can interfere with it. . . . Our hopes of prosperity depend upon this measure, and on it I believe I know the West to be undivided in opinion and sentiment. . . . There is nothing of a party character connected with it—and *I assure you I would go for the Erie Canal enlargement against all parties.*" Andrews to O'Reilly, March 22, 1841, Henry O'Reilly Papers, NYHS.

[54] New York *Evening Post,* January 7, 1841.

of the Oswego route to the lakes.[55] Still more drastic demands for retrenchment emanated from two Democratic assemblymen from Herkimer County, a county which bordered the eastern section of the canal. In days to come, when control of the canals would pass from Whig to Democratic hands, both would dominate the policy of their party. Michael Hoffman proposed in the session of 1841 that a doubling of the locks throughout the canal would suffice without further enlargement of the channel and that the lateral canals which did not pay their way should be abandoned. It was left to his fellow assemblyman, Arphaxad Loomis, to introduce the famous "people's resolution" which proposed an amendment to the state constitution limiting the power of a legislature to create a debt without the specific approval of the people at the following general election. Ominously for the Whigs, the Loomis resolution failed by a tie of 53 to 53, and it would haunt them in the New York constitutional convention only five years hence.

For the moment, the Whigs had voted down the Democracy, and they emerged once more as the fast friends of the Erie Canal. The state debt had risen to a staggering eighteen millions, but the *Evening Journal* congratulated itself as the legislators left the capital: "Thanks to the Whigs, the public credit is preserved, the public works will go on, the people will not be taxed, and New York will march onward in her career of glory."[56]

It was the fate of the Whigs in New York, however, to march onward to a crippling defeat in the fall elections of 1841. With control of the legislature at stake and their victory of 1840 razor thin, they placed the issue of

[55] S. G. Andrews to O'Reilly, March 22, 1841, Henry O'Reilly Papers, NYHS.

[56] Albany *Evening Journal*, May 13, 1841.

internal improvements above all others. Contractors, laborers, and *"every man* who has an interest in the prosecution of the Public Works" were warned of the impending threat to their livelihood in a Democratic victory. For all to read, the Democratic New York *Evening Post* declared unequivocally: "The democracy stands pledged to arrest that wild and reckless system, which, in nine cases out of ten, is miscalled internal improvements."[57] The Whigs looked hopefully to Henry Clay's Distribution Bill in Congress for aid to the sagging credit of New York. A public meeting was held in Buffalo demanding enlargement of the Erie Canal on the western section, and Whig papers carried the complaints of those unable to ship their goods because of the great press of freight moving east in October and November.

"Let no true friend of Internal Improvements fail now to support this cause by supporting the Whigs' candidates," cried Weed in the *Evening Journal*. As the election drew closer, Weed bent to the cause of saving the Whigs, and, he believed, the Erie Canal. The canal had become a "mine of wealth" to the state. Lateral canals and railroads were "tributaries to the main artery." The West only now began to send its surplus which would soon swell the coffers of the state with tolls. "To bring about so glorious a result, at once the wish and hope of every citizen, has been the object of the Whigs." But should the Regency return to power, "the giant sinews of the State are to be . . . bound as with chains of iron, so as effectually and forever to cripple her energies and humble her in the dust."[58] Exhortations to save the canal followed almost daily. Two days before the ballot boxes were to be opened, the *Journal* printed a full-page picture

[57] New York *Evening Post,* October 21, 1841.
[58] Albany *Evening Journal,* October 29, 1841.

of a ship under full sail emblazoned with the appeal, "Friends of Internal Improvement rally to your cause!" Boatmen, laborers, and farmers were warned that the Democratic creed was "opposed to the ENLARGEMENT OF THE ERIE CANAL."[59] But all to no avail. The Democrats carried all before them and control of both branches of the legislature fell securely into their hands. Right as Seward may have been on the need to speed the enlargement of the Erie Canal and add other improvements to draw Western trade to New York, the electorate had rebelled at the cost and the indebtedness Seward's program had incurred. The voters had resolved to return to a program of expenditures based upon surplus revenues alone.

Clearly the mandate was for more drastic retrenchment. But just how this should be done was now the primary problem confronting the Democratic victors. Already plans were afoot in western New York to call another state canal convention to meet in Rochester in January. Seth C. Hawley in Buffalo warned O'Reilly that "there is a growing impression that our canal policy will be this winter in danger and need all the vigilance of all its friends."[60] A note of caution was heard in the New York *Herald* as its editor advised "no violent change of public policy to injure Whig officers or contractors—but a just and liberal administration of government, carried out for the good of the whole State."[61] This caution the Regency threw to the winds when they inaugurated the "stop and tax" policy of 1842.

[59] *Ibid.*, November 2, 1841.
[60] Hawley to O'Reilly, December 29, 1841, Henry O'Reilly Papers, NYHS.
[61] New York *Herald*, November 8, 1841.

17

The Democratic Stop Policy, 1842-1846

THE LEGISLATIVE SESSION of 1842 produced a radical change in the fortunes of the Erie Canal. The New York lawmakers enacted a stop law on state indebtedness which was written into the constitution in 1846 and remained a bitterly contested issue until it was reversed in 1854. The stop policy of that session not only widened the gulf between Whig and Democrat over internal improvements, but it caused also an irreparable schism in the Democratic party itself.

There was no doubt that a financial crisis of the first order faced the Albany solons. Marcy feared that the "new impulse" which had brought the Whigs to power in 1839 had "propelled the state to the brink of the precipice."[1] The new spirit which pervaded the halls of the capitol was limned in William Cullen Bryant's *Evening Post,* which warned in December, "We must stop the extravagant expenditures which are now going on, . . . listen to no more schemes of state canals and state railroad companies, . . . and lay a direct tax to meet and pay the debt which is impending."[2] It would be Michael Hoffman and his Committee of Ways and Means who would dominate the session, bringing to an end the heyday of the Committee on Canals and Railroads.

On the fourth of January, Seward addressed a legislature which had been elected upon the repudiation of his program. Loyal as ever to the Erie Canal, he traced the history of the enlargement to "invoke in its behalf, in an important crisis, a return of the general confidence it obtained in its inception."[3] He sought to capitalize on the sudden increase of lockages to 30,320 at Alexander's Lock, up 12½ percent in 1841 over 1840 and the nearly constant figures which had held for some five years before. This brought the passage of one boat every ten and a half minutes at Schenectady. He reported that thirty-six hours had been added to the voyage from Buffalo to Albany because of detentions at the locks. If New York was to preserve its commercial advantages and political influence, maintain public faith, prevent general distress, and guard against Canadian rivalry for Western trade, she must "complete the enlargement of the Erie Canal throughout, and with all convenient diligence." For Seward internal improvements had become a panacea.

The reaction to Seward's appeal was partisan, as was to be expected, but there was room for honest doubt concerning the ability of the state to go on with its public works. Given the indebtedness of the state, the pressure of the times, and Seward's recommendation of further appropriations of seventeen millions, the *Argus* reported that Seward's message could not "be too strongly characterized as visionary dreaming, or a gross assault upon the public intellect."[4]

The credit of the state was, as the *Argus* put it, "on a lee shore." Its 5 percent stock was at a discount of 30 percent and its 6 percent stock was selling at 20 percent

---

[1] Marcy to P. M. Wetmore, December 31, 1842, William L. Marcy Papers, LC.

[2] New York *Evening Post*, December 2, 1841.

[3] Lincoln, *Messages from the Governors*, III, 957.

[4] Albany *Argus* (s.w.), January 11, 1842.

below par. Temporary loans for payment of interest ran
to more than three millions and contractors went unpaid.
Hoffman, leading the attack on Seward's program in the
assembly, showed a total state debt of twenty-seven and
a half millions. At fifty-four, Hoffman had already served
eight years in Congress before coming to the New York
legislature. A contemporary saw him as "a tallish man,
past middle age, with iron-gray locks drooping on his
shoulders," and hearing him speak, found him "so method-
ical and lucid in his argument, that, where all had
appeared confused before, everything now seemed clear."[5]
Hoffman was from Herkimer, where the canal ran close
by the Mohawk River and opened that beautiful valley
to the commerce of the West. Still he cried in an emotional speech during the debate on the enlargement, "Can
any man, native or foreign, hesitate between stopping
these expenditures, and going on at the expense of credit,
honor, and character?"[6]

In the course of these debates the Democratic members
of the assembly prepared the way for the stop policy
soon to be adopted, while the Whigs urged on the
completion of the public works wherever money could
be borrowed at 6 percent. The Democratic majority
promptly named six new canal commissioners, only one
of whom, Jonas Earll, had had experience on the canal
before. Azariah Cutting Flagg was returned to the post
of comptroller, which he had occupied in the days before
the Whigs came to power in 1839, and from that fortress
of statistics promptly exposed the near prostration of the
credit of the state. Flagg labored to show "that a sound
system of finance is *not* unfriendly to the advancement of
the public works," while the *Argus* called out to the "*true*

[5] Stanton, *Random Recollections,* p. 85.
[6] Hammond, *Political Parties,* III, 270.

friends" of internal improvement that fiscal solvency was "the only base upon which these works can ever progress."[7] Flagg's report, said the *Argus*, would be "the great question" in the November elections.

Acting on Flagg's report, Hoffman reported on state finances for the Committee of Ways and Means and brought in a bill to the assembly entitled, "an act to provide for paying the debt and preserving the credit of the state." This, the famous "stop and tax" bill, provided for the suspension of expenditures on the public works and the imposition of a mill tax to begin payment on the state debt. Washington Hunt, a young Whig from Lockport, moved to strike out the tax and to go on with the unfinished canals, but his motion was roundly defeated. On March 17, by a strict party vote of 67 to 23, the stop and tax bill passed the assembly.[8] Only Whig votes were cast against it.

In the senate, a compromise was attempted by Daniel S. Dickinson, a Democrat friendly to internal improvements, which would impose a tax but allow the public works to go on. But it failed even of Whig support.[9] Some Democrats in the senate, on the other hand, wished to retrench so severely that they proposed amendments to limit even the maintenance of the public works. These also were defeated. The stop and tax bill passed the senate as it had come from the assembly, opposed by the Whigs, but not entirely to the taste of all Democrats either. Governor Seward professed to believe that "the Executive could not consistently with the spirit of the Constitution, attempt to control the deliberate action of

[7] Albany *Argus* (s.w.), February 22, 1842.

[8] New York, *Assembly Journal*, 65th Sess., pp. 528-33.

[9] Hammond wrote that since many Whigs held bank stock which would appreciate with passage of the stop law, they were not unwilling to see it go into effect. Hammond, *Political Parties*, III, 285n.

the legislature in regard to such measures," and on March 29 he signed the stop and tax bill into law.

After rolling back the accumulated evils of three years of Whig extravagance, the New York Democracy hoped to build a firm financial base on which they would raise again the edifice of Regency control in Albany. But even as the walls of the new structure took shape, deep fissures revealed fatal weaknesses in the design. The division in the senate over the severity of the stop and tax policy exposed the split of the Democracy into Conservatives or "Hunkers" and Radicals or "Barnburners."[10] Hunkers supposedly "hunkered" for the spoils of public office and private speculation while the Barnburners were likened to the farmer who would burn down the barn to rid it of rats. Dickinson had spoken for the Conservatives, and he was joined in his support for a moderate spending policy by some of the most prominent leaders of the party.

Edwin Croswell put the most influential Democratic paper in the state at the service of the Conservatives. Bouck was neither by temperament nor past record likely to join with the Radicals. He visited Albany while the stop and tax bill was under debate and raised the ire of the Radicals by opposing suspension of the public works until a mission could be sent to Holland to borrow money. Marcy's six years as governor from 1833 until 1839 had long since placed him on the Conservative side of the Democracy in opposition to the banking and internal improvement views of Silas Wright. Marcy was now in Washington, as was Wright, but both still wielded immense power in New York politics. Moreover, young Horatio Seymour of Utica was Marcy's protege and had begun his first term in the assembly. Seymour's father

[10] Herbert D. A. Donovan, *The Barnburners* (New York, 1925), pp. 9, 32-33, 94.

had been a canal commissioner from 1824 until 1830, and the son had been reared within sight of the Erie Canal. Seymour cast his lot with the Conservatives at the outset of a public career which would lead him to the governorship in 1853 and make him Democratic candidate for the presidency in 1868. When Michael Hoffman and his Radical followers sought to implement the stop and tax law of 1842, these men would be counted, in varying degrees, among the opposition.

The act itself quickly accomplished its purpose. Within two months 7 percent state stocks were sold at par, within six months the 6 percents were at par, and in fifteen months the 5 percent stock was sold at face value.[11] The banking community rallied behind the new policy as their stocks rose. It was also possible, to a limited degree, to have it both ways on the matter of canal construction. While the new law provided for suspension of expenditures on the canals, exceptions were made. Construction necessary to continue navigation or to preserve work already done went on.[12]

In the villages and cities along the canal reactions to the stoppage of construction varied with party allegiance, but the stop and tax law enjoyed widespread support. The Schenectady *Reflector* commented that "the great body of the people are becoming anxious to commence paying before they incur any more debt" and added that the law was "not looked upon as a party measure, but, as a public measure essential to the welfare and credit of the state."[13] In Syracuse, the Onondaga *Standard* reported at the end of April that the measure was "fast becoming popular with the people."[14] In Oswego, the

[11] Hammond, *Political Parties*, III, 286.
[12] Albany *Argus* (s.w.), June 17, 1842.
[13] Quoted in *ibid.*, April 5, 1842.
[14] *Ibid.*, April 29, 1842.

Palladium found "little fear in these days of cold water, of the people being dazzled by the glories of a forty million debt."[15] The Batavia *Spirit of the Times* stood ready "to meet the evil at the threshhold and submit at once to taxation."[16] Even Henry O'Reilly's Rochester *Daily Advertiser* supported the stop policy with the observation that the public works had already been suspended by the Whigs: "Ask the contractors in this region, how they got along with their works for months before the assembling of the Legislature, and they will reply, by borrowing from banks and from their own means."[17] O'Reilly's mercurial temperament allowed him not only to support the stop law but to endorse Gerrit Smith's campaign to sell the canals to private owners.[18] In Albany, Croswell's *Argus* reported that if ever a measure were supported by "the honest popular sentiment" on "all sides," it was the stop law.[19]

Democratic representatives in the assembly from New York City had long seemed perversely opposed to the construction or enlargement of the Erie Canal, and now the New York press rallied behind the Radicals in Albany. The *American* broke from the Whigs, supported the stop policy, and reported a "perfect willingness" among the propertied men of the city to pay off the debt.[20] The *Sun*, unaffiliated as to party, noted that "even those who were at first most deeply infected with this internal improvement fever, now admit the necessity of a tax."[21] The *Journal of Commerce*, which devoted itself almost exclu-

15 *Ibid.*, August 9, 1842.
16 *Ibid.*, March 4, 1842.
17 *Ibid.*, May 31, 1842.
18 Smith to O'Reilly, November 14, 1842, Henry O'Reilly Papers, RPL; Buffalo *Commercial Advertiser and Journal*, June 8, 1842.
19 Albany *Argus* (s.w.), March 22, 1842.
20 Quoted in *ibid.*
21 *Ibid.*

sively to mercantile affairs, reported that the stop and tax law "has been favorably received here, although it is well known that the burden will fall heaviest on this city."[22] William Cullen Bryant's *Evening Post*, while censuring the state government as "the clumsiest of all contrivances for the public accommodation," hailed the stop law as "a most popular measure."[23]

The New York Whigs had been sent "Up Salt River." They sought to save face by publicizing the progress of the canal revenues which had grown from $1,292,023 in 1837 to $2,034,882 in 1841. They sought to spread the blame for an empty treasury with their long-repeated charge that Regency legislation had originated the debt, and then took the offensive with a challenge to the Democratic "Bourbons" to find a way to carry out their stop law without at the same time diverting Western trade to rival routes to the Atlantic.[24] The Whigs played their strongest card when they kept before the public the fallacious estimates on which the Regency had based the construction of the enlarged Erie Canal and the lateral canals. Stung into editorial fury, Thurlow Weed castigated the "wild, crazed estimates of incompetent Engineers and bewildered or dishonest Canal Commissioners" and ridiculed " 'the Forty Million Debt' which has been dropped, foundling-like as guilty parents leave their illegitimate offspring, at the street-door of the Whig Administration."[25]

Ironically, not quite a month after the passage of the suspension law, the first fourteen miles of the enlargement west of Albany were opened for use. To celebrate, the

[22] *Ibid.*, April 5, 1842.
[23] *Ibid.*
[24] Albany *Evening Journal*, March 22, 23, 1842; New York *Commercial Advertiser*, March 22, 1842.
[25] Albany *Evening Journal*, March 25, 1842.

comptroller, a canal commissioner, and the engineers boarded two boats, one named *Enlargement,* and with colors waving, a band playing and salutes sounding from a six-pounder carried on board, passed from the lower Mohawk aqueduct down the line to Lock No. 1 at Albany. But the *Journal* ribbed the Regency celebrants: "Why should a party that has arrested the progress of the Enlargement, celebrate the completion of an unavailable fragment of that work?"[26]

The Whig espousal of the enlargement from Salt River was dramatized by the unfinished structures left everywhere along the line of the Erie Canal. After the rebuilding of the five-lock combine at Lockport was called to a halt, stone left strewn in the fields became almost common property, some of which went into the portico of the Eagle Tavern in Rochester while other pieces became part of the foundations of buildings near Spalding's Mill. Daniel P. Bissell, the Democratic canal commissioner on the western section, complained to Flagg that he "was daily beset by a hungary [sic] & starving throng of contractors upon our public works, begging for money or State stocks, or even a promise of money. . . ."[27]

At the same time, expenditure of relatively small amounts of money would allow suspended but nearly completed work on the enlargement to be put into use. At Schoharie Creek, for example, only $45,000 was needed to bring $550,000 worth of new work into operation.[28] The magnificent new aqueduct was done, two double locks were finished, and six miles of canal were completed. All that was required for these works to be put

[26] *Ibid.,* April 25, 1842.

[27] Bissell to A. C. Flagg, May 7, 1842, New York (State) Comptroller Papers, NYPL.

[28] George W. Little to William C. Bouck, November 28, 1842, William C. Bouck Papers, Cornell University Library.

into service was the completion of a mile of new canal and a portion of a small aqueduct.

It was clear that the Whigs would make the stop and tax law a primary issue in the fall election, and the Regency Radicals hedged neatly by nominating two Conservatives, Bouck and Dickinson, on their ticket for governor and lieutenant governor. Seward declined renomination and the Whigs named Luther Bradish and Gabriel Furman to oppose the Regency on a platform which condemned the state tax and the suspension of the public works. If it was whistling in the dark to hope to elect a Whig successor to Seward and reverse the stop law, the Whigs nevertheless had a record to defend and a future to prepare for. No other issue was of greater moment than that of the canals and the Whigs drew the lines with utmost clarity. "The Regency candidates are pledged to the TAX AND STOP law side of the issue," declared the *Evening Journal*. "The Whigs regard the tax as oppressive and unnecessary, and go for resuming the public works moderately but surely. For which policy are you?"[29] If the Democratic stand was blurred by the pro-internal improvements record of Bouck and Dickinson, the Whigs could make the Democratic nominations an admission that the Regency "*dare not* go to the polls on the issues which they themselves have made up!"[30] The Whig New York *Daily Express* chided Bouck with being "a Whig *inside*, only with a Loco Foco coat on the *outside*."[31]

Few Democrats cared to sound as radical on the issue as Michael Hoffman when he told an extra session of the legislature meeting in August and September that it would

29 Albany *Evening Journal*, September 29, 1842.
30 *Ibid.*, September 12, 1842.
31 New York *Daily Express*, July 15, 1842.

be "intended arson" to adopt Seward's proposals to go on with the public works. Instead the Democrats were increasingly careful to construe the stop policy as necessary for the future completion of the enlargement, and this was especially so in the villages and cities along the canals. The Lockport *Democrat and Balance* assured its readers that "the Democrats stopped the public works, that they might be enabled hereafter to go on."[32] A resident of Nunda on the Genesee Valley Canal wrote Bouck in September requesting "an explicit avowal" that Bouck had not been won over to the Regency stop policy, for his answer would "make many hundred & perhaps thousand votes difference." Bouck answered so agreeably that the correspondent found Bouck's views "entirely satisfactory to the democracy of this part of the state," and added, "it being the same doctrine that many Whigs pretend to hold they have stopped from saying anything against you."[33]

Despite such equivocations, and even the genuine affection which Bouck had won on the canals, it was the Radical and not the Conservative Democratic policy on the canals which was before the people in 1842. Even the Hunker presses in the Democracy were without the Whig conviction that growing Western trade created imperative demands for an enlarged Erie Canal. "Indeed," concluded the *Argus*, as its mythical eyes looked to the future, "there is little ground to apprehend that the canal is not capable to transact all the business thrown upon it, or likely to be so for years to come."[34] It was for the more nationalistic Whigs to talk of the trade of the "mighty West," rising cities, and national

[32] Quoted in *Albany Argus* (s.w.), August 16, 1842.
[33] B. Bagly to Bouck, September 10, October 10, 1842, William C. Bouck Papers, Cornell University Library.
[34] Albany *Argus* (s.w.), August 26, 1842.

growth. "Shall not a policy, so full of promise for the wealth, the glory and the greatness of the Empire State receive the sanction and support of the People at the ensuing election?" asked the *Journal*.[35]

The answer of the electorate in November was once more a resounding negative. Bouck defeated Bradish by a majority of nearly 22,000, more than four times that by which Seward had been reelected in 1840. The Democrats carried all but one of the senate districts and elected a solid majority in the assembly. The legislature that passed the stop and tax law was sustained by the *vox populi* at the polls. Clearly it was the will of the majority that enlargement of the Erie Canal must stop until the debt of the state had been reduced.

But now it was Bouck who held the tail of a tiger running down the path of Radical canal policy. The schism between the Radicals and the Conservatives in the Democracy widened, and the stop law itself became a litmus test for party loyalty.[36] Bouck found himself surrounded with state officers who were Radicals and in whose eyes Bouck's loyalty to the stop law would always be suspect. Flagg was comptroller and Samuel Young was secretary of state; both were commissioners of the Canal Fund and both were determined to fight any retreat from the Radical stand taken by the legislature and sustained in the recent state-wide elections. But Bouck's first message to the legislature confirmed his desire for further prosecution of the enlargement at Schoharie Creek, Syracuse, Lockport, and numerous other points on the line of the Erie Canal. Greater heresy still, he recommended work on the Black River and Genesee

---

[35] Albany *Evening Journal*, October 12, 1842.

[36] The Radical Albany *Atlas* opposed the "bank democrats," who wished the increase of state stocks for the creation of banking capital. Albany *Atlas*, Extra, December 1, 1846.

Valley canals, and it helped little to ask in the same breath for "caution" in increasing the state debt. Both Marcy and Van Buren assisted Bouck with his message, and the latter counseled the Conservatives against allowing divisions over the debt policy to produce "a ruinous schism in our ranks."[37] Marcy thought that Bouck should "put himself right" on the debt question, and could not see why Bouck would not trim his sails to the prevailing winds.[38] In the legislature the Radicals struggled to contain a Hunker movement to appropriate half a million dollars to the lateral canals while Flagg reminded Van Buren that "the equivocal language of the message" had sown the dragon's teeth.[39]

The Whigs were quick to exploit the divisions of the Democracy as they were daily exposed to public view. Weed asked in the *Journal* for an interpretation of the "Executive riddle" on internal improvements in Bouck's message. Bouck was nicely trapped by his own endorsement of a circular sent abroad by the canal commissioners to secure laborers for the enlargement which promised an expenditure of twenty millions on 500 miles of canals. Weed gleefully watched the embarrassed governor *"dismissing from employment* the thousands of laborers whom he had lured over from Europe. . . ."[40] In the legislature, a Whig senator charged that Bouck had spent excessively for the masonry on the enlarged canal between Albany and Schenectady while he was canal commissioner, a charge which was not proven but which placed the governor on the defensive. Meanwhile, the Democratic Radicals added to Bouck's tribulations by defeating the nomination of one of his canal associates as canal appraiser

[37] Martin Van Buren to Marcy, January 13, 1843, William L. Marcy Papers, LC.

[38] Quoted in Garraty, *Silas Wright*, p. 293.

[39] Flagg to Van Buren, April 15, 1843, Martin Van Buren Papers, LC.

[40] Albany *Evening Journal*, February 14, 1842.

and reducing the number of acting canal commissioners from four to three.

The movement of the Democratic Radicals against Bouck reached its climax in 1844, during the second year of his term. They were strengthened by the steadily improving credit of the state, which was marked by the sale of 6 percent stock at a premium of 9 percent. Canal tolls were rising at the rate of some 7 percent a year while there was less than 3 percent average annual increase in the tonnage carried.[41] Even when the Wabash and Erie Canal was opened in 1843, the number of lockages rose only slightly in consequence. The Democracy could advertise that the state was "reaping the harvest of Western trade" without increasing its debt.[42]

But Bouck was also under pressure to go on with the enlargement of the Erie Canal. John B. Jervis admonished the governor from New York City that "so much has been expended, that with the growing magnitude of its trade, it cannot be that it will be abandoned. If our party too long adhere to suspension, we must expect our opponents will profit by it." David Murray wrote from Oriskany Falls that Bouck's annual message was "looked for with almost feverish anxiety by friends and foes." As a close friend of long standing, Murray pleaded with the governor for "a frank, open avowal of your honest opinions, showing that while you opposed the wild reckless and visionary schemes of the whigs, that you remain the fast friend of our Canals. . . ."[43]

The governor went before the legislature and recommended that the canal board be authorized to complete new work on the canals which could be done more eco-

[41] Albany *Argus* (s.w.), April 14, 1843.

[42] *Ibid.*, December 15, 1843.

[43] Jervis to Bouck, November 17, 1843, Murray to Bouck, November 27, December 6, 1843, William C. Bouck Papers, Cornell University Library.

nomically than to maintain work which had been suspended. The Radicals, led by Hoffman and Young, countered with a proposal to amend the constitution to limit the power of the legislature to increase the public debt by constructing canals and railroads or to loan money to corporations. This failed, but it was the germination of a seed which would flower in the Constitutional Convention of 1846. Bouck's friends next tried without success to get passage of a resolution pledging the state to complete the public works as soon as finances should permit. Meanwhile, damage claims by contractors on suspended contracts reached so large a figure that the Whigs parodied the Regency for paying "MILLIONS FOR DAMAGES BUT NOT A CENT FOR IMPROVEMENT."[44] It was a senate bill for the protection and preservation of the public works which brought the issue to a head.

The Democracy divided against itself in two conflicting reports brought before the legislature. That of the Radicals was made in the senate and did little more than repeat the holy writ that the act of 1842 "must be rigidly observed until the debt be paid." The report of the Conservatives, or Hunkers, was made in the assembly by young Horatio Seymour, now chairman of the Committee on Canals, and just entered upon his second term in the legislature. As in the days of Clinton, the man became as important as the cause. Seymour was a rising figure in the assembly and had been talked of for speaker. He was persuasive, logical, even eloquent. Printed, Seymour's report ran seventy-one pages and Hammond pronounced it "one of the ablest and best-written documents ever presented to a legislative body."[45] It would become the basis for the canal policy of the state for twenty years.

[44] Albany *Evening Journal,* April 27, 1844.
[45] Hammond, *Political Parties,* III, 410; New York, *Assembly Documents,* 67th Sess., Doc. 177, pp. 1-71.

Seymour recommended the application of any surplus revenues, over and above those required to carry out the act of 1842, to enlarging the locks, preserving the unfinished works, and continuing construction on the Genesee Valley and Black River canals. Where the Radicals would use all surplus revenues for the reduction of the debt, Seymour would go on with the canals. Still, he proposed no new debt and thus kept his distance from the Whigs, though he knew he could count on their support for any program that would go on with construction. He had earned a hearing from the Radicals by his support for the stop and tax law when it was passed, but now he warned against hostility to the canals themselves. With a touch of Seward's optimism he dwelt upon the returns certain to come after completion of work on the canals.

Along with his report, Seymour introduced a bill which embodied his recommendations. So skillful were his forensic sallies and so conciliatory was his manner that the bill passed the assembly by a vote of 67 to 38. In the senate the vote was closer, but Whig votes added to those of the Hunkers saw the measure through. "Indeed," writes Alexander in his history of the state, "the history of the session may be described as the passage of a single measure by a single man whose success was based on supreme faith in the Erie Canal."[46] The soul-searching required of the Democrats in the defense of the more doctrinaire position they had adopted is attested to by the remark of a Radical at the end of the session: "We all claimed to be in favor of the law of 1842, but we varied in opinion whether this law clashes with that policy."

What the Hunkers had won with Seymour in the session, they lost with Silas Wright in the fall elections. Seymour sought vainly to secure the renomination of

[46] DeAlva S. Alexander, *A Political History of the State of New York*, II (New York, 1906), 63.

Bouck on the strength of his stand on state issues, but the New York Democracy had bigger fish to fry. The famous Baltimore Convention of 1844 had jettisoned Van Buren in favor of Polk for the presidency, and Polk's victory over Henry Clay was widely believed to depend on the outcomes of the contest in New York. Wright's personal popularity with New York Democrats, together with his stand on the explosive issues of Oregon and Texas, and his status as a senator in the national legislature were deemed of far greater moment than his long-held opposition to state indebtedness for internal improvement.

Wright himself was as unwilling a candidate as ever wore political harness. He knew that he could not sacrifice his principles on questions such as internal improvements, and he was equally certain that the division within the New York Democracy would not suffer him to maintain them without the loss of Hunker friends such as Marcy and Dickinson, or without detraction from the position he had earned as a national Democratic leader. "I will not pretend to believe that I am not fairly popular with the democracy of this State," he wrote to Polk, "but with the untrue portion, those whose politics hang on banks, canals and railroads . . . I never was, and never expect to be a favorite."[47]

The contest between Wright and Millard Fillmore of Buffalo, the colorless Whig nominee, turned as much on the national issues of bank and tariff, Texas and Oregon, as it did on state policies. Even at the state level, the canal issue vied with the Anti-Rent riots on the feudal estates in New York and with anti-Catholic nativism in attracting public attention. Nevertheless, the campaign was heavily burdened with partisan use of the canal record of both Whig and Democrat. John A. Dix, former

[47] Quoted in Garraty, *Silas Wright*, p. 326.

Regency canal commissioner, lectured a series of mass meetings across the state on the subject of "Arabian Nightism," which derived from his earlier remark that Ruggles' proposals for a forty-million-dollar debt for internal improvements in the midst of the depression of 1837 belonged in the same class with the Arabian Nights entertainment. For the time being, the two wings of the Democracy worked in a temporary alliance against the Whigs. A strident new paper, the Albany *Atlas*, which became the mouthpiece of the Radicals, carried the attack to the Whigs rather than to fellow Democrats with the charge of "the State Debt, its whig origin, and its whig consequences." Croswell's *Argus* spoke for the Conservatives, but he announced on the eve of the election that "the principal question so far as this state is concerned is this, and only this:—*Shall the reckless, profligate and debt-contracting policy of 1840 and 1841 be renewed?*"[48] Although the Democratic ranks remained riven with feuding so severe that Jacob Gould of New York complained to Van Buren that the two factions were "doing all they can to annoy and perplex each other, and comparatively nothing against the common enemy," in the end Bouck's followers voted for Wright.[49]

Silas Wright carried the state in a solid triumph, running well ahead of Polk whose victory over Clay in New York won him the presidential election. But the reluctant candidate now became the reluctant governor. Wright's worst fears of Democratic factionalism were soon realized. In the new legislature, where the Conservative and Radical Democrats shared almost equal strength, Horatio Seymour narrowly won the contest for speaker over the Radical William C. Crain of Herkimer.

48 Albany *Argus* (s.w.), November 1, 1844.
49 Gould to Van Buren, April 15, 1844, Martin Van Buren Papers, LC.

The Hunkers demanded and won half of the state offices giving them a majority among the commissioners of the Canal Fund. The election of the Radical John A. Dix to complete the remainder of Wright's term in the United States Senate and of Daniel S. Dickinson to a six-year term in that august body brought the Democratic feud to such intensity that the selection of the latter became a triumph of the Conservatives over the new governor. In Washington, Polk responded with seeming ungratefulness for Wright's victory in New York by giving to a Hunker the plum of collector of New York.

Having won so much in Albany and Washington, the Hunkers found little to be gained and much to be risked in a drive by Crain and Hoffman for a constitutional convention which would put the "People's Resolution" into law and put the stop policy beyond reversal by any future legislature. Hunker-sponsored amendments to limit the power of the legislature to make debts or loans had already been passed in the session of 1844 and upheld by the electorate in the fall elections. A two-thirds vote of approval in the session of 1845 would tack them onto the constitution without risking more sweeping and potentially dangerous reforms in a convention. Governor Wright also favored this mode of action, but he could not hold the Radicals in check and he was outmaneuvered by the Whigs.

The Radicals wanted an unlimited convention. They were motivated primarily by a desire to strike down the state's indebtedness, but their actions were symptomatic of the leaven of reform at work in the 1840s. The time had come for a more thorough revision of the constitution of 1821 than could be achieved through the process of amendment. Whigs, Anti-Renters, and Native Americans joined the Radical Democrats in the opinion that the constitution should more perfectly express the sovereignty of the people, that all state offices—whether executive, legislative, or judicial—should be elected directly by popular vote. At least on the face of it, the People's Resolution was written in this same spirit of democratic reform, proposing as it did to place the final power of creating a state debt in the hands of the people themselves.

Ironically, the Radicals were aided at this juncture by the Whigs, who had given their votes to pass the Conservative canal bill in 1844. Although the Whigs were more frequently found in the lists on the side of conservatism and the existing social order, the party leaders saw an opportunity to go before the people as the champions of reform. John Young, whose rise as a Whig spokesman in the assembly had been even more rapid than that of Seymour among the Conservatives, seized upon a convention bill brought in by Crain and transformed it into a Whig measure.

First, he skillfully manipulated the balance of power in the hands of the Whigs to defeat the amendments favored by Wright which were already before the assembly. Then, in a long and masterful debate, he overcame Seymour and the Hunkers on Crain's convention bill. The bill passed the assembly, was approved by the senate, and in a final triumph for the rising Whig leader, received the signature of the governor.[50]

While Young's generalship had dealt the Hunkers a hard blow in the matter of a constitutional convention, the Whigs finessed by supporting a Hunker measure to make still another breach in the stop policy of 1842.

[50] Stewart Mitchell, *Horatio Seymour of New York* (Cambridge, 1938), pp. 54-55; Donovan, *Barnburners*, pp. 68-69; Alexander, *Political History of the State of New York*, II, 95-100.

Public meetings and petitions in western New York reminded the Albany legislators that up-staters were growing impatient for the completion of the public works.[51] It was well known that four millions of the state debt fell due in 1845 and 1846, and the Hunkers came forward late in the session with a new appropriation of $197,000 to go on with the enlargement of the Erie Canal and with the lateral canals. Whig votes turned the trick; the bill passed both houses of the legislature, only to be returned by Governor Wright with a veto. The governor opposed the bill as "putting an end to the policy of a suspension of the public works" dictated by the stop and tax law to which the state was bound.

Wright's veto followed the uncompromising dictates of his principles, but its consequence was to widen the gulf between Radical and Hunker over the canals. It diminished still further the acquiescence of the Conservatives in the stop policy as it was ever more rigorously defined by the Radicals. Defeated by Young on the issue of the convention and now by Wright's veto of the Hunker canal bill, Seymour retired to eight years of private life in Utica. On the other hand, the Radicals had suffered too much from Wright's ineptness as a party leader to be content with his identification as a Radical in the canal veto.

Still, the full impact of the widening schism in the Democracy would not be revealed until Wright stood for reelection in 1846. Together the two wings of the party carried the fall elections of 1845, doubling their strength in the assembly and winning five of the eight senate seats up for contest. The Radicals emerged in clear

[51] A *Memorial to the Legislature of the State of New York, upon the Effects of the Passage of the Trade of the Western States, through the Welland and Oswego Canals, upon the Income of the State and the Interests of its Citizens* (Rochester, 1845).

control of the legislature. Sixty of the seventy-two Democrats in the assembly could be expected to vote with the Radicals and to sustain both Wright and the stop and tax policy with regard to the canals. Hoffman's Radical colleague from Herkimer, William Crain, was easily elected speaker, and that arch-opponent of the Seward program, Samuel Young, was elected to the senate from the fourth district.

Riding hard against their Hunker rivals, the Radicals on the Canal Board drove the Conservatives from the canal offices and appointed their own political servants to their places. The Utica *Observer* protested that "the whole canal influence" in that section of the state was being turned against the Hunkers.[52] In Albany, the Radical *Atlas* declared open warfare on Croswell and the *Argus*, accusing the Hunker editor of insufficient loyalty to the stop policy of 1842. Croswell desperately thwarted a Radical bill to take the state printing from the *Argus* and give it to the *Atlas* only by getting the office of state printer abolished and then by printing the state notices for nothing.

The greater threat to the canal policies of Hunker and Whig alike, however, lay in the Radical control of the state just as preparations were being made for the Constitutional Convention of 1846. The referendum on the convention had been carried by an overwhelming majority and sessions were scheduled to open in Albany in June. As we have seen, the movement for a convention had originated with the Radical attempt to put the Loomis Resolution, or People's Resolution, into the constitution, and to do this by constitutional revision rather than by amendment. For all the victories of the Radicals at the polls and the apparent popular support for the policy of

52 Quoted in Albany *Argus* (s.w.), May 8, 1846.

stop and tax, there was genuine concern in the state as to just what disposition the convention would make of the many-faceted issue of the canals and the state debt.

Moreover, although Governor Wright's austere messages to the legislature gave no indication that the public works would be resumed in the immediate future, traffic on the New York canals began to reach the levels predicted in the days of Ruggles and Seward. Trade on the Erie Canal passed the million-ton mark in 1845 and tolls climbed to more than two and a third millions. By 1847, the canal receipts would reach the annual three millions anticipated in the Ruggles report. During a single week in November of 1845, 280 boats went east from Buffalo in the heaviest week's business ever transacted at that city. A Lockport paper gave notice at the same time that "freights have doubled, and yet produce from the west is moving down, forming an almost continuous fleet of canal boats."[53] The Albany *Journal* chided the Democrats that "the Canals, even in the hands of dry-nurses, are doing their duty nobly. Every dollar of increase in tolls rebukes the men who have madly arrested the progress of the public works."[54]

Canal advocates in western New York met publicly to frame resolutions to be put before the convention. That at Lockport resolved that a "speedy resumption" of the enlargement of the Erie Canal was demanded, and that "complicated and impractical constitutional restrictions" should not be imposed on future canal legislation. The largest canal gathering of all met at Buffalo and was attended by delegates from every county west of Oneida. Many men at these meetings, such as William Peacock, Samuel Wilkeson, and Lot Clark, were associated with

[53] Niagara *Democrat,* November 12, 1845.
[54] Albany *Evening Journal,* May 6, 1842.

the first construction of the Erie Canal in western New York. What was feared most of all was that constitutional restrictions would make future canal legislation even more difficult than in the past. Henry Steward of Niagara County admitted that the people had assented to a suspension of the enlargement, but he added that "they did not consent to a perpetual suspension." Benjamin Cooper of Oneida called it heresy to apply the philosophy that "that people was best governed which was governed least" to the enlargement of the Erie Canal. Samuel Wilkeson told of pork lying exposed to the sun at Buffalo for thirty days for want of transportation east, and of freight costs rising higher than goods could bear. On the motion of the Buffalo Whig, Millard Fillmore, the meeting petitioned the convention "remonstrating against any provision in the Constitution, imposing restrictions upon the Legislature" in the prosecution of the public works.[55]

The imposition of restrictions upon the legislature in adding to the indebtedness of the state was, of course, the primary purpose of the convention. The general election of delegates had given a solid majority to the Radical Democrats, and at the head of the Committee on Canals stood Michael Hoffman. Perhaps most conspicuously absent from the convention was William Henry Seward, who more than any other man had been charged with creating the debt which Hoffman now inflated to thirty-eight millions. Seward refused to become a delegate from any but his own assembly district, and his own at Auburn would not have him.

The report of Hoffman's committee became the basis for the financial article of the constitution, Article II. Hoffman proposed that the constitution set aside $1,500,000 from the canal tolls for the canal debt and provide

[55] *The Canal Convention* (1846), Henry O'Reilly Papers, NYHS.

another $672,000 for the use of the state before further construction on the public works could be authorized. He would allow no debt to be created without at the same time levying a direct tax to redeem it within eighteen years. His speech exaggerated the canal debt, minimized canal revenues, and depreciated the income from the salt and auction duties; but his was the strongest and most respected voice in the financial debates of the convention. He was the "schoolmaster of the convention" on financial matters and a delegate from western New York who rose to speak against him thought himself challenging "the Ajax Telemon" of the session.[56]

It was almost foreordained that the convention should become a "battle of the factions" over the public works. The Whig minority pursued the divide-and-conquer strategy which had been executed so successfully by John Young in the legislature and looked to victory in the fall elections when the governorship would again be at stake. The Hunkers, with former Governor Bouck as their spokesman, sought to reduce the large annual installment on the canal debt proposed by Hoffman, cut the required contribution from canal revenues for the expenses of the state, and leave a larger surplus to be applied specifically to the Erie Canal enlargement and the two laterals, the Genesee Valley and Black River canals. Hunker and Whig, especially from western New York, combined against the Radicals in obstinate opposition and forced them to accept amendments and compromise. Hoffman fought like a man possessed to preserve "his favorite offspring," the stop law, and when the convention receded from his more extreme recommendations, Arphaxad Loomis carried his cudgel for the Radicals.

[56] Hammond, *Political Parties*, III, 651-52; Alexander, *Political History of the State of New York*, II, 108.

WEIGHLOCK BUILDING, SYRACUSE, BUILT IN 1850

*Courtesy of the Onondaga
Historical Association*

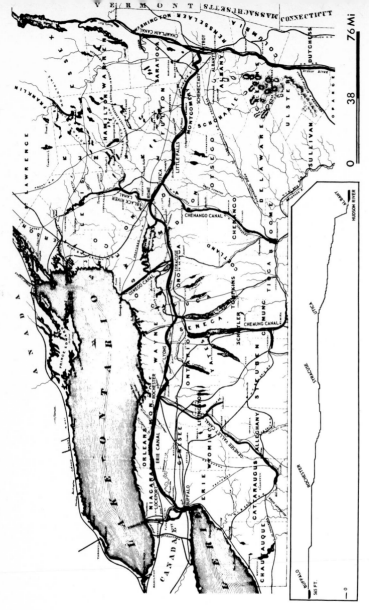

THE NEW YORK CANAL SYSTEM IN 1854

*Based on a map of the
State Engineer and Surveyor*

But the compromises to which the Radicals were driven were minor rather than major, and Hoffman emerged with essentially what he had demanded. One and a half million dollars must be taken annually from the canal tolls to reduce the canal debt. Two hundred thousand dollars more would be applied to the general fund for the expenses of the state. Only the remainder could be applied to canal construction. Never again would the credit of the state be loaned to a private corporation, such as the New York and Erie Railroad, and further debt for canals or railroads would no longer be left to legislative discretion alone. Every debt must carry a tax, and such debt and tax must win approval from the people at a general election. When the financial article of the constitution had finally been adopted, Hoffman looked upon the Radical handiwork and called it good. By thus providing for the indebtedness of the state, the Herkimer Radical assured his fellow delegates, they had "overcome the greatest disgrace ever attempted to be cast on free institutions."[57]

If the grand design of Ruggles and Seward had been reversed with finality by the convention, the Hunkers and Whigs had exacted their price for the Radical triumph. Not only the Erie Canal enlargement, but the Radical-despised Genesee Valley and Black River canals as well, would be specifically and certainly provided for until they were completed. Moreover, further provision was made that "they shall remain the property of the State and under its management forever." Weed summed up for the Whigs in the *Journal*: "On the whole we are satisfied; first, because the Constitution devotes the Surplus Revenues of the Canals to their completion—and second, because the question of Internal Improvements

[57] Quoted in Hammond, *Political Parties*, III, 656.

is no longer to be made a foot-ball to be kicked about by demagogues."[58] But the satisfaction of the Whigs and the predictions of the "Dictator," as Weed was called by his rival editors, would scarcely outlast the fall elections.

The constitutional convention adjourned in September and its work was submitted to the voters in November. It was ratified handily, with so few votes cast against it that there appeared a remarkable consensus on its provisions for the canals. But in the general elections of 1846 the increasing virulence of the Hunker-Radical conflict and the campaign of the Whigs showed the issue of the canals to be anything but at rest. Although a Democratic convention renominated Governor Wright, the two wings of the Democracy separated into virtually independent parties. Wright drew closer to the Radicals, and the Hunkers either sat upon their hands or bolted to the Whigs. The Whigs put up for the governorship their brilliant assembly leader, John Young, and rode to victory on the feuding of their opponents. More than that, it was a Whig sweep which won the Whigs a majority in the assembly, five out of eight senate seats, and twenty-three of New York's thirty-four congressmen.

Weed oversimplified the causes for the Whig windfall when his analysis of the election concluded: "The State was fairly ours upon an issue of principles. The People were indignant at Governor Wright's Canal and President Polk's Harbor Vetoes." The canals were only one of the factors in the overturn of the Democracy. Wright was opposed by the Anti-Renters whose riots he had put down with uncompromising severity in 1845. President Polk appeared to serve notice of his displeasure with Wright's candidacy when he named the leading Hunker, Bouck, to be subtreasurer in New York City under the new Inde-

[58] Albany *Evening Journal,* September 25, 1846.

pendent Treasury system and only too late did he throw the power of the national administration behind the governor. Slavery, Texas, and the war with Mexico created deep divisions between Democrat and Democrat, and Democrat and Whig.

Nonetheless, Wright was hobbled in the canal counties by his veto of the spring, where much of the Hunker defection to Young grew out of the governor's stringent interpretation of the stop law. In the verbiage of the campaign, laborers were reminded that "Silas Wright's 'Stop Policy'" had caused the discharge of thousands of workers from the public works, "many of whom are now destitute of employment." Farmers were told that "the Stop-Policy of Silas Wright" cost them an extra eighteen cents on the bushel to get their wheat to market.[59] Young, on the other hand, had completed his coup in the assembly by his part in the passage of the canal appropriation bill which Wright had vetoed. The new Whig governor garnered a harvest from seed sown in a decade of Whig support for the canals in particular and internal improvements in general. A Whig orator in New York, for example, repeated the familiar theme that while the Democrats had constantly impeded the progress of canals and railroads, "the great whig principle was to encourage internal improvements and every thing domestic. . . ."[60]

The postmortem of the defeated Radicals put the blame for the loss of the election only indirectly. For them, the dispute over the canals was but one facet of the real cause for their defeat, which was to be found in the factionalism and "treachery" of the Hunkers. A series of articles appearing in the Albany *Atlas* in December traced the long defection of the Conservatives back to 1837,

59 *Ibid.*, October 28, 1846.
60 New York *Herald*, October 31, 1846.

1838, and 1839, when they had opposed Van Buren's plan for an independent treasury and then, with the aid of Seward and the Whigs, "married together the internal improvement and bank interests in the democratic party." When the new constitution blasted their hopes for further profit from the public works, ran the Radical thesis, the Hunkers turned their labors and their votes to the defeat of Wright and the Radicals, and to the election of the Whigs. The Radicals thus concluded that the canal veto was *a* cause and Anti-Rentism was *a* cause, but *the* cause for Wright's defeat lay with the Hunker defection.[61] This interpretation, pronounced orthodox in the Radical presses, held that Wright's canal veto became merely a convenient reason in the canal counties for opposition that had its true basis in speculation and factionalism.

At the other extreme, Alexander gives us an exercise in "iffy" history in his account which viewed the political fortunes of both Wright and Young as turning on their policy toward the canals. Summarizing Wright's administration as governor, Alexander speculated:

He was opposed to a constitutional convention as well as to a canal appropriation, and, by wisely preventing the former, it is likely the latter would not have been forced upon him. Without a convention bill and a canal veto, the party would not have divided seriously, John Young would not have become a popular hero, and the Anti-Renters could not have held the balance of power. To prevent the calling

[61] Garraty, *Silas Wright*, p. 382; Wright to Van Buren, November 10, 1846, Martin Van Buren Papers, LC. Ranson H. Gillet, Wright's close friend and later his biographer, wrote that the canal veto was regarded by the Radicals "as deeply affecting, if not controlling, the question of his re-election." But, he added, since the Hunkers knew that Wright would veto the bill and its appropriation was "too trifling" to accomplish anything substantial, their real purpose was the overthrow of the governor. R. H. Gillet, *The Life and Times of Silas Wright* (Albany, 1874), II, 1693-95.

of a constitutional convention, therefore, . . . was the Governor's great opportunity. It would not have been an easy task. William C. Crain had a profound conviction on the subject, and back of him stood Michael Hoffman, the distinguished and unrelenting Radical, determined to put the act of 1842 into the organic law of the State. But there was a time when a master of political diplomacy could have controlled the situation.[62]

Thus the canal issue proved to be the undoing of Silas Wright, and brought John Young to the governorship.

Difficult and dangerous as such a generalization about New York politics in the 1840s may be, no question seems more central to the Radical–Conservative division in the Democratic party than that of the canals and the debt incurred in their construction. Explaining the ills of the party in New York to Polk, Silas Wright wrote in 1845 that "two great points of principle now occupy the commanding position in the eyes and minds of the freemen of this State. The first in importance and interest is the question of our public debt. . . . These are the points upon which our division line in this State is run, and it is not influenced at all by men, but by these questions of principle."[63] The primacy of the canals and the canal debt in Democratic divisions continued even when conflict between Locofoco and Conservative over banks and between Barnburner and Hunker over slavery widened and embittered the schism. Similarly, the canal policies of Ruggles, Seward, and Young were fundamental to

[62] Alexander, *Political History of the State of New York*, II, 122-23.

[63] In March of 1846, Wright wrote to John L. Russell that the Conservatives, led by Croswell in the *Argus*, were motivated by selfish speculations: "They have deeply and firmly and desperately resolved that they will have irresponsible banks, public debt, internal improvements and stock jobbing, or they will sink the democratic party." Wright to Russell, March 10, 1846, quoted in Gillet, *Life of Silas Wright*, II, 1731.

the philosophy and program of the New York Whigs, and perhaps no event cast a longer shadow upon the politics of the decade than the stop and tax law of 1842.

At the same time, every indicator in the latter half of the 1840s foreshadowed the close of the era when dispute over internal improvements, banks, and tariffs had dominated the political stage. The twin questions of slavery and westward expansion were crowding the older Jacksonian issues from the scene. But while the public eye in New York turned increasingly to the more disquieting sectional conflicts over slavery in the territories, the problem of the enlargement of the Erie Canal and the completion of the lateral canals would not reach its climax for another decade. The limitations upon the indebtedness of the state in the new constitution remained to slow the progress of construction while a large segment of popular opinion and the victorious Whigs in Albany chafed at the delay.

For the Radical Democrats, bitter in defeat, it was something that they were safe at least from a repetition of the Whig extravagances of Seward's day. "There is one consolation in all our political afflictions," wrote Churchill C. Cambreleng (who had been a Radical leader in the convention) to Van Buren, "the new Constitution binds the Whigs hand and foot and renders them harmless as doves."[64] Harmless as doves on the issue of canals, neither the Whigs nor their Hunker allies would prove to be.

[64] Cambreleng to Van Buren, November 30, 1846, Martin Van Buren Papers, LC.

18

The Canal Goes On,
1847-1854

E VEN BEFORE the victorious Whigs took control of the
state, the Whig press prepared the way for a new
policy toward internal improvements. The national conflict over the Wilmot Proviso, which would prohibit
slavery in territory which might be acquired in the war
with Mexico, divided their ranks between "Conscience"
and "Cotton" Whigs, and all but pushed canal controversy
into the realm of party history. Nevertheless although
the New York Whigs divided over slavery in the territories, they set out to vindicate their past canal program,
to pin responsibility for four years of inactivity in canal
construction upon the Democrats, and to prepare the
public mind for a liberal application of money to public
works.

An unusually large traffic crowded the Erie Canal in
November, leading the Albany *Journal* to announce that
"the Canal is not large enough to do the business it
attracts! The West cannot get its Produce to market!"[1]
Freight rates on eastward-moving cargoes doubled in
consequence of the pressure. Although the commissioners
filled the canal "brim-full" of water to enable boats to
carry a third more freight, in doing so they increased the
frequency of breaks and delays. All along the line the
Whigs could point to "Half-finished Locks and Aque-

ducts—rotting Timber—crumbling banks" and unused construction materials as the fruit of Democratic retrenchment. In New York City, the *Courier and Enquirer* of the
Whig editor, James Watson Webb, blamed "all this evil"
on the stop policy of the Democrats, and Webb brought
the financial article of the new constitution itself under
attack. "Unless we are greatly mistaken," warned the
influential New York editor, "the whole State will soon
feel the evils consequent upon this provision of the Constitution."[2]

When the legislature met in Albany in January, the
Whig majority heard Governor Young ask "not for special
or local, but for general resumption of the public works."
The echo of the last Whig governor's messages on the
canals and Western trade was unmistakable. "Secure the
trade of the great opening west, by enlarging the Erie
Canal," said Young, "and how unimportant is our present
indebtedness considered in connection with the revenue
that may reasonably be expected."[3] The address became
the opening sally of a six-year campaign against the debt-
restricting clauses of the constitution of 1846.

Notwithstanding the hobbles of the constitution, a
modest resumption of the public works was launched in
May of 1847. Nearly a million dollars were appropriated
to canal construction each year of Young's term, 15 miles
were added to the Erie enlargement to open 113 miles to
improved navigation, and eighty-one new structures were
finished. But progress was frustratingly slow. Some 250
miles of the Erie Canal remained to be enlarged, and
more than half of the enlarged structures were yet to be
completed. Crop failures in Europe stimulated the flow

[1] Albany *Evening Journal*, November 9, 1846.

[2] *Morning Courier and New York Enquirer*, November 13, 1846.

[3] Albany *Argus* (s.w.), January 5, 1847; Lincoln, *Messages from
the Governors*, IV, 372.

of goods down the canal in 1847, and tolls reached nearly three and a half millions, a level calculated by Ruggles and Seward not to be reached until 1849. With this vindication of the Whig "Forty Million Debt," Young told the legislature that "it is now clearly seen, by the demonstration of time and experience, that if the State had firmly and prudently persevered in that policy to the end . . . our great system of inland navigation would have been completed and perfected. . . ."[4]

Unlike Seward, Young was not to be allowed a second term in which to push the enlargement toward its conclusion. In the face of the growing divisions between Cotton and Conscience Whigs, the canal offered only a watery glue for the party. Young sided with the Conservatives, earned the opposition of Weed and the Conscience Whigs on grounds of both patronage and principles, and was passed over for renomination in 1848 in favor of Hamilton Fish of New York City. Fish was only thirty-nine years old, wealthy and respected, and his greatest years of public service would not come until he took a place in the cabinet of Ulysses S. Grant.

The election which sent Hamilton Fish to Albany became a three-cornered fight among Free-soilers, Hunker Democrats, and Whigs, with parties so bitterly divided over the extension of slavery that the canal was only incidentally at issue. The divided Democrats gave the national election to General Zachary Taylor, "the hero of Buena Vista," and enabled the minority Whigs to sweep the state offices in New York. In the legislature the fratricidal voting of the Democracy gave the Whigs a windfall majority of 104 seats in both houses. The victors entered a slavery fight of their own over the selection of Seward for the Senate seat of John A. Dix,

---

[4] Lincoln, *Messages from the Governors,* IV, 389-90.

but turning to local affairs, the Whigs continued to vote appropriations for the enlargement of the Erie Canal. Nearly $1,000,000 went to the enlargement in 1849, and more than $600,000 was added in 1850. Indeed, the Whig assemblymen and senators voted funds with a zeal which was far ahead of the perfunctory references to the public works in the messages of the new Whig governor. Hamilton Fish was the down-state exception in the succession of Whig executives in New York who ardently gave themselves to the cause of internal improvements.

By contrast, the gubernatorial contest of 1850 was between two candidates almost equally devoted to the cause of the canal. Horatio Seymour stood at the head of a Democracy struggling to return to unity, and the Whigs turned to Washington Hunt of Lockport, who had grown to manhood in a village owing its very existence to the Erie Canal. In the crisscrossing personal and political loyalties of the day, Horatio Seymour was the fast friend of Hamilton Fish, while Washington Hunt had joined with William L. Marcy in the operation of a mill and factory at Lockport which were dependent upon the surplus waters of the canal for their power. Since the fall elections of 1849 Seymour and Marcy had labored to find a formula on the extension of slavery by which the two wings of the Democracy could unite, and so successful were their efforts that only the want of 262 votes kept Seymour from the governorship. Washington Hunt, meanwhile, eked out his victory from a Whig party now split into Woolly Heads and Silver Grays, bedeviled as it was by Seward's "Higher Law" in the debates on the Compromise of 1850.[5]

Hunt returned the canal issue to the forefront of state politics, where it would remain until the constitutional

[5] Van Deusen, *Thurlow Weed*, p. 182.

limitations on the enlargement would finally be broken in 1854. Although the slavery conflict overshadowed all others in New York and the nation, his views on internal improvements belonged with the half-century just closing. His close friend and confidant was Samuel B. Ruggles, whose philosophy Hunt shared and whom he sought to persuade to take the office of comptroller which he himself had just vacated to become governor. "Acting together," Hunt wrote to Ruggles, "we can make New York a great state, great at home, potential abroad. We can preserve the Whig party, and carry out its principles on a generous scale."[6]

Generosity of scale in Hunt's first message to the legislature in January, 1851, meant the immediate completion of the enlargement of the Erie Canal. In the spirit, if not the handwriting, of Ruggles, the message declared that the Erie Canal had doubled the trade and population of New York, benefited the state beyond estimation, and was "destined to pour into our lap, during all future time, a stream of tribute rich and inexhaustible beyond any example in history, ancient or modern."[7] Looking back over the sixteen years of construction since the enlargement was authorized in 1835 and recalling the nearly sixteen millions already spent upon it, the governor thought it remarkable "that any portion of our people should deem it wise or necessary to occupy a quarter of a century in enlarging and perfecting a work, which was constructed originally under circumstances far more difficult, in less than one-third of that period."

Hunt recognized three possible plans for proceeding with the enlargement. First the state might issue revenue certificates pledging future canal revenues, at the risk of

---

[6] Washington Hunt to Ruggles, November 23, 1850, Samuel B. Ruggles Papers, NYPL.
[7] Lincoln, *Messages from the Governors*, IV, 543.

the purchaser, for their redemption. Second, a loan might be authorized meeting the constitutional requirement of a direct tax for the payment of the interest on the debt. And third, the plan favored by the governor called for a loan of seven or eight millions, sanctioned by an amendment to the constitution, to allow the entire enlargement to be completed by 1856.

Reaction to the message was partisan as ever, but Webb reported in New York that in that city there were "very few individuals of any party, who do not frankly avow, that to persevere in the present ridiculously slow mode of enlargement, is palpable folly."[8] For the opposition, the Radical New York *Evening Post* called the revenue certificate plan "a trick, . . . a paltry and dirty evasion of the prohibition of the constitution," and the proposal for a loan authorized by an amendment, "a direct attack upon the constitution."[9] Hunt complained to Marcy that the *Atlas* was "very savage" upon him and he feared himself vulnerable to charges that his investments at Lockport with Marcy lay behind his canal proposals. Moreover, though Hunt joined Hamilton Fish and Weed in efforts to reconcile the "Woollies" and the Cotton Whigs in New York and Washington, it was easy to believe that the plums of canal patronage would be used to bolster the Woolly Heads in their domination of the party. By March the governor was ready to act. Believing that public opinion was "right in all quarters," and hearing the voice of the people "calling loudly for prompt action," he opened consultations with the Democrats to gain their backing for a canal bill. He urged Ruggles to prepare an address to the merchants of New York to show them that "they can have Ohio, Western Pennsylvania, Michi-

[8] *Morning Courier and New York Enquirer*, January 9, 1851.
[9] New York *Evening Post*, January 8, 1851.

gan, Indiana, Illinois, Wisconsin, Iowa, Minnesota and Upper Canada for customers." A petition was framed to be sent to western New York for signatures, in the expectation of overwhelming response. "The prospect of success fills my soul with exultation," was his elated comment to Ruggles.[10]

The way was further prepared by the report of the state engineer and surveyor, H. C. Seymour, showing that during the next session the utmost capacity of the canal would be exceeded.[11] He put the limit of traffic going from and arriving at tidewater at 2,600,000 tons and estimated that this limit would be exceeded by nearly three hundred thousand tons in 1852. Only a "speedy and *progressive* enlargement" of the Erie Canal, said the state engineer, would allow it to challenge the New York railroads or the rival routes to Canada, Philadelphia, or Baltimore.

Unfortunately for the governor as well as the state, the legislature chose the plan of the sale of revenue certificates to go on with the enlargement. A bill emerged from the Committee on Canals, sponsored by Whigs and Conservative Democrats, which soon became notorious as the "Nine Million Bill." It would provide for the completion of the Erie Canal, as well as the Black River and Genesee Valley canals, by the sale of nine million dollars of certificates based on the future revenues of the canals. These certificates would serve as banking capital and add to the circulating currency of the state. Petitions poured into the assembly in support of the bill; the Whig press throughout the state backed it, and it was passed by the Whig majority by a vote of 76 to 27. Only four Democrats voted for the bill, and two of these were

[10] Washington Hunt to Ruggles, March 31, 1851, Samuel B. Ruggles Papers, NYPL.
[11] New York, *Assembly Documents*, 74th Sess., III, Doc. 45.

contractors. Behind this vote was the hand of Thurlow Weed, the "Wizard of the Lobby," whose consummate skill guided the bill through the session. The Dictator's *Evening Journal* predicted that the measure, "so palpably proper, and fraught with so many bright results," would allow the completion of the enlargement within four years, "without an increase of the State Debt and without a resort to taxation. By anticipating our revenues, the Canal is permitted to enlarge itself."[12]

Although Whig ingenuity denied the creation of a state debt, the Radical Barnburners decried a "New Nine Million Debt," much as they had the forty-million debt a decade earlier. In the senate the Democratic minority prepared to block the measure by whatever means possible. They took strength from the report of the Democratic attorney-general, Levi S. Chatfield, who rejected the scheme as "a direct, open and palpable infraction of the constitution," and whose arguments were widely distributed in a pamphlet entitled, *Pay as You Go*.[13] The Whigs countered by enlisting the aid of none other than Daniel Webster, then visiting in Albany. The "Godlike" studied the act and found it no violation of the state or national constitutions. To the Barnburner opposition, Webster's opinion was "foreign" interference by "this mercenary of the bar."

A party vote among the Whigs would have seen the bill through the senate and into law, had not the Barnburners resorted to a desperate stratagem. To prevent the necessary three-fifths quorum from voting, twelve senators resigned, leaving three Democrats to join the Whigs for the passage of necessary appropriation bills. The Whigs refused even to act on these, a thirteenth

12 Albany *Evening Journal*, March 29, 1851.
13 Quoted in New York *Evening Post*, April 12, 1851.

Democrat withdrew, and the legislature adjourned. On the last day of the session, the resigning senators presented a "Manifesto," which excited Weed to warn in the *Journal* that the state was "in the midst of a Revolution."[14]

The governor responded with a proclamation calling for an extra session of the legislature to meet in June. Of the "Immortal Thirteen," as the *Evening Post* called the opposition senators, eleven promptly stood for reelection. All six of them from canal districts were defeated save Henry B. Stanton from Seneca County, who was reelected by a majority of only 5 votes. Of the seven new senators elected, four were Whigs and three were canal Democrats. "It has rarely, if ever, happened in this state," observed the *Evening Post*, "that a political issue so recently formed . . . has so suddenly and thoroughly aroused the attention of the people."[15]

The special elections to fill the seats of the seceding senators became a twin referendum on the Nine Million Bill and on the method of opposition chosen by the seceders. When Benjamin N. Huntington defeated Abijah Mann in Oneida County by a large majority, James Watson Webb found Huntington "one of the best witnesses to the value of the Canals, that could be found in the State. He knew Oneida County as it was when the Canal was not in existence, and in its transition to the opulence, and industry, and population that distinguishes it from the sparsely settled wilderness of other days, he sees the real worth of the Canal policy." The Whigs made the most of the irregular method chosen to block the bill, as Webb, for example, called the senatorial resignations "little short of treason." They quoted from the opinions of Judge Ambrose Spencer and Judge Daniel

---

[14] Albany *Evening Journal*, April 18, 1851.
[15] New York *Evening Post*, June 4, 1851.

Lord, as well as from the opinion of Webster, for the constitutionality of their measure, and they emphasized the value of the canal revenue certificates in augmenting the currency of the state.

It was the prospect of the inflationary effect of the Nine Million Bill which most alarmed the business community. The New York *Journal of Commerce*, usually unaffiliated politically, feared that if the bill were to pass, business would take flight "on the wings of paper money."[16] Speculation would increase, bankruptcy would result, and "years of calamity" would follow.

The Democrats found themselves in an embarrassing dilemma. From Utica, Daniel Wager wrote to Marcy, "Our friends here with great unanimity condemn the Canal Bill. With nearly equal unanimity, they condemn the resignation of the Senators as anti-republican and revolutionary, tending in no degree to defeat the bill, but directly tending to prostrate the democratic party." Marcy agreed that the senators had taken "a false step from which we shall suffer some."[17] A canal meeting of Democrats in Buffalo revealed the pain of the Democrats as they were thrust into a stance opposing the enlargement of the Erie Canal. One Denson rose to declare himself a "barnburner of the darkest hue," but also "an unswerving friend of our State Canals and their early enlargement."[18] Israel T. Hatch of Oswego complained that "a great wrong has been done to *Western New York*," while an avowed Hunker, H. K. Smith, defended the Nine Million Bill and denounced "*the attempt at Albany to array the Democratic party without consulting it against the enlargement of the State Canals.*" The Barnburners took what comfort they could from a

16 New York *Journal of Commerce*, May 1, 1851.
17 Marcy to A. Campbell, May 28, 1851, William L. Marcy Papers, LC.
18 New York *Express*, April 25, 1851.

Lock No. 36 on the enlarged Erie Canal at Little Falls, from a recent photograph

REMAINS OF THE RICHMOND AQUEDUCT ACROSS THE SENECA
RIVER AT MONTEZUMA

meeting of fifty-five members of the constitutional convention who gathered in Albany in May and pronounced the Nine Million Bill repugnant to the constitution which they had written in 1846.

Moreover, in the very month of the senatorial secession, the New York and Erie Railroad was completed to Lake Erie, allowing travel over the 450 miles from Dunkirk to New York in twenty hours. Radical prints such as the *Atlas* had long warned against "intemperate zeal" for the enlargement because railroads crossing the central and southern parts of the state would soon claim an increasing share of Western trade. Compounding the problem of railroad competition, the legislature of 1851 removed the tolls that had been placed upon the railroads to protect the commerce of the canals. In New York City, a correspondent to the *Journal of Commerce* warned that "we shall see that Railroad transportation . . . will supersede canal transportation almost entirely," while the *Evening Post* anticipated that the railroads would turn the Erie Canal into "a useless ditch."[19]

The extra session of the legislature called by the governor sat for a month and in July of 1851 passed the ill-fated Nine Million Bill. Within another month, more than three million dollars in revenue certificates were authorized. At the request of the governor, Judge Greene C. Bronson, former judge of the state supreme court, gave an opinion that the new law was constitutional and that the certificates were secured by a fourth mortgage on the canal revenue.

With the excitement aroused by the passage of the canal bill fresh in the minds of the voters, the Whig leaders willingly avoided the slavery question and made the en-

[19] New York *Journal of Commerce*, April 28, 1851; New York *Evening Post*, May 2, 1851.

largement of the Erie Canal the first issue of the fall elections of 1851. Weed made the canal "the burden of his song" and Webb was emphatic that "beyond all question, the coming election is to determine forever, the Canal Policy in this State."[20] In Utica, the Oneida *Weekly Herald* urged that the issue of "immediate Enlargement, or no Enlargement" hung upon the election. That print pulled out all the stops and promised that with a Whig victory "every laborer in the State will have enough to do, and fair wages. No children will be crying for bread, and no wives or mothers shivering in the winter's cold, for want of the necessaries of life."[21]

Publicly, at least, the Democrats joined the Whigs in subordinating the slavery question to the canal. Their state ticket was divided between Hunkers and Barnburners, and as their candidate for state treasurer, Benjamin Welch of the Buffalo *Republic*, reported, "Other subjects have been dropped, and all the energies of the Democracy will be directed to the protection of the honor of the State and the integrity of the Constitution."[22] The Buffalo editor listed seventy presses throughout the state that opposed the Nine Million Bill, and the New York *Evening Post* warned that the Whig cry of "the Canal in Danger" covered "one of the most bare-faced violations of the constitution ever devised by the mind of man." But canal Democrats in Buffalo, Rochester, and Syracuse bolted the ticket in sufficient numbers to bring Marcy the report of a "wide-spread system of secret treachery." In Utica, Horatio Seymour watched the returns come in and prayed for a majority on the Canal Board. "If we have," he assured Marcy, "all will be well."[23]

[20] *Morning Courier and New York Enquirer,* September 25, 1851.

[21] Oneida *Weekly Herald,* October 21, 1851.

[22] Quoted in *ibid.,* November 9, 1851.

[23] Seymour to Marcy, November 11, 1851, William L. Marcy Papers, LC.

All, or very nearly all, was well. The Democrats carried all but two of the state offices at contest; they tied the Whigs in the senate, and gained a majority of two in the assembly. Marcy admitted that "the canal issue weighed us down," but it had been more than counterbalanced by the defection of the Cotton Whigs in New York City from the Whig ticket. With the Canal Board secure in Democratic hands, Marcy found himself besieged with applicants for places as collector, superintendent of canals, canal auditor, and lesser posts. The despondent Whigs had staked all on the canal and lost. J. L. Talcott wrote to Weed, "Can you see any light ahead?—Is there a 'good time coming'? If so please mention the date."

Had the election turned thumbs down on the Nine Million Bill and the enlargement of the Erie Canal? Notwithstanding the vote of no confidence for the Whigs, the Whig vote in the canal counties had shown a strong desire that the enlargement should go on. Governor Hunt reported to the legislature that every officer elected to the Canal Board had been elected upon a public pledge "supposed to be binding in honor and morality" to support the law.[24] It was clear that the Canal Board must implement a law at best clouded in public support.

The "big letting" was made in December. "From all parts of the State, from other states, from all walks of life —from every profession, pursuit and trade, from every division and sub-division of political sects," reported a legislative committee, a legion of applicants swarmed upon the capitol for a share of the melon soon to be cut. Canal revenue certificates worth a million and a half dollars were issued before the year was out in a dispensation wholly political. The work was equally divided between "the democratic and whig bidders, without

[24] Lincoln, *Messages from the Governors,* IV, 627.

regard to their being the lowest bidders."[25] Charges cir-
culated that political favorites often devoid of experience
in canal building had won the contracts over the lower
bids of their competitors. If "one tithe of the stories"
were true, advised the Whig Buffalo *Advertiser,* the contracts should be rescinded and the offenders punished.
An Albany reporter found it "known and notorious" that
gross favoritism had prevailed in the contracts, with "a
thousand witnesses to prove it, throughout the state."[26]
Seward Whigs and Hunker Democrats had gathered in
the windfall, while Barnburners and Cotton Whigs had
been denied.

Protest action against the lettings appeared almost
simultaneously in the legislature, in the banking community, and among contractors who had lost out. In
February of 1852 a joint legislative committee launched
an investigation which produced 1,200 pages of testimony
and upheld the lettings of the Canal Board.[27] However,
George W. Newell, auditor of the Canal Department,
refused to pay a draft of $110 on a contract let under
the Nine Million Bill. The case of *Newell v. People*
became a test case and reached the Court of Appeals.
When the decision came in May, the court held the Nine
Million Bill unconstitutional. The state engineer promptly
ordered a stoppage of work on contracts let under this
act and the Whigs found themselves thwarted in the
execution of the law they had worked so long to procure.

The Democratic Radicals were jubilant. With the death
of the disputed law just a year after its passage, the
Evening Post in New York could crow, "Its friends and
advocates have polluted themselves to no purpose with
the foul means which were taken to procure the passage

25 New York, *Assembly Documents,* 75th Sess., III, Doc. 89, p. 24.
26 New York *Evening Post,* January 19, 1852.
27 New York, *Assembly Documents,* 75th Sess., III, Doc. 89.

of the bill and to turn its execution to their own personal profit."[28] The more prosaic *Journal of Commerce* reported "a very general and cordial approval in business circles" of the decision. In western New York, however, the Democracy was far from content. A public canal meeting in Rochester voted resolutions petitioning the governor to call the legislature into session for the passage of a constitutional amendment to enable the enlargement to proceed. "In western New York," said a delegate, "it is a rare instance to find a Democrat who is not in favor of the Canal Enlargement." Replying to the Rochester resolutions, Hunt assured his friends in western New York that the controversy would end yet in support for the enlargement. "You and I, who have spent most of our days in Western New York," he wrote to Mayor Hamblin Stilwell of the Flour City, "have witnessed the wonderful and beneficent influences of the Erie Canal, in the growth of cities and the rapid settlement and improvement of the country."[29]

For the defeated Whigs with two years of labor gone for nought, all that remained was to attempt to secure a constitutional amendment to remove the prohibition against borrowing for the canals. James Watson Webb summed up the Whig predicament in this hour of defeat: "The Enlargement of the Canal is a measure which the Whig party of this State cannot abandon if they would. Their whole history of the last thirty-five years has pledged them to it. . . ."[30] Both parties, meanwhile, looked to the fall elections for returns on the events of the preceding spring. For their part, the Whigs hoped to use the defeat of the Nine Million Bill to dramatize their support for the canal.

[28] New York *Evening Post*, May 12, 1851.
[29] Quoted in *Morning Courier and New York Enquirer*, June 7, 1852.
[30] *Ibid.*, May 18, 1852.

As in nearly every election for a decade, the greater problem so far as the canal was concerned was presented to the Democrats. They must make choices which would preserve the appearance of unity yet secure the canal policy of one or the other faction. Seymour's close vote in 1850 and his advocacy of Marcy's cause in the presidential nomination at Baltimore in June virtually assured him a place at the head of the state Democratic ticket. Seymour, however, had also stumped the state for the "Fugitive Senators" who had resigned to defeat the canal law of 1851. Since this equivocation had identified Seymour with the opposition to the "speedy enlargement policy," William F. Russel of Saugerties pleaded, "let us take some Western man that goes Canal enlargement first, last, and all the time. . . ." Israel T. Hatch of Oswego urged the party leaders to put someone on the ticket "whose local and pecuniary interest place his fidelity to the Enlargement beyond a question."[31] But Marcy's choice prevailed, and the Democratic convention emerged from their labors in September of 1852 with Seymour as their candidate for governor.

With Seymour, the Democrats renominated Sanford B. Church, a Barnburner, to repeat their ticket of 1850. Church was wanted on the Canal Board in part to balance the renomination of Frederick Follett of Genesee County as canal commissioner. Follett had had a part in the tainted contracts of 1851 and had publicly opposed the decision of the Court of Appeals on their legality. In August, Marcy had written, "I wish above all other *temporal things* the triumph of the Democracy, and the rescue of the State Treasury from the hands of the robbers." But now with Follett renominated, Marcy made

[31] Hatch to William L. Marcy, June 28, 1852, William L. Marcy Papers, LC.

the best of a bad nomination in the name of party unity. "To appease the canal interests we put upon the ticket one of the old commissioners who in truth is not worthy of the place," he wrote in September. "Though a rotten piece of timber he strengthens our fabric."[32] James A. Wadsworth was less sanguine. He feared that "an honest administration of our finances cannot be looked for," and added, "I hope we will not be entirely dwarfed by this infamous canal business."[33]

Follett's renomination almost immediately embarrassed the Democracy when the canal auditor made his report to the Canal Board in September. George Washington Newell had become the focus of the struggle over the 1851 lettings in the court fights during the spring. As auditor of the Canal Department he stood for honest administration of the canals, and as the brother-in-law of Marcy and a loyal Democrat, he worked for the interests of the party. Newell reported to the board on the expenditures made between August of 1851 and August of 1852. His figures revealed that expenditures under the Democratic commissioners, Follett and Mather, were more than 50 percent higher in 1852 than in 1851, while those under the Whig commissioner, Henry Fitzhugh, were up only 23 percent. The auditor was required by law to notify the Canal Board when reports of the superintendents were unsatisfactory, and he so judged the accounts on portions of the canal under the commissioners elected by his own party. "If I shall not have credit for a desire to protect the public interest," wrote Newell at the conclusion of his report, "I shall have at least endeavored to save myself from censure, where silence and

[32] Marcy to A. Campbell, September 8, 1852, William L. Marcy Papers, LC.
[33] Wadsworth to William L. Marcy, September 14, 1852, William L. Marcy Papers, LC.

inaction on my part would tend to prolong what I believe to be a wasteful and improvident expenditure of public money. . . ."[34]

Newell's exposé gave the Whigs a field day against their economizing opponents. They renominated Washington Hunt for the governorship and, on state issues, directed their attack against Seymour's defense of the Fugitive Senators. Seymour was made out to be the embodiment of Democratic perfidy on the question of the canals, first pledging the Democracy to carry out the Nine Million Bill before the election of 1851 and then joining in the Barnburner movement to stop work on the canals and attack the constitutionality of the law. Seymour himself published a pamphlet in opposition to the controversial law, even translating his views into German since, as he said, "the Germans are very much opposed to debt and taxation." Although the Whigs were grievously divided over the slavery question and Weed was almost certain of impending defeat, Charles Stebbins of Carmonia warned Marcy that if the Democrats should be beaten, "it will be owing in my judgment to the unfortunate position of the canal question." He saw arrayed against Seymour not only the "ultra canal interest" but also the "army of contractors" whose private interests governed their votes. "The canal subject," he lamented, "has been about as badly handled by our friends as it could be and gives the Whigs a tremendous advantage."[35]

Seymour, however, kept the support of the canal Democrats. The *Argus* came to his rescue with public assurance that "his friendship was strong for the canals, but stronger for the constitution." Seymour's canal record could be traced back to 1844 when he had supported a

[34] New York, *Assembly Documents*, 76th Sess., II, Doc. 15, p. 125.
[35] Stebbins to Marcy, October 14, 1852, William L. Marcy Papers, LC.

bill for the Schoharie Creek aqueduct and enlargement of the Jordan level. "If any one man in the state is more entitled to credit than another for calling into life the public works after their suspension in 1842," wrote Croswell, "it is Horatio Seymour."[36] As the nation preferred Franklin Pierce to General Winfield Scott in 1852, so New Yorkers gave Seymour 22,000 more votes than Hunt. Although Hunt carried every canal county west of Ontario, Seymour won forty-three out of the fifty-nine in the state, and in the assembly, Democrats outnumbered the Whigs nearly two to one.

When Seymour took office as the first Democrat since Bouck to occupy the governor's chair in New York, he devoted half of his opening address to the legislature on the subject of the public works. Once more the long history of the Erie Canal and its enlargement was recited by a New York governor. Seymour recommended immediate improvements to allow the use of new boats loaded to 150 tons throughout the canal and the further expenditure of a million dollars a year for six years until these new boats could carry full capacity of 240 tons and the lateral canals could be completed as well. Whether the requisite money should be raised by taxation, loan, or constitutional amendment, the governor left for the legislature to determine. It was evident that he had moved steadily toward the Barnburner side of the dispute over financing the canals when he added, "A strict regard for economy and the mandates of organic law are of vital importance in republican governments."

Early in the legislative session it became clear that 1853 would be the year of decision to bring the enlargement to completion. The rival Democratic factions placed

[36] Albany *Argus*, October 21, 1852.

two plans for action before the legislature, each providing for an amendment to the constitution. That of the Barnburners emerged from resolutions proposed by Arphaxad Loomis and became known as the "Assembly plan" or "West plan." This would authorize a new debt of one and a half million dollars a year for six years to be repaid by direct taxation. The plan of the Hunkers was drawn in the senate by John Vanderbilt, a canal Democrat from Long Island. Vanderbilt would have the state borrow two and a half million dollars a year for four years to create state stock to be redeemed from the future canal revenues without resort to taxation. To this plan rallied the Hunkers, the Whigs, and the canal commissioners. The latter, Follett, Mather, and Fitzhugh, produced a report to show that the greater delay in repayment under the Vanderbilt plan would cause a greater share of the cost of the enlargement to be borne by tolls on goods from Western states rather than from New York.

For two months the legislature debated little else and their dispute reverberated throughout the state. "Canals, canalling and canallers, are all that is talked of," reported the *Evening Post* in New York; "this subject governs all the politics of the state. What Buffalo wants, what Oswego won't submit to, what Rochester has declared in her Whig Convention, what Lockport requires for her milling property, these are the questions which are asked. . . ."[37] The Democracy divided under new names of Hardshells and Softshells. Seymour and Marcy were the leaders of the "Softs" as they were alleged to have made unconscionable concessions to the Barnburners while the Hunkers held hard and fast to their canal program. Thus the Hardshell *Argus* ridiculed the "free-soil and soft scheme

[37] New York *Evening Post*, February 22, 1853.

of taxing the people of the entire state for the means to scratch the bottom and tickle the sides of the canal. . . ."[38]

The Democratic majority in Albany legislated on the canals under the gun of popular censure at the polls. John L. Pruyn of Albany warned that the assembly plan would not do with the public, for "the tone of our press and of a large portion of the party has been such as to justify the expectation that we would propose to amend the constitution, [and] raise money to a moderate amount in that way, to go on with canals." From Penn Yan in the central part of the state, D. A. Ogden warned Marcy that the canal question was "the great disturbing element" in Democratic prospects for the fall elections; while from the sidelines, Webb's *Courier and Enquirer* gleefully reported the agonies of the Democracy. "That on the Canal question the party is widely broken up," wrote the New York editor, "cannot and will not be denied."[39]

Seymour worked for the assembly plan, opposed that of Vanderbilt, and placed the blame for the division of the Democrats over the canals at the door of Edwin Croswell and the *Argus*. "The whole power of the opposition" was centered there; "without him and his press the rest of the concern could do nothing," he advised Marcy.[40] But Vanderbilt's Hunker ally in the senate, James E. Cooley, assured Marcy that it was Seymour himself who was responsible for the impasse as the governor sought to "browbeat the legislature." "The Governor, as you very well know, is kind-hearted, amicable but exceedingly timid, and in some respects, a weak man," wrote the

---

[38] Albany *Argus*, March 24, 1853.

[39] *Morning Courier and New York Enquirer*, March 25, 1853.

[40] Horatio Seymour to Marcy, March 20, 1853, William L. Marcy Papers, LC.

senator to Marcy, and Cooley feared that Seymour was "in the hands, almost entirely, of bad advisers."[41] Seymour entered the legislative lists in April of 1853 with a special message calling for an immediate appropriation of only a little more than half a million dollars to allow the use of new boats on a "150 ton canal." He did not refer to the rival plans to amend the constitution before the legislature, but his sympathies were clearly with the plan supported by the assembly. He recommended a "modest annual appropriation" to complete the enlargement because the history of the canals had shown that even more important than the amount of the funds provided was "the wisdom, economy and fidelity with which they are applied." To the Hunkers the special message was an attempt to check the growing sentiment for the Vanderbilt plan. Weed's *Evening Journal* taunted that unless the assembly could be induced to take the Vanderbilt amendment, the legislators would have to "go home to their constituents and confess that the 'Democracy' were unable to do anything for the Canals."

Weed and the Whigs prepared to profit from the chronic inability of the Democrats to survive their own success. The Radical opposition to the Hunkers had helped the Whigs to "use up Gov. Bouck," wrote the Dictator, and now Seymour's abuse of the Hunker senators would only help to elect the Whigs in November. As on so many occasions in the past, the New York Whigs played their cards from the strength of their devotion to the trade of the West. The Buffalo *Commercial Advertiser*, a Whig print, warned that New York stood on "the verge of a crisis" in her control of Western trade, which "once allowed to slip, may not be easily recovered." Weed watched the completion of the Pennsylvania railroad

[41] Cooley to Marcy, March 23, 1853, William L. Marcy Papers, LC.

system as the Keystone State "extends her arms toward the West" and repeated a perennial theme:

> The fatuity which governs our councils—which *creates* and *sustains a party in this State in opposition to the Canals,* is entirely beyond our comprehension. The people of Ohio, of Indiana, of Michigan, of Illinois, and of Wisconsin, witnessed with amazement the resignation and flight of Senators from this Capitol, and the disorganization of the government, in 1851, to prevent the passage of bills for the Speedy Completion of our Public Works. They watched with intense anxiety . . . the defeat and rebuke of the Anti-Canal faction.
>
> When the enemies of the Canals stole into power . . . to renew their assaults upon our improvement system, . . . They saw their own hopes cut down and destroyed; and saw New York rejecting the richest boon of commercial supremacy ever offered to man—equally her exclusive natural right, and the ungrudged tribute of the great valleys which covet a highway to the markets of the world through her borders.[42]

The factional fight over the enlargement reached its climax in mid-April, with a result that had been predicted, if not foreordained. The Vanderbilt resolutions came to a vote in the senate and there passed handily, eight Democratic senators voting "aye" with the Whigs and six Democratic senators casting the only opposing votes. In the assembly, the Vanderbilt resolutions met the hardened opposition of the Barnburners, backed by Seymour and by Marcy in Pierce's cabinet in Washington. It appeared that Pierce had thrown the patronage of the national government against the "Softs" when he appointed Greene C. Bronson and other Hunkers to federal offices in New York. The Barnburner Levi S. Chatfield appealed in desperation to Marcy, "Is it the desire and intention of the President to blow us to Hell in the fall? . . . The

[42] Albany *Evening Journal,* April 1, 1853.

President has so plainly indicated his preferences for the enemies of the constitution and our financial safety that all is lost."[43]

But party lines held firm. When the vote was taken, the Vanderbilt resolutions failed in the assembly, the assembly plan could not succeed in the senate, and no agreement could be reached before the session ended on April 13. The assembly used its final hours for the impeachment of the Hunker canal commissioner, John C. Mather, for unauthorized and excessive expenditures on the eastern division of the Erie Canal. The alleged political motive was to allow the Barnburners to get "full swing at an offending Hunker." To Webb, in the *Courier*, the assembly vote and the impeachment of Mather were a quixotic repetition of the Democratic removal of De Witt Clinton in 1824, with retribution at the hands of the people to follow as surely in their wake. It was against this almost certain sequel that Seymour called the legislature into extra session the day after its adjournment with the demand that it provide for the enlargement to go on. The governor's personal support, however, remained with the assembly plan in the belief that it would "be received with more favor by the people of the State, as it is not open to the suspicion of being designed to advance private interests."

The legislature received the governor's message and then adjourned to meet again in the last week of May. By that time, a "Soft" assured Marcy, "I think returning sanity will take the place of discord. We shall have a canal law submitted to the people." But D. A. Ogden was less confident. "There is much bad feeling & bitterness, and what the end is to be no one can tell," he wrote from the canal appraisers office; "If matters go on as they now

[43] Chatfield to Marcy, April 11, 1853, William L. Marcy Papers, LC.

promise to do, we shall very likely loos [*sic*] the state next fall & for years to come."[44] Meanwhile pressure for decision or compromise built up throughout the state. It was strongest from the Hunker and Whig presses which wished the speedier program of the Vanderbilt plan enacted into law.

"The produce of the west and of our State, is pouring in, crowding along, wedging up, and all upon account of the inability of the canals to accommodate the demand," wrote Croswell in the *Argus* on the first of May. For the next three weeks the Hunker editor developed the theme of the necessity of the enlargement of the Erie Canal for the commerce of the West and for revenues which would diminish the taxes of the state. Down-state the New York *Times* reported that the "newly awakened sentiment of the people, not only on the line of the canal, but throughout the state, [is] in favor of speedy and effectual enlargement." A Brooklyn Common Council meeting passed resolutions which endorsed the Vanderbilt plan. The Herkimer *Democrat*, from Loomis' home district, asserted that "nine-tenths of the tax payers of Herkimer county" favored the Vanderbilt plan, and insisted that "the people will look for some provisions for the completion of the canals." Farther west, the Seneca County *Courier* called upon the legislature "to act decisively and finally upon it in some form."[45]

From western New York, the Buffalo Board of Trade petitioned the legislature that the wealth of "the Great West" was "piled up waiting the means of reaching New York." In Lockport, former governor Washington Hunt labored "to give an impulse to public opinion," and a canal meeting at Rochester resolved that the Erie Canal

[44] Ogden to Marcy, April 27, 1853, William L. Marcy Papers, LC.
[45] Quoted in Albany *Argus*, May 21, 1853.

must be enlarged "at the earliest practicable period . . . without any resort at any time to taxation." The Rochester Daily Advertiser found it futile "to attempt to resist the mighty current of Popular Sentiment which is setting so irresistably in favor of the onward progress of our Public Works." In Syracuse, the *Daily Journal* served notice that "every word and movement" relating to the canal question in the legislature would be watched and every member held to "strict accountability" for his vote. Back in Albany, Weed's *Evening Journal* quoted the New Orleans *Picayune* as saying that "the question of the New York Canal Enlargement is familiar to the whole country . . . ," and reported that the pressure of public sentiment was bearing upon the legislature "with crushing force."[46]

The legislature reconvened on the twenty-fourth of May. The first break in the stalemate came when the assembly bill went to the senate. In spite of the application of what Senator Cooley called "the most abominable piece of Inquisition thumb-screw ever devised," the Hunkers won partial victory by cutting the tax provision from the assembly bill, although the six-year provision was retained. To Weed, who was in effective control of the Whigs in the legislature, this was still the "snail-pace policy," and Loomis fought to substitute "may" for "shall" in the clause providing for the borrowing and expenditure of money for the canals. Loomis was so far successful that when the assembly concurred with the senate deletion of taxation, the bill was made permissive rather than imperative. But this the Hunkers and Whigs refused to accept. "It is without qualification a cheat—which settles nothing, and accomplishes nothing, with certainty,"

[46] Quotations cited here are found in Hunt to Samuel B. Ruggles, May 22, 1853, Samuel B. Ruggles Papers, NYPL; Albany *Argus*, May 24, 30, 1853; Albany *Evening Journal*, April 30, 1853.

wrote Croswell, for the enlargement might be interrupted "as often as a legislature can be elected hostile to the canal policy of the State."[47] The senate refused to concur and requested a conference committee with the assembly, which ironically was what Senator Cooley had been refused at the opening of the regular session in January.

While the legislature went off on a railroad excursion to Niagara Falls, Seymour and the administration leaders worked for compromise. The conference committee met on June 8 and agreement was reached. Two and a quarter million dollars would be spent each year for four years on the enlargement and the laterals, and one and a half million dollars would be set aside for redemption of the canal certificates of 1851, making in all, a debt of ten and a half million dollars. All hope of further opposition lost, the assembly voted unanimously for the compromise, and in the senate, only Jones of Newburgh voted against it.

The result was victory for the Hunkers and Whigs. The enlargement would be completed two years sooner than Seymour had recommended and the expenditures were mandatory. Croswell exulted in the *Argus* that "the result could scarcely have been more gratifying to the friends of the canals, or more conducive to the great interests of the state, under any circumstances." Weed took it as a triumph "extorted from the enemies of the Canals," and Webb's *Courier and Enquirer* fairly glowed with satisfaction. "The canal controversy is virtually at an end," Webb wrote; "the passage of this bill will be the most signal defeat the radical section of the Democratic party has ever experienced in this State."[48]

Worsted though they had been, the Radicals were relieved that the issue was settled. Seymour himself had

[47] Albany *Argus*, June 4, 1853.
[48] *Morning Courier and New York Enquirer*, June 14, 1853.

taken a major role in the compromise, fearing a coalition between the "Hard Shells & the Whigs to run a 'canal ticket'" in the fall elections. Curiously, he looked upon the victory as his own. Writing to Marcy his own version of the passage of the canal bill, he explained that "all of the discontent, disaffection & factious feeling have been 'Hived' in the Canal question. When we found the Swarm had settled on that point we put a box over them and I am mistaken if the plans of the Conspirators are not thwarted."[49] Congratulations poured in upon Marcy from those who had backed the union movement in the Democracy since 1849. "The settlement of this vexed and disturbing question, through our agency, and by democratic influence," wrote John C. Wright, "takes away from the factionists all pretext for defection." Another assured him that "we have got the Canal question in good shape," adding with an eye to the fall elections that "the Whigs have no Capital to trade on & the bolters will be too insignificant to crush." The Whigs, with Weed as their spokesman, claimed prior and higher virtue, but gave public recognition to the Democratic achievement. "Having from the beginning urged the completion of the Erie Canal Enlargement as a question superior to Party," wrote Weed, "we now freely award to Democrats the credit so justly due to them." At the same time, he warned that "to ensure the final triumph our friends must keep their Arms bright and their Powder dry."[50]

The vote in New York drew comment from the West as well. The Milwaukee *Sentinel* rejoiced that provision had been made "for prosecuting the noblest work of

[49] Horatio Seymour to Marcy, June 12, 1853, William L. Marcy Papers, LC.
[50] Albany *Evening Journal*, June 15, 1853.

Internal Improvement on the globe," and a Detroit print considered the measure of such "vital and widespread benefit to the west" that "its progress has been watched all the closer from the fact that though deeply interested, we are nevertheless powerless in regard to it."[51]

If the outcome of the long struggle over the canal bade as fair to the fortunes of Seymour and the Softs as they allowed themselves to believe, they were once more confronted with the problem of surviving a victory. The difficulties of the leaders of the Democracy lay not so much in their stars as in themselves. Their continued ascendency in the state depended upon the fall elections, and these they were not to win.

When the state Democratic convention met in Syracuse in September, the Hunkers bolted and named a separate ticket of their own. The bolt involved no dispute over the canal, but the nominations and the canvass fanned the embers of the enlargement issue. More important, this Democratic split virtually insured a Whig victory. The Hunkers endorsed the constitutional amendment and named George W. Clinton, the son of the famous canal governor, to head their ticket as secretary of state. They nominated Cooley for comptroller and selected Mather for canal commissioner. Seymour himself appeared in the ranks of the Softshells and, after the Hunkers had bolted, forced through a resolution supporting the amendment and his own administration. In Washington, Marcy and Pierce came belatedly to the aid of the Softs with the removal of Greene C. Bronson as collector of New York. Judge Bronson's appointment had been particularly grievous to the Barnburners as he had given a favorable opinion on the constitutionality of the Nine Million Bill

[51] Milwaukee *Sentinel*, quoted in Albany *Evening Journal*, June 21, 1853; Detroit *Daily Advertiser*, quoted in Albany *Argus*, June 21, 1853.

and had remained outspoken in his opposition to Radical canal policy. Bickering among the Democrats over the canals played directly into the hands of the Whigs.

Quick to exploit the Hunker bolt, Thurlow Weed wrote in the *Journal* that "the people can have no confidence in the Canal professions of the Barn Burners," for their conversion to the constitutional amendment had been too sudden to be sincere. Weed sang his familiar refrain: "The Canals are only safe in the hands of their friends." Friendship for the canals, however, would include Hunkers as well as Whigs. Weed urged that "the canal triumph should be COMPLETED as it was COMMENCED, by the united action of its Whig and Democratic friends." Weed hoped for a coalition with the Hards and professed to have desired a "Canal Organization, irrespective of old party lines," in preference to separate Whig and Hunker tickets.[52]

Although their doom was written in the bolt of the Hunkers, the Softshells explained their impending defeat by the plunder to be derived from the completion of the enlargement. Seymour expected to see "a horde of speculators" in Albany when the canal contracts were let. "Prince John" Van Buren thought the state besieged by the band of "thieves & robbers who marshalled under Croswell & Weed. . . ." Despite the overwhelming vote for the canal amendment in the summer session of the legislature, the question of the enlargement became paramount in all parties and factions as election day approached. The *Argus* put "CLINTON AND THE CANALS" at its masthead and reminded the electorate that the new legislature must concur in the amendment to the constitution before it could pass "through the ordeal of a popular vote." Softshell candidates for the legislature

[52] Albany *Evening Journal,* October 11, 1853.

were the "disguised enemies of the public works," warned Croswell.

As sober judgments had long predicted, the Democratic split threw the election to the Whigs. They carried both houses of the legislature and the Canal Board as well, electing Elias W. Leavenworth as secretary of state and James M. Cook as comptroller. Among the Democratic candidates, the Hardshell Hunkers ran far ahead of the Softshells. The latter were convinced that it was Whig votes from "Weed & Co." that had swelled the Hardshell columns. "As the Whigs were sure of the State, they voted freely for the Hard ticket," wrote Seymour in his post-mortem on the election.[53] Together the Whigs and the Hards had defeated the Softs, and the canal issue had been the cause of the defeat of the latter. Although the Bronson removal had been badly bungled by Pierce, James G. Dickie wrote from Buffalo to explain that it was the canal question and not the policies of the national administration which had produced the defeat. There and elsewhere, three out of five votes for the Hardshells were on the canal issue, Dickie explained; " 'Clinton & the Canals,' was rung in our ears for six weeks previous to the Election from morn until night, and then the *alleged* bad faith on the part of the present state officers was made quite a handle by the Adamantine Canal men, and obtained them many votes, in this section of the state."[54]

While the national crisis over free soil and slavery poisoned the politics of the Democracy in New York, the local issue of the Erie Canal hurried the breakup of the party which had dominated the state in all but four terms since the death of De Witt Clinton. The Demo-

[53] Seymour to Marcy, November 11, 1853, William L. Marcy Papers, LC.

[54] Dickie to Marcy, December 25, 1853, William L. Marcy Papers, LC.

cratic coalition was now "forever broken" by the anti-canal record of the Barnburners, declared Croswell in the *Argus*. "No coalitions, no unions, no compromises, no hypocritical resolutions, could have renewed the lease of power which the anti-canal faction had so disgracefully abused." The only hope of the Democracy, as Croswell saw it, was in a ticket of candidates friendly to the canals. "The people have said it," he wrote, "and the annihilation of a dozen parties, if necessary for the end, would be assured. The canals will be enlarged and completed."[55]

In the months following the election of 1853 the separation of the two wings of the Democratic party in New York widened. The *Argus* noted "the quiet but thorough separation daily going on in every county," and in Rochester, the *Daily Advertiser* joined other Hunker presses in shunning any thought of reunion. "It is the answer of every man that we know," said that print, "who voted with us in November." In less than a year the Kansas-Nebraska Act would complete the collapse of the old political order in New York, driving many of the Democratic Radicals into the new-born Republican party and reshaping the Democracy to which the Hunkers would give their allegiance. The defeat of the Radicals over the issue of the canal gave particular poignance to the letter of Auditor Newell to Marcy when his term expired in January of 1854. He looked back upon his opposition to the Nine Million Bill, the lettings of 1851, and the Vanderbilt amendment as an almost single-handed effort to save the credit of the state. "I know there is egotism in talking thus of myself," he wrote to his father-in-law, "but as it is *the* event of my life you must excuse me."[56]

55 Albany *Argus*, November 30, 1853.
56 Newell to Marcy, January 3, 1854, William L. Marcy Papers, LC.

With the new legislature controlled by Whig votes and marshaled by Thurlow Weed, the constitutional amendment for the completion of the enlargement faced no opposition. Weed reported an "almost universal desire, in and out of the Legislature" for early action. "It is true that the Erie Canal is the pet of the People," he added, "but there is abundant reason for this. It is the 'goose that lays the golden egg'. . . ." By mid-January the amendment was passed by both houses and had received the signature of Governor Seymour. The third Wednesday of February was designated for the referendum required to complete the amendment process under the constitution.

Victory for the enlargement of the canal was now tacitly assured. No party took the field to defeat it, though Barnburner presses, such as the Syracuse *Standard*, the Albany *Atlas*, and the New York *Evening Post*, opposed the measure in their columns. By this election, concluded the *Standard*, "the people are to decide whether they will, or will not, saddle the canal revenues with an additional ten and a half millions of debt, with no present prospect of payment without a resort to taxation." A Whig canal meeting in Syracuse repeated the familiar charge that the Radical Democrats were yet the "enemies of the Canals," and in Albany the *Journal* warned that "they will leave no stone unturned" to defeat the amendment. The day before the election Weed called upon his readers to "Stand by the Canals!"[57]

Thurlow Weed's final exhortation in the *Journal* in defense of the Erie Canal so thoroughly identified the enlargement with the growth of Western trade that despite its length, it deserves quotation here. Weed wrote that the question of the enlargement was still a question of whether:

[57] Albany *Evening Journal*, February 14, 1854.

New York shall or shall not continue to control the vast trade of the Great West; . . . whether a channel which has rendered her the 'Empire State' of the Union, shall assume proportions commensurate with the demands upon it; and whether what has continued the chief glory of our People shall continue to pour its exhaustless streams of wealth into the coffers of the State. . . . Let but the work of tomorrow be well done, and New York will have a richer heritage than has ever before been vouchsafed to any State or People on Earth. . . . And the Erie Canal has been the chief instrument of this unparalleled prosperity. But for that great work, there would, to-day, have been no Chicago, no Milwaukee, no Cleveland, and but a hamlet at Detroit. . . . What Son of New-York, who is proud of her present prosperity, will prove so recreant to her future glory, as to vote against a measure fraught with such sublime results? Let us, then, GIVE ONE DAY TO THE STATE![58]

An eleventh-hour controversy stirred the presses of the state over the impact of railroad competition as doubters warned that the speedier iron horse would claim all the increase in Western trade. Whig presses such as the Rochester *Daily American* answered that the railroad and the canal were complementary avenues of trade rather than rivals. As canal and railroad aided the growth of the West, noted that print, "A country so extensive, fertile and populous, will yield travel, transportation and trade enough for all the great thoroughfares of New York." The consolidation of the New York Central in 1853, meanwhile, raised the cry of monopoly.[59]

On the fifteenth of February the electorate went to the polls with no other question before it except that of the amendment to the constitution for the Erie Canal enlargement and the completion of the laterals. Some 246,000

[58] *Ibid.*

[59] David Maldwyn Ellis, "Rivalry Between the New York Central and the Erie Canal," *New York History*, XXIX (July 1948), 279.

votes were cast, nearly two-thirds the number in the preceding fall elections. The amendment was carried, 185,000 to 80,000; not even the constitution of 1846 itself had been ratified by so large a majority. "For the third, and we trust the last time," wrote Weed in the *Journal*, "the People have literally 'crushed out' the opposition to the Canals. . . . The Enlargement of the Erie Canal is now a part of the Constitution of the State."[60]

The long fight over, the legislature and the Canal Board began to resume large-scale construction. To protect the new contracts from charges of fraud and plunder, new laws were enacted to prevent false estimates by engineers and penalizing contractors if their contracts were not completed by themselves under the terms of their proposals. State officers, members of the legislature, and those employed on the canals by the state were prohibited from interest in any contract, and a stricter administration of state money was enjoined upon the superintendents. Even so the estimates for completion of the enlargement and the laterals proved too low. "There is a tendency, almost always, to underestimate the cost of the Public Works," admitted Weed in the *Journal*. "If it had been known at the beginning what our Public Works were to cost, they would either have not been undertaken, or, when authorized, pushed vigorously forward to completion."[61]

Contracts were let for further work on the enlargement during the summer and fall of 1854. Attacks by the *Atlas* and others on the cost of the enlargement led the Whigs to make the canal a rallying cry once again in the gubernatorial election in November. On the eve of the election, Weed's *Journal* cried out, "THE CANALS ARE

[60] Albany *Evening Journal*, February 16, 1854.
[61] *Ibid.*, April 12, 1854.

IN DANGER." The reelection of Governor Seymour, he wrote, "will be a verdict against the Canals; and those who contribute to his election will be parties to that verdict." But more to the point in 1854 was the letter of Henry S. Randall written in June from Cortland Village. He predicted "a sharp fiery, exciting canvass, on the count of the 'liquor question' & all the voters will be out."[62] Conflict between railroad and canal interests became increasingly bitter in the 1850s as revenues fell below those necessary to sustain the enlargement, but the Erie Canal had ceased to be a major issue dividing the parties of New York state. The long-contested enlargement program was officially completed in 1862.[63]

As the canal ceased to divide the parties of New York, it worked its unifying influence on the nation. The Democratic Hunkers had combined their labors for the enlargement with efforts to maintain the sectional compromise reached in Congress in 1850, and in spite of Seward's "Higher Law" on slavery, the Whigs had long sought to join West and East. Paradoxically, the year that saw the adoption of the constitutional amendment to complete the rebuilding of the Erie Canal saw also the shattering impact of the Kansas-Nebraska Act in Congress, which broke the sectional truce and hurried the nation toward civil war. Less than a year after war came, construction on the enlargement was finally completed. The Erie Canal could now be employed to fulfill one of the purposes for which it had been constructed, the preservation of the Union.

[62] Randall to Marcy, June 24, 1854, William L. Marcy Papers, LC.

[63] The estimated cost of enlarging the Erie Canal had been $23,402,863. The actual cost of construction was $32,008,851. *Annual Report of the State Engineer and Surveyor, on the Canals of New York for the Year 1863* (Albany, 1864), p. 4.

19

A Canal for the Nation

FROM THE perspective of today, perhaps the most striking element in the history of the Erie Canal was its nationalism. Less strident than the nationalism of more recent times, that of the Erie Canal belonged to an era when nationalism was directed primarily to the unification of the nation state.[1]

The Erie Canal was built by the state of New York alone, but it was by its very nature a national enterprise which related the growth of the other states to New York. Almost from the beginning of its existence as a state, New York successfully strengthened its own economy through mercantilistic aid to private and public improvement. In consequence, the loans to meet the cost of constructing the Erie Canal were borrowed with remarkable ease.[2] But the enlargement of the Erie Canal after 1835, pursued simultaneously with the construction of the lateral canals such as the Genesee Valley and Black River canals in the midst of the depression of 1837, was a more difficult matter. It is tempting to conclude that as the Erie Canal increasingly fulfilled the national function for which it was designed, its enlargement was more properly within the scope of the nation than of a single state.[3]

The contribution of the Erie Canal to the growth of New York as the "Empire State" is a ready key to its national significance. Yet its nationalism was derived most of all from what Carlton J. H. Hayes has defined as a "condition of mind" in which loyalty to the nation is superior to other loyalties.[4] While motive in historical actions is seldom easy to assess, one of the most striking aspects of the literature of the Erie Canal is its constant identification of local with national interest.

The projectors of the Erie Canal in New York, such as Gouverneur Morris, Elkanah Watson, Jesse Hawley, and De Witt Clinton, proposed a canal which would pass through the Mohawk gap, cross the frontier, and bring to New York City the trade of the Old Northwest. Before the building of the Erie Canal, the St. Lawrence and the Mississippi were the chief avenues for this trade, as all the difficulties of overland transportation deterred the movement of products through New York. Thus the Erie Canal would overcome fundamental geopolitical disadvantages of the United States. Furthermore, local isolation would be destroyed, and the Old Northwest and New York would come to share more fully in a common American patriotism.

[1] Carlton J. H. Hayes, *The Historical Evolution of Modern Nationalism* (New York, 1931), Chapter 5.

[2] Miller, *Enterprise of a Free People*, pp. 109-11.

[3] National, state, and local aid to canals and railroads is studied by Carter Goodrich in *Government Promotion of American Canals and Railroads 1800-1890* (New York, 1960). He notes the contributions to American development made by all levels of government and comments that "the achievements of public investment might well have been still greater if federal resources had been used in the early decades to carry out a national plan of internal improvements or if certain of the states had provided a sounder fiscal basis for their more promising projects" (p. 281).

[4] Carlton J. H. Hayes, *Essays on Nationalism* (New York, 1937), p. 6. Criteria of nationalism have been taken from the works of Hayes; Hans Kohn, *The Idea of Nationalism* (New York, 1944); Merle Curti, *The Roots of American Loyalty* (New York, 1945); and Edward M. Earle, ed., *Nationalism and Internationalism* (New York, 1950).

While achieving this goal, the canal planners sought the development of western New York, which remained in an essentially frontier condition in the first two decades of the nineteenth century. Parochial as the American frontier of this era may often have been, this development of the frontier in western New York itself produced a strong nationalizing influence.[5] It was from western New York that there came the first demands for a canal. Jesse Hawley of Canandaigua and Joshua Forman of Onondaga each claimed credit for originating the plan of an overland canal to Lake Erie, and Joseph Ellicott, agent of the Holland Land Company at Batavia, nurtured the canal project with invaluable support. Jesse Hawley's plans for a "Genesee Canal," published in 1807 and 1808, contained a strong plea for public rather than private construction, and he proposed that the national government should pay for the canal.[6] In 1808, Joshua Forman introduced the first resolution in the New York legislature for the exploration of the best route between the Hudson and Lake Erie for a canal to be financed by Congress, and then carried his appeal for national aid to Washington only to be rebuffed by Jefferson and ignored by the national legislature. Joseph Ellicott sought to advance his company's interests by opening western New York to settlement, but he regarded the projected canal as "an object of vast importance to the United States."[7] Also from western New York, Congressman Peter B. Porter of Black Rock sought funds in Washington in 1810 for the canal as part of a national system of internal navigation

[5] Frederick J. Turner, *The Frontier in American History* (New York, 1920), pp. 24-27.

[6] Hosack, *Memoir of De Witt Clinton*, pp. 324-25.

[7] Ellicott to Simeon De Witt, July 30, 1808, *HCL-WNY Canal Documents*, p. 3.

which would "preserve the integrity of this government."[8]

The following year the New York commissioners appointed to report on the feasibility of a canal advised against reliance on private enterprise to reach western New York by water, as had been attempted by the Western Inland Lock Navigation Company. They predicated their plans on national aid and warned: "Too great a national interest is at stake. It must not become the subject of a job, or a fund for speculation."[9]

The Federal aid so persistently sought by the New Yorkers never materialized. Congress failed to act on Porter's bill in the House or a similar measure introduced by Senator Pope of Kentucky in the Senate. A visitation to President Madison in 1811 by Clinton and Morris yielded enthusiastic interest but no better results; and even the passage of Calhoun's Bonus Bill in 1817 to set aside for internal improvements the dividends of the stock held by the national government in the Bank of the United States met with Madison's veto.

That New Yorkers should use this fulsome nationalistic argument in their efforts to procure national aid might be expected. Moreover, the purity of this nationalism is called into doubt by the threat of Joseph Ellicott to Congressman Micah Brooks during the debate on the Bonus Bill that if national assistance was not forthcoming, the state might control the canal in a manner "extremely injurious to the U. S. territories, and exclusively beneficial to the State." But the nationalism of New Yorkers building the Erie Canal seems more than a device to enable New York to tap the national treasury.

The nationalism of the Erie Canal was expressed most

[8] Hosack, *Memoir of De Witt Clinton*, p. 10.
[9] *Laws*, I, 68.

directly in the prevalent belief that the canal would serve as a bond of union to prevent the detachment of the West from the East. The fears held by Washington in his *Farewell Address* that the new nation might split along its Appalachian backbone were reiterated again and again by those who worked for a canal in New York. Jesse Hawley's remarkable essays predicted that the number of states in the Union would grow tenfold and must be bound together by a national canal system. The binding together of the Union was a favorite theme of De Witt Clinton, whose efforts as canal commissioner and as governor during the years of canal construction earned him a reputation as the guiding spirit behind the Erie Canal. Clinton adjured the state legislature in the memorial sent to Albany from New York City in 1816, which made no mention of the possibility of federal aid, that New York was uniquely "both Atlantic and Western" and that a canal from the Hudson to Lake Erie would provide a lasting "cement" to the Union. "Standing on this exalted eminence," wrote Clinton, "with power to prevent a train of the most extensive and afflicting calamities that ever visited the world (for such a train will inevitably follow a dissolution of the union) she will justly be considered an enemy of the human race if she does not exert for this purpose the high faculties which the Almighty has put into her hands."[10]

Clinton exhibited here the nationalistic sense of mission felt by canal advocates in New York who saw in the Erie Canal the means of preserving American liberties for the world. Moreover, he drew on the popular romantic notion that, in placing Lake Erie 565 feet above the Hudson, God had foreordained a path for the canal

[10] *Ibid.,* p. 140.

(though by this reasoning God had also given the natural outlet of the Lakes through the St. Lawrence to the Canadians), and that it was for the people of New York only to complete the divine intentions.[11]

Clinton's private secretary, Charles G. Haines, who was an ardent canal propagandist in his own right, put the strengthening of the Union above all other expectations from the canal. In an introduction to a volume of canal documents published in 1821, Haines wrote: "But paramount to all other considerations, is the influence to be anticipated from the Western canal in giving strength and durability to our national confederacy. . . . We must bring the north, and the south, and the east, and the west, nearer each other, by the attractions of interest. This will destroy asperities, soften contrasts of character, and create those moral ligaments which will grow strong through time. . . . The Western canal will unite the two most populous and powerful sections of the nation, and form one of the strongest safeguards of the union, that either state or national policy is capable of devising."[12]

The threat to national unity most frequently envisioned by the canal planners in New York came from the rivalry with Canada for the trade of the Old Northwest. At the outset it was the critical argument in the long contested dispute over the route of the canal to Lake Erie. The proposal that the canal should follow the Mohawk and Oswego rivers to Lake Ontario with a second canal cut around the falls of the Niagara to Lake Erie was vigorously opposed by the New York canal

[11] "The liberality of Nature has created the great ducts and arteries," asserted Clinton, "and the ingenuity of art can easily provide the connecting veins." *Ibid.*, p. 133.

[12] The New-York Corresponding Association, *Public Documents*, pp. xlii-xliii. See also Charles G. Haines, *Considerations on the Great Western Canal* . . . (Brooklyn, 1818), pp. 5, 9, 11, 12.

commissioners. Repeatedly they asserted that western trade once afloat on Lake Ontario would go on to Montreal. "True it is," said the commissioners in their report of 1811, "that as regards the pecuniary benefit of those who may settle along the lakes the route by which their products are sent abroad . . . must be to them a matter of little consequence. But the political connexion which would probably result from a commercial connexion, certainly deserves the consideration of intelligent men."[13]

The feeble operations of the War of 1812 centering on the New York frontier brought canal plans nearly to a standstill, but the conflict added nationalistic fuel to the demands for a canal. The war itself turned on the control of the very waterways which the New York canal system would unite. Furthermore, the failure of the American attempt to acquire Canada meant that the geopolitical features of the Canadian-American border would remain for an undetermined time. Only two years after the end of the war, the commencement of the canal was written into law and eight years after that, it became a reality.

The flood of petitions demanding the beginning of canal construction in 1815 and 1816 almost without exception voiced concern over continued Canadian rivalry. That from Niagara County, for example, emphasized the need for strengthening the frontier after the "melancholy experience of the late war," and the memorial from New York City warned that use of the Ontario route would "inevitably enrich the territory of a foreign power."[14] These petitions helped to overcome the long-standing opposition to the canal that had arisen from the southern

[13] *Laws*, I, 51; see also pp. 74-78, 118.
[14] *Ibid.*, p. 131; see also *A Serious Appeal to . . . the Legislature of the State of New York . . .*, p. 18.

tier of counties and from anti-Clintonians throughout the state. Fear of Canada, moreover, became a critical factor in the final passage of the bill to begin construction of the Erie Canal in 1817 when it faced possible veto in the Council of Revision. It was the prospect of a renewed war with Great Britain that induced Chancellor Kent to cast the deciding vote which enabled the canal bill to become law.

During the eight years of canal construction, western New York occupied the key position for the success of the nationalistic goals of the canal planners.[15] Partly to insure that the western section of the canal would be completed, digging was begun in the middle and progressed toward both ends. It was in western New York that some of the greatest engineering feats were accomplished, with the 70-foot high embankment across the Irondequoit Valley, the 800-foot long aqueduct across the Genesee at Rochester, and the two miles of deep cutting through solid rock at Lockport. The villages that grew up along the path went through a hothouse growth. Gradually, as the influence of the canal began to be felt, the people of these western settlements were woven into the social fabric of the state. What Hans Kohn has described as the widening "circumference of sympathy" characteristic of nationalism grew in New York.[16] Cadwallader D. Colden, grandson of the famous lieutenant-governor of New York, described the formation of this new society when he wrote in 1825, "We thought, and spoke of the borders of the Lakes as of some distant territory, a journey which was not so often made, as a voyage across the Atlantic. Now a citizen of New York thinks much less of a journey to Buffalo, than he did formerly of going to Albany; and

15 *Laws,* I, 438-39.
16 Kohn, *Idea of Nationalism,* p. 4.

persons who never would have known each other, mix in our familiar circle, with mutual good feelings."[17] In this manner the Erie Canal helped to mold American nationality itself.

When all 363 miles of the canal were dug, the people of New York conducted a gala celebration which was replete with nationalistic symbolism. The "Grand Salute" which signaled the entrance of the *Seneca Chief* into the canal on the way to New York was fired with guns from Admiral Perry's fleet at the battle of Lake Erie. "Who that has American blood in his veins can hear this sound without emotion?" asked Colden. "Who that has the privilege to do it can refrain from exclaiming, I too, am an American citizen; and feel as much pride in being able to make the declaration as an inhabitant of the eternal city felt, in proclaiming that he was a Roman."[18]

The *Seneca Chief*, joined by a procession of boats carrying symbolic products from western New York, sailed down a banner-bedecked canal amidst speeches praising Clinton, internal improvements, and republicanism. In the ceremony off Sandy Hook Clinton poured a keg of Lake Erie water into the Atlantic with all the mysticism of a nationalistic rite. But not every drop. Clinton was careful to leave some of the now almost sacramental liquid to be sent to General Lafayette in a box made by Duncan Phyfe from cedar wood on board the *Seneca Chief*. As if there could be no end to nationalistic symbolism, Dr. Samuel Latham Mitchill poured into the Atlantic his vials of water from more than a dozen great rivers of the world.

In these celebrations there were earmarks of nationalism

[17] Colden, *Memoir of the New York Canals*, p. 92-93.
[18] *Ibid.*, p. 379. The New York legislature resolved in 1825: "There is certainly a national glory to the enterprise, calculated to excite the pride of every patriot." *Ibid.*, p. 52.

deserving of special emphasis. New Yorkers displayed a keen sense of history, which Merle Curti has described as a prime factor in American patriotism.[19] They believed that they had earned a unique place in historical progress which would be recognized by all posterity.[20] As early as 1821 the New-York Corresponding Association for the Promotion of Internal Improvements collected the public documents relating to the New York canals in order that "nothing concerning them should be left to conjecture" for future historians.[21] An elaborate history of the canal was prepared by Cadwallader D. Colden at the request of the Common Council of New York City and copies were sent to all the living signers of the Declaration of Independence. Even if the panegyrics of the New Yorkers distorted national history, the Erie Canal was frequently pronounced to be the greatest American achievement since the signing of that document. "Next to the establishment of American Independence," noted a New York gazeteer in 1822, "it is the greatest achievement of the age."[22] Here we find the paradox suggested by R. W. B. Lewis in *The American Adam* of "the dedicated absorption with history at a moment when it was being claimed that a new history had just begun. . . ."[23] Jesse Hawley

[19] Curti, *Roots of American Loyalty*, p. 50. Writing from a different point of view, Wesley Frank Craven has argued that "sectionalism, provincialism, and other forms of localism and particularism" were more important forces than nationalism in shaping the popular interest in American history in the period 1832-1876. Wesley Frank Craven, *The Legend of the Founding Fathers* (New York, 1956), p. 86.

[20] As has been noted above, in Chapter 3, p. 50, the report of the canal commissioners to the legislature in 1812 stated: "And even when . . . the records of history shall have been obliterated, . . . this national work shall remain. It will bear testimony to the genius, the learning, the industry and intelligence of the present age." *Laws*, I, 81.

[21] New-York Corresponding Association, *Public Documents*, p. iii.

[22] Goodenow, *A Brief Manual*, p. 22.

[23] R. W. B. Lewis, *The American Adam* (Chicago, 1955), p. 159.

sent the *Seneca Chief* down the canal from Buffalo with a speech praising the union of the Lakes and the Atlantic as "an epoch that will be recorded in the tables of history."[24] In Rochester, the *Telegraph* observed on the completion of the canal that "its first projection seems to have been one of the boldest, most sublime, and important conceptions of the human mind."[25] The builders of the Erie Canal knew full well that they were innovators, constructing the first large-scale canal in the nation, but they consciously related their innovation to their past.

Moreover, those who witnessed the construction of the Erie Canal left no doubt that they considered it the product of American democratic institutions. For example, when Buffalonians numbering fewer than 3,000 souls broke ground for the canal in 1822, the editor of the Buffalo *Patriot* attributed the canal to the happy efficacy of the American political system. After extolling the establishment of American independence, which "gave to liberty an asylum in the bosom of our country," and the formation of a government which "unfolds every resource of wealth and honor" and "invigorates every faculty of the human mind," he concluded: "It is to such a government that we owe the intelligence and enterprize, which have led our citizens to encompass the great work of connecting the waters of Lake Erie with those of the Hudson."[26] Thurlow Weed, young editor of the Rochester *Telegraph*, described the five-tier combine of locks at Lockport as "a work which will probably remain for ages as a monument of American genius and American patriotism."[27] On the locks themselves, a marble slab was placed bearing the inscription, "Let posterity be

---

[24] Buffalo *Emporium and General Advertiser*, October 29, 1825.
[25] Rochester *Telegraph*, July 19, 1825.
[26] Buffalo *Patriot*, August 13, 1822.
[27] Rochester *Telegraph*, June 28, 1825.

excited to perpetuate our Free Institutions, and to make still greater efforts than their ancestors, to promote publick prosperity, by the recollection that these works of Internal Improvement, were achieved by the spirit and perseverance of Republican Freemen."[28]

Furthermore, in their celebrations New Yorkers shared the belief set forth in the Monroe Doctrine that American institutions were fundamentally different from those on the other side of the Atlantic, and they crowed over the Erie Canal as proof that American ingenuity had outstripped any work of European hands.[29] In young and promising Brockport, then a tiny canal village near Rochester, Hial Brockway signalled the completion of the canal that far west with the toast: "The United States —cutting canals while Europe is cutting heads." One canal pamphleteer thought the Erie Canal a work which "beggars to insignificance all similar undertakings in the old world."[30] Cadwallader Colden suggests a national sensitivity to the power status of the United States when he confessed that the ceremonies of 1825 were partly to attract the attention of foreign nations. "They have told us that our government was unstable," he wrote, "that it was too weak to unite so large a territory—that our Republic was incapable of works of great magnitude. . . . But we say to them, see this great link in the chain of our union—it has been devised, planned and executed by the free citizens of this Republican state."[31] New York canal

[28] *Ibid.*, June 21, 1825.

[29] "Foreign nations will gaze in admiration upon the boldness of our enterprise," commented an Albany print as the Canal Bill became law in 1817; ". . . America is destined to become the greatest nation in the world; and the state of New York the greatest in the confederacy." Albany *Gazette and General Advertiser*, May 17, 1817.

[30] *A View of the Grand Canal, from Lake Erie to the Hudson River* (New York, 1825), p. 11.

[31] Colden, *Memoir of the New York Canals*, p. 5.

propagandists enjoyed a sense of optimistic superiority over Europe and ridiculed the European efforts to glorify their past. Charles G. Haines taunted in 1821, "Where is there a work of their hands which will compare in grandeur and utility with the great Western canal?"[32]

The completed canal fulfilled many of the prophecies of its projectors and its commerce exceeded their wildest dreams. But its original dimensions were really large enough only for the needs of New York, and without enlargement it could not be made to serve the more national purpose which had also motivated the canal planners. The rebuilding of the Erie Canal to dimensions nearly twice as large was begun in 1835 in the midst of the Jacksonian boom, and the project was pushed most vigorously by the more nationalistic Whigs.

The report in 1838 by Samuel B. Ruggles, chairman of the Committee on Ways and Means in the assembly, on the state finances fairly glowed with predictions of national growth through internal improvements. The alleged "Forty Million Debt" charged against the Whigs for canals and railroads was based on Ruggles' confident estimates of the increase in Western trade, and Ruggles' recommendations were adopted by William Henry Seward when he became governor in 1839.

Seward was as ardent a nationalist as ever guided the fortunes of the Empire State. His annual message of 1839 pledged the state to a sweeping program of canal and railroad construction "to preserve the integrity of the Union, and by the paramount duty we owe to mankind, to illustrate the peacefulness, the efficiency, the beneficence and the wisdom of republican institutions."[33] Subsequent messages to the legislature during his four years

---

[32] New-York Corresponding Association, *Public Documents*, p. xlvii.
[33] Lincoln, *Messages from the Governors*, III, 738.

as governor dwelt upon the fears of disunion in Washington's *Farewell Address* and Jefferson's interest in roads and canals. At the end of his second term, he congratulated his constituents that by means of the New York canal system, "the States are bound together with bands stronger than those of merely political compact, and the danger of dismemberment is happily averted." The New York canals, said Seward, had been "designed and shaped by herself, to strengthen and perpetuate the national structure."

To meet the cost of Seward's ambitious schemes of canal and railroad construction, loans were floated which swelled the indebtedness of the state. Seward relied in part upon Henry Clay's bill in Congress for a division among the states of the revenues derived from the sale of public lands. The New York governor held that the Erie Canal was the principal cause for the rising value of those lands and provided the major outlet for the productions of their soil. In 1841 he appealed for aid to Western canals and railroads through the distribution law and, in nationalistic fashion, showed the consequent benefits to the internal improvements of New York. "One might suppose, [he addressed the legislature] from the cold speculations sometimes heard among ourselves concerning the improvidence of those States, that they were hostile or at least rival powers, and that our security and prosperity rose with the decline of theirs. Yet it is far otherwise. They are communities bound to us by interest, as well as by consanguinity between their citizens and our own; their prosperity is our prosperity, and no calamity falls upon them by which we do not suffer, although we may withhold our sympathy."[34]

As New York itself became financially embarrassed and

[34] *Ibid.*, p. 902.

was forced to a policy of retrenchment, Seward placed the blame on the worsening depression of the national economy rather than on the loans floated by the Whigs for the enlargement of the Erie Canal.

The Democratic opposition in New York could with good cause find extravagance in the Whig program, but it was equally true that Jacksonian convictions on internal improvements ran counter to the national dream. The *laissez faire* philosophy of the Jacksonians and their abhorrence of debt inhibited the use of the state or national governments for national growth. Even the Democratic Hunkers, who were closely allied with the banking community and were responsible in the 1850s for the ultimate completion of the enlargement of the Erie Canal, were less touched than the Whigs by the spirit of American nationalism.

The New York Whigs such as Seward, Ruggles, Thurlow Weed, and Washington Hunt, subscribed to Clay's American System with its emphasis on internal improvements as a means of developing the resources of the nation and they were eager to use the credit of the state government to that end. And, it must be added, canal meetings gathered in western New York "without distinction of party" to urge the completion of the enlargement of the Erie Canal at the earliest possible period. Whigs, Hunkers, and non-partisan canal meetings, all engaged in the canal movement of the 1840s and 1850s, articulated many of the nationalistic ideas which we have seen with the canal project from the start.

The frontier continued to exercise a nationalizing influence as the amazing growth of the hinterland provided the fundamental premise for those who worked for a larger canal. New Yorkers felt a responsibility to those who had built canals and railroads in the West depending upon the Erie Canal for an outlet to the sea.[35] We continue to find the idea that the Erie Canal followed a God-given path which would be improved still further under divine protection. "If in five years, this great work is accomplished," noted the Rochester *Daily Democrat* in 1837 while discussing the enlargement, "New York will . . . remain what Nature designed her to be, the highway between the Atlantic and the Lakes."[36] A foreign visitor traveling on the canal during the period observed that "the yeomanry, the bone and muscle of these regions, make you see in their countenances that they esteem it to be little short of a gift of the Gods."[37]

New Yorkers were proud that canal commerce came to exceed that carried on any channel of the Old World, and viewed the canal as an instrument for the preservation of American liberties. The editor of the Rochester *Daily Democrat* feared in 1844 that the spirit of the Democratic stop policy would gain still wider support among the people and asked, "Apply such logic to the past, present, and future enterprises of the nation, and where would it lead us? I answer, in the safe-keeping of some warring despot or haughty king."[38] Just as Colden had written in 1825 that the Erie Canal had brought western New Yorkers into "our familiar circle, with mutual good feelings," Levi Woodbury wrote from Vermont in 1835 to Azariah C. Flagg praising the people of New York for

[35] A canal meeting in Niagara County in 1846 resolved: "That we consider the State of New York as pledged to the policy of enlarging the Erie Canal, not only to our own citizens interested in its use and in its revenues, but to our Western sister States, who have constructed canals and railroads for transportation to the Great Lakes, relying on the Erie Canal as the great outlet of their trade." Buffalo *Courier*, June 5, 1846.

[36] Rochester *Daily Democrat*, January 18, 1837; see also Jesse Hawley, *An Essay on the Enlargement of the Erie Canal* . . . (Lockport, 1840), p. 6.

[37] Quoted in Mansfield, *History of the Great Lakes*, I, 224.

[38] Rochester *Daily Democrat*, February 8, 1844.

opening new opportunities for the people of his mountainous state. He thanked Flagg for a copy of a state canal report and added: "When I reflect on the small territory, rocky mountains and barren soil of my native State and look to the vast resources and high destinies of the empire State I can almost submit to be envious. But a moment's further consideration, that you open your generous arms to welcome the emigrants from our frosty hills & to patronize her sons, whenever their enterprise and industry merit favour—I feel again friend, that we are in many respects but *one People* and that the success of a part is in some degree the success of the whole."[39]

The completion of the Welland Canal around Niagara Falls in 1829 and its enlargement in 1841, together with the canalization of the St. Lawrence, once more placed Canadian markets in competition for the trade of the Old Northwest and evoked a nationalist response from the canal advocates in New York. It must be admitted that nationalistic loyalties did not keep American engineers from assisting in the building of the Welland Canal, and a Utica newspaper reported that the locks of the Canadian waterway were constructed chiefly by "Yankee" contractors.[40] A "New Yorker" from Niagara Falls protested that Wall Street stock jobbers had taken the stock of the Welland Canal Company and thus helped to divert to Canada "one fourth of the canal revenue" in New York.[41] But for all such equivocations, the New York Whigs raised the specter of Canadian gain from American

[39] Woodbury to Flagg, January 22, 1834, Azariah C. Flagg Papers, NYPL.

[40] Utica *Sentinel and Gazette*, August 2, 1825; Henry Seymour to Thomas, April 17, 1826, David Thomas Papers, NYSL. See also Alfred Barrett to William C. Bouck, February 8, 1843, William C. Bouck Papers, Cornell University Library.

[41] Utica *Sentinel and Gazette*, August 2, 1825. Considerable stock was also held in the Welland Canal by Buffalonians. Buffalo *Emporium and General Advertiser*, April 16, 1829.

trade in their campaigns to reverse the Democratic stop policy. Thurlow Weed, writing in the Albany *Evening Journal,* warned when the stop law was passed in 1842 that while New York slept, "the Canadian Government, our National and natural rival," was vigorously enlarging the Welland Canal.[42] The Whigs stigmatized their opponents as the "British Party" for their failure to go on with the enlargement.[43] On the other hand, some Democrats were no less sensitive to Canadian rivalry. The Hunker Buffalo *Courier* complained in 1845 of "this unnatural alliance between the citizens of the State of New-York and British subjects."[44] In 1845 and 1846 a series of public meetings were called in western New York to protest "the diversion of the Trade of the West through the Welland Canal."[45]

It was but a short step from competition to cooperation between Canada and the United States as New Yorkers sought to control the flow of Western trade to the East and to share in the trade of the St. Lawrence themselves. The Champlain Canal, which was constructed at the same time as the Erie Canal, drew the northern counties of New York and the western counties of Vermont away from "the commercial empire of the St. Lawrence" and into that of New York.[46] Despite the alarms of the New York Whigs, the Welland Canal sent more trade to Oswego and New York City than to Montreal because the passage from Lake Ontario to Montreal remained fraught

[42] Albany *Evening Journal,* May 5, 1842; see also August 11, 30, 1842.

[43] Rochester *Daily Democrat,* July 6, October 14, 15, 18, 28, 31, 1842, January 17, 1845; Buffalo *Commercial Advertiser and Journal,* November 25, 1841, June 25, 1842.

[44] Buffalo *Courier,* May 29, 1845; see also June 21, 1845.

[45] Buffalo *Commercial Advertiser,* January 4, 6, 1845; Buffalo *Courier,* April 2, June 2, 1846; Rochester *Daily Democrat,* January 7, 8, 1845.

[46] John Bartlet Brebner, *North Atlantic Triangle* (New Haven, 1945), p. 121.

with risk.[47] Simultaneously with their demands that the state proceed more rapidly with the completion of the Erie Canal, New Yorkers supported the movement of the national government toward commercial reciprocity with Canada which culminated in the Reciprocity Treaty of 1854. Levi Beardsley of Syracuse on the Erie Canal wrote to Marcy in Washington that as a result of reciprocal trade, "The canal tolls would be greatly increased while a thousand reciprocal benefits would flow from it which need not be enumerated."[48] Two years later, the New York *Evening Post* reported that the people of New York "would be glad to possess the free navigation of the St. Lawrence, and to see some of the obstructions removed which prevent a profitable trade with their neighbors."[49] In the same spirit of cooperation, some in New York looked to the future annexation of Canada by the United States. "Geographic position, kindred interests, language and laws, sympathy of origin and destiny, to say nothing of the oppressions of a hard-hearted step-mother, must ultimately, sooner or later, place the Canadas under the *Aegis* of this empire," predicted the New York *Evening Star* in 1835.[50] When such a union had been consummated, the Erie and Oswego canals would offer the Canadians an easier route through "sister states" to the sea. Samuel B. Ruggles, writing in 1852 to Lord Elgin, the Governor General of Canada, forecast that British colonial policy would lead "if not to a formal Confederation, at least to a close political alliance between the two great Nations whose destiny it is to guide the civilization and preserve the liberties of Mankind."[51]

47 *Ibid.*, p. 122.
48 Beardsley to Marcy, February 21, 1849, William L. Marcy Papers, LC.
49 New York *Evening Post*, January 25, 1851.
50 New York *Evening Star*, January 29, 1835.

Nationalists in New York during the Middle Period of American history shared the ambivalence of loyalties to state and nation inherent in the compromises of the federal system. They rebelled at the "odius claim" of the national government to tonnage duties on goods entering the Erie Canal at Buffalo.[52] They lost some of their zeal for national internal improvements after their own Erie Canal had been constructed without national aid, and they feared the prospect of taxation to support the improvements of others. Clinton and Gouverneur Morris had ardently sought national assistance in 1816, but Van Buren could report to Old Hickory in 1830 the enormous popularity in New York of his Maysville Road veto.[53] To New York canal builders, the Erie Canal was a state work with a national function. Jesse Hawley, who had first laid out a design for an overland canal to Lake Erie in 1807, petitioned the legislature in 1840 for a speedier enlargement of the canal and the retention of its full dimensions against the efforts of those who wished to economize by building a smaller canal. His petition neatly blended the state and national elements in the construction and enlargement of the Erie Canal as he wrote that "no single act—no public measure—except the Declaration of Independence, and the formation of the United States Constitution, has done so much to promote the public prosperity and produce a new era in the history of the country, *as the construction of the Erie Canal*. It is the father of canals in America; and of the State system of internal improvements which has grown up under its

---

[51] Ruggles to the Earl of Elgin, October 27, 1852, Samuel B. Ruggles Papers, NYPL.

[52] Utica *Sentinel and Gazette*, May 30, 1825, May 23, 1826; Buffalo *Emporium*, December 4, 1824.

[53] Van Buren to Andrew Jackson, July 25, 1830, Martin Van Buren Papers, LC.

benign influences; and that its political influence and importance to the Union, for the construction of the internal improvements by *State funds*—as *State properties* —for *State revenues*, on the principle of State Rights is equal to its commercial value."[54]

In 1854, at the close of the period considered in this volume, Governor Horatio Seymour devoted much of his annual message to a discussion of the New York and national constitutions. He wished the citizens of New York "to cherish fraternal feelings among the people of the different states of the Union" and he was personally interested in promoting the Fox and Wisconsin Canal to connect the Great Lakes with the Mississippi. But now that the Erie Canal enlargement was on its way to certain completion by an amendment to the state constitution which he had only reluctantly endorsed, he urged a strict construction of the national constitution to prevent "profuse expenditures" on "extravagant systems of internal improvement."[55]

While the rival Democratic factions and the Whigs in New York battled over the means and speediness of the rebuilding of the Erie Canal, its growing commerce gave it a primary place in the economic growth of the nation. Other states were stimulated to build canals which would link the Ohio River Valley to the Atlantic, connect the Ohio and Mississippi rivers with the Great Lakes, and improve transportation between the upcountry and tidewater in the Atlantic states.[56] Western products on the Erie Canal came to exceed in volume those from New York by 1847; the peak year of tonnage carried on the New York canal system was 1872. The great staples

[54] Hawley, *Essay on the Enlargement of the Erie Canal*, p. 14.
[55] Lincoln, *Messages from the Governors*, IV, 746-47.
[56] George Rogers Taylor, *The Transportation Revolution 1815-1860* (New York, 1951), p. 37.

of wheat, flour, beef, wool, and lumber came east on the canal, while merchandise and great batches of immigrants moved west. Tonnage going to Western states on the Erie Canal was largest in 1854. American industrial development was speeded as well. As the most successful canal of the Canal Era, the Erie Canal contributed to what the economist W. W. Rostow has called the "take off" stage of national economic growth in the 1840s.[57] Moreover, the ties between North and West which were created by the Erie Canal, antedating those of the railway network of the 1850s, would strengthen the Union in the Civil War. "By 1824," wrote George Dangerfield in his study of the Era of Good Feelings, "it was clear that the great trans-Allegheny route was to be shifted away from the Potomac, away from the slave-holding South, and towards the industrial North."[58]

The Erie Canal was the work of the state of New York, constructed after the failure of its efforts to secure national aid. Yet the spirit of enterprise with which it was built was the spirit of nationalism. The summation of this spirit is found in William Henry Seward's last gubernatorial address to the legislature in 1842, just twenty-five years after the passage of the Canal Bill of 1817, as he declared that the state was required to go on with its canals and other internal improvements "by every consideration of duty to ourselves, to posterity, to our country, and to mankind."[59]

[57] Rostow, *Stages of Economic Growth*, pp. 25, 38.
[58] George Dangerfield, *The Era of Good Feelings* (New York, 1952), p. 323.
[59] Lincoln, *Messages from the Governors*, III, 1050.

Essay on Bibliography

1. MANUSCRIPT COLLECTIONS

The first efforts to improve the Mohawk route to the interior of New York State in the 1790s by the Western Inland Lock Navigation Company can be followed in greatest detail in the voluminous Philip Schuyler Papers in the New York Public Library and in the Elkanah Watson Papers in the New York State Library at Albany. For the political history of the Erie Canal after 1810, the basic manuscript source is the De Witt Clinton Papers in the Columbia University Library. This collection is essential for the background of the canal laws of 1816 and 1817, the politics of canal construction, and the operation of the canal until Clinton's death in 1828.

Political opposition to Clintonian sponsorship of the Erie Canal is best traced in the Martin Van Buren Papers in the Library of Congress. Even after Van Buren left New York for Washington, letters to and from Democrats in New York show the Erie Canal as a major issue in Jacksonian politics. The William L. Marcy Papers in the Library of Congress supplement the Van Buren Papers and are more directly related to canal policies as Marcy was comptroller from 1823 to 1829 and governor from 1833 to 1839, and was caught in the Barnburner-Hunker feud which divided the New York Democracy.

The Peter A. Porter Papers at the Buffalo and Erie

County Historical Society are useful as they include the papers of General Peter B. Porter, canal commissioner, anti-Clintonian political leader from Black Rock, and contestant in the Buffalo-Black Rock struggle for the canal terminus harbor. Also at the Buffalo and Erie County Historical Society are the Joseph Ellicott Letter-books, containing fair copies of Joseph Ellicott's correspondence relating to the support of the canal project by the Holland Land Company.

The William C. Bouck Papers in the Collection of Regional History of the Cornell University Library and the Samuel B. Ruggles Papers in the New York Public Library and the Library of Congress have particular usefulness as both men were political leaders in their respective parties and served also as acting canal commissioners. The Bouck Papers reveal the Hunker support for the enlargement program and contain detailed reports of canal engineers to Bouck as canal commissioner or party leader. The Ruggles Papers show the Whig attitude toward internal improvements and Ruggles' experiences on the western section of the canal. Also basic for Whig canal politics are the Thurlow Weed Papers at the University of Rochester Library.

Papers of engineers active on the construction of the Erie Canal or the enlargement are the Canvass White Papers in the Collection of Regional History at Cornell, the David Thomas Papers in the New York State Library, and the John B. Jervis Papers in the Jervis Public Library at Rome. The manuscript of the Jervis autobiography affords an excellent account of the training of an engineer on the Erie Canal. The Myron Holley Papers in the New York State Library show Holley's contribution as an acting commissioner and loyal Clintonian to the construction of the canal and also his defense against the charges of his misuse of state funds. The Simon Newton Dexter Papers at Cornell University include the records of the first packet boat navigation company on the Erie Canal, and the New York State Comptroller Papers in the New York Public Library are a rich source for the reports of officials charged with the day-by-day operation of the New York canals.

One of the most extensive canal collections in New York State is found in the Henry O'Reilly Papers at the New-York Historical Society. As a resident of Rochester and Lockport and a Democratic editor, O'Reilly worked zealously for the speedy completion of the enlargement of the Erie Canal. With his papers are materials he gathered for a history of the New York canals. A smaller collection of his papers is held by the Rochester Public Library.

2. PUBLISHED LETTERS AND MEMOIRS

A basic source for any study of the New York canals is the commemorative volume by Cadwallader Colden, *Memoir, Prepared at the Request of a Committee of the Common Council of the City of New York and Presented to the Mayor of the City, at the Celebration of the Completion of the New York Canals* (New York, 1825). Colden surveys the history of the Erie Canal and an appendix contains detailed accounts of the celebration of 1825. Drawings and lithographs by George Catlin appear as illustrations in the volume. David Hosack, *Memoir of De Witt Clinton: with an Appendix, Containing Numerous Documents, Illustrative of the Principal Events of His Life* (New York, 1829) is most useful for its appendix which makes up three-fourths of the volume. Excerpts are reprinted from diverse sources relating to the history of the

Erie Canal, such as letters to and from Clinton, canal pamphlets, Jesse Hawley's essays in the Genesee *Messenger,* the speech of Peter B. Porter on internal improvements delivered before Congress in 1810, debates on the canal bills of 1816 and 1817, and accounts of Clinton's removal as canal commissioner in 1824.

For the contribution of Elkanah Watson to the canal movement in New York, see Winslow C. Watson, ed., *Men and Times of the Revolution: or, Memoirs of Elkanah Watson, Including His Journals of Travels in Europe and America, from the Year 1777 to 1842, and his Reminiscences and Incidents of the American Revolution* (second edition, New York, 1856). In response to a pamphlet by Robert Troup on Watson's claims as projector of the canal policy of New York State, De Witt Clinton published a letter under the pseudonym, Tacitus, *The Canal Policy of the State of New York; Delineated in a Letter to Robert Troup, Esquire* (Albany, 1821). For Troup's reply, see Robert Troup, *A Letter to the Honorable Brockholst Livingston, Esq., One of the Justices of the Supreme Court on the Lake Canal Policy of the State of New York* (Albany, 1822).

Letters pertaining to the Erie Canal in western New York and the Buffalo and Black Rock Harbor controversy by De Witt Clinton, Joseph Ellicott, Peter B. Porter, and many others, are found in Volume XIV of the *Buffalo Historical Society Publications,* Frank H. Severance, ed., *The Holland Land Co. and Canal Construction in Western New York; Buffalo-Black Rock Harbor Papers; Journals and Documents* (Buffalo, 1910). This volume also includes the "Journal of a Tour from Albany to Lake Erie in 1826" kept by George W. Clinton, son of the governor, as he accompanied Amos Eaton on his scientific and educational tour of that year.

Two published autobiographies are of particular importance to the political history of the canal. Harriet A. Weed, ed., *Autobiography of Thurlow Weed* (Boston, 1883) and John C. Fitzpatrick, ed., "The Autobiography of Martin Van Buren," American Historical Association, *Annual Report for the Year 1918* (Washington, 1920), give personal accounts of men and events in the history of the Erie Canal as viewed by leaders of rival political parties. Also useful is Henry B. Stanton, *Random Recollections* (second edition, New York, 1886). Though brief, it recounts many political controversies in which the Erie Canal was involved.

3. NEW YORK STATE LEGISLATIVE DOCUMENTS

The legislative history of the Erie Canal in the period 1792-1854 can be traced in the *Journal of the Assembly of the State of New York* and the *Journal of the Senate of the State of New York*, although newspaper accounts are necessary for a more complete record of speeches or debates in the legislature. The *Assembly Documents*, 1830-1854, and the *Senate Documents*, 1830-1854, provide the reports of legislative committees on canal affairs and also include reports of the canal commissioners and the commissioners of the Canal Fund. After 1849 the statistical information on the trade, tonnage, and tolls of the New York canals is given in the annual report of the auditor of the Canal Department.

For the history of the Erie Canal before 1825 the most valuable and convenient legislative source is the *Laws of the State of New York in Relation to the Erie and Champlain Canals, Together with the Annual Reports of the Canal Commissioners and other Documents*, 2 vols. (Albany, 1825). It includes the legislative proceedings leading to the enactment of canal laws and documents such as the memorial of the citizens of New York of 1816, and is readily available in libraries throughout the state. Much less comprehensive is the volume published by the New-York Corresponding Association, for the Promotion of Internal Improvements, *Public Documents, Relating to the New-York Canals, which Are to Connect the Western and Northern Lakes, with the Atlantic Ocean* (New York, 1821). This volume is notable for its nationalistic introduction written by Charles G. Haines. Those portions of the messages of New York governors relating to the Erie Canal can be found in Charles Z. Lincoln, *Messages from the Governors,* 11 vols. (Albany, 1909).

Two legislative documents, published separately, deserve special mention. Samuel B. Ruggles, *Report upon the Finances and Internal Improvements of the State of New York* (New York, 1838) became a Whig blueprint for the expansion of internal improvements in New York State. *The Report of the Select Committee of the Assembly of 1846, upon the Investigation of Frauds in the Expenditure of the Public Monies upon the Canals of the State of New York* (Albany, 1847) is an assembly document of 866 pages containing testimony on costs and procedures in the construction of the New York canals in the late 1830s and 1840s.

4. NEWSPAPERS

The newspapers used most extensively in this volume because of their statewide influence were the Albany *Argus,* the Democratic organ edited by Edwin Croswell, and the Albany *Evening Journal,* organ of the Whigs edited by Thurlow Weed. In New York City, the editorial opinion of the *Morning Courier and New York Enquirer* for the Whigs and the New York *Evening Post* for the Democrats offered partisan contrast on canal issues. While these papers have been cited most frequently, others in Albany and New York City have been used and many newspapers were examined in Utica, Syracuse, Rochester, Lockport, and Buffalo.

An attempt has been made in this study to see the Erie Canal as it appeared to its contemporaries, conflicting and contradictory though such views may have been. Newspapers thus provide a major body of source material for information about the origins, construction, enlargement, and operation of the canal, and also for contemporary opinion on the canal issue in politics. A consequent risk, however, is the acceptance of newspaper opinion at face value, particularly as it ascribes motive or rationalizes political policy. For example, use of newspaper sources may have suggested a greater degree of nationalism in New York than actually existed. In the controversy over the western terminus harbor, however, the files of the Buffalo *Patriot,* Buffalo *Journal,* and the Black Rock *Beacon* were indispensable.

5. POLITICAL HISTORIES AND BIOGRAPHIES

Study of the political history of New York State for the period discussed here must begin with Jabez D. Hammond, *The History of Political Parties in the State of New York,* 3 vols. (fourth edition, Syracuse, 1852). Hammond was an astute political observer who was a member of several of the legislatures which directed the building and early operation of the New York canals. De Alva S. Alexander, *A Political History of the State of New York,* 4 vols. (New York, 1906-23) is a standard survey of New York politics. A classic study by Dixon

Ryan Fox, *The Decline of Aristocracy in the Politics of New York* (New York, 1919) emphasizes the Federalist landlord interest in the construction of inland waterways in New York and presents the Clintonians and Whigs as heirs of the Federalists. A brief but groundbreaking study of the Barnburner-Hunker split over internal improvements is that of Herbert D. A. Donovan, *The Barnburners; A Study of the Internal Movements in the Political History of New York and of Resulting Changes in Political Affiliation, 1830-1852* (New York, 1925).

Party attitudes toward canals in New York have been reexamined in several more recent political studies. The volume by Robert V. Remini, *Martin Van Buren and the Making of the Democratic Party* (New York, 1959) finds the Bucktails not against canals but rather opposed to state indebtedness in the course of Van Buren's organization of a political base in New York from which to launch a national Jacksonian party. Lee Benson's challenging study, *The Concept of Jacksonian Democracy; New York as a Test Case* (Princeton, 1961) chooses Rockland and Chautauqua counties to illustrate his thesis that socioeconomic issues such as the Erie Canal were less important than ethnocultural, religious, and localistic influences in determining political divisions. Like Benson, Alvin Kass finds an economic interpretation of New York politics untenable in his new study, *Politics in New York State 1800-1830* (Syracuse, 1965) and describes instead factions and parties bent on gaining power in political contests governed more by opportunism than by principle.

A definitive biography of De Witt Clinton remains to be written. An older work is that of James Renwick, *Life of De Witt Clinton* (New York, 1840). The biography by Dorothy Bobbé, *De Witt Clinton* (New York, 1933), is marred by its eulogistic tone.

Other biographies which are useful for the history of the Erie Canal before 1854 are Glyndon G. Van Deusen, *Thurlow Weed: Wizard of the Lobby* (Boston, 1947); John A. Garraty, *Silas Wright* (New York, 1949); Frederick Bancroft, *The Life of William H. Seward*, 2 vols. (New York, 1900); Ivor Debenham Spencer, *The Victor and the Spoils; A Life of William L. Marcy* (Providence, 1959); and Stewart Mitchell, *Horatio Seymour of New York* (Cambridge, 1938).

6. ECONOMIC AND SOCIAL STUDIES

General studies of the canal era in nineteenth-century American transportation history are found in Caroline E. MacGill and a Staff of Collaborators, *History of Transportation in the United States before 1860* (Washington, 1917) and George Rogers Taylor, *The Transportation Revolution 1815-1860, The Economic History of the United States*, IV (New York, 1951). On American canals alone, an older survey is Archer B. Hulbert, *The Great American Canals* (Cleveland, 1904). In the recent study by Carter Goodrich, Julius Rubin, H. Jerome Cranmer, and Harvey H. Segal, *Canals and American Economic Development*, Carter Goodrich, ed., (New York, 1961), chapters by Rubin and Segal offer new approaches to the history of the Erie Canal. See also Carter Goodrich, *Government Promotion of American Canals and Railroads, 1800-1890* (New York, 1960), which has a brief discussion of the Erie Canal as the first and most successful effort in the Appalachian competition for western trade in a period characterized by the emulation of states and cities for internal improvement.

First in any list of economic studies of the Erie Canal is that of Nathan Miller, *The Enterprise of a Free People:*

Aspects of Economic Development in New York State During the Canal Period, 1792-1838 (Ithaca, 1962), which analyzes the ways in which state construction of the Erie and Champlain canals furthered the economic development of New York and emphasizes in particular the contribution of the Canal Fund. The basic engineering study of the Erie Canal is Noble E. Whitford, *History of the Canal System of the State of New York together with Brief Histories of the Canals of the United States and Canada,* 2 vols. (Albany, 1906). These volumes go far beyond the details of the construction to include the history of canal laws, statistical tables, diagrams, a chapter on the influence of the Erie Canal, biographies of engineers, and a bibliography of printed canal sources in the New York State Library. Henry W. Hill, *An Historical Review of Waterways and Canal Construction in New York State, Buffalo Historical Society Publications,* XII (Buffalo, 1908) reveals the personal interest taken in the New York waterways by its author as a canal advocate in the state senate at the turn of the twentieth century.

Several local or regional studies relate the Erie Canal to particular parts of New York State. Among those most useful are Robert Greenhalgh Albion, *The Rise of New York Port, 1815-1860* (New York, 1939); David Maldwyn Ellis, *Landlords and Farmers in the Hudson-Mohawk Region, 1790-1850* (Ithaca, 1946); Codman Hislop, *The Mohawk,* Rivers of America Series, Hervey Allen and Carl Carmer, eds. (New York, 1948); Neil Adams McNall, *An Agricultural History of the Genesee Valley, 1790-1860* (Philadelphia, 1952); Blake McKelvey, *Rochester: the Water-Power City, 1812-1854* (Cambridge, 1945); Paul D. Evans, *The Holland Land Company* (Buffalo, 1924); John T. Horton, Edward T. Williams, Harry S. Douglass, *History of Northwestern New York; Erie, Niagara, Wyom-*

ing, Genesee and Orleans Counties, 3 vols. (New York, 1947); and Whitney R. Cross, *The Burned-over District* (Ithaca, 1950).

The Erie Canal has received more popular treatment in Alvin Harlow, *Old Towpaths* (New York, 1926); Madeline Sadler Waggoner, *The Long Haul West, the Great Canal Era, 1817-1850* (New York, 1958); Harvey Chalmers II, *The Birth of the Erie Canal* (New York, 1960); and Lionel D. Wyld, *Low Bridge! Folklore and the Erie Canal* (Syracuse, 1962). Samuel Hopkins Adams, *The Erie Canal* (New York, 1953) and Ralph Andrist, *The Erie Canal* (New York, 1964) are accounts written for younger readers, the latter having one of the best available collections of canal illustrations in color. A stimulating study which interprets the canal in its relation to the cultural patterns of a society is Lewis Mumford, *Technics and Civilization* (New York, 1934).

7. TRAVEL ACCOUNTS AND TRAVELERS' GUIDES

Printed and manuscript accounts of travel on the Erie Canal in the Canal Era are abundant. Some of the printed travel accounts used in the preparation of this study are A. Levasseur, *Lafayette in America in 1824 and 1825: or, Journal of a Voyage to the United States,* 2 vols. (Philadelphia, 1829); [Charles Frederick] Bernhard, Duke of Saxe-Weimar Eisenach, *Travels Through North America During the Years 1825 and 1826,* 2 vols. (Philadelphia, 1828); Anne Royall, *The Black Book, or, A Continuation of Travels, in the United States,* 2 vols. (Washington, 1828); Basil Hall, *Travels in North America in the Years 1827 and 1828,* 3 vols. (Edinburgh, 1829); S. A. Ferall, *A Ramble of Six Thousand Miles Through the United States of America* (London, 1832); E. T. Coke, *A Subal-*

tern's Furlough: Descriptive of the United States, Upper and Lower Canada, New Brunswick, and Nova Scotia, During the Summer and Autumn of 1832, 2 vols. (New York, 1833); Frances Trollope, *Domestic Manners of the Americans,* Donald Smalley, ed. (New York, 1949); [James Boardman], *America, and the Americans* by a Citizen of the World (London, 1833); Thomas Hamilton, *Men and Manners in America,* 2 vols. (Edinburgh, 1833); Carl D. Arfwedson, *The United States and Canada in 1832, 1833, and 1834,* 2 vols. (London, 1834); Edward S. Abdy, *Journal of a Residence and Tour in the United States of North America from April, 1833, to October, 1834,* 3 vols. (London, 1835); Tyrone Power, *Impressions of America During the Years 1833, 1834, and 1835,* 2 vols. (Philadelphia, 1836); Charles Augustus Murray, *Travels in North America During the Years 1834, 1835, & 1836,* 2 vols. (London, 1839); Harriet Martineau, *Retrospect of Western Travel,* 2 vols. (New York, 1838); Robert B. Allardice, *Agricultural Tour in the United States and Upper Canada, with Miscellaneous Notices* (Edinburgh, 1842); [James Lumsden], *American Memoranda, by a Mercantile Man, During a Short Tour in the Summer of 1843* (Glasgow, 1844); and Alex. Mackay, *the Western World; or, Travels in the United States in 1846-47,* 3 vols. (second edition, London, 1849).

Among the many travelers' guides which include a description of the route of the Erie Canal are Horatio G. Spafford, *A Pocket Guide for the Tourist and Traveller, Along the Line of the Canals, and the Interior Commerce of the State of New York* (New York, 1824); William Cobbett, *The Emigrant's Guide* (London, 1829); Oliver O. Steele, *Steele's Western Guide Book, and Emigrant's Directory, Containing Different Routes Through the States of New York, Ohio, Indiana, Illinois and Michigan, with*

Short Descriptions of the Climate, Soil, Productions, Prospects, &c. (fifth edition, Buffalo, 1836); John Disturnell, *The Traveller's Guide Through the State of New-York, Canada, etc., Embracing a General Description of the City of New-York; the Hudson River Guide, and the Fashionable Tour to the Springs and Niagara Falls; with Steamboat, Rail-road, and Stage Routes Accompanied by Correct Maps* (New York, 1836); and O. L. Holley, ed., *The Picturesque Tourist; being a Guide Through the Northern and Eastern States and Canada: Giving an Accurate Description of Cities, and Villages, Celebrated Places of Resort, etc., with Maps and Illustrations* (New York, 1844).

One of the best descriptions of canal travel is found in Warren S. Tryon, ed., *Mirror for Americans: Life and Manners in the United States, 1790-1870, as Recorded by American Travellers*, 3 vols. (Chicago, 1952).

8. ARTICLES

For a detailed account of the Western Inland Lock Navigation Company see Nathan Miller, "Private Enterprise in Inland Navigation: The Mohawk Route Prior to the Erie Canal," *New York History*, XXXI (October 1950), 398-413. Charles Sydnor, "The One-Party Period of American History," *The American Historical Review*, LI (April 1946), 439-51, offers background for the politics of canal construction in New York between 1817 and 1825. For Whig attitudes toward internal improvements see Glyndon G. Van Deusen, "Some Aspects of Whig Thought and Theory in the Jacksonian Period," *American Historical Review*, LXII (January 1958), 305-22. The thousands of wage reports in the Erie Canal Papers in the New York State Library form the basis for a study by Walter B. Smith, "Wage Rates on the Erie Canal, 1828-1881," *The*

Journal of Economic History, XXIII (September 1963), 298-311. The Erie Canal in urban history is described by Blake McKelvey in "Rochester and the Erie Canal," *Rochester History,* XI (July 1949), 1-24, and "The Erie Canal, Mother of Cities," *The New-York Historical Quarterly,* XXXV (January 1951), 55-71. For the rivalry of Albany and Troy for both canal and railroad commerce, see David Maldwyn Ellis, "Albany and Troy—Commercial Rivals," *New York History,* XXIV (October 1943), 484-511. For the rivalry of canal and railroad see the same author's "Rivalry between the New York Central and the Erie Canal," *New York History,* XXIX (July 1948), 268-300. An interesting account of Amos Eaton's scientific tour of 1826 is Samuel Reznecx, "A Travelling School of Science on the Erie Canal in 1826," *New York History,* XL (July 1959), 255-69. Life on the canal since the 1850s as it was experienced by the Moran family, made famous by its tugboat fleet, is told in Eugene F. Moran, "The Erie Canal as I have Known It," *Bottoming Out,* III, No. 2 (1959), 1-18. *Bottoming Out* is published periodically by the Canal Society of New York State at Syracuse and contains articles, notes, and illustrations relating to the history of the New York canals.

Index

Adams, John Quincy, 164, 172, 179-80, 304
Albany: in Jesse Hawley's essays, 26; and canal completion celebration, 187; canal arrivals at, 239; canal basin at, 280-81
Alexander's M.lls, 134, 135
Allen, S. F., 312-13, 325
American Bethel Society, 229
American Revolution: transportation in, 11
Appropriations, canal: for surveys of 1808, 30, 33; in canal law of 1811, 45; in canal law of 1816, 63; in canal law of 1817, 70-71; in 1820, 110; in 1821, 115, 117, 119, 180; in enlargement act of 1838, 312; for enlargement to 1840, 323; in 1841, 326; and progress of enlargement in 1847-1849, 362; in 1849-1850, 364; in canal compromise of 1853, 387; to complete enlargement in 1862, 396
Aqueducts: over Genesee River, 124, 127-28, 129-30, 292; at Little Falls, 134; over Mohawk River, 135, 279; classical style of, 232; over Seneca River, 292; progress on enlarged, 292; at Schoharie Creek, 338-39, 379
"Arabian Nightism," 346-47
Assembly plan in 1853 for enlargement: origin of, 380; and Seymour, 381, 382

Astor, John Jacob, 98, 304
Atticus. See Clinton, De Witt

Barnburners. See Democratic Radical faction
Barrett, Alfred, 324
Barton, Benjamin, 140, 145n
Barton, James L., 145n, 148, 162, 270, 271, 288
Bates, David S., 89, 157
Bayard, William, 56, 135, 183
Beach, Samuel, 54-55
Beardsley, Levi, 415
Betts, Samuel R., 77
Biddle, Nicholas, 257
Bird, William A., 145n
Birdseye, Victory, 166
Black River Canal, 240, 242, 306, 341, 345, 354, 367, 397
Black Rock: as port of transfer, 6; and rivalry for canal terminus, 140-63; joined with Buffalo, 162; trade integrated with Buffalo, 271-72
Black Rock Harbor Company: formed, 145
Bleecker, Barent, 17
Board of (Canal) Commissioners. See Commissioners, canal
Boatmen's Friend Society, 224
Boatmen's Magazine, The, 234
Bonus Bill of 1817, 67, 68, 69, 400
Bouck, William C.: as canal commissioner, 86, 117, 162, 312, 323; and Sabbatarianism, 226;

Weed, Thurlow (*continued*):
canal estimates, 395; nationalism of, 407; belief of in Clay's American System, 411

Weighlocks: locations of, 243; and canal museum in Syracuse, 243n; operation of, 246; complaints on, 248

Welch, Benjamin, 372

Welland Canal: and Oswego Canal, 297; American engineers on, 413; completion and enlargement of, 413; trade on to Oswego and Montreal, 414

West plan. *See* Assembly plan

Western Inland Lock Navigation Company: incorporated in 1792, 15; backers of, 16; work of at Little Falls, Rome and German Flats, 17; dividends of, 20; purchase of properties by state, 20, 51, 56; and Holland Land Company, 31-32; efforts of for renewed support, 38; and federal aid to canal, 400

Weston, William, 18, 64

Whig party: and canal patronage, 253-54; and Canal Fund, 258-59; support of for canal enlargement, 307, 313, 314, 321-23, 325-26, 338, 361, 364, 375; canal policy of, 308-11; and Western trade, 309, 340-41, 382-83; economic philosophy of, 318-19; and canal tolls, 320; defeated on canal issue in 1841, 327-29; and stop and tax policy, 337; makes stop policy election issue in 1842, 339; and Democratic schism, 342; support of for constitutional convention, 348-49; in convention of 1846, 354; uses canal issue to defeat Wright in 1846, 356; divisions in, 361, 363, 364, 373; in election of 1848, 363; support of for Nine Million Bill, 368, 369; and resignation of Democratic sen-

Whig party (*continued*):
ators, 369-70; makes canal primary issue in 1851, 371-72; and canal lettings of 1851, 374; canal program of declared unconstitutional, 374, 375; attacks Democratic canal policy in 1852, 378; support of for Vanderbilt amendment, 385; and enlargement victory of 1853, 387-88; combines with Hardshell Democrats in 1853, 391; wins legislature and Canal Board in 1853, 391; and the West, 396; nationalism of in canal enlargement policy, 409; and Canadian rivalry, 413-14

White, Canvass, 95-96

Wilkeson, Samuel: and Buffalo harbor, 142, 144-45, 146-47, 150-51, 153; on removal of canal commissioners, 166; and railroads, 288; at Buffalo canal meeting, 352, 353

Williams, Elisha, 72, 73, 77

Woolly Heads, 364, 365

Worth, G. A., 315

Wright, Benjamin: and inland lock navigation companies, 19, 21; role of in canal resolution of 1808, 29-30; surveys on canal line in 1810, 41; at groundbreaking ceremonies, 84; as chief engineer, 87, 88, 125n; runs test level in 1818, 88; and Canvass White, 95; engineering problems of in Mohawk gorge, 134; on canal terminus, 149; anticipates canal trade, 193; advises larger canal in 1834, 241

Wright, John C., 388

Wright, Silas: leader of Albany Regency, 164; internal improvements policy of, 307; elected governor, 345-46; as governor, 347-48, 350, 352; and constitutional convention of 1846, 348; defeated in gubernatorial election of 1846, 356, 357-59